UNDERSTANDING CHINA THROUGH HER POETRY, HER FICTION, HER FOLKLORE, HER HISTORY, HER ASTONISHING PEOPLE...

By examining China's three thousand years of history, we can also bring into sharper focus some of the prejudices held by Westerners. For example, that all Chinese are "thrifty," "superior and cultured," or "hardworking" or "devious," "inscrutable," and "heathen."

Yet if our efforts to provide a less stereotyped picture of China have succeeded, this new vision will perhaps not be so simple as before. A new picture will be richer, more complex, kaleidoscopic. Closer to the Chinese reality...

CHINA
YESTERDAY AND TODAY

Edited by Molly Joel Coye,
Jon Livingston,
and Jean Highland

Third Edition

Revised and Updated

BANTAM BOOKS
TORONTO · NEW YORK · LONDON · SYDNEY

RL 10, IL age 15 and up

CHINA YESTERDAY AND TODAY

A Bantam Book / September 1975
2nd printing .. September 1977

Revised Bantam edition / October 1979
2nd printing .. December 1980

3rd printing .. May 1982

Bantam Third edition / February 1984

ISBN 0-553-23876-0

COPYRIGHT NOTICES AND ACKNOWLEDGMENTS

Contents

III. CHINA AND THE WEST
1800–1937

IV. NEW CHINA:
1937 to the Present

Sources for the readings in this book are listed in the
order in which they appear on the copyright pages, iv-viii.

CHINA
YESTERDAY AND TODAY

Introduction

All peoples must solve the same basic problems: they must find food, clothing, and shelter. Beyond this, they also share a common desire for the company of other people; and because of this, a social group is born. How these men and women will behave among themselves and with other groups marks the beginning of their own particular kind of society. As they develop a religion, a family system, a government, and other forms of organization, this group will have to adjust to the climate and geography of their part of the world. They will have to learn to defend themselves and to produce food for themselves. Ultimately, their lives will form a pattern that we call "Chinese" or "French" or "American." But each society will have a different way of solving some of the same basic problems.

Approached from this perspective of "problem-solving," perhaps even the vast history of China seems more understandable and less mysterious. We will also find that the Chinese, like all other people, have changed their way of solving these problems many times. Organized Chinese society began with the Shang dynasty in 1790 B.C., when hunting tribes warred against the growing kingdom and much of the work was done by slaves; but the size of the kingdom eventually became too great for rule by a central king, and the Chou dynasty established a system of feudal nobles with more independent powers. These nobles in turn became too powerful to be controlled, and the kingdom broke apart; it was reunited under the Ch'in and Han dynasties, and during this period the foundations of what we call Imperial China were laid. Although the empire endured for two thousand years after Ch'in, it continued to evolve, and a Chinese subject of the Ching dynasty in A.D.

1800 would have had difficulty recognizing the life of his ancestors in 200 B.C.

Even greater changes occurred after the first Westerners arrived. China was in almost constant turmoil from the nineteenth century until the Communist victory in 1949. This was a time of cataclysmic change, change that touched every aspect of life—not only government and economy but also literature, art, religion, family patterns, and even language—so that today's China is really, as her people say, a "New China." The basic human needs and problems that we discussed earlier are still being met, but in ways quite different from those of traditional China.

By examining China's three thousand years of history from this viewpoint, we can also bring into sharper focus some of the prejudices about China commonly held by Americans. For example, is it true that all Chinese are "thrifty" or "superior and cultured" or "hardworking"? Or are they "devious," "inscrutable," and "heathen"? Is China really so "mysterious," or can it be understood like France or Mexico?

Perhaps the most difficult thing for anyone reading about another country is to break down such stereotypes. We have tried to correct the worst of the misconceptions that underlie them and to construct a new, more comprehensible image of China's history, culture, and society.

Yet if our efforts to provide a less stereotyped picture of China have succeeded, this new vision will perhaps not be so simple as those before. A new picture will be richer, more complex, kaleidoscopic. But this is also, we hope, closer to the Chinese reality.

The selections have been organized into four parts. The first provides a physical description of China: people, climate, religions, rivers, languages. In the second, "Imperial China," the selections are broken down into sections covering government, philosophy, family and society, and other topics. For the third part, "China and the West," selections follow a roughly chronological order from 1800 to 1937. The final part, "New China," records the early history of the People's Republic and then shifts to topical divisions on women, foreign policy, the communes, and so on. We have included several maps to give a visual guide to major geographical features, historical events, and political boundaries. At the end of the book there is a brief annotated bibliography with suggestions for simple and readable materials covering each of these three major periods of Chinese history.

Note on the Transliteration of Chinese

The most widely used transliteration system for Chinese has, for the past four years, been *pinyin*, the system adopted in 1959 and put into universal use by the People's Republic in 1979 for publications in Western languages. Since 1979 the use of *pinyin* in the American media has gradually increased and is now the standard in all but scholarly publications. Selections in this anthology published since this changeover feature *pinyin*; thus, most contemporary political figures and many place names will be immediately familiar to American readers. However, in selections dealing with pre-1949 China and in most works published before the general acceptance of *pinyin*, spellings appear in the old transliteration system, Wade-Giles. Furthermore, some names will appear differently in different articles. See page 328 for an explanation of how to pronounce Chinese in *pinyin* and for a conversion table of the most common names and places.

PART I

THE LAND, THE PEOPLE, AND THEIR LANGUAGE

MAJOR ADMINISTRATIVE DIVISIONS OF
THE PEOPLE'S REPUBLIC OF CHINA

·········· Borders of provinces, autonomous regions, and the
3 special districts of Beijing (Peking), Tianjin (Tientsin),
and Shanghai

O   Provincial capitals

500 km

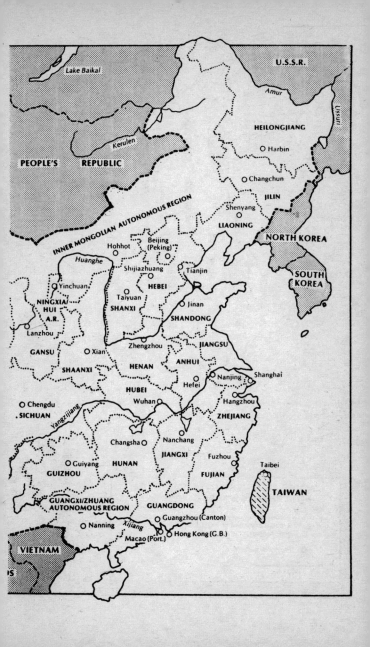

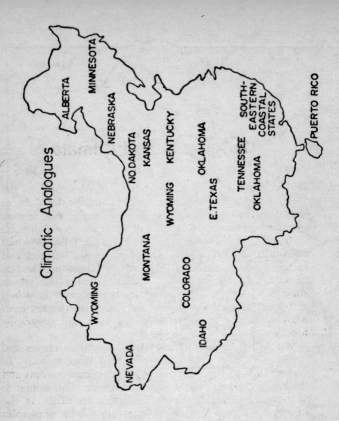

Climatic Analogues

ALBERTA
MINNESOTA
NEBRASKA
NO. DAKOTA
KANSAS
KENTUCKY
OKLAHOMA
SOUTH-EASTERN COASTAL STATES
PUERTO RICO
TENNESSEE
OKLAHOMA
WYOMING
E. TEXAS
MONTANA
COLORADO
WYOMING
IDAHO
NEVADA

Map of China with North American States labelled to indicate climate comparable to locations in China

Geography and Climate

In the north are the great steppes of Mongolia; to the west, caravans are swallowed by the sands of the Gobi; to the southwest, beyond the Kunlun range, the Tibetan plateau lies hidden; to the south, smaller mountains are carpeted by thick jungles. To the east, the Yellow Sea and the China Sea send typhoons howling toward the land; and in the center lies China, the Middle Kingdom. Despite these formidable barriers, China's isolation was never complete. Even in ancient times the barriers were breached as traders crossed the desert and sailed up the southern coast seeking contact; in this way men and geography together shaped history.

Within her natural borders, both mountain ranges and great rivers divide China into several large regions. In each of them, people have evolved their own customs and their own dialect of the Chinese language. This influence of geography has been most important, perhaps, in the history of China's minority peoples—in the life of peoples such as the nomadic Mongols of the north and the Uighurs of the western oases, as well as in their relations with the Han Chinese.

The selections in this part introduce the geography and peoples of China; a knowledge of these will give insight in later selections on her history and culture. Anna Louise Strong was an adventurous American journalist who first visited China in 1925. She returned five times for periods of extended travel and writing, and finally settled in China in 1958.

An Air View of China
by Anna Louise Strong*

Let us take an air view of China—China in space and time! It lies in a sheltered pocket of southeastern Asia, held in a natural isolation by barriers on all sides—tropical jungles, earth's highest mountains, widest deserts and largest ocean. In a great semicircle its southeastern coast bulges into the waters of the South Pacific, catching the warm rains. Southwest it is bounded by the steaming Malayan jungles. Westward in Tibet the Himalayas' mighty range divides it from India; the lowest passes are higher than the highest mountain peaks of America or Europe. Northwest these drop to the desert plateaus of Turkestan and Mongolia, two thousand miles of wastes, pierced perilously by a few difficult caravan routes. Only from the north is there easy access to China, by the pioneer plains of Inner Mongolia and Manchuria, across which, at intervals down the centuries, invaders came. China herself reached out, with cultural and at times political domination, a thousand miles beyond all these barriers, but within them are the million and a half square miles of "China Proper," about one-half the size of the United States.

And now we fly northwest, following a wide river, thickly beset with cities, villages and farms. This is the Yangtze, the mightiest river of Asia, which drains with its tributaries the farms of 200,000,000 people, one-tenth the population of the world. Cutting China in half, it flows eastward from the high mountains of Tibet to the Pacific Ocean; its great valley is known as Central China. Just north of it and paralleling its course, the sharp backbone of the Tsinling Range forms the climatic boundary between the two great parts of China.

China south of this range—all the way south to Canton— is a land of many hills and abundant rainfall which drains into rivers and lakes. Because of its hills and water-filled valleys, travel has always been difficult here. Access was by sea and river courses to the main centers, and thence

*Strong, *One Fifth*.

on foot by stone paths across rice fields and mountain trails through the hills. Only recently have there been roads on which wheeled vehicles could travel, and these are not yet many. China of the South has therefore been split into many separate regions in which different races and dialects have long remained. To most of its provinces the Yangtze and its tributaries act as thoroughfare, but the three southernmost provinces are reached by sea-coast or by other rivers which meet at the great port of South China, Canton.

Every bit of level land in this China of the South is intensely cultivated, and terraces creep up the gentler hills. A sub-tropical climate, reaching tropical in the southern provinces, makes it possible for the hardworking Chinese farmers to raise two or three crops a year. The largest areas of the level land are found in three places: the Canton delta in the South, the Yangtze delta on the central sea-coast, and the Red Basin fourteen hundred miles up the Yangtze in far west Szechwan. These are among the world's most highly developed farm areas. In them are most of China's 200,000 miles of canals, especially in the Yangtze delta, which is sometimes known as "sea on land." The Red Basin, which because of isolation is less known to foreigners than the other two regions, but which gains in importance now as China's center of life moves inland, supports a farming population of 2,150 per square mile on crops that range from wheat to rice, sugar cane and cotton. It is one of earth's loveliest garden spots, famous for its hill terracing and for its remarkable series of irrigation canals built by the great engineer Li Ping two thousand years ago.

North China—north of the Tsinling Range—is in every aspect of nature a contrast to the China we have just described. Instead of the warm, moist breezes from the South Pacific, it is swept by dust-laden storms from the deserts of Central Asia. It is a land of fertile soil but uncertain rainfall. In the Northwest, driest and nearest to the desert, are the highlands of "Yellow Earth," or loess, a wind-blown silt hundreds of feet deep. Despite the inexhaustible fertility of this soil, this is the "famine belt." For water is infrequent; it runs in deep river beds cut in the porous earth.

This is the land of the famous Yellow River, so heavy with silt that it seems half-mud, half-water. It sweeps in

great snake-like bends, southward between Shensi and
Shansi, then east across the central plain of Honan to the
coastal plains of Shantung, which have been built up
through the ages with earth brought from the heart of Asia
by this river to the sea. The process of this building is a
constant war between man and nature. Century by century the river raises its muddy bottom higher and higher
above the surrounding plain, while the toiling people of
China confine its waters by dikes. Yet often at high water,
especially when war or internal disorder have slackened the
eternal vigilance of the people, it breaks through its banks
in floods which destroy hundreds of villages, yet leave behind increased fertility of soil for the generations to come.

All parts of China, north and south, are filled to capacity
with people. More people probably have lived on China's
level areas than in any similar area in the world. Four-
fifths of them are, and have always been, farmers—the
most industrious, patient, thrifty farmers on earth.

Within the Great Wall and Without
by Molly Joel Coye and Jon Livingston

The Great Wall of China is a huge stone barricade more
than fourteen hundred miles long, twenty to thirty feet
high, and fifteen to twenty feet thick. It was built in
segments by succeeding Chinese dynasties in order to
keep the "barbarian" nomadic tribes to the north out of
China proper, and was finished around 1600. Within the
Great Wall lie the eighteen provinces of China proper.
This is the homeland of the Han people, the original
Chinese. Here the first dynasties rose along the Yellow
River in the north Chinese plain. In succeeding generations the empire expanded until the Chinese had settled
lands south below the Pearl River, west to the plateaus of
Yunnan and Kweichow and the steep terraces of Szechuan,
north into the hills of Kansu and Shensi and Shansi. By
the height of the Tang dynasty in A.D. 800 China proper
had reached the physical barriers of mountains, steppes,
forests, and jungles that still define it and have kept it
always partially in isolation. China proper was far more
than a geographical term, however; it was intended to

define that group of people who spoke Chinese, shared the Chinese culture, and together regarded those "outside the wall" as barbarians.

Outside the wall lay the lands of the Manchus, Mongols, Uighurs, Tibetans, and many other peoples who over time became a part of China as well. Twice they ruled all of China—the Mongols under Genghis Khan, and the Manchus three hundred years later—and several times large parts of the north fell to them. In peace they traded with the Chinese, exchanging horses for food and luxuries, and sent tributes to the Chinese emperor acknowledging his sovereignty over "all under heaven." This pattern was also followed in contacts between the Chinese and tribes along the southern borders with Vietnam, Laos, Thailand, and Burma. Although these tribes were never a serious military threat to the Empire, their support and trade were considered desirable. Today the Miao, Yao, and other tribes are part of the non-Han minority in China.

Together, China proper and the lands outside the wall total 3,657,765 square miles. About ninety percent of the population lives in the eastern third of the country, and ninety-four percent are of the Han peoples. The remaining six percent are made up of more than fifty minority groups. These are the regions of China:

Northern China. China's civilization arose along the Yellow River on the north Chinese plains. Here in northern Honan the people of Shang conquered neighboring tribes and established the first dynasty; later rulers continued the pattern of defeating and then encompassing citystates on the fringes of the empire. Today this region is bounded on the north by the Great Wall, the Huai River to the east, and the Tsinling Mountains to the south. The climate is like that of the North American plains, except for an even more undependable rainfall. Almost all of the population is Han, and it is the Mandarin dialect of this region which is used as the national language in China today. The economy of northern China consists primarily of agriculture, growing industrialization, and coal mining.

The Northwest. From the Taihung Mountains beginning in Shansi, the northwest stretches to the deserts of Sinkiang over mountain passes and the steppes of western Inner Mongolia. Here the people are spread thinly over the land. In Kansu the Han are mixed with the Hui (Muslims);

in the provinces farther to the west live the Uighurs, Kazakhs, Kirghiz, and other groups of Aryan descent. All of them except the Hui speak their own language in addition to Chinese. Some of them are as tall and fair as northern Europeans, while the Mongolians resemble North American Indians. Since this area is too dry for farming, much of the northwest is devoted to the livestock industry; in the last two decades the oil and mineral reserves of Sinkiang have been developed rapidly.

The Northeast. This region was formerly known as Manchuria, named after the Manchu people who conquered China and founded the Ching dynasty in the fifteenth century. For more than two thousand years, however, the Han Chinese have migrated to and from the northeast to farm the rich lands of the central Manchurian plain; more recently they have come to work in the growing industrial centers there. To the far north are great forests yielding lumber and furs, and the mountain ranges which cross the northeastern provinces contain rich deposits of iron ore, coal, copper, manganese, gold, lead, and sodium. To the west of these provinces lies the great autonomous region of Inner Mongolia, where the steppes are beginning to be farmed, as well as used for raising livestock.

Southern China. Warmer and wetter than the north, southern China is the most productive region in agricultural terms. The main crop is rice (in the north it is wheat), although cotton, tea, silk, soybeans, sweet potatoes, and tobacco are also produced in large quantities. The rich lands are ribboned with rivers and lakes, making fish another staple food and making transportation easier than in the north. This region is also the most densely populated— Shanghai, the largest city in the world, stands on the eastern coast—with well-developed industry and commerce. The south consists of Hupeh, Hunan, Kiangsi, and parts of Shensi, Anhwei, Kiangsu, and Chekiang.

The Southeast. The coastal provinces of southern Chekiang, Fukien, and Kwangtung, with the islands of Taiwan and Hainan, are very hilly, with less arable land than in the central-south. Rice terraces cover the hills, and sugar cane, bananas, pineapples, oranges, and litchis are raised for export as well. Above the farming land, forests are found, and lumbering is an important industry. The irregular coastline is dotted with fishing villages, and a large part of the catch is dried and salted for shipping inland. The people of this region speak two main dialects—Amoy or Min in in the north, and Cantonese in the south. It is Cantonese that we hear most often in the United States, for the southeast coast was the center of overseas commerce, and the difficulties of the last century caused many inhabitants of the region to emigrate. The British colony of Hong Kong and the Portuguese colony of Macao lie on the coast, and Taiwan has been held by Chiang Kai-shek and the remnants of the old Kuomintang government for the past two decades.

The Southwest. The four provinces of the southwest are Yunnan, Kweichow, Kwangsi, and Szechuan. The first two form the Yun-Kwei plateau, where, despite a mild climate, the rugged terrain makes agriculture difficult; the population is consequently comparatively low. Szechuan is the "Heavenly State"—for the mountains surround rich and well-watered valleys where rice, soybeans, cotton, wheat, corn, sweet potatoes, and sugarcane are grown for export as well as consumption. Ancient salt wells continue to produce, and there are light industries producing tung oil and raw silk. Railroad connections between Szechuan and the rest of China have been improved to facilitate transport of her goods outward.

Tibet and Mongolia. Historically, Tibet was divided into a Chinese territory called Tibet and a province called Sikang; in the mid-1950s Sikang was divided into two sections, and one became part of the autonomous region of Tibet, while the other became part of the province of Szechuan. Both Tibet and Mongolia are autonomous regions (Mongolia is called Inner Mongolia to distinguish it from Outer Mongolia, which is now an independent country). Tibet is high, rocky, and largely unfit for agriculture; the people raise livestock, including the all-purpose yak, which occupies a place in their life akin to that of the buffalo among the North American Indians. Mongolia is also thinly populated, and here only the oasis can support farming. The traditional livestock of horses and sheep, once raised by nomads, are now raised by the same peoples on large ranches. Mongolia is distinguished, however, by its mineral resources of coal, iron ore, sodium, and sulfur. The people of both Tibet and Mongolia speak and are educated in their own languages as well as in Chinese, and efforts have been made to preserve their folk culture.

Understanding Chinese

Today all Chinese know and use one form of Chinese—Mandarin—as well as their own local dialect. Until 1949, however, China was both divided and united by her language: divided, because people from one region could not understand the *spoken* dialect of other regions; and united, because every group and region used the same basic *written* form. The "original" Chinese, which developed in North China, spread to the south and west. There, isolated by mountain ranges and poor transportation, the language diverged into new forms so different from each other that it is perhaps wrong to call them dialects at all. Cantonese, which we hear spoken in Chinese communities in the United States, varies from Mandarin almost as much as spoken French does from Spanish, even though both are written alike.

Chinese have written their language with "Chinese characters" for thousands of years and have developed a unique culture around their unusual script. The complex picturelike characters are not an alphabet, which all Western languages use, but are a form of "logographic" script. Each character represents a separate word (word = "logo-") in Chinese. Instead of showing individual sounds, Chinese characters indicate both the meaning and the sound for a *whole word*.

In ancient China, characters began as simple drawings of natural objects—trees, water, mountains, horses, humans. The earliest characters are thus "pictographic" in quality. Later, as Chinese developed, characters were stuck together to form compound words of more than one syllable, usually on the basis of sound value. A character was often borrowed to represent another word which sounded like it—for without an alphabet, new words could not be invented simply by stringing together the right letters.

The most important difficulty of this system is that each character must be memorized individually, and there is usually no way to guess the pronunciation of a character by looking at it—learning their language is thus more of a chore for Chinese children than for children who learn an alphabetic language. One important advantage, however, is that written Chinese characters can be read by all Chinese, whatever dialect they may speak, since characters have standard meanings all over China. Both the difficulty of

The Evolution of Written Chinese
by Derk Bodde*

EARLY	MODERN	MEANING AND EXPLANATION	EARLY	MODERN	MEANING AND EXPLANATION
厂	厂	Cliff	米	木	Tree, wood (tree with roots and branches)
ㅂ	口	Mouth	从	比	To compare (file of 2 men)
▢	口	Enclosure	平	毛	Hair, feathers (piece of fur or down)
夕	夕	Evening, dusk (crescent moon)	屮屮	艸	Grass (growing plants)
大	大	Large (frontal view of "large" man)	宐	虫	Insect, reptile (snake or worm)
子	子	Child, boy (child with upraised arms)	見	見	To see (exaggerated eye on legs)
門	廾	To lift, great (joined hands)	語	言	Speech (vapor or tongue leaving mouth)
弓	弓	Bow (Chinese reflex bow)	豆	豆	Eating vessel (vessel on pedestal)
心 心 忄 小	心 忄 小	Heart, mind (picture of physical heart)	豸	豸	Feline, reptile (cat-like animal)
尸	户	Door, house (left leaf of double door)	魚	魚	Fish
半	扌	Hand (showing five fingers)	鳥	鳥	Birds
攴	攴	To beat, tap (hand holding stick)	麻	麻	Hemp (hemp plants drying under shed)
日	日	Sun	黽	黽	Toad
曰	曰	To speak (mouth with protruding tongue?)	鼎	鼎	Sacrificial urn (two-handled tripod vessel)
夕	月	Moon, month	鼓	鼓	Drum (drum on stand; hand with stick)

Early and Modern Forms of Chinese Pictographs. Other Chinese characters can be much more complex than these. The "early" forms are in many cases not the earliest known. The "modern" ones became current around the first century A.D. (Adapted from Raymond D. Blakney, *A Course in the Analysis of Chinese Characters*, Peiping, 1948)

*Bodde, *China's Cultural Tradition*.

traditional written Chinese and the diversity of spoken forms were important factors in the development of Chinese society, as explained here by two well-known "sinologists" (China scholars): Derk Bodde of the University of Pennsylvania and John K. Fairbank of Harvard University.

The Language of Scholars
by John K. Fairbank

Most Chinese characters are combinations of other simple characters. One part of the combination usually indicates the root meaning, while the other part indicates something about the sound.

For example, take the character for east, 東, which in the Peking dialect has had the sound "tung" (pronounced like "doong," as in Mao Tse-tung's name). Since a Chinese character is read aloud as a single syllable and since spoken Chinese is also rather short of sounds (there are only about four hundred different syllables in the whole language), it has been plagued with homophones, words that sound like other words, like "soul" and "sole" or "all" and "awl" in English. It happened that the spoken word meaning freeze had the sound "tung." So did a spoken word meaning a roof beam. When the Chinese went to write down the character for freeze, they took the character for east and put beside it the symbol for ice ㇀, which makes the character 凍 ("tung," to freeze). To write down the word sounding "tung" which meant roof beam, they wrote the character east and put before it the symbol for wood 木 making 棟 ("tung," a roof beam).

These are simple examples. Indeed any part of the Chinese language is simple in itself. It becomes difficult because there is so much of it, so many meanings and allusions, to be remembered. When the lexicographers wanted to arrange thousands of Chinese characters in a dictionary, for instance, the best they could do in the absence of an alphabet was to work out a list of 214 classifiers, one of which was sure to be in each character in the language. These 214 classifiers, for dictionary purposes, correspond to the 26 letters of our alphabet, but are more ambiguous and less efficient.

In spite of its cumbersomeness the Chinese written language was used to produce a greater volume of recorded literature than any other language before modern times. One sober estimate is that until 1750 there had been more books published in Chinese than in all the other languages in the world put together.

Perhaps enough has been said to indicate why written Chinese became a monopoly of the scribes. The Chinese language had the character of an institution, rather than a tool, of society. Men worshipped it, and devoted long lives to mastering even parts of its literature, which was a world of its own, into which one might gain admittance only by strenuous effort. The Chinese writing system was not a convenient device lying ready at hand for every schoolboy to pick up and use as he prepared to meet life's problems. It was itself one of life's problems. If little Lao-san could not find the time for long-continued study of it, he was forever debarred from social advancement. Thus the Chinese written language, rather than an open door through which China's peasantry could find truth and light, was a heavy barrier pressing against any upward advance and requiring real effort to overcome—a hindrance, not a help to learning.

PART II

IMPERIAL CHINA

1765 B.C.–1800 A.D.

Introduction

Part II is titled "Imperial China," but the readings in it have been selected to show that phrases like "imperial China" and "traditional China" are usually misleading. China did not develop and maintain one unchanging form of society. A peasant from "traditional China" of the early Han dynasty (c. 200 B.C.) would find the urbanized, sophisticated cities of "traditional China" in the late Sung dynasty (c. A.D. 1100) hard to recognize. He would notice the immense changes which had taken place, but he would probably not remark upon the fact that many aspects of Chinese society had remained essentially the same, from the written language to the organization of the bureaucracy.

We are faced with a contradiction between continuity and change. It is a basic contradiction in all histories, and it is the central theme of our study of China during the 3,565 years from the founding of the earliest dynasty, the Shang, to the height of the last, the Ching. To investigate these elements of continuity and change we have combined chronological and topical forms of organization. This is instead of following the more common and purely chronological approach which describes one dynasty after another and emphasizes the cyclical and repetitive elements of Chinese history.

The first chapter on the rise of Imperial China gives historical background for the early dynasties and the establishment of a feudal-bureaucratic system of government in the Han dynasty. This is followed by topical chapters on philosophy and culture among the upper classes and on commerce, spanning the period from the Han to the Tang dynasties. The Mongol Yuan dynasty serves as the focus for readings on Chinese relations with the border tribes. A chapter on peasant life includes descriptions of the rural gentry-scholars who dominated village politics, and several accounts of family life; here, as in other topical chapters, the readings are drawn from many periods in traditional China to counter images of a static society. After this description of family life, chapters on Secret Societies and Rebellions and on Folk Culture introduce forms of political and social expression among the peasantry. Part II ends with readings on urbanization and commercial development in the Sung and later dynasties, and on the difficult question of why China's economic development did not lead to classic Western forms of capitalism.

Some aspects of Chinese civilization will appear at first to be almost entirely continuous, without marked changes. A good example is the large "extended" family organized on Confucian principles of deference and obedience. But we discover in reading poetry from the earliest dynasties that women were considerably freer then; they were more independent and marriage for love was more acceptable. On the other hand, aspects which appear to have changed greatly may have remained much the same in essence. The bureaucracy is an example of this: despite refinements in the examination and appointment systems, officials continued to represent the educated upper classes and to function in support of existing patterns of authority in traditional society.

These two cases show the importance of thinking as you read. Don't accept any of these selections entirely at face value. Often the point of view expressed by an author (or by the editors) is the subject of great disagreement among "China experts." If you look for the author's argument, it will be easier to consider the opposite; and through the evaluation of both, you can reach your own conclusions.

Chronology for Imperial China

Because Chinese history is so long, and because the names of the dynasties are sometimes confusing for Western readers, a simple chronology of events helps to organize the study of Imperial China. This one lists only the most important dynasties, together with some of the great changes in Chinese society that occurred during them. The chronology ends with the reign of Chien Lung, the emperor whose life spanned the "golden age" of Ching China, just before the Westerners arrived in force.

Mythical Five Dynasties—Neolithic Age	Agricultural communities in Yellow River Valley.
Shang Dynasty 1765–1122 B.C. *Bronze Age*	City states, slavery; irrigation, wheeled vehicles; writing, oracle bones.
Chou Dynasty 1122–221 B.C.	Feudal states, hereditary military lords; iron, glass; Confucius, Taoism.
Ch'in Dynasty 221–206 B.C.	Break-up of feudalism, unification of China, Great Wall; legalists, burning of Confucian classics.
Han Dynasty 206 B.C.–A.D. *222*	Civil service and bureaucratic feudalism; expansion of empire; Yellow Turban Revolt; Buddhism arrives from India, Confucianism is state religion; paper invented.
Three Kingdoms, Six Dynasties A.D. *222–589*	Political disintegration; Buddhism spreads; tea used.
Sui Dynasty A.D. *589–618*	Reunification, Grand Canal links northern and southern parts of empire; repression of Buddhism begins.
Tang Dynasty A.D. *618–907*	Empire expands to south, commerce advances into Indian Ocean; state examinations for bureaucracy; cultural flowering, influence on Japan and Korea; printing; footbinding begins.

Sung Dynasty A.D. *960–1127*	Northern tribes threaten, dynasty forced to move capital to south; urbanization; compass, paper money.
Yuan Dynasty A.D. *1278–1368*	Mongols conquer China, take dynastic name "Yuan"; Mongol Empire reaches from Pacific to Central Europe; novels, opera develop; first Western travelers.
Ming Dynasty A.D. *1368–1644*	Explorers reach Africa; clash with Japan over Korea; Portuguese traders set up post at Macao; White Lotus Rebellion; Jesuit missionaries in Peking; reassertion of Chinese cultural ethnocentricity in reaction to Mongols.
Ching Dynasty A.D. *1644–1912*	Manchu conquest, new rulers establish Ching dynasty. Height of Imperial China under Emperor Chien Lung (1736–1795); borders expand to greatest extent, population increases rapidly, economic stress begins to weaken empire. Western pressure for trade and settlement rights escalates; Ming loyalist scholars, anti-Manchu sentiment; popular literature and drama.

The Rise of Imperial China

Until the rediscovery of the oracle bones of Anyang, modern historians were skeptical that the Shang dynasty described in Chinese records actually existed. With the evidence of the bones, however, the horizon of history has been pushed back to a millennium before Christ, and some historians have estimated the date of the founding of the dynasty as 1766 B.C. It is possible that more archaeological "finds" in the future will confirm the existence of the mythical first rulers of China—of the Yellow Emperor, whose wife taught the people to raise silkworks; or Fu Hsi, who invented writing; or Yu, who drained the floods and opened the waterways. But for the present, we begin with the people of Shang.

Life in Shang China
by John K. Fairbank, Edwin O. Reischauer and Albert M. Craig

The Shang economy was mainly agricultural. The Shang also had sheep and cattle but already seem to have had the traditional Chinese abhorrence for milk and milk products. Since bronze was rare and costly, agricultural tools were made of wood or stone. Cowrie shells were used as a sort of primitive money. These shells from southern waters have left their mark on the writing system: many characters having to do with wealth and trade have the "shell" signific. Jade was highly prized, as it has been throughout Chinese history.

Succession among the Shang rulers was often from brother to brother (thirteen cases) rather than from father to son (seventeen cases). Two of the successive capitals of these rulers were undoubtedly the cities unearthed near Cheng-chou and An-yang. How far beyond their walls they actually ruled is not known. Shang cultural remains are found scattered over a wide area in North China from the great bend of the Yellow River to central Shantung; but much of this area may have been ruled by vassal or even rival states, and the effective area of Shang control may have been fairly small. The Shang rulers were frequently at war with nearby neighbors and marauding herdsmen.

On the other hand, the state was big enough to field armies of three thousand to five thousand men, and the remains at Cheng-chou and An-yang are impressive. The style of architecture was essentially the same as that of modern China, contrasting with the stone architecture of the ancient West. The roof was carried by rows of wooden pillars, and the walls, at first made of pounded earth but in later times usually of brick, were merely nonstructural screens. The pillars rested on individual foundation stones set on a platform of pounded earth. As is still the custom in North China, buildings were carefully oriented to face south.

Unlike the palace buildings, the houses of the common people appear to have been crude pit dwellings, as in Neolithic times. The gap between ruler and ruled is further illustrated by the grandiose scale of the royal tombs at An-yang. These were great pits, as much as forty-three feet deep and covering up to five thousand square feet, subsequently filled with beaten earth. It was customary to bury with the corpse articles of use and value, presumably for the benefit of the deceased in some afterlife. In the tombs have been found war chariots, which show that Shang was part of the war chariot culture that in the middle of the second millennium B.C. swept over the civilized world all the way from Greece to China.

Many bodies of both aristocrats and humble followers were also buried with the rulers, and there were other forms of human sacrifice, usually in multiples of ten and sometimes hundreds at a time. Some historians have concluded that the Shang was a slave society. In any case, the cleavage between ruler and ruled was very great. The Shang sovereigns, who may have started as little more than chief shamans mediating between the people and their ancestors and deities, developed during the roughly five centuries of Shang ascendancy into rulers of very great authority. Thus the tendency of the Chinese to establish and accept a unified, authoritarian state goes back to very early times.

The Chou Dynasty: Chinese Feudalism

Chinese legends say that the last emperor of the Shang was so wicked and despotic that King Wu of Chou rose up against him. With the help of his brother, the Duke of Chou, King Wu destroyed the Shang and established a new dynasty. The Chou dynasty ruled a territory much larger than the Shang, and the empire now spread across the plains of North China. As a result, the new rulers could no longer maintain direct control over all their subjects. Instead, they were forced to delegate authority to relatives and friendly nobles, allowing them to operate semi-independent fiefdoms in return for loyalty, soldiers, and tax revenues. This was the feudal era of Chinese history, comparable in some ways to the feudalism of Europe in the Middle Ages.

Culturally the Chou greatly resembled the Shang. They spoke the same language, continued to develop written characters, used oracle bones, and adopted some of the same rituals. Chou conquests brought other tribes into the empire; by this time we can already see China's traditional pattern of absorbing "barbarian" peoples into her civilization while adopting whatever in their culture might be an improvement.

At one point the Chou dynasty collapsed and was reestablished to the east of its old capital. For this reason the dynasty is divided into Western and Eastern periods. But in the Eastern period the Chou never regained their former strength. The feudal lords ruled their territories independently, and after the end of the Eastern Chou none of them were strong enough to establish control over all the others. This was the time of the "Warring States," famous in Chinese history for intrigues and continual battles. But the weak Eastern Chou and the Warring States are also famous for the flourishing of Chinese culture and technology.

This was the era of Confucius, of philosophical debates and vigorous literary development. At the same time, the Chinese began to use iron extensively; undertook large-scale irrigation and water-control projects; constructed canals for transport; and used metal coins, glass, and chopsticks. Rapid increases in population stimulated trade, and a large class of wealthy merchants arose. This threatened the old aristocratic families who had based their power on wealth from the land and on their literary achievements. They responded to the merchants by creating the idea of the "four classes": the highest class were the scholars (in fact, the land-holding families); after them, the ordinary farmers; then the artisans; and lowest of all, the merchants. This ranking system lasted until the fall of Imperial China.

In this time also, the first walls were erected against the barbarian horsemen to the north, and the various states began to tighten and centralize their systems of government. Salt and iron monopolies were introduced by their governments to finance bureaucracies. New states to the south, including the areas below present-day Shanghai, joined in the struggle to unite and conquer all of China. These developments are discussed by Wolfram Eberhard of the University of California.

Economic and Cultural Changes
by Wolfram Eberhard*

In the course of the wars much land of former noblemen had become free. Often the former serfs had then silently become landowners. Others had started to cultivate empty land in the area inhabited by the indigenous population and regarded this land, which they themselves had made fertile, as their private family property. There was, in spite of the growth of the population, still much cultivable land available. Victorious feudal lords induced farmers to come to their territory and to cultivate the wasteland. This is a period of great migrations, internal and external. It seems that from this period on not only merchants but also farmers began to migrate southwards into the area of the present provinces of Kwangtung and Kwangsi and as far as Tonking.

As long as the idea that all land belonged to the great clans of the Chou prevailed, sale of land was inconceivable; but when individual family heads acquired land or cultivated new land, they regarded it as their natural right to dispose of the land as they wished. From now on until the end of the medieval period, the family head as representative of the family could sell or buy land. However, the land belonged to the family and not to him as a person. This development was favoured by the spread of money. In time land in general became an asset with a market value and could be bought and sold.

Another important change can be seen from this time on. Under the feudal system of the Chou strict primogeniture among the nobility existed: the fief went to the oldest son by the main wife. The younger sons were given independent pieces of land with its inhabitants as new, secondary fiefs. With the increase in population there was no more such land that could be set up as a new fief. From now on, primogeniture was retained in the field of ritual and religion down to the present time: only the oldest son

*Eberhard, A History of China •

of the main wife represents the family in the ancestor worship ceremonies; only the oldest son of the emperor could become his successor. But the landed property from now on was equally divided among all sons. Occasionally the oldest son was given some extra land to enable him to pay the expenses for the family ancestral worship. Mobile property, on the other side, was not so strictly regulated and often the oldest son was given preferential treatment in the inheritance. . . .

Together with the economic and social changes in this period, there came cultural changes. New ideas sprang up in exuberance, as would seem entirely natural, because in times of change and crisis men always come forward to offer solutions for pressing problems. We shall refer here only briefly to the principal philosophers of the period.

Mencius (c. 372–289 B.C.) and Hsün Tzŭ (c. 298–238 B.C.) were both followers of Confucianism. Both belonged to the so-called "scholars", and both lived in the present Shantung, that is to say, in eastern China. Both elaborated the ideas of Confucius, but neither of them achieved personal success. Mencius (Meng Tzŭ) recognized that the removal of the ruling house of the Chou no longer presented any difficulty. The difficult question for him was when a change of ruler would be justified. And how could it be ascertained whom Heaven had destined as successor if the existing dynasty was brought down? Mencius replied that the voice of the "people," that is to say of the upper class and its following, would declare the right man, and that this man would then be Heaven's nominee. This theory persisted throughout the history of China.

Finally one of the Warring States, the Ch'in, managed to conquer the others. The Ch'in owed their victory in part to a man named Shang Yang, a brilliant organizer who tried to bring all the territories under direct control of the central government and broke much of the power of the old feudal lords, but he died before the final unification of all the states in 221 B.C.

The state of Ch'in became the empire of Ch'in (from which we get the name "China"), and the king proclaimed himself Ch'in Shih Huang Ti, the first emperor of China. He foretold that his dynasty would extend for ten thousand generations— but it ended in 206 B.C., only fifteen years later. In the years it took him to conquer the contending states, however, and in his short reign, Imperial China first took shape.

China Reunited
by Anna Louise Strong*

The era of feudal warlords came to an end not through philosophy but with the rise in 221 B.C. of the first Emperor of All China, a harsh dictator from the region which is now Shensi. He abolished the feudal lords in his own domain and established a somewhat freer relation of classes, in which soil-tillers paid with grain for their use of land, instead of with labor and "feudal duties." This, together with his possession of the biggest irrigation canal and of more of the recently invented iron implements, led to a more productive kind of farming, and so strengthened his rule that he was able to conquer all his rivals and establish himself as Emperor Shih Huang-ti. He ordered the abolition of feudal rights throughout the empire, created a uniform legal code, a uniform written language, uniform weights and measures, and even uniform wagon axles to enable all the peasant carts to travel easily in the same deep ruts. He extended the Great Wall of China, of which parts had been previously built, till it reached from the sea fourteen hundred miles to the western mountains, a formidable barrier against invading tribes. His ruthless use of the forced labor of tens of thousands of criminals and disbanded soldiers aroused hate among the common people. He also burned the books of the past and thereby aroused the hatred of the scholar-officials, who had served earlier rulers. These twin hates overthrew his dynasty fifteen years after it began. This was in the time of his son, for he himself ruled only eleven years. From that brief rule he left to succeeding centuries the ideal of a unified empire and a name as ruthless dictator, which is still mentioned with hatred by the Chinese people after twenty-one hundred years.

---

*Strong, *One-Fifth*.

A common soldier started the uprising that overthrew this first dictator; the whole empire of oppressed farmers and soldiers "answered him like an echo." After seven years' struggle, a man of humble origin, Liu Pang, sat on the throne as founder of the great Han dynasty, which built the greatest empire then known in the world. The expanding power of this regime was based on the building of great public works for irrigation, on the widening use of the newly discovered metal, iron, and on the trade made possible from this surplus wealth. Merchants grew rich, sought to buy land and to advance into new regions. These forces did more to break down feudalism than had the edicts of Huang-ti. Liu Pang identified himself with the new rising class of merchants. He was a realist; it was said of him that he lost more battles than he won, but never the final battle, for his sense of social and political forces always gave final victory. He passed a law that all sons should inherit equally from their fathers, thus gradually extinguishing the feudal families by making them many, but small and powerless. He made scholarship, rather than feudal rank, a qualification for high office; men proficient in philosophy and ethics were given government jobs. Thus he won support both from conservative scholars and the new businessmen, and established on the ruins of feudalism a new society in which men might rise through trading to wealth, and through knowledge to government posts.

Imperial China under the Han dynasty was the product of almost two thousand years of social and political evolution. All succeeding dynasties took their basic form and organization from this one, and today the Chinese still call themselves the "people of Han." Although the next chapters will emphasize the many changes which followed, the thread of continuity is there as well.

Here Étienne Balazs, an eminent French China scholar, presents his ideas on the basic elements of traditional Chinese society. The examination system he mentions required all those who wished to serve the government as officials to pass a difficult test on classical literature; the examinations were begun in Han times but attained their final form in the Tang dynasty four hundred years later.

Imperial China: The Han Dynasty
by Étienne Balazs

You may paste on labels (Antiquity, Early or Late Middle Ages, Modern Times); you may cut it up into longer or shorter slices; but, whatever you do, you cannot conjure away the sheer length of time the Chinese Empire lasted, founded in 221 B.C. and still surviving at the beginning of the twentieth century, or deny the permanence of the imperial institutions and the perenniality of certain phenomena such as Confucianism, which endured in spite of successive metamorphoses. Explanations may differ, interpretations contradict each other, but the underlying reality persists, a majestic mountain of solid, incontrovertible fact.

Now, it seems to me that the only valid method for letting light into this solid mass of historical fact is to seek out the causes of continuity—that is, try to discover the specific and significant features of Chinese social structure. I shall have to confine myself to discussing the social structure of imperial China, for it would take me far beyond the limits of the present essay to make comparisons with earlier periods, however interesting and instructive that might be. And I can only point out the more striking of its distinctive features, since anything approaching a complete description of the social structure of imperial China would require not an essay but several large tomes.

What, then, were its most striking features?

In the first place, China was a large *agrarian* society, highly developed but using traditional techniques, and established on a subcontinent that lacks any marked geographical articulation. Its cells, scattered over an immense territory whose main arteries were a system of waterways, existed in an economic autarchy that made each of them an individual unit, and isolated each unit from every other. These cells were the peasant families that composed the overwhelming majority of the population. They were self-sufficient; but without the system of economic exchanges and the organizational framework imposed from above, they would have disintegrated irremediably into their component particles, into an anarchy that would have made impossible not only the distribution, but also the production of goods, and indeed the maintenance of life itself. It was, in other words, a pre-industrial, nonmaritime society, based on a peasant subsistence economy.

This society was *bureaucratic* because the social pyramid—which rested on a broad peasant base, with intermediate strata consisting of a merchant class and an artisan class, both of them numerically small, lacking in autonomy, of inferior status, and regarded with scant respect—was capped and characterized by its apex: the mandarinate.

The class of *scholar-officials* (or mandarins), numerically infinitesimal but omnipotent by reason of their strength, influence, position, and prestige, held all the power and owned the largest amount of land. This class possessed every privilege, above all the privilege of reproducing itself, because of its monopoly of education. But the incomparable prestige enjoyed by the intelligentsia had nothing to do with such a risky and possibly ephemeral thing as the ownership of land; nor was it conferred by heredity, which after all can be interrupted; nor was it due solely to its exclusive enjoyment of the benefits of education. This unproductive elite drew its strength from the function it performed—the socially necessary, indeed indispensable, function of coordinating and supervising the productive labor of others so as to make the whole social organism work. All mediating and administrative functions were carried out by the scholar-officials. They prepared the calendar, they organized transport and exchange, they supervised the construction of roads, canals, dikes, and dams; they were in charge of all public works, especially those aimed at forestalling droughts and floods; they built up reserves against famine, and encouraged every kind of irrigation project. Their social role was at one and the same time that of architect, engineer, teacher, administrator, and ruler. Yet these "managers" before their time were firmly against any form of specialization. There was only one profession they recognized: that of governing. A famous passage from Mencius on the difference between those who think and those who toil perfectly expresses the scholar-officials' outlook: "Great men have their proper business, and little men have their proper business.... Some labor with their minds, and some labor with their strength.

Those who labor with their minds govern others; those who labor with their strength are governed by others. Those who are governed by others support them; those who govern others are supported by them. . . ."

A final totalitarian characteristic was the state's tendency to clamp down immediately on any form of private enterprise (and this in the long run kills not only initiative but even the slightest attempts at innovation), or, if it did not succeed in putting a stop to it in time, to take over and nationalize it. Did it not frequently happen during the course of Chinese history that the scholar-officials, although hostile to all inventions, nevertheless gathered in the fruits of other people's ingenuity? I need mention only three examples of inventions that met this fate: paper, invented by a eunuch; printing, used by the Buddhists as a medium for religious propaganda; and the bill of exchange, an expedient of private businessmen.

In view of its contemporary relevancy, one additional feature of the bureaucratic state may be worth mentioning here: the panicky fear of assuming responsibility. To avoid getting into trouble was the Chinese bureaucrat's main concern, and he always managed to saddle his responsibilities on to some subordinate who could serve as a scapegoat.

The scholar-officials and their state found in the Confucianist doctrine an ideology that suited them perfectly. In ancient times, Confucianism had expressed the ideals of those former members of the feudal aristocracy who had formed a new social stratum of revolutionary intelligentsia, but in Han times (206 B.C.–A.D. 220), shortly after the foundation of the empire, it became a state doctrine. The virtues preached by Confucianism were exactly suited to the new hierarchical state: respect, humility, docility, obedience, submission, and subordination to elders and betters.

During the turmoil of Eastern Chou and the Warring States, Chinese philosophical and political thought developed at a rapid pace. Then, with the unification of China, a great catastrophe occurred: Ch'in Shih Huang Ti ordered the burning of every book in the empire. He saved only his own library and those of seventy court officials, along with a few useful volumes on medicine, agriculture, and the history of the state of Ch'in. All other volumes were destroyed, wiping out the written record of much of early Chinese civilization. For years after this, embittered scholars labored to reconstruct the lost works from remembered passages and surviving manuscripts, but a large part was never recovered.

Despite this blow, the Chinese continued to record and discuss their history in greater detail than any other ancient civilization. This tradition of historical writing produced Sze-ma Chien (also written Ssu-ma Ch'ien), the greatest scholar of China. In the following passages John King Fairbank and Edwin O. Reischauer introduce Sze-ma Chien and another famous historian, Pan Ku, and consider the question of dynastic cycles. After this is an excerpt from Sze-ma Chien himself, in a passage translated by Lin Yu-tang. Mr. Lin has translated many works from Chinese and has written numerous scholarly books of his own.

Early Chinese Historians: Ssu-ma Ch'ien and Pan Ku
by Edwin O. Reischauer and John K. Fairbank

Ssu-ma Ch'ien (died about 85 B.C.) inherited a post as court astrologer and had access to the resources of the imperial library. He also had traveled throughout most of the empire in his youth. He claimed to be simply completing the historical work which his father, Ssu-ma T'an, had commenced, but this may have been partly a pious excuse for what was in reality a most presumptuous undertaking— the continuation and amplification of what was supposed to be Confucius' greatest accomplishment, that is, the arrangement of the record of the past in proper form. Ssu-ma Ch'ien was obviously a man of great daring as well as prodigious learning. In 99 B.C. he came to the defense of a prominent Chinese general who had been forced to surrender to the Hsiung-nu, and Wu Ti repaid him for his audacity by having him castrated.

Ssu-ma Ch'ien not only set the pattern for most later Chinese historical works but also determined their style and scholarly approach. He limited himself to a concise and straightforward statement of the facts as he knew them, avoiding the dramatic but largely imaginary embellishments of historical incident that characterized some of the earlier Chinese histories as well as those of the ancient Occident. His technique was to quote with a minimum of alterations those sources which he felt to be the most reliable. On dubious points that he did not feel he could himself resolve, such as the variant traditions regarding high antiquity, he simply copied the different accounts side by side. His book, therefore, like those of later Chinese historians, is for the most part a complicated patchwork of passages and paraphrases from earlier books and documents. Ssu-ma Ch'ien thus set a standard for historical scholarship in China that was probably not equaled in the West until relatively modern times. His succinct prose style also set a literary standard that strongly influenced later generations of historians. . . .

The Chinese practice of compiling records of the past in dynastic chunks is partially responsible for the traditional interpretation of Chinese history as a series of repetitive dynastic cycles. The lack of a belief in progress and the idea that there was a golden age in antiquity have strengthened this tendency, for the most that could be expected of history as it unfolded was the repetition of past glories. As a result, the fascinating story of the growth of Chinese civilization has been made to seem like one vast human treadmill. After reading the story of one dynasty, the student may feel that the next is just more of the same.

The Han historians, with their assumption that ancient China had enjoyed the same imperial unity they knew, managed to hide many of the fundamental changes between Shang times and the Early Han under a surface pattern of repetitive motifs. Later historians made the succeeding 2000 years seem an even more monotonous series of more or less successful attempts to repeat the story of the Earlier Han dynasty. The concept of the dynastic cycle, in other words, has been a major block to the understanding of the fundamental dynamics of Chinese history. Even today historians are only beginning to grope their way toward the establishment of such useful generalizations as are afforded in Western history by its division into ancient, medieval, and modern periods. . . .

All the great dynasties have an initial period of prosperity. The group that has seized the throne is relatively small and closely knit. The wars that have brought it to power have eliminated most of its rivals, and therefore the wealth of the nation pours largely into its coffers. The country prospers in its newly established peace, the population seems to increase rapidly, and the treasuries and granaries of the central government overflow.

But an excess of *yang* leads to the rise of *yin*. The affluent central government builds great palaces, roads, canals and walls. The imperial clan, the nobility, and the high bureaucracy grow in numbers and become accustomed to an ever more luxurious mode of life. The very military successes of the empire have established far-flung defense lines that are costly to maintain. More and more lands and their peasant-cultivators are used for the personal support of the ruling classes and fewer and fewer tax-paying contributors remain to the central administration. Because of constantly increasing expenditures and often a slight decline in income, each dynasty begins to experience serious financial difficulties within a century of its founding.

Economic and administrative reforms are then carried out and may halt the financial decline for a while. The downward trend, however, eventually reasserts itself. Economic and administrative difficulties accumulate. Official self-seeking and corruption become worse, leading to a decline in administrative efficiency and an intensification of factional quarrels at court. The potential rivals of the imperial family become politically and economically more independent of the central government and challenge it with greater impunity. To meet government deficits, the burden on the tax-paying peasant is increased to the breaking point. Because of the government's financial difficulties, canals and dikes are allowed to fall into disrepair, making floods and droughts more probable. Crop failures that once could have been offset by stores from the government granaries now result in famines, and these lead to banditry and eventually to peasant uprisings. Inadequately maintained frontier defenses begin to crumble. Provincial officials and their armies begin to defect, and the central government starts to go to pieces. Then follow the wars that liquidate the old regime and clear the slate for a new dynastic beginning.

Szema Chien on Retribution
by Lin Yu-tang

*The name of "Poyi" (twelfth century B.C.) is synony-
mous with that of a saintly hermit or recluse. He and
his brother Shuchi were princes of a small kingdom.
They both declined the throne and finally it was given
to another brother. When a conquering dynasty was
founded, they refused to serve under the conqueror
and escaped to the mountains where they subsisted on
beans and eventually died of starvation. They were
made immortal by Confucius's calling them "true
men." Szema Chien therefore posed the problem whether there is justice in the world. I have omitted here
the beginning, which expresses the author's doubt
that they died without regret, thus contradicting
Confucious.*

Some people say [quoting the *Book of History*], "God is
impartial. He is with men who walk in righteousness." We
should say that Poyi and Shuchi were righteous men,
should we not? They were men of great strength of
character and of stern principles, yet they died of starvation!
Furthermore, of the seventy disciples of Confucious, the
one who received the highest praise from him as a true
lover of learning was Yen Huei. But Huei was always poor,
eating his coarse meals without complaint, and he died
young! Is this the way God rewards the good men? On the
other hand, we see the famous bandit Chih, who killed the
innocent, ate human liver, and ran roughshod marauding
the country with thousands of his gang, killing and robbing,
and yet he died a natural death in his old age! What did he
do to deserve it? These are well-known examples of the
past. In modern days, we see people who break the law
and commit acts against justice, get rich and live a comfortable life, and their families go on enjoying luxury and
prosperity. Others, on the other hand, observe the strictest
principles, turn their backs on the short cuts to success,
and are moreover careful with their words, speaking only
out of motives for the public good when there is a great

injustice. Yet countless of these people run into personal disasters. Is this the God's way which the people speak of? Or is the contrary the case? I have great doubts about it.

Confucius says, "People who do not believe in the same things cannot do business with one another," by which he means that all one can do will be just to follow his own convictions. That is why Confucious says of himself, "I would even be willing to be a carriage driver if I knew that by so doing I could get rich by my own effort. Since I cannot be sure, I will do what I like to do." Again he says, "When winter comes, then one finds out that the pines and cypresses stand the cold best." A pure-hearted man stands out in a world of general corruption. He knows what he values most, and disregards the rest.

"A gentleman hates to die without leaving a name for posterity" [says Confucius]. And Chiatse* says, "A greedy man dies of money-making, a heroic knight dies for fame, a successful man dies of striving after power, and the common people avoid death." "Those of the same light attract each other and animals of the same kind seek each other"; "The clouds follow the dragon, and the winds follow the tiger"; "The sage arises and all things become clear" [quotations from the *Book of Changes*]. Poyi and Shuchi became immortal through the praise of Confucius, and Yen Huei became known to posterity because he followed the Master, although they all had their merits. But there are many retired philosophers who are admirable in their conduct and character but whom no one ever hears about. Is it not sad? Common people who are strict with their conduct and wish to be known to posterity have no other way except to associate themselves with scholars of great reputation.

The Philosophers of China

The most famous philosopher of late Chou was, of course, Confucius. But our knowledge of the man has been obscured

---

*Chia Yi (201–169 B.C.), about two generations before Szema Chien. Chia and the great poet Chuyuan (343–290 B.C.) are great examples of honest, brilliant scholars who would not compromise on principles and who both committed suicide later.

since his death by a multitude of legends, by the Ch'in burning of the earlier records of his life and ideas, and by the continual rewriting and reediting of later versions. The first reading is the story of Confucius' life as it has been reconstructed by modern historians; the second is the story of how his philosophy was changed as it became the official "state religion" during the Han dynasty.

Life and Ideas of Confucius
by Wolfram Eberhard*

. . . Priests of the earlier dynasty of the Shang developed into the group of so-called "scholars." When the Chou ruler, after the move to the second capital, had lost virtually all but his religious authority, these "scholars" gained increased influence. They were the specialists in traditional morals, in sacrifices, and in the organization of festivals. The continually increasing ritualism at the court of the Chou called for more and more of these men. The various feudal lords also attracted these scholars to their side, employed them as tutors for their children, and entrusted them with the conduct of sacrifices and festivals.

China's best-known philosopher, Confucius (Chinese: K'ung Tzŭ), was one of these scholars. He was born in 551 B.C. in the feudal state Lu in the present province of Shantung. In Lu and its neighbouring state Sung, institutions of the Shang had remained strong; both states regarded themselves as legitimate heirs of Shang culture, and many traces of Shang culture can be seen in Confucius's political and ethical ideas. He acquired the knowledge which a scholar had to possess, and then taught in the families of nobles, also helping in the administration of their properties. He made several attempts to obtain advancement, either in vain or with only a short term of employment ending in dismissal. Thus his career was a continuing pilgrimage from one noble to another, from one feudal lord to another, accompanied by a few young men, sons of scholars, who were partly his pupils and partly his servants. Many of these disciples seem to have been "illegitimate" sons of

---

*Eberhard, *A History of China*.

noblemen, i.e. sons of concubines, and Confucius's own family seems to have been of the same origin. In the strongly patriarchal and patrilinear system of the Chou and the developing primogeniture, children of secondary wives had a lower social status. Ultimately Confucius gave up his wanderings, settled in his home town of Lu, and there taught his disciples until his death in 479 B.C.

Such was briefly the life of Confucius. His enemies claim that he was a political intriguer, inciting the feudal lords against each other in the course of his wanderings from one state to another, with the intention of somewhere coming into power himself. There may, indeed, be some truth in that.

Confucius's importance lies in the fact that he systematized a body of ideas, not of his own creation, and communicated it to a circle of disciples. His teachings were later set down in writing and formed, right down to the twentieth century, the moral code of the upper classes of China. Confucius was fully conscious of his membership of a social class whose existence was tied to that of the feudal lords. With their disappearance, his type of scholar would become superfluous. The common people, the lower class, was in his view in an entirely subordinate position. Thus his moral teaching is a code for the ruling class. Accordingly it retains almost unaltered the elements of the old cult of Heaven, following the old tradition inherited from the northern peoples. For him Heaven is not an arbitrarily governing divine tyrant, but the embodiment of a system of legality. Heaven does not act independently, but follows a universal law, the so-called "Tao." Just as sun, moon, and stars move in the heavens in accordance with law, so man should conduct himself on earth in accord with the universal law, not against it. The ruler should not actively intervene in day-to-day policy, but should only act by setting an example, like Heaven; he should observe the established ceremonies, and offer all sacrifices in accordance with the rites, and then all else will go well in the world. The individual, too, should be guided exactly in his life by the prescriptions of the rites, so that harmony with the law of the universe may be established.

A second idea of the Confucian system came also from the old conceptions of the Chou conquerors, and thus originally from the northern peoples. This is the patriarchal idea, according to which the family is the cell of society, and at the head of the family stands the eldest male adult as a sort of patriarch. The state is simply an extension of the family, "state," of course, meaning simply the class of the feudal lords (the "chün-tzŭ"). And the organization of the family is also that of the world of the gods. Within the family there are a number of ties, all of them, however, one-sided: that of father to son (the son having to obey the father unconditionally and having no rights of his own); that of husband to wife (the wife had no rights); that of elder to younger brother. An extension of these is the association of friend with friend, which is conceived as an association between an elder and a younger brother. The final link, and the only one extending beyond the family and uniting it with the state, is the association of the ruler with the subject, a replica of that between father and son. The ruler in turn is in the position of son to Heaven. Thus in Confucianism the cult of Heaven, the family system, and the state are welded into unity. The frictionless functioning of this whole system is effected by everyone adhering to the rites, which prescribe every important action. It is necessary, of course, that in a large family, in which there may be up to a hundred persons living together, there shall be a precisely established ordering of relationships between individuals if there is not to be continual friction. Since the scholars of Confucius's type specialized in the knowledge and conduct of ceremonies, Confucius gave ritualism a correspondingly important place both in spiritual and in practical life.

Here, in several selections from the *Analects* of Confucius, the Master describes proper relationships among men and the correct conduct of a king. These dialogues between Confucius and his disciples and visitors reveal their belief that virtuous men, by serving as examples for others, create a harmonious and orderly world around them.

From *The Analects of Confucius*

TRANSLATED BY ARTHUR WALEY

Book xii

2. Jan Jung asked about Goodness.* The Master said, Behave when away from home** as though you were in the presence of an important guest. Deal with the common people as though you were officiating at an important sacrifice. Do not do to others what you would not like yourself. Then there will be no feelings of opposition to you, whether it is the affairs of a State that you are handling or the affairs of a Family.***

Jan Yung said, I know that I am not clever; but this is a saying that, with your permission, I shall try to put into practice. . . .

4. Ssu-ma Niu asked about the meaning of the term Gentleman. The Master said, The Gentleman neither grieves nor fears. Ssu-ma Niu said, So that is what is meant by being a gentleman—neither to grieve nor to fear? The Master said, On looking within himself he finds no taint; so why should he either grieve or fear?

5. Ssu-ma Niu grieved, saying, Everyone else has brothers; I alone have none.† Tzu-hsia said, I have heard this saying, "Death and life are the decree of Heaven; wealth and rank depend upon the will of Heaven. If a gentleman attends to business and does not idle away his time, if he behaves with courtesy to others and observes the rules of ritual, then all within the Four Seas‡ are his brothers." How can any true gentleman grieve that he is without brothers? . . .

7. Tzu-kung asked about government. The Master said, sufficient food, sufficient weapons, and the confidence of

---

*I.e., ruling by Goodness, not by force.
**I.e., in handling public affairs.
***A ruling clan, such as that of the Chi in Lu.
†This may merely mean that his brother Huan T'ui, being an enemy of Confucius, could no longer be regarded by Niu as a brother. When Niu died in 481 B.C. he left behind him at least three brothers.
‡That bound the universe.

the common people. Tzu-kung said, Suppose you had no choice but to dispense with one of these three, which would you forgo? The Master said, Weapons. Tzu-kung said, Suppose you were forced to dispense with one of the two that were left, which would you forgo? The Master said, Food. For from of old death has been the lot of all men; but a people that no longer trusts its rulers is lost indeed. . . .

11. Duke Ching of Ch'i* asked Master K'ung about government. Master K'ung replied saying, Let the prince be a prince, the minister a minister, the father a father and the son a son. The Duke said, How true! For indeed when the prince is not a prince, the minister not a minister, the father not a father, the son not a son, one may have a dish of millet in front of one and yet not know if one will live to eat it. . . . **

16. The Master said, The gentleman calls attention to the good points in others; he does not call attention to their defects. The small man does just the reverse of this.

17. Chi K'ang-tzu asked Master K'ung about the art of ruling. Master K'ung said, Ruling (*chêng*) is straightening (*chêng*). If you lead along a straight way, who will dare go by a crooked one?

18. Chi K'ang-tzu was troubled by burglars. He asked Master K'ung what he should do. Master K'ung replied saying, If only you were free from desire, they would not steal even if you paid them to.†

---

*Died 490 B.C. The last of a long line of powerful and successful dukes. The closing years of his reign were clouded by the intrigues of the Ch'ên Family, which menaced the security of the dynasty (the prince was no longer a prince; ministers, i.e. the leaders of the Ch'ên faction, were no longer content to be ministers); and by succession-squabbles among his sons (the father no longer had the authority of a father; the sons were not content to be sons).

**Figure of speech denoting utter insecurity. Legend makes Duke Ching haunted by the fear of death. Advice very like that which Confucius gives here was given to Duke Ching's ancestor Duke Huan by Kuan Chung.

†This is a rhetorical way of saying that if K'ang-tzu did not accumulate valuables, he would not be robbed. But coupled with this meaning is the suggestion that the ruler's moral force operates directly on the people, as a magic, not merely as an example.

Some of the ideas that Confucius wrote about are very familiar. We can even find in the *Analects* the sentence "That which you do not desire, do not do unto others," and in Mo Tsu (another philosopher of the same era), "Spread love, do not make war."

Familiar Ideas:
Other Chinese Philosophers
*by Anna Louise Strong**

The words of some of those ancient Chinese philosophers sound strangely modern. Mo Tsu (fifth century B.C.) taught—in opposition to Confucius—an all-embracing love of humanity reaching beyond the family and the state. "The man of Ch'u is my brother," he said. Modern, indeed, is his denunciation of war:

> The murder of one person is called unrighteous and incurs a death penalty . . . the murder of a hundred persons is a hundredfold more unrighteous and there should be a hundredfold death penalty. But when it comes to the great unrighteousness of attacking states, the gentlemen of the world do not know that they should condemn it; on the contrary, they applaud it, calling it righteous. Shall we say that these gentlemen know the difference between right and wrong?

In many others there is the same timeless note—for example, the lines of Hsun Tse, 208 B.C.:

> You glorify nature and mediate on her.
> Why not domesticate and regulate her?

Or the musings of Chuang Tsu (third century B.C.) on ultimate reality:

> Once Chuang Tsu dreamed that he was a butterfly, flying about enjoying itself. It did not know that it was Chuang Tsu. Suddenly he awoke and veritably was

*Strong, *One-Fifth*.

Chuang Tsu again. But I do not know whether it was Chuang Tsu dreaming that he was a butterfly, or whether now I am a butterfly dreaming that I am Chuang Tsu.

─────────────

After the fall of the Han dynasty, men found more freedom to explore new ideas. The next selection relates the rise of Taoism and Buddhism, the two great philosophies of China after Confucius.

Taoism and Buddhism
by John K. Fairbank, Edwin O. Reischauer and Albert M. Craig

Taoism. Next to Confucianism, the most important stream in Chinese thought is Taoism (pronounced *dowism*). It was in large part a philosophy of retreat and withdrawal on the part of thinkers who were appalled by perpetual warfare, instability, and death and so turned away from the struggle for power, status, and wealth. In the face of infinite time and space, they accepted the unimportance of individuality except as human beings are individual manifestations of vast cosmic forces. This philosophy constituted a protest of common men against the growing despotism of rulers. It also expressed the rebellion of the very uncommon man of intellect or sensitivity against the growing rigidity of the moralists. who were following in the footsteps of Confucius. Where both the moralists and rulers sought to bring men into conformity with social patterns, the Taoists stoutly championed the independence of each individual, whose only concern, they maintained, should be to fit into the great pattern of nature. This was the *Tao*, literally the "Road" or "Way," a term used by Confucius to describe the social system he advocated but given a metaphysical interpretation in Taoism.

Some scholars have associated early Taoism with the state of Ch'u in the Yangtze Valley, suggested that it may represent an enrichment of Chinese thought derived in part from "barbarian" sources. Its attempt to fit human life into nature's rhythms may also represent a philosophical expression of the interest of the early Chinese in nature dieties, fertility cults, and the ruler's role as mediator between nature and man. Taoist mysticism, which may have been at the core of the movement, might also have derived from the early shamans. The latter, through self-induced trances, had communicated directly with the spirits; the Taoists, through "sitting and forgetting" and "fasts of the mind," experienced trance-like ecstasies in which they achieved the state of the "true man" and directly apprehended the oneness of the universe. Such practices may have been influenced by Indian yoga, for the Taoists, like the Indians, emphasized breathing exercises. . . .

The Spread and Development of Buddhism. Buddhism is a universal religion, in which all men are equal in the Buddhist "law," or teachings. Like Christianity and Islam, the two great universal religions of the Mediterranean area, it spread widely. Indian traders and travelers carried it by sea throughout Southeast Asia and to South China. It also spread among the Greek kingdoms left over by Alexander's conquests on the northwestern frontiers of the Indian subcontinent. Gandhara in the border region between the present Pakistan and Afghanistan became a particular stronghold of Buddhism. The greatest monarch of the Kushan Empire of the Yüeh-chih, who ruled around 100 A.D. from North India to the Tarim Basin, also was an ardent patron of Buddhism. He championed the faith in Central Asia, and from there it spread into North China. . . .

Buddhism, unlike Christianity in the Roman Empire, apparently was taken up by the rich before it spread downward to the poor. At first it seems to have made more rapid progress in the "barbarian" North than in the South, perhaps because the non-Chinese rulers of this area felt no prejudice against it as a foreign religion. The greatest imperial patrons of the new religion were the emperors of the "barbarian" Northern Wei dynasty (386–534). Two groups of Buddhist cave temples, at Yün-kang near their first capital in northern Shansi and at Lung-men near their second capital of Loyang, contain some of the finest artistic remains of early Chinese Buddhism. By the sixth century, however, the South was as thoroughly permeated by Buddhism as the North.

Part of Buddhism's success was due to its readiness to compromise with Taoism and Confucianism, tolerating the former as an inferior level of truth and the latter as a political and social philosophy that was not incompatible with its own basic teachings. Ever since there has been a strong tendency among the Chinese to synthesize "the three religions" or to maintain them side by side. At this time, however, Buddhism was definitely the dominant member of the trio, and a great proportion of the higher intellectual capacities and artistic genius of the Chinese was devoted to the translation and interpretation of its scriptures and the building and beautifying of its temples and monasteries.

The whole epoch from the fourth century to the ninth might well be called the Buddhist age of both Chinese and Asian history. During this period, Buddhism blanketed the whole of the Asian continent, except for Siberia and West Asia, giving to this vast area a degree of cultural unity that has never again been matched. This, however, was but a brief moment of religious unity. Buddhism began to decline in India as early as the sixth century and by the fifteenth had virtually disappeared. It was wiped out in Central Asia in the ninth century by the inroads of Islam. Meanwhile, the Hinayana of Southeast Asia and the Mahayana of East Asia had begun to drift apart, and a serious decline had commenced in Chinese Buddhism.

In our account of the rise of Taoism and Buddhism we have covered a good deal of time. For three and a half centuries after the fall of Han, China was divided—first into the Three Kingdoms and then into the Northern and Southern Dynasties. Unlike in the time of the Warring States, the political units in this period were still fairly large and comparatively stable. North China was conquered by the nomad Huns, but the south remained under Chinese rule. There, trade and other contact with non-Chinese societies to the south and west expanded in the wake of Buddhist travels. The south was wealthy, and the arts flourished; the gentry painted, composed poems, cultivated music, and studied the past glories of China. Finally, one of the many lesser competing "dynasties" overcame its neighbors and reunited China. Like Ch'in Shih Huang Ti, the first unifier of China, this new house, the Sui, did not last long (only thirty-eight years).

The Sui faced new difficulties. During the previous 360 years of division, social and political development in the north and south had diverged. The peoples of north and south had begun to speak different languages (or dialects), as they still do today. The north was heavily populated. The south was relatively less so, and was less directly under the control of the capital. Partially to facilitate political control and the collection of taxes, the Sui began construction of what became the great canals running north and south to connect the Yellow River and the Yangtze River. The canals were built at enormous expense, and at the same time pressures by the barbarian tribes and the extravagance of the second Sui emperor's court weakened the dynasty. Finally it was overthrown, and for five years China again lay fragmented, until she was reunified by the Tang—a dynasty that lasted three hundred years.

The Flowering of the Tang Dynasty
by Edward H. Schafer

Out of these centuries of ferment came the splendor of medieval civilization in the Far East, when China, finally known by that name, became the wonder of the world. The hallmarks of the house of T'ang, which ruled the reunified Middle Kingdom during the Seventh, Eighth and Ninth Centuries A.D., were its prosperity, its freedom, its gaiety, its experimentation and its unique contributions to art, music, literature and gardening. It was an age of faith in which the old ways of thinking became thoroughly impregnated and altered by Buddhist beliefs and attitudes, just as early medieval Europe had been profoundly altered by Greek and Roman Christianity. It was a second imperial age, comparable to the age of Han, but much richer, more cosmopolitan and sophisticated. Finally, it was an age of security and confidence, supported by successful wars against such neighbors as the Korean peoples of the north, the Vietnamese peoples of the south and the Tibetans and Turks to the west. It was during this age that the T'ang empire became the colossus of Asia.

In their conquests the T'ang armies converted the monsoon coasts of the distant southern frontier, long claimed but little absorbed, into a truly Chinese land, safe for settlers and for the benevolent activities of the Confucian magistrates, propagators of Hua civilization. Even in medieval times these tangled forests and green shorelines—in our time thoroughly tamed, cleared and planted in rice—were only partly explored, and remained largely the haunts of aliens and infidels.

Still, it was greatly desired country. Here Persian merchant princes repaired their great seagoing vessels with the fine wood of the schima, a relative of the tough southern oaks. The hot hillsides were covered with endless stands of cinnamon and camphor trees, from which came supplies for the medicine chests of the north. Camellias and tea, which are intimately related, grew wild there, and were becoming widely appreciated. The halcyon kingfisher provided iridescent turquoise feathers for the headdresses of noble northern ladies; the dark patterning of rosewood attracted dealers in carpentry supplies, and the heavy scent of kanari lured the makers of incense for Buddhist temples.

The adventurous immigrant into the new tropical south of T'ang learned to eat bananas and tangerines and lichees, and made them familiar to his friends in the north; he learned to make furniture of the tangled liana vines of the forest, and brought back red and yellow hibiscus for his gardens. He seized green peacocks in their primeval roosts and sent their tail feathers north to become expensive fans, and he captured green turtles in the phosphorescent sea to make soup for royal banquets.

The vivid, vivacious and complex culture of T'ang—in which seemingly disparate and incompatible elements from many parts of the world and many levels of society were welded into a glittering whole—represents the climax of a civilization that we now identify as "Chinese." During the twelve centuries that separated Szu-ma Niu in his bronze-fitted chariot from the silk-robed, jade-belted T'ang rulers of much of Asia, China had developed intellectual, technical and artistic resources that made it both the Greece and Rome of the Far East.

The Upper Classes and Their Culture

With the reunification of the Empire and the founding of the Tang dynasty, China reached a major watershed in her history. Up to this point, periods of relative stability and dynastic strength had alternated with long periods of disintegration. The Shang dynasty had been followed by the feudal warring and tumult of the Chou dynasty; the Han dynasty was so weakened halfway through its reign that it was forced, as the Chou dynasty had been, to move its capital. The fragmentation and instability of the Three Kingdoms and Six Dynasties lasted for more than three hundred years after the Han dynasty, until finally the Sui managed to reunify most of central China. Less than thirty years later, the Tang dynasty followed the Sui—to rule for three hundred years. With the Tang expansion into the south the empire finally had found the means to sustain itself; the militarily crucial north (first line of defense against the border tribes) could be supplied by way of the newly opened canal system from the rich agricultural regions of the south. These foundations, laid during the Tang dynasty, were so strong that for the next twelve hundred years no challenge could destroy them. Temporary retreat during the later Sung and Mongol Yuan dynasties caused only limited disintegration, more easily controlled and more rapidly restored than in previous periods. Imperial China had been established.

The wealthy and leisured gentry of Tang China produced some of the most beautiful art and poetry the world has known. The peasantry, largely excluded from this culture, developed their own culture in folktales such as the "Yellow Millet Dream." Such folktales were often then adopted by the scholars and made part of elite culture.

As the "Yellow Millet Dream" suggests, it was only the rich who had time to fully enjoy life, and the educated who had the time to create the art we find today in the great museums of the world. But it is important to remember that this art is only one of two kinds of art in traditional China. Throughout China's history two levels of culture existed side by side. The culture we study in the West as "Chinese art" is the sophisticated and highly literate culture that was the monopoly of the wealthy and leisured class. The arts that this class developed were closely related to literacy: calligraphy and brush painting, poetry and essays—very different from the folk culture we will read about later.

In this section we will explore the nature of the upper classes who produced the "literate" arts, and then consider some of their essays and poems. We include a discussion by the historian Dun Li, who contrasts the "four classes" of classical Confucianism with the idea of Mencius, who was a famous Confucianist; their differences demonstrate how many different points of view took the name "Confucianism." Dun Li then presents arguments for and against the examination system that provided educated men for the bureaucracy; many of those who failed the examinations went on to become great poets and artists. Those who did pass were usually employed by the government but were paid very low salaries. The expectation was that the officials would either live on their private incomes (from land rents or other investments) or on bribes; there was no attempt to avoid "conflicts of interest." Not surprisingly, the officials were easily influenced; but what we would see as outright corruption was built into the system. This is discussed in a reading from French sinologist Jacques Gernet's *Daily Life in China on the Eve of the Mongol Invasion*.

The Yellow Millet Dream
by Étienne Balazs

Tradition and Revolution in China

I shall begin by telling a story. One evening in A.D. 731 a poor peasant and an old Taoist called Liu met together in an inn on the road to Han-tan. In order to forget how hungry they were, they started to chat while the innkeeper prepared a bowl of gruel for their supper. The peasant spoke of the cares and anxieties of his poverty-stricken life, but when the strange old man offered him a curious porcelain pillow, scarcely had he laid his weary head upon it than he was transported to a wonderful land of dreams, where he possessed a house of his own, was married to a daughter of one of the best families, was rich, looked up to, and respected, and had passed the civil service examinations with distinction. After filling a number of important posts, he was appointed governor of the capital, and in this capacity, conquered an army of barbarians. As a reward, the Emperor made him a minister; but a rival faction was successful in its plot to bring about his downfall, and his headlong plunge from the heights of power to the depths of a dungeon nearly ended in his being decapitated. Only at the last minute did he escape execution, and he was then restored to office, and given a title to make up for the injustice he had suffered. His five sons, all high officials, provided him with numerous descendants, and he had come to the point of contemplating retirement, happy to end his days in peace, and looking forward to a final resting place with his ancestors, when he suddenly wakened to find himself once again in the vile inn, where the pot of gruel was still heating on the stove, and the old Taoist was smiling at him and saying, with a wink: "That's the way life passes, quick as a flash."

This little tale, known in Chinese as "The Yellow Millet Dream," dates from the end of the eighth century, and later supplied the theme for a number of stories and plays. The story is remarkable, because it contains the dream of happiness shared by all Chinese, and expresses it with the utmost conciseness yet without leaving out a single salient feature. It is as if the writer had striven to put all his experience into a nutshell, and in doing so he has summarized two thousand years of history, during which the ideal of every Chinese had always been to become an official, this being regarded as the height of power and the sum of happiness. It was, however, an ideal that could be realized only by a tiny minority of the elect, and the fate of the vast majority was to remain a peasant, an artisan, or a merchant— in short, one of the *misera plebs,* the humble subject to those remote, haughty, flesh-and-blood divinities of the terrestrial universe, the officials.

The Four Classes
*by Dun Li**

Customarily the Chinese spoke of their society as composed of four classes: the scholars, the farmers, the artisans, and the merchants. The scholars were given the highest status because they performed what the Chinese regarded as the most important function: the transmission of an

---

*Dun Li, *Ageless Chinese*.

ancient heritage and the personification of Chinese virtues. The farmers' standing was second only to the scholars because they were the primary producers, feeding and clothing the nation. The artisans processed what the farmers had produced, and their function was not regarded as so essential as that of the farmers. At the bottom of the social scale were the merchants whom the Chinese regarded as outright exploiters, making profits from what others had produced or processed and contributing nothing themselves. Two other classes were often added to the four described above. One was the soldiers, whose expected role of burning and killing was very distasteful to the Chinese. Inasmuch as they took away the most valuable things from society, their standing in society was inferior to that of the merchants. Their image in the eyes of the public was not improved during modern times when the idle and adventurous swarmed to their ranks as mercenaries. The other class ws the so-called "mean people" (*chien-min*), consisting of domestic slaves, prostitutes, entertainers, and members of lowly professions such as barbers. Though the contempt shown for this group could be explained historically, it was nevertheless a prejudice. It should be added, however, that the total number of this group was very small at any given time.

A more accurate classification of the Chinese people was perhaps the one advanced by Mencius some 2,300 years ago. He believed that in an ideal society there were two kinds of people: the educated who ruled and the uneducated who were the ruled. Though Mencius was only speculating on what an ideal society should be, the Chinese applied his theory almost to the letter until modern times. If we transcribe the customary division of classes (scholars, farmers, etc.) into his classification, all but the scholars would belong to the ruled category. Among the ruled it was difficult to say which group actually had a higher standing. Though traditionally the farmers were exalted and the merchants were condemned, such an evaluation of their comparative worth was done more in principle than in fact. It did not affect to any large extent the estimation of each class in the eyes of the general public. With the exception of the Former Han dynasty, discrimination against merchants was more theoretical than actual, though this discrimination, even on a theoretical plane, did discourage young men of talent from pursuing a commercial career. While it is true that a great landlord enjoyed more prestige than a rich merchant, it is not correct to say that a shopkeeper was regarded as inferior to a small, independent farmer. In the eyes of most people he was definitely superior to a tenant farmer. In China as in other societies, income crossed over the established social boundaries to become an important factor in determining social prestige. What made the traditional Chinese society seem unique was that income played only an auxiliary rather than a dominant role in the matter of social standing.

While the difference between farmers, artisans, and merchants was comparatively minor insofar as social standing was concerned, there was no question that scholars towered above them all in social prestige and general esteem. A number of reasons can be advanced to explain their exalted position. First, without an established religion (Confucianism was not a religion), China did not have a clerical hierarchy. On the other hand, some of the essential, useful functions traditionally carried on by the clergy in the West had likewise in China to be performed by someone. The teaching of morals, for instance, was such a function. Under the circumstances no one was in a better position to perform such functions than Confucian scholars. Second, the ultimate goal of practically all Confucian scholars (including Confucius) was to secure a position with the government, and in China as in many other agricultural societies, there was no higher prestige than that of becoming a king's minister. Since government officials were selected from scholars as a matter of principle, the prestige generally ascribed to government officials was also shared by scholars. Third, there was the difficulty of the Chinese written language. Though to learn colloquial Chinese (*pai-hua*) was perhaps no more difficult than to learn the English or Russian languages, it was definitely much more difficult to learn to read and write literary or classical Chinese. This required not only the mastering of more than 10,000 separate characters and their numerous combinations but also a fair knowledge of the great accumulation of Chinese literature. Unless the learner was a born genius, it would take a considerable part of his life just to learn to write in a presentable style. His style could always be improved no matter how good it was, and to improve it would be a life-long process. Most Chinese just could not afford the time. Thus, true mastery of a literary education was bound to be limited to a few. Knowledge, like commodities, commanded a high price when it was difficult to obtain.

The Examination System
by Dun Li*

Like all other systems, the examination system had its advantages and disadvantages. On the positive side, it might be said that it had broadened the government's base by drawing officials from all levels of society and thus introduced a democratic element into an otherwise oligarchic society. Theoretically at least, it was entirely possible for a man of the humblest origin, by passing the specified examinations, to rise in power, wealth, and prestige. More than anything else, the examination system accounted for the absence of a caste system in China and the large degree of social mobility denied to many other authoritarian societies. Second, to find the right man for the right task, nothing could be more objective than a test impartially administered, and the civil service examination system was adopted precisely for that purpose. Many great statesmen in China were a product of this system. Third, the examination system brought to mind the importance of education and learning and thus indirectly raised the cultural level of the country as a whole. While in other countries landlords, merchants, or industrialists might be men of the greatest prestige, in China the most respected had always been the scholars.

However, those who criticized this system could point out that the examination which at best was a test of literary learning should not be used as the sole criterion to judge a man's true ability, since a good administrator was more often a man of the world than a man learned in Confucian classics or skillful in writing poetry. Moreover, while the examination system might have increased social mobility, it did not end social stratification. A barber's son might pass

---

*Dun Li, *Ageless Chinese*.

the examination and thus be accepted as one of the social elite, but this did not help the rest of the barbers who were still regarded as the "mean" people. Furthermore, except for the wealthy few, who could afford to spend years of study just to prepare for the examinations? The so-called democratic outlook of the examination system was perhaps more apparent than real. Critics of this system were anxious to point out that the over-emphasis on literary learning at the expense of other intellectual pursuits had done great damage to other areas of learning of equal importance. This accounted for, at least in part, China's lag behind some other countries in the field of science and technology, despite its achievement in the humanities. Individual scientific talents did occur from time to time, but as society did not attach much importance to the study of natural science and offered no reward for its development, and as people generally looked down upon manual work, there was no intellectual tradition outside the study of humanities. Last, perhaps the most serious indictment against the examination system was its contribution to the development of despotism. After this system was adopted, a man could no longer attain political authority or social recognition through any channel but one, which was controlled by the government. Forever looking for favor and patronage from the central government, the country's educated lost their political initiative and independence and became the ardent defenders of the status quo. As the educated class went, so went the country as a whole.

Imperial Justice
by Jacques Gernet

There was very little contact between the government and the rural population. The sub-prefect lived in town, within a fortified citadel containing his residence, the administrative offices, the audience-hall and the prison. He was a distant being who was hardly ever seen and who was surrounded by an aura of dazzling prestige. The State for its part did not interfere in the life of the peasant communities, or rather only did so for essential purposes: collecting taxes, collecting men for the forced labour that was demanded for public works, when sometimes as many as several hundred thousand men were required, and for taking defensive measures against subversive movements. For these, villages and families were held collectively responsible—and sometimes organized into groups of families with collective responsibility—so that whenever a rebellion broke out anywhere, the repression was terrible.

The principle underlying the whole administrative system in China was that above all, peace must reign. There was to be no stirring up of trouble: a sub-prefect who allowed disturbances to arise in his area of jurisdiction was a bad administrator, and it was he who was blamed, whatever the origin of the disturbances might have been. His immediate superiors ran a considerable risk of having their promotion retarded. From another point of view, the people administered were hesitant about referring to the public authorities for settling their differences, and it was only when all other solutions (compromise or arbitration) had failed that they presented themselves before the court of justice held by the sub-prefect. An accused person was immediately thrown into prison: even an innocent person wrongfully accused was guilty of having disturbed the peace of the locality and the tranquillity of the judge. Besides, since the idea of accusing him had arisen, his innocence was not complete. As for the accuser, he too was regarded with the greatest suspicion. Furthermore, it was expensive to have recourse to public justice, since an accusation could not be laid without making the usual offerings to the judge: it was a matter of decorum.

Chinese justice insisted on certain kinds of objective proof (a thief could not be condemned if the object stolen had not been found, nor a supposed murderer if there was no trace of violence on the corpse), but at the same time it was one of the most cruel systems of justice that has ever existed. All the penalties consisted of extremely severe corporal punishments. The accused were kept in prison for lengthy periods in wretched conditions. They received no nourishment except from their relations, who, however, were needed for work in the fields. Torture (whipping, beating, the iron collar and manacles) was normally employed to induce recalcitrant prisoners to confess. Also miscarriage of justice was comparatively frequent. In short, it was a system of justice apparently designed to discourage people from acquiring a taste for legal proceedings, and it is easy to understand why the peasants preferred to settle their quarrels among themselves, either by coming to an agreement, or by arbitration. Only the most serious cases came before the official courts of justice.

Collective responsibility, the cruelty of repressive measures, the authority of the elders of the village and the local district, the authority of heads of families, village solidarity and the horror of legal proceedings—these are the factors which explain why peace reigned in the countryside. Only a great famine or the most crying and widespread injustice stirred up troops of rebels. It was troops of this kind, inflamed with messianic hopes and grown to the size of veritable armies, that usually put an end to dynasties and sometimes swept one of their leaders to the throne of the Son of Heaven.

The Poets

The gentry, scholars, court officials, and their relatives gathered taxes and rent from the peasantry; with this wealth they supported an elegant, sophisticated civilization famous for its art and literature. The Tang period (A.D. 618–907) was especially renowned for its music, painting, and poetry. While the poets by and large were of elite origins themselves, many sympathized with the common people and wrote about them. Tu Fu, for instance, is still known as a "people's poet," and Po Chü-yi wrote in everyday language rather than in a learned style. Moreover, many poets were far from rich; some lived on the fringes of upper-class society and supported themselves by tutoring children of wealthy families or by taking official posts when they could be found.

Li Po (A.D. 701–762), one of China's great poets, was fond of wine and is also remembered for his romantic descriptions of nature. In "On the Mountain" he expounds on a hermit's reasons for withdrawing into the wilderness.

On the Mountain: Question and Answer
by Li Po

You ask me:
                    Why do I live
on this green mountain?
        I smile
        No answer
                    My heart serene
    On flowing water
                        peachblow
                        quietly going
                        far away
    This is   another earth
               another sky
    No likeness
                to that human world below

Translated by Cyril Birch

Drinking Alone Under Moonlight
by Li Po

Holding a jug of wine among the flowers,
And drinking alone, not a soul keeping me company,
I raise my cup and invite the moon to drink with me,
And together with my shadow we are three.
But the moon does not know the joy of drinking,
And my shadow only follows me about.
Nevertheless I shall have them as my companions,
For one should enjoy life at such a time.
The moon loiters as I sing my songs,
My shadow looks confused as I dance.
I drink with them when I am awake
And part with them when I am drunk.
Henceforward may we always be feasting,
And may we meet in the Cloudy River of Heaven.

Translated by Robert Payne

A more serious poet than Li Po, Tu Fu (A.D. 712–770) lived through the turmoil of the An Lu-shan rebellion and wrote about the wars that regularly swept over China. The setting of "Advent of Spring" is the ruins of a destroyed city after a war.

Advent of Spring

by Tu Fu

The city has fallen: only the hills and rivers remain.
In spring the streets were green with grass and trees.
Sorrowing over the times, the flowers are weeping.
The birds startled my heart in fear of departing.
The beacon fires were burning for three months,
A letter from home was worth ten thousand pieces of gold.
I scratch the scant hairs on my white head,
And vainly attempt to secure them with a hairpin.

Translated by Robert Payne

Though he enjoyed a successful career in government, Po Chü-yi (A.D. 772–846) here gives a personal impression of injustices in Tang society. The title refers to the fact that taxes were partially paid in grain.

The Grain Tribute

by Po Chü-yi

There came an officer knocking by night at my door—
In a loud voice demanding grain-tribute.
My house-servants dared not wait till the morning,
But brought candles and set them on the barn-floor.
Passed through the sieve, clean-washed as pearls,
A whole cart-load, thirty bushels of grain.
But still they cry that it is not paid in full:
With whips and curses they goad my servants and boys.
Once, in error, I entered public life;
I am inwardly ashamed that my talents were not sufficient.

In succession I occupied four official posts;
For doing nothing,—ten years' salary!
Often have I heard that saying of ancient men
That "good and ill follow in an endless chain."
And to-day it ought to set my heart at rest
To return to others the corn in my great barn.

Translated by Arthur Waley in 170 Chinese Poems

In addition to civil strife, the people of the Tang era suffered through border wars against foreign barbarians and wars aimed at expanding the empire's territory. Li Po gives a memorable picture of the human victims of war, while Tsán Shān and Wáng Hàn sketch life for soldiers on the distant frontier. As an official, Tsán was stationed on the northwest border of the Tang domain.

Fighting South of the Ramparts
by Li Po

Last year we were fighting at the source
of the Sang-kan;*
This year we are fighting on the Onion River†
road.
We have washed our swords in the surf of
Parthian seas;
We have pastured our horses among the snows
of the T'ien Shan,
The King's armies have grown grey and old
Fighting ten thousand leagues away from home.
The Huns have no trade but battle and carnage;
They have no fields or ploughlands,
But only wastes where white bones lie
among yellow sands.
Where the House of Ch'in built the great wall that
was to keep away the Tartars.

---

*Runs west to east through northern Shansi and Hopei, north of the Great Wall.
†The Kashgar-darya, in Turkestan.

There, in its turn, the House of Han
                       lit beacons of war.
The beacons are always alight, fighting and
                       marching never stop.
Men die in the field, slashing sword to sword;
The horses of the conquered neigh piteously
                       to Heaven.
Crows and hawks peck for human guts,
Carry them in their beaks and hang them on
                       the branches of withered trees.
Captains and soldiers are smeared on the
                       bushes and grass;
The General schemed in vain.
Know therefore that the sword is a cursed thing
Which the wise man uses only if he must.

Translated by Arthur Waley in Poetry and Career of Li Po

In the Wasteland
by Tsán Shān

into the west I walk my horse,
                    into the very skies
since leaving home, I've seen the moon
                    twice round before my eyes*
I cannot think where I shall stop
                    to spend the night tonight—
from level sands, for a myriad miles,
                    no smokes of men arise

Translated by E. Bruce Brooks

Verses from Lyángjōu
by Wáng Hàn

lovely grapewine in the cups
                    of noctilucent jade
urged on, as they're about to drink,
                    by lutes on horseback played

———————

*I.e., for two months.

drunk, they lie upon the sands,
  but let milord not laugh—
the journey back from the battlefield
  how many men have made?

Translated by E. Bruce Brooks

Chinese poets were often critical of the established state religions of Confucianism and Buddhism. Here Po Chü-yi makes fun of Lao Tzu, the author of the *Tao Te Ching* and a central figure in Taoism.

Lao Tzu

by Po Chü-yi

"Those who speak know nothing;
Those who know are silent."
Those words, I am told,
Were spoken by Lao-tzu.
If we are to believe that Lao-tzu
  Was himself one who knew,
How comes it that he wrote a book
  Of five thousand words?

Translated by Arthur Waley in Chinese Poems

Merchants

In theory the merchants were the lowest social group, despised by the scholars and officials. But it is not surprising that many merchants found that their actual position varied according to their wealth. Here Dun Li describes the growth of trade and commerce in Imperial China and the power of the wealthy merchants. His picture of these merchants is quite different from that implied by the traditional idea of the "four classes."

The Rise of the Merchants
by Dun Li*

Together with the political factors described above, there were social and economic causes that slowly undermined the feudal structure. One of these was the rise of the merchant class and the growth of cities. Feudalism thrived best in a self-sufficient economy within a small area, but geographical specialization in production was bound to destroy such self-sufficiency and eventually feudalism as well. While basic crops such as rice and wheat were raised practically all over China, different sections specialized in producing different products: "lumber, bamboo, and precious stones in Shansi; fish, salt, lacquer, silk and musical instruments in Shantung; fruits in the Yangtze River valley; and copper and iron in the mountainous regions in Szechuan." As society became more advanced, people desired more and better goods. This was especially true with the nobles who, being wealthy, could afford and consequently demanded luxuries produced in other areas. As such demands increased, each area, besides producing for its own needs, had to produce a surplus to exchange for what it needed and did not have. Hence there arose the merchant class which shipped goods from one place to another by performing a necessary economic service. Barter was no doubt the earliest form of trade, but as trade increased, money had to be used. Money in various forms was in use as early as the Shang dynasty, but it was not until the seventh or the sixth century B.C. that governments began to mint metallic coins. They came to different states at different times. The comparatively backward state of Ch'in, for instance, did not coin money until the fourth century B.C. After the fifth century B.C. gold began to circulate in large quantities. While the princes used it for rewarding their own ministers as well as bribing the ministers of other states, the merchants employed it as a medium of exchange. The use of precious metals as money unquestionably facilitated trade.

---

*Dun Li, *Ageless Chinese*.

Trade also benefited from the increasing mobility of the people. Despite the fact that China was politically divided, there was no restriction of movement across state lines. A merchant could move freely from one state to another without encountering harassment from government on either side of the border line. No state would persecute a merchant simply because he came from another state; nor would it discriminate against him on behalf of its own merchants. It seemed that all governments had recognized the importance of his services. Under this benevolent atmosphere, many merchants became powerful and wealthy, so wealthy that in many cases they outshone the feudal lords in the display of luxuries. Often they doubled as money-lenders and even had kings and princes as their regular customers. One of the Chou kings, we are told, was so much in debt that he rarely chose to emerge from his palaces because he was afraid that he might bump into his creditors. As wealth increased, influence increased proportionally. The big merchants were granted audiences and were treated as equals by reigning princes in whichever states they happened to be. Often they exercised great influence over domestic and interstate affairs. It was said that Tzu Kung, a powerful merchant and also a former student of Confucius, in one trip, "saved Lu, deranged Ch'i, destroyed Wu, strengthened Tsin, and raised Yüeh to a position of supremacy." His feats were no doubt exaggerated. The fact nevertheless remains that the merchants were a powerful group to reckon with during this period.

The increase of commercial activities was reflected in the growth of cities. Cities became larger and more numerous, especially those located along the trade routes or chosen as state capitals. . . .

Cities with a population of almost 100,000 were common all over China. This booming scene was particularly noticeable in South China. Through the efforts of the southern states, Ch'u, Wu, and Yüeh, the Chinese frontier was extended steadily southward to the modern Fukien province and the southern portions of the modern Kiangsi and Hunan provinces. Here natural environment was more rewarding, land was more productive, and people were generally more spirited and carefree. All these, of course, were favorable conditions for the growth of commercial activities. There was the famous merchant Fan Li who, after retiring from an official career as Yüeh's chief minister early in the fifth century B.C., amassed a huge fortune in a period of nineteen years. He distributed much of his wealth among his friends and relatives, still leaving a large amount to his descendants. Today his supposed image is still hung in many Chinese stores whose owners are no doubt hoping to duplicate the achievement of this ancient financial wizard.

In the cities life was lively and interesting. Whenever a large number of people congregated, community activities existed; some of them were secular and others were religious. In the northern city of Lintzu, one of the most important events was the annual spring festival in honor of the Earth God. On that day all were dressed in their best, and the city provided a variety of entertainments including songs, dances, dramas, and acrobatics. Country people flowed into the city for the occasion, and many young maidens could enjoy overt flirtations without being criticized. After all was over and when evening drew near, there was plenty of wine for people to get intoxicated. The temple of the Earth God was perhaps the most important building in the city besides the palaces. Before a military campaign, meat and wine were offered to the Earth God to bring about good luck. After the campaign, victory was reported to him; sometimes the captured enemy commanders were killed in the temple as sacrifices. Natural disasters like flood and drought had also to be reported so he could give counsel with regard to the best of possible remedies. In a lawsuit when the judge was unable to render a judgment because of the lack of evidences, both sides were required to swear before the Earth God and waited for miracles to happen. Whenever there was an eclipse of the sun or the moon, people gathered in front of the temple, beating drums loudly to scare off the evil spirit who was about to swallow up the heavenly body.

The Middle Kingdom and the Barbarians

In peaceful times the Chinese traded with their neighbors and great caravans crossed the mountains and deserts to the west. All the peoples with whom they had contact, save only for the Buddhists of India, regarded China as the center of civilization and acknowledged the Chinese emperor as the Son of Heaven. Periodically, when dynasties declined and their military defenses weakened, the nomads to the north and west would rise in revolt. The strongest were often able to dominate northern China, and twice in history they conquered all of China: the Yuan dynasty of the Mongols, and the Ching dynasty of the Manchus.

The first reading is by Owen Lattimore, an American historian who has traveled widely in Mongolia and China's northwest since the early part of this century; it is about the troubled history of Chinese conflicts with these border nomads to the north. The next two readings describe Genghis Khan and the Mongol conquest which founded the Yuan dynasty, and the last is a Chinese explorer's account of his voyages.

Border Lands
by Owen Lattimore

One of the master keys to Chinese history is an understanding of the balance of power between China and the "barbarians" of the outlying regions.

Between the Pacific Ocean and the Pamir plateau and curving southward from the Pamirs into the bleak highlands that divide China from India, lie the North-eastern Provinces, Mongolia, Chinese Turkistan, and Tibet. These are the Inner Asian barrier lands, one of the least known frontiers in the world, which limit the geography and history of China on one side as the sea limits them on the other.

The Great Wall, for a score of centuries the most colossal tide mark of the human race, stands as the symbol of this entire frontier. It runs from the sea westward into the deserts of Central Asia for a distance about as great as from New York City to the Rockies. Parts of the Great Wall were built by several ancient Chinese kingdoms. In the third century B.C. the Chin emperor Shih Huang Ti, the first imperial unifier of China, joined these local walls into a complete national walled frontier. Later the walled frontier was modified more than once by succeeding dynasties.

The idea of the Great Wall was to divide the settled Chinese people from the nomad shepherd peoples. Actually, however, the Great Wall never worked very satisfactorily as a sharp dividing line. If you went far enough north of the wall you came to people who were only shepherds; if you went far enough south you came to people who were only farmers. But the region of the wall itself stubbornly insisted on remaining a region, not a line of cleavage—a region in which some people were herdsmen and some farmers. Because they combined two ways of life these people were pulled two ways in their political allegiance. Sometimes they came under the control of the nomads; at other times they were under the control of agricultural China. The real political frontier, accordingly, often lay either to the north or to the south of the Great Wall.

Directly to the north of the Great Wall lies the main expanse of the grassy steppes of Mongolia. What makes Mongolia important in the history of China and Inner Asia is the natural scope of movement of nomad peoples. In a nomad society there can never be as many people to the square mile as in a farming society. On the other hand, when war or politics makes it necessary, nomads can gather together from great distances more readily than farmers. Hence in the wars of the past between wandering peoples and settled peoples, the nomads normally had the advantage of sudden and concentrated impact. . . .

In China as in other settled countries, nomad conquerors and the garrisons they brought with them were always "absorbed" simply because they relinquished the source of their strength, which was mobility, by becoming sedentary. On the other hand, when nomads were defeated and driven away from the frontiers of "civilization," this very defeat normally lead to a renewal of the strength of nomadism, for the nomads were thrown back completely on the pure techniques of herding and mobility which gave them strength.

Moreover, while nomads were from time to time absorbed among the settled people, there were also many settled people who became converted into nomads. These included farmers along the frontier, merchants who traveled among the nomads, and prisoners of war. In the upshot, the conflict between the tilled lands and the pasture lands always renewed itself because each kind of society was capable of recovering vitality even after severe defeat. . . .

Westward from Mongolia and northwestward from China, the steppes of the nomads thin out into deserts where no herds can be grazed. On the western side these deserts run at last up to the foot of the highest mountains in the world, which shut off Tibet and India and Afghanistan. On the northern side other mountains bar access to Siberia and the Soviet Central Asian republics, except for a few gaps through which trade and migration have flowed for centuries. In narrow curving lines where the mountains meet the deserts lie the thinly strung oases of Sinkiang or Chinese Turkistan.

Each of the oases of Central Asia is like a miniature China. Its bearded men and fair-skinned women differ from the Chinese in physical appearance and in many other respects. For the most part they are Turkish by speech and Moslem by religion but they belong in the main to a white race, descended in unbroken line from ancestors who are known to have lived in the same regions in the Stone Age. These ancestors at one time spoke languages belonging to the Indo-European system, and they were closely akin to the people who still live in Switzerland and the Tyrol, whom anthropologists call "Alpine." These differences, however, only disguise the fact that in its essential structure the life of the oases is like that of China. It is closely dependent on agriculture; the agriculture is of a specialized, intensive kind, with a maximum of irrigation and hand cultivation; and as in China a walled city stands at the heart of each agricultural district. . . .

Between the oases lie stretches of desert. There are big oases and little ones, but otherwise any oasis is almost exactly like any other, so that there is a minimum demand for trade and exchange. Trade, in both the recent and the ancient past, has largely been the concern of alien merchants dealing in such commodities as can stand the high cost of transport over very long distances.

In the Middle Ages, at an oasis like Turfan, where routes from the deserts and the steppes and from China, Persia, and India converged on each other, there dwelt whole communities of alien traders. Turfan, in the eighth century, for example, was like a landward Shanghai. In each foreign trading quarter, people wore the costumes and spoke the languages of their distant homes, and worshipped at the temples and chapels of their own religion; but when war interrupted the caravan trade, the merchants vanished and the people of Turfan were left to their ancient occupations, tending their canals and irrigating their fields.

Genghis Khan, the conqueror of China, was a Mongol chieftain who lived from about 1167 to 1227. His personal name, Temujin, is used throughout the selection by Harold Lamb. The Mongols were an Asiatic tribal people who lived in and migrated across a vast area of barren windswept steppe stretching from the Great Wall of northern China to the forests of southern Siberia. Their conquest of China took more than a generation, from the early 1200s to 1279, and was finally completed by Kublai Khan, Genghis' grandson. Today the People's Republic of Mongolia occupies only a small part of the original Mongol territory between Russia and China.

The Life of Genghis Khan
by Harold Lamb

The Desert

Children of this corner of the northern Gobi were not hardened to suffering; they were born to it. After they were weaned from their mother's milk to mare's milk they were expected to manage for themselves.

The places nearest the fire in the family tent belonged to the grown warriors and to guests. Women, it is true, could sit on the left side, but at a distance, and the boys and girls had to fit in anywhere they could.

So with food. In the spring when horses and cows began to give milk in quantity, all was very well. The sheep grew fatter, too. Game was more abundant and the hunters of the tribe would bring in deer and even a bear instead of the lean fur-bearing animals like the fox, marten and sable. Everything went into the pot and was eaten—the able-bodied men taking the first portions, the aged and the women received the pot next, and the children had to fight for bones and sinewy bits. Very little was left for the dogs.

In the winter when the cattle were lean the children did not fare so well. Milk existed then only in the form of *kumiss*—milk placed in leather sacks and fermented and beaten. It was nourishing and slightly intoxicating, for a young chap of three or four years—if he could contrive to beg or steal some. Meat failing, boiled millet served to take the edge off hunger after a fashion.

The end of winter was the worst of all for the youngsters. No more cattle could be killed off without thinning the herds too much. At such a time the warriors of the tribe were usually raiding the food reserves of another tribe, carrying off cattle and horses.

The children learned to organize hunts of their own, stalking dogs and rats with clubs or blunt arrows. They learned to ride, too, on sheep, clinging to the wool.

Endurance was the first heritage of Genghis Khan, whose birth name was Temujin.* At the time of his birth his father had been absent on a raid against a tribal enemy, Temujin by name. The affair went well both home and afield, the enemy was made prisoner, and the father, returning, gave to his infant son the name of the captive foeman.

His home was a tent made of felt stretched over a framework of wattled rods with an aperture at the top to let out the smoke. This was coated with white lime and ornamented with pictures. A peculiar kind of tent, this *yurt* that wandered all over the prairies mounted on a cart drawn by a dozen or more oxen. Serviceable, too, because its dome-like shape enabled it to stand the buffeting of the wind, and it could be taken down at need. . . .

Temujin—the youthful Genghis Khan—had many duties. The boys of the family must fish the streams they passed in their trek from the summer to winter pastures. The horse herds were in their charge, and they had to ride afield after lost animals, and to search for new pasture lands. They watched the skyline for raiders, and spent many a

---

*Temujin signifies "The Finest Steel"—*Tumur-ji*. The Chinese version is *T'ie mou jen*, which has another meaning altogether, "Supreme Earth Man."

night in the snow without a fire. Of necessity, they learned to keep the saddle for several days at a time, and to go without cooked food for three or four days—sometimes without any food at all.

When mutton or horse-flesh was plentiful they feasted and made up for lost time, stowing away incredible amounts against the day of privation. For diversions they had horse races, twenty miles out into the prairie and back, or wrestling matches in which bones were freely broken.

Temujin was marked by great physical strength, and ability to scheme—which is only another way of adapting himself to circumstances. He became the leader of the wrestlers, although he was spare in build. He could handle a bow remarkably well. Not so well as his brother Kassar who was called the Bowman. But Kassar was afraid of Temujin.

They formed an alliance of two against their hardy half brothers, and the first incident related to Temujin is the slaying of one of the half brothers, who had stolen a fish from him. Mercy seemed to these nomad youths to be of little value, but retribution was an obligation.

And Temujin became aware of feuds more important than the animosity of boys. His mother, Houlun, was beautiful, and so had been carried off by his father from a neighboring tribe on her wedding ride to the tent of her betrothed husband. Houlun, being both sagacious and willful, made the best of circumstances after a little wailing; but all in the *yurt* knew that some day men from her tribe would come to avenge the wrong.

At night by the glowing dung fire Temujin would listen to the tales of the minstrels, old men who rode from one wagon-tent to another carrying a one-stringed fiddle, and singing in a droning voice the tales of a tribe's forebears and heroes.

He was conscious of his strength, and his right of leadership. Was he not the first-born of Yesukai the Valiant, Khan of the Yakka or Great Mongols, master of forty thousand tents?

From the tales of the minstrels he knew that he came of distinguished stock, the Bourchikoun, or Gray-eyed Men. He harkened to the story of his ancestor, Kabul Khan who had pulled the emperor of Cathay by the beard and who had been poisoned as a consequence. He learned that his father's sworn brother was Toghrul Khan of the Karaïts, the most powerful of the Gobi nomads—he who gave birth in Europe to the tales of Prester John of Asia.

But at that time Temujin's horizon was limited by the pasture lands of his tribe, the Yakka Mongols.

"We are not a hundredth part of Cathay," a wise counselor said to the boy, "and the only reason why we have been able to cope with her is that we are all nomads, carrying our supplies with us, and experienced in our kind of warfare. When we can, we plunder; when we cannot, we hide away. If we begin to build towns and change our old habits, we shall not prosper. Besides, monasteries and temples breed mildness of character, and it is only the fierce and warlike who dominate mankind."*

The Mongols
by John K. Fairbank, Edwin O. Reischauer and Albert M. Craig

In the history of the Northern Wei, the Liao, and the Chin we can see a number of repetitive features which become still clearer in the periods of Mongol and Manchu conquest: (1) Invaders seized power in North China usually during periods of disorder. (2) The "barbarians" enlisted Chinese advice and aid, especially from Chinese of the border region. (3) The superior "barbarian" cavalry was supplied with more and better horses from the steppe than could be maintained in an agricultural region. (4) Through a policy of tolerance, if not appeasement, local Chinese leaders were attracted and used to enlist a larger corps of Chinese tax collectors and administrators. (5) The invaders made use of the Chinese institutions of government and also let the traditional administration and Chinese social and cultural life continue. (6) But for them-

---

*It must be remembered that the Mongols were not of the same race as the Chinese proper. They were descended from the Tungusi of aboriginal stock, with a strong mixture of Iranian and Turkish blood—a race that is now called Ural-Altaic. These were the nomads of high Asia that the Greeks named Scythians.

selves the invaders maintained a homeland of their own beyond the Wall in order to preserve their own conscious existence as a people and avoid absorption. (7) A dual, Sino-"barbarian" administration was conducted at the local level, largely by Chinese under the supervision of the conquerors. (8) The invaders also employed other foreigners in their administration. (9) They preserved control through military force held in reserve—including both a territorial army into which Chinese could be recruited, and units of the invading horde, which garrisoned the capital and key areas. (10) Toward tribal peoples in Inner Asia, dynasties of conquest developed a divide-and-rule policy. (11) In the long run, the invaders in the midst of overwhelming numbers of Chinese subjects would begin to borrow elements of Chinese culture: food, clothing, names, and even the language. (12) The result was eventual absorption or expulsion. All these features were illustrated during the Mongol conquest.

Like other nomad groups who conquered smaller parts of China, the Mongols used Chinese bureaucrats and the existing government to rule this part of their empire. They realized it would be impossible to impose their culture on the agrarian and highly cultured Chinese, and instead held themselves apart as a separate class, above the Chinese in theory but in fact closely dependent on them.

Over time it became increasingly difficult for the Mongols to maintain their identity. With the adoption of Chinese customs and intermarriage, their exclusive control was eroded and the dynasty rapidly declined. Floods and famines in the early 1300s depleted the state granaries and provoked rebellions. Finally a rough peasant and former Buddhist monk named Chu Yuan-chang joined a secret society and began to attract a following. In 1356 he seized Nanking in the Yangtze Valley and by 1368 had taken Peking, overthrown the Mongols, and proclaimed himself the first emperor of the Ming dynasty.

The historians of this newly established dynasty did not deal kindly with the earlier barbarians of the Yuan, and a selection by Michael Sullivan reflects this Chinese image of the Mongols. The Ming scholars also disapproved of Imperial missions to explore the south seas. In spite of their opposition, several voyages reached the coast of Africa, but finally the voyages ceased, and China again turned inward.

The Fall of the Mongols and the Rise of the Ming Dynasty
by Michael Sullivan

During the twelfth century China had come to uneasy terms with her northern neighbours and, after her custom, civilized them. But beyond them across the deserts of Central Asia there roamed a horde which Fitzgerald called "the most savage and pitiless race known to history"—the Mongols. In 1210 their leader, the great Genghis Khan, attacked the buffer state of Chin, and destroyed their capital at Peking. In 1227 he destroyed the Hsia, leaving only one hundredth of the population alive, a disaster by which the northwest was permanently laid waste. Three years later Genghis died, but still the Mongol hordes advanced, and in 1235 they turned southward into China. For forty years the Chinese armies resisted them, almost unsupported by their own government, But the outcome was inevitable, and when in 1279 the last Sung pretender was destroyed, the Mongols proclaimed their rule over China, calling themselves the Yüan. China was spared the worst of the atrocities which had been visited upon all their other victims for, as a Khitan adviser had pointed out, the Chinese were more useful alive, and taxable, than dead. But the wars and break-up of the administration left Kubilai master of a weak and impoverished empire, whose taxpayers had been reduced from a hundred million under the Sung to less than sixty. Although Kubilai was an able ruler and a deep admirer of Chinese culture, the Mongol administration was not only utterly out of touch but ruthless and corrupt to boot. Seven emperors succeeded one another in the forty years following the death of Kubilai in 1294. Chinese discontent against the harsh rule of the last Khan broke into open rebellion in 1348. For twenty years rival bandits and warlords fought over the prostrate country, which the Mongols had long since ceased to control effectively. Finally, in 1368, the last Khan fled northwards from Peking, the power of the Mongols was broken for ever, and the short, inglorious rule of the Yüan Dynasty was at an end. In conquering China they had realised the age-long dream of all the nomad tribes, but in less than a century the Chinese drained them of the savage vitality which had made that conquest possible, and threw them back into the desert, an empty husk.

Although the Chinese have not been known as a seafaring people, they proved their abilities at overseas exploration during the Ming dynasty. In the early 1400's, Cheng Ho, a court official, commanded a series of maritime expeditions which took Chinese ships through the East Indies, into the Indian Ocean and to the Persian Gulf, and down the east coast of Africa. Thus, before Portuguese explorers rounded the Cape of Good Hope at Africa's southern tip, Chinese armadas had already "discovered" India and Arabia. After Cheng's adventure, however, the Chinese decided not to continue his naval exploits and ceased sending ships far from China's coastal waters. Here Jeannette Mirsky, an historian and chronicler of explorers in many parts of the world, gives us an idea of the conflict these voyages caused within the court at Peking.

Cheng Ho's Naval Expeditions
by Jeannette Mirsky

During the previous century (1260–1368), when the Mongols dominated Asia, traffic between East and West had been very lively; with their downfall and the break-up of the vast Mongol empire, the caravan routes were cut and the imports to which the Chinese had become accustomed ceased to flow. Chinese attitudes toward foreign trade were always mixed. From a practical point of view, foreign trade brought prosperity to the great numbers of people profitably engaged in it, especially to the southern provinces, and the treasury was enriched by the import duties. Although the outflow of cash was an evil, the advantages of foreign trade were considerable. Now all overseas commerce had chiefly to do with articles of luxury—precious stones, fragrant woods, spices, rare objects—and the consumers of these goods were the wealthy classes, especially and most markedly, the court and its harem ladies. Ideologically, however, this state of affairs was never admitted because the Confucian theory regarded trade as something inferior, almost sordid, with which the emperor could have nothing to do. Therefore trade relations with overseas nations always took the form of tribute-bearing: barbarians, attracted from afar, recognized the overlordship of the Son of Heaven by bringing tribute; after this they were graciously allowed to trade. In the past Chinese envoys had repeatedly been sent to induce foreign nations to come to China offering tribute, thus increasing the prestige of the Chinese emperor as well as their own. The greater the number of foreign envoys present at the New Year's court audiences, the more illustrious was the glory of the emperor, who, like the Duke of Chou of old, succeeded by his sage government in attracting foreign barbarians.

These mixed motives, the longing for the exotic and precious felt particularly at court and the desire to increase the imperial prestige by the traditional tribute gifts, must have prompted the third emperor of the Ming Dynasty to undertake a series of missions overseas. In the official annals another, a political motive, is given: to search for the emperor's young nephew to whom the throne had been bequeathed and who, when he had been deposed, disappeared. Because it was rumored that he had fled overseas, a fleet was sent out to try and bring him back from the country of the barbarians where he was supposed to be hiding. The excuse is transparent; to search for the deposed, missing heir, it would not have been necessary to send expeditions on so large a scale as sailed, not merely once, but at least seven times, not counting minor ones. Some of the fleets consisted of sixty-two vessels and carried 37,000 soldiers; more than thirty countries in the Indian Archipelago and Indian Ocean were visited, as well as ports in the Persian Gulf; the great markets of Aden and Mecca were visited; and the Chinese ships sailed all the way to Africa.

These fleets were placed under the command of a Chinese Muslim, native of the province of Yunnan, a court eunuch, Cheng Ho, popularly known as the "three-jewel eunuch." The ships under his command were designated "jewel ships." From the days of the Emperor Wu-ti (second century B.C.), eunuchs were entrusted with overseas expeditions. . . .

Unfortunately, the official reports of Cheng Ho's voyages no longer exist—a direct consequence of his having been a eunuch. Whereas the overland expeditions into Central Asia led by various generals are part of the nation's historical tradition and are regarded as deeds reflecting China's greatness, knowledge of Cheng Ho's expeditions, equally notable, was deliberately erased. It is said that, about 1480, another eunuch who had risen to great power wished to emulate Cheng Ho and lead a maritime expedition against Annam. When he attempted to organize an expedition and asked for Cheng Ho's official records, to frustrate him the records were destroyed with the connivance of the high officials of the War Office. For during the Ming Dynasty a strong rivalry existed between the eunuchs, who were privately employed by the emperor in various important functions, and the official classes, who, as good Confucians, despised trade and luxury and foreign barbarians. Thus the whole matter of overseas relations became a moral issue to the official classes, inextricably bound up with their deep sense of disapproval of the extravagances and usurpation of power by the notorious eunuchs. In official eyes, China, economically self-sufficient, could very well do without the products of foreign countries which were nothing but curiosities. And it was indeed true that the expeditions were expensive and unprofitable.

These expeditions then, a major event in Chinese history, are only known in a most fragmentary way; it was a fortunate accident that enabled us at least to fix the dates of the various expeditions with certainty and to ascertain the places visited by each of them. The accident ultimately rests on a miracle.

Some years ago in the yamen at Ch'ang-lo, in the province of Fukien, a stele was discovered; it had been brought there at an earlier date from the Temple of the Celestial Spouse in the same city....

The texts give the answer. That at Ch'ang-lo reads:

"The Imperial Ming Dynasty, in unifying the seas and continents, surpassing the three dynasties, even goes beyond the Han and T'ang Dynasties. The countries beyond the horizon and at the ends of the earth have all become subjects; and to the most western of the western or the most northern of the northern countries, however far they may be, the distances and the routes may be calculated.

Thus the barbarians from beyond the seas, though their countries are truly distant, with double translation have come to audience bearing precious objects and presents.

"The emperor, approving of their loyalty and sincerity, has ordered us [Cheng Ho] and others at the head of several tens of thousands of officers and flag troops to ascend more than a hundred large ships to go and confer presents on them in order to make manifest the transforming power of the Imperial Virtue and to treat distant people with kindness. From the third year of Yung-lo [1405] till now we have several times received the commission of ambassadors to the countries of the Western Ocean. The barbarian countries we have visited are: by way of Chan-ch'eng [Champa], Chao-wa [Java], San-fo-ch'i [Palembang], and Hsien-lo [Siam], crossing straight over to Hsi-lan-shan [Ceylon]; in South India, Ku-li [Calicut, not Calcutta] and K'o-chih [Cochin]; we have gone to the western regions of Hu-lu-mo-ssu [Hormuz], A-tan [Aden], Mu-ku-tu-shu [Mogadishu, in Africa], all together more than thirty countries large and small. We have traversed more than one hundred thousand *li* of immense water spaces and have beheld in the ocean huge waves like mountains rising sky-high, and we have set eyes on barbarian regions far away hidden in a blue transparency of light vapors, while our sails, loftily unfurled like clouds, day and night continued their course, rapid like that of a star [the designation for an Imperial Embassy], traversing the savage waves as if we were treading a public thoroughfare. Truly, this was due to the majesty and good fortune of the court and moreover we owe it to the protecting virtue of the Celestial Spouse.

"The power of the goddess having been manifested in previous times has been abundantly revealed in the present generation. In the midst of the rushing waters it happened when there was a hurricane, that suddenly there appeared a divine lantern shining in the mast; as soon as this miraculous light appeared the danger was appeased, so that even in the peril of capsizing one felt reassured that there was no cause for fear."

The "divine lantern" in the mast was the well-known St. Elmo's Fire; but to the men caught in a hurricane it was a sign of celestial protection. This miracle, which occurred on the first voyage, inspired the inscription which preserved knowledge of these maritime expeditions. By imperial decree the Celestial Spouse was given a title of twelve characters: "Protector of the Country and Defender of the People, whose miraculous power manifestly answers prayers and whose vast benevolence saves universally."

The Tillers of the Soil

The gentry who governed China and enjoyed a sophisticated culture actually constituted only a small slice off the top of traditional society. Below them, and apart from the merchants and artisans, existed the great mass of the people: the peasants. Because most peasants were illiterate—and would have had no time to write even if they had known how—historical records deal mostly with the concerns of the scholars and tell us little about the life of the common people. In this chapter we have selected readings on the working life of the peasants, on the role the gentry played in village affairs, and on the development of Chinese marriage and family systems. The first reading is a description of peasant life and work by the American journalist Anna Louise Strong. It was written in the 1920s, but the author could easily have been describing China of the Ming or Ching dynasties instead.

The Farmers
by Anna Louise Strong

All parts of China, north and south, are filled to capacity with people. More people probably have lived on China's level areas than in any similar area in the world. Four-fifths of them are, and have always been, farmers—the most industrious, patient, thrifty farmers on earth. Pressing for forty centuries hard on the limits of subsistence, they have penetrated steadily into every corner of the available land. With canals and hill terraces they have modified the appearance of nature. "Trillions of men and women have made their contribution to the contour of hill and valley and the pattern of the fields." In the cultivated parts of China the blue-trousered farmers seem a living part of the landscape; nature has been adjusted to man and man to nature in interaction for four thousand years.

These toiling farmers utilize every resource. Land is economized; lowlands are protected by dikes, hills are terraced. Many—sometimes too many—river and lake bottoms have been generations ago reclaimed. Roads are narrow in the North; in the South they shrink into footpaths. Water is economized; the same canal furnishes transportation and irrigation to a long succession of fields, and mud dug up from its bottom is applied as fertilizer to the soil. Human and animal wastes are utilized; even from large cities they are collected and carried painstakingly to manure the fields. By-products are utilized; straw and stalks go into building or for fuel. By hard, continuous work, skillful practices, and exceptional economy in using soil, water, human and animal wastes, the Chinese farmer still gets good crops on the same earth after four thousand years. . . .

Fighting through centuries for survival, the Chinese farmers have learned a grim economy of food. They hope for three meals a day during harvest labors, but in winter their diet drops to two scant meals of rice (in the South) or millet (in the North), flavored with a rough vegetable. Meat is a rare luxury for feast days and is then used in tiny slivers to extract its utmost flavor. The food supply has conditioned even the village transport. Since fodder-grass is plentiful in the North, they have draft-animals with two-wheeled carts. But the narrow valley-lands of the South, with their three annual crops, are too precious for grass; southern transport is by canalboats and on the backs of human beings, who are cheaper to feed than animals.

Generations have taught a close economy of fuel. Houses in the cold north are built facing southward to catch the sun and avoid the harsh desert winds from the northwest. As much as half of the interior is filled with the "kang," a platform of clay brick raised two feet above the floor and gently heated by the exhaust of the family stove and by straw fires inserted from outside the house. This slightly raises the temperature of the whole room, especially at night when the kang serves as a bed for many people. Even in zero weather Chinese farmers do not wastefully heat their homes. Chilled hands are kept warm over little charcoal fires in metal basins. Bodies are kept warm by layers of padded cotton garments, far warmer than our woolen clothes. These garments saved the lives of thousands of Chinese soldiers this past winter, for they are thick enough to turn back shrapnel if its impact is not too hard.

Generations also have taught the efficient cherishing of every bit of metal and wood. Since wood is especially scarce in the North, its use in building is limited to upright posts, roof beams, and door and window frames—all of which are family heirlooms, taken from house to house as the mud walls crumble with the years. Stoves are made of clay bricks. I recall even a small portable stove made of clay held together by a framework of iron wire, which served in Shansi to heat water for our tea. Our host fed charcoal a piece at a time into a two-inch hole in the middle of the stove-top. Over the tiny flame a wide-bottomed but narrow-topped copper kettle was raised on three small stones just high enough to allow the fire to draw. The shape of the stove, of the kettle, and their relation to each other, had all been carefully adjusted to use every smallest bit of heat. In the summer the stove could easily be carried outdoors; in summer, to cool the house, the paper is torn from the windows and replaced—if the householder has funds for such luxuries—by a net.

Since land is the source of life and is tilled by the family's labor, each family has been held together for centuries by its land. It was a partiarchal family under "the old man," who directed the toil of his children and ruled their lives, even when he could no longer toil. Sons grew up and the family secured wives for them, bringing these to the family homestead, building perhaps an annex of clay or bamboo walls. Receiving the land from the fathers, the family treasured it for the children, improving it that they might live in after years. As the parents died they were buried in their own soil, and remained a part of the family life through the tablets erected to their memory, to which their descendants did reverence as the source from which they and their means of life had come.

These large, self-sufficient families lived in villages. Heads of families chose the village chiefs, who managed the common life and carried on relations with other villages in such matters as irrigation, water supply and minor trade. Village life has changed little since a poet of the T'ang dynasty described it thus:

Each family maintains its rural occupations,
Men grow white-haired, yet never go abroad.
Alive, they are the villagers.
And dead, they are the village dust.

Sharp class divisions, however, arose even in this seemingly placid countryside. Richer families became landlords, exploiting both share-croppers and hired labor; they became moneylenders, extorting robber-rates of interest. Poorer families, hard-pressed in years of drought, sold daughters into slavery. Village officials bowed to the will of the rich and did "justice" against the poor.

Gentry families were the link between the peasants and the state. One gentry family could perform several different functions. Some sons would pass the examinations and go on to the capital as officials. Other sons, also educated, would remain behind to collect rents and administer local government. Thus a peasant complaining about his landlord would find that the town judge was his own landlord's son-in-law or best friend, or in any case a landlord himself and not likely to encourage tenant complaints. Appeals to higher officials would fall on equally unsympathetic ears. Reischauer and Fairbank describe the functions of these gentry families at the village level, including periodic conscription of village labor for public works.

The Gentry

by John K. Fairbank and Edwin O. Reischauer

"Gentry" Functions. The peculiar strength of Confucian government lay in the fact that the "gentry" performed so many public functions in the local community without official remuneration. They commonly lived in the market towns or in the "big houses" in the villages, but also maintained contact or even establishments in the administrative cities. They were the bearers of the Confucian doctrine. As learned men and often also as men of wealth and political influence, they assumed responsibility for many activities which today are performed by officials.

They raised funds for and supervised public works such as the building and maintenance of irrigation ditches and canals with their dikes and dams, and roads with their bridges and ferries. The "gentry" also took responsibility for public morals, maintaining the local Confucian temple or other shrines and the ceremonies which inculcated proper social behavior among the masses. They set up and supported local private schools and academies. They compiled and published the local histories or gazetteers. In time of plenty they sponsored orphanages and care for the aged, even though philanthropy in China did not become as public and impersonal an institution as in the modern West. In time of disaster the "gentry" supported relief activities. They also organized and led the local militia as defense corps for maintaining order. In most of these activities they received official encouragement or recognition but not specific appointment to office or any pay.

These public functions were of course inextricably intermixed with the private affairs of the "gentry" in their dealings with the peasantry below and officialdom above. A partial comparison might be made in this respect with other classes that have functioned in very different societies, such as the equestrian order of ancient Rome, the modern American business class, or other non-official groups that have provided local community leadership.

The "gentry" naturally tended to support the government, and it was to the interest of the latter to maintain a type of public spirit among the "gentry," as opposed to selfish opportunism. To this end the Confucian doctrines were regularly recited in the local Confucian temple and the Son of Heaven issued his moral exhortations for repetition in every community. The six imperial injunctions of Hung-wu were ordered posted in all villages in 1397. These said, in effect, "Be filial, be respectful to elders and ancestors, teach your children, and peacefully pursue your livelihood." In a similar formative period of the Ch'ing, the Emperor K'ang-hsi in 1670 issued his famous *Sacred Edict*, to be expounded semi-monthly by the officials and "gentry" in the villages. These sixteen maxims, each in seven characters, repeated, in effect, "Be filial and respect the social relationships, be frugal and diligent, esteem scholarship and eschew unorthodoxy, be law-abiding and pay taxes."

Thus the great tradition of learning, under the patronage of the head of the state, was used to indoctrinate the "gentry" class as the local elite, and they in turn provided leadership in the orderly life of the villages. Though not aristocratic in a hereditary sense, this was indeed an elitist system, for the degree-holders with their immediate families formed certainly no more than two per cent of the population but held the highest prestige and social authority outside the small official class itself. A comparison with the modern party elite of totalitarian states would be more accurate than a comparison with the hereditary elite in early modern Europe.

When the emperor's mandarin arrived at his yamen, in a province not his own (according to the "law of avoidance"), the local dialect might be quite unintelligible to him. He became at once dependent on the advisors and assistants he had brought with him and on the yamen clerks—a low-level sort of "permanent civil service" which handled his office's daily contact with the populace. His public, however, were particularly the local "gentry," who were in the best position to present local problems to him, to help him in meeting such problems, and to criticize his conduct of office. The empire of the Ming and Ch'ing, seen in modern terms, was governed by officials, to be sure, but with the indispensable assistance of the "gentry"—one might almost say, by officials and "gentry" together.

Confucian ideals of the "five relationships" and extended families were the basis of Chinese social patterns, although usually only the wealthier families could afford large households. The stress of poverty created tensions between family members, and in hard times families often broke up, homes were abandoned and children were sold or given away. Sad stories of the difficulties many people had conforming to these traditional ideas of filial piety and obedience make up much of the literature and folktales of China.

The Death of Prince Shen-sheng
by Ssu-ma Ch'ien

TRANSLATED BY DUN LI*

In the fifth year of Duke Hsien's reign (672 B.C.), the Duke attacked Li-jung** and acquired Madame Li. Both Madame Li and her younger sister became the Duke's favorites. . . .

In the twelfth year (665 B.C.) Madame Li gave birth to a son named Hsi-ch'i. The Duke began to think seriously about the possibility of replacing Shen-sheng by Hsi-ch'i as the crown prince. . . .

In the seventeenth year (660 B.C.) the Duke ordered crown prince Shen-sheng to head an army to attack Tung-shan. . . .†

"I have several sons," said the Duke to Li K'e.‡ "I do not know which one of them should be designated as my heir apparent." Li K'e did not reply. Later he went to see the crown prince.

"Is it true that I am going to be replaced as the crown prince?" Shen-sheng asked.

"You should do your best while you are commanding the army," said Li K'e. "As long as you believe that you are respectful towards your father, why should you be afraid of being replaced? Moreover, a man should be more concerned with his performance as a loyal son than with the possibility, or the lack of it, of being designated as the heir apparent. You will be very safe indeed if you diligently cultivate your virtue and never place any blame on others."

One day in the nineteenth year (658 B.C.) the Duke told Madame Li privately that he intended to replace Shen-sheng by Hsi-ch'i as the crown prince. "No, you should not," Madame Li protested in tears. "The fact that Shen-sheng is the crown prince is known to all the states throughout the country. Moreover, he is at the head of an

---

*Dun Li, *Essence of Chinese Civilization*.
**A non-Chinese tribe.
†A non-Chinese tribe.
‡A minister.

army and is very popular with the people. You must not replace the eldest son of a legal wife by the young son of a concubine on my behalf. If you insist on carrying out your plan, I will commit suicide."

Despite what she said in front of the Duke, Madame Li secretly sent her agents to spread rumors for the purpose of slandering the crown prince, though outwardly she kept on praising him. She, of course, wanted her own son to be installed as the crown prince.

One day on the twenty-first year (656 B.C.) Madame Li told the crown prince that she had dreamed about Madame Chiang, the crown prince's deceased mother, and that he, the crown prince, should proceed to Ch'üfu* to offer sacrifices to comfort his deceased mother. After the ritual of offering sacrifices had been completed, the crown prince brought back the sacrificial meat to his father as tribute. The Duke was then in a hunting trip outside the capital, and Madame Li ordered her servants secretly to place poison in the meat.

Two days later the Duke returned from his hunting trip, and the royal chef presented the sacrificial meat. The Duke was about to eat it when he was stopped by Madame Li. "Since the meat comes from a place faraway, it should be tested before you eat it," she said. The Duke threw the meat to the ground, the ground began to bulge.** Fed with it, a dog died immediately. Tested on a slave, the slave also dropped dead. "How cruel the crown prince is!" Madame Li said in tears. "He wants to kill his own father whom he is anxious to replace. How can he possibly have mercy on others? You, sir, are very advanced in age, and yet he cannot wait. The reason he wants to kill his father is because he cannot stand me and my son Hsi-ch'i. Under the circumstances I and my son can either flee to another country before it is too late, or commit suicide before the crown prince slaughters us with his own hands. Formerly when you wanted to replace him as the crown prince, I was strongly opposed to it. Now I know how wrong I was."

As soon as he learned that he had been implicated by Madame Li in the alleged attempt to murder his father,

---

*The former capital of Tsin, located in modern Shansi province.

**According to Chinese hearsay, an object unusually poisonous, once thrown to the ground, could make the ground rise slightly.

the crown prince fled to Hsinch'eng.* Unable to locate the crown prince, the Duke was furious enough to kill the prince's tutor Tu Yüan-k'uan as a substitute.

Some one told the crown prince that the poison was placed by Madame Li and that he should inform his father about his innocence. "My father is very old," said the crown prince. "He needs Madame Li for his old age. Without her he could not eat or sleep well. If I tell him the truth, he will be very angry with her. I cannot bear to see that his only comfort is taken away from him during his old age." Some one suggested that he should flee to another state. "With a bad reputation such as I have,† which state in the country will take me in as its guest?" said the crown prince. "The only course open to me is to commit suicide."

On the *wu-shen* day of the twelfth month, crown prince Shen-sheng committed suicide at Hsinch'eng.

Marriage

by Dun Li‡

In bygone days the sexes were segregated, and a maiden was not supposed to see a male stranger under any circumstances. The higher the family standing was, the stricter the segregation. Such being the case, marriages had to be arranged. In looking for a prospective wife or husband for their son or daughter, the parents had to consider a number of factors, and the most important factor was the other family's reputation and standing. The personal attributes of the prospective groom or bride came second: the boy should be talented and promising (for gentry families) or strong and hard-working (for peasant families), and the girl should be even-tempered, know her household work (such as sewing), and look wholesome, preferably on the plump side. The interested family revealed its intention to a go-between who approached the other family in the most casual manner; it had to be casual to avoid embarrassment. For a gentry family of high standing, the

---

*Located in modern Shansi province.
†This refers to the alleged attempt of murdering his own father.
‡Dun Li, *Ageless Chinese*.

marriage procedure consisted of "six rituals" (*liu-li*), from the initial inquiry to the wedding itself. Most families, however, could not afford the expenses and passed over most of them. One ritual they could not pass over was the exchange of birth information: the hour, day, month, and year the prospective groom or bride was born. A fortune-teller was called in, and he would decide whether the proposed marriage was an auspicious one. A girl born in the Year of the Tiger would have a much more limited choice. She could not marry a man born in the Year of the Lamb because she would surely swallow him. But it would be all right for her to marry a man born in the Year of the Monkey because the monkey could always jump up to the back of the tiger. Needless to say, many prospects of happy marriages were ended right there.

In the Chinese thinking, a marriage was as much a marriage of two families as it was between the two persons directly involved. Its major purpose was the propagation of the male family line. Children bore their father's name, never their mother's. Individuals submitted themselves to their family's decisions, and rarely were they consulted about their prospective mates. Two great friends, learning that each other's wives were pregnant, might decide right then that their unborn babies were engaged if they turned out to be opposite in sex. Instead of seeing anything wrong with this kind of arrangement, the traditional Chinese society glorified it. Since marriage was arranged, the groom would be an ingenious man indeed if he had seen his wife before the wedding night. A woman performed her function well as a wife if she had borne her husband a son: it was then that her position with the family became absolutely secure. If she failed to perform such a function, her husband would be strongly pressed to take a concubine, mostly by his parents and sometimes by his wife as well. Socially and legally, a man could take as many concubines as he could afford. Since few could afford it, concubinage was confined to a small fraction of the population. Chinese emperors, who could best afford it, had scores or even hundreds of concubines.

Grim as Chinese marriage might seem, there is no indication that it was less happy than marriages arrived at any other way. Even though divorce was socially disapproved, it was legally permissible, and divorced persons could remarry if they chose to. Yet there were few cases of divorce. The concubine system may have saved many marriages, but it did not seem to be the main factor in the scarcity of divorce cases. Social disapproval was definitely a deterrent, and the families involved would normally exercise great pressure to prevent marriages from breaking up. Strange as it may seem, the fact that marriages were arranged might have been beneficial in some respects. A good family background as emphasized by the Chinese was perhaps a more important factor in happy marriages than a prospective mate's physical appearance. The customary subservience of wives to husbands and the Chinese attachment of great importance to children might be another contributing factor. It is not known, however, how many people remained married though unhappy. It will remain unknown, because the Chinese, as a matter of principle, did not believe that they should reveal to outsiders their feelings towards their spouses. Outward affection was taboo, even towards one's own wife. When a man and his wife had to appear together in public, the woman customarily walked ten paces behind.

How did sexual segregation come into being? Certainly there was no such thing at the beginning of recorded history. Then boys and girls enjoyed each other's companionship as much as they have under any other culture. Here is an example:

You, shy, beautiful lass, my beloved,
    Failed to meet me in a city corner you'd promised.
Here I come; nowhere could you be found.
Should I leave or should I have waited?
For a long time I hesitated.

You, shy, beautiful lass, my beloved,
    Gave me a river reed flashing red;
I love the river reed,
I love more my beloved.

I love the river reed, beautiful and enchanting;
What beauty would it possess,
Had it not caressed my beloved?*

---

*Translated from a poem in the *Book of Odes*.

In those ancient years a woman could be equally romantic:

> Are you thinking of me?
> Your love I cannot see.
> What prevents you from crossing the stream
>   That separates you and me?
>
> If you stay your adoration for me,
>   Others will not, certainly!
> Oh, how stupid you can be,
>   How stupid you can be!*

As late as the second century B.C. it was still possible to conduct courtship. The Han poet Ssu-ma Hsiang-ju (179–117 B.C.) courted a rich widow with his lute and succeeded in persuading her to elope with him. Four centuries later the handsome P'an Yo (A.D. 247–300) was reported to have been mobbed by women every time he went out. Such an occurrence would have been unthinkable in a later period. The indications are that sexual segregation became more and more rigid with the passage of time and was strictly enforced after the Sung dynasty. What caused the change? The acceptance of Confucian moralism was unquestionably one of the major reasons, especially the Sung School of philosophy. Chu Hsi, for instance, not only advocated strict sexual segregation but glorified widowhood as well; he thought he did society a great service by encouraging widows to join their dead husbands at the earliest possible moment. As his philosophy dominated the intellectual and ethical scene for the next seven hundred years, his bleak, puritanical ideas began to be accepted as the lofty goal which every gentry family strove to achieve. With the popularity of his ideas, the status of women declined.

Nothing can illustrate better the decline of women's status in society than the custom of foot-binding. It is not known exactly when or how this custom began. One reputable source maintains that it began in the court of Li Yü where a court dancer "bent her feet with silk so they were shaped like a crescent and whirled around as if she were dancing in the clouds." By the Sung dynasty foot-binding was widely practiced among the gentry families.

---

*Translated from a poem in the *Book of Odes*.

The binding process began when a girl was four or five and continued until the desired result was achieved. The net result was a pair of crippled feet, only half the normal size. (Many mothers did such a thorough job that their daughters could barely walk.) Why did this inhumane custom ever get established and moreover persist for almost 1,000 years? Men, for unknown reasons, prefer small feet on women. A Western woman responds by squeezing her feet into shoes of smaller size, and Chinese women, perhaps more eager to please, bound their feet so they could walk forever as a modern ballerina dances. Chinese gentlemen of older generations would not consider a woman attractive unless she had a pair of bound feet.

In 1867 in the small city of P'eng-lai on the Shantung coast, the Hsu family welcomed a new member, "Little Tiger"; seventy years later Little Tiger, now an aged but still vigorous woman, told the story of her life to Ida Pruitt, an American who had grown up in China herself. Her story is a colorful and detailed account of family life in China, and could easily be an account of life in Ming or earlier times.

The Story of Little Tiger
by Ida Pruitt

Growing up

When I was three or four years old we moved to the Chou Wang Temple neighborhood, to be near the garden. We had the three northern *chien** in the court, the ones facing south. There was a two-chien east house in which the neighbors lived. This was the first time our family had lived in a court with others. The house had a thatched

---

*A chien is a unit of space with a constant relationship between height, width, and length—the space between the supporting pillars, the floor, and ceiling. In a large house, therefore, the chien is large and in a small house, small. The usual house in this part of the country was three or five chien. Some of the smaller side houses might be two chien. The partitions from pillar to pillar, front to back, could be put in or taken out at will. A room could be from one to five chien. In poor families such as these, a chien tended to be a room.

roof. Before we had always lived in houses with tile roofs.

The house was convenient to the garden where my father worked part of the time. It was also convenient for my mother and my aunt to see the plays on the open stage across the street. My father was very strict and would not let them out to see the plays. My mother and my aunt took benches and stood on them so they could look out the high north windows.

I was a difficult child to manage. I liked to play too much. I played with my brother and sister and the children of the neighbors. We played on the streets and in the garden next door.

I climbed trees, and hanging by the rope from the windlass I would let myself down into the well. I would put my toes into the cracks between the bricks that lined it. My mother did not know that I did this. She would have been frightened had she known. There was nothing that I did not dare to do. I was the baby and my parents favored me.

They did not begin to bind my feet until I was seven because I loved so much to run and play. Then I became very ill and they had to take the bindings off my feet again. I had the "heavenly blossoms" and was ill for two years and my face is very pockmarked. In my childhood everyone had the illness and few escaped some marking.

When I was nine they started to bind my feet again and they had to draw the bindings tighter than usual. My feet hurt so much that for two years I had to crawl on my hands and knees. Sometimes at night they hurt so much I could not sleep. I stuck my feet under my mother and she lay on them so they hurt less and I could sleep. But by the time I was eleven my feet did not hurt and by the time I was thirteen they were finished. The toes were turned under so that I could see them on the inner and under side of the foot. They had come up around. Two fingers could be inserted in the cleft between the front of the foot and the heel. My feet were very small indeed.

A girl's beauty and desirability were counted more by the size of her feet than by the beauty of her face. Matchmakers were not asked "Is she beautiful?" but "How small are her feet?" A plain face is given by heaven but poor bound feet are a sign of laziness.

My feet were very small indeed. Not like they are now.

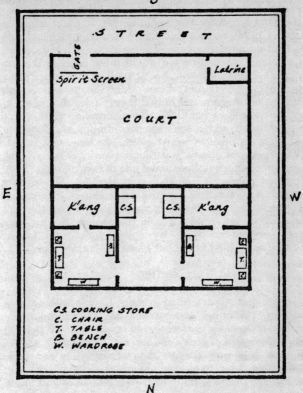

S

STREET

GATE

Spirit Screen

Latrine

COURT

E   W

K'ang   C.S.   C.S.   K'ang

C.S. COOKING STOVE
C. CHAIR
T. TABLE
B. BENCH
W. WARDROBE

N

FLOOR PLAN OF A THREE-CHIEN HOUSE

Note: A *K'ang* is a raised brick platform on which the family sleeps at night and sits during the day. It is heated by a flue running underneath it from the cooking stove.

When I worked so hard and was on my feet all day I slept with the bandages off because my feet ached, and so they spread.

When I was eleven we moved into a house in the corner of the garden. The wall between the house and the rest of the garden was low. I was a very mischievous child. When

I was naughty and my mother wanted to beat me I would run and jump over the wall and she could not catch me.

One day we wanted to go out to play, a neighbor's little girl and I. My mother said that we could go when I had finished grinding the corn. The neighbor's child said she would help me so that we would finish sooner. We ran round and round the mill, but to grind so much corn takes time. We were impatient, so while she ground I took handfuls of the corn and buried them under the refuse in the mill house, a handful here under some dust and a handful there under some donkey droppings. Then we told my mother that we were through. She came and saw that the hopper was empty. But the chickens did not give us face. They scratched here and a pile of corn showed. They scratched there and another pile showed. My mother scolded us. "You naughty, mischievous children." She started after us to beat me, but we ran and jumped over the wall and climbed into a pear tree in the garden. By this time there were several of us. My mother came to the foot of the tree and called to me but I would not come down. . . .

Marriage

Seeing that my sister had so much trouble with a young husband, my father and mother said that I should be married to an older man who would cherish me. When the matchmaker told of such a one and that he had no mother— she was dead—my parents thought that they had done well for me. I was to have an older husband to cherish me, but not too old, and no mother-in-law to scold and abuse me.

Our neighbor, the man who carted away the night soil, made the match for me. He was a professional matchmaker. He did not care how a marriage turned out. He had used the money. As the old people say, "A matchmaker does not live a lifetime with the people he brings together." The matchmaker hid four years of my husband's age from us, saying that the man was only ten years older than I. But he was fourteen years older. I was twelve when the match was made, and I became engaged—a childhood match. I still had my hair in a plait. I did not know anything. I was fifteen when I was married.

They told me that I was to be a bride. I had seen

weddings going down the street. I had seen brides sitting
on the k'angs on the wedding days when all went in to see
them. To be married was to wear pretty clothes and
ornaments in the hair.

I sat on the k'ang, bathed and dressed, in my red
underclothes and red stockings. The music sounded and
they took me off the k'ang. I sat on the chair and the
matrons combed my hair for me into the matron's knot at
the nape of my neck. They dressed me in my red embroidered bridal robes and the red embroidered bridal shoes
and put the ornaments in my hair. An old man whose
parents and wife were still alive carried me out and put
me in the wedding chair that was to carry me to my new
home. I knew only that I must not touch the sides of the
chair as he put me in, and that I was dressed in beautiful
clothes. I was a child, only fifteen by our count, and my
birthday was small—just before the New Year. We count
ourselves a year old when we are born and we all add a
year at the New Year. I was counted two years old when I
was a month old, for I was born near the end of the old
year. I was a child. I had not yet passed my thirteenth
birthday.

I was frightened. I was homesick.

It was the year of the broom-tailed star. I can still see it
distinctly. And there were many rings around the sun that
year.

The Wedding

The musicians in their green uniforms and red tasseled
hats sat by the table in the court. There were those who
played on bamboo reed flutes and those who played on
wooden horns. At times the cymbals clashed. But during
the ceremony of clothing the bride and while the groom,
who had come to fetch the bride, drank in another room
with the men of the bride's family, it was the flute that
sounded. By the different motifs played those who passed
by in the street or stopped to watch knew which part of
the ceremony was in progress.

The table where the musicians sat and drank tea and
played at intervals was next to the gate. It was time for the
groom to take the bride home. The musicians stood and
played. The wooden horns joined the flutes. The cymbals

clashed. The drums boomed. The groom came out of the house door. He was clothed in hired bridal robes, patterned like those of a mandarin's full dress. Once or twice at least in a lifetime every man and woman is equal to the highest in the land. When they are married and when they are buried they are clothed in the garments of nobility.

The father and the brother and the uncle of the bride escorted the groom. They bowed him to his chair. Then the red sedan chair of the bride was brought to the gate and placed against the gateway. The gateway was too small to allow the chair to enter the court as would be done in great households. All cracks between the chair and the gate were covered with pieces of red felt held by the chairmen to make sure that no evil spirit should enter. A long note of the horn was sounded and the bride was carried out kneeling on the arms of an old man. He was a neighbor, a carpenter who was no longer working but was spending the last years of his life in pleasant social pursuits. He was also a doctor—not the kind who had many honorary boards hanging outside his walls telling in poetic allusion of his healing powers, but a homely man who knew what to tell the mothers when their children's bellies ached, and how to keep their faces from scarring when the children broke out with smallpox, and how to break a fever when the inner fires got too hot. He was also a manager for weddings and funerals, and he was peacemaker for the neighborhood. Long days he would sit squatted on his heels in the lee of a sunny wall and listen to all sides of any quarrels. He was what was known as a whole man. Destiny had been kind to him. His father and mother still ate and slept in his house and not in the small brick vault he had prepared for them deep in the steepest slope of his wheat field. His wife, his old partner, was the one with whom he had started forty years ago as a boy of sixteen. He had sons and grandsons. Therefore at wedding ceremonies he was much sought after to bring good luck to the new couples. Dressed in his ceremonial black coat he carried the red-robed bride to the chair. She knelt on his arms and her head, heavy with ornaments, drooped over his shoulder. She was a bow of red arched over a bow of black. He sat her on the broad low seat of the sedan chair.

Matrons whose husbands were alive patted the bride's garments into place as she folded her arms and legs. They dropped the red curtain before her. The gong sounded and the bearers seized the chair. They ran the poles through the loops and lifted the chair to their shoulders. The procession started, and as both families were poor, it was not a long one.

The little procession started off. There were pairs of red lanterns on poles, red banners, and red wooden boards on which were great gold ideographs. The band followed and then came the green chair of the groom. This was followed closely by the red chair of the bride. Her brother walked beside it. He carried a piece of red felt in his hands. It was his duty to hold this between her chair and all the wells and dark corners and temples they passed. He must protect her from the hungry ghosts, the souls of those who have drowned themselves in these wells and are doomed to stay there until they can persuade others to drown themselves and release them. He must protect her from the elementals that lurk in dark corners, the weasel spirits and the fox fairies, and from the little demons in the temples who might follow her home and possess her and make her leave the path of reason and do those things which people do not do. The passers-by looked curiously at the brother, trying to gauge the bride's beauty by his features. Behind came the cart carrying the perfect couple, the whole couple, a middle-aged man and wife whose parents and children lived, who were to act for the family in giving her over to her new home.

The bearers strutted as they walked, mincing in their gait, with one arm akimbo and the other swinging, for they carried a virgin bride and she was sitting in an official chair, wearing robes, though rented, patterned after the great.

The procession filed out of the narrow side street where the elbows of the bearers almost touched the rough stone walls on either side, built from the hills on which the city stands. They came into the main street of the city paved with great blocks of granite. They turned north past the temple where the Taoist priest told fortunes and his hunchbacked wife sold sweetmeats to the neighborhood children. They went out of the city through the vaulted tunnel of the North Gate.

Outside of the city the procession veered to the east and followed the cart track along the city wall. It crossed the wheat fields and went toward the sea and a village lying low and gray on the rocks of a small promontory.

It was a village of fishermen and the groom owned one of the fishing boats. He was also a farmer. He owned twenty mu of the wheatland that lay near the village. It was the family village of the Ning clan. All in the village were of this one clan. Their names were recorded in the books in the family temple in the middle of the village. Twelve hundred years ago they had been brought by the emperor of the Sui dynasty to replace those who had been killed in the wars that had ravaged China after the breakup of the great Han dynasty. The Sui emperor had brought them from Yünnan, on the borders of Szechwan and Kweichou, many thousand miles, to repopulate the peninsula. There they had lived ever since on the lands the emperor had given them.

When I got to my new home and the wedding guests had left I found that there was a woman living in the house, a cousin's wife. She had lived there for many years and had borne a son to my husband. We all slept on one k'ang, the four of us. I was such a child that I told her I was glad she was there for I was frightened. Her husband had been gone many years and none knew whether he was alive or dead. She had an older son who had also gone to Manchuria. His name was Fulai, "May Fortune Come." The little boy's name was Fats'ai, "May Wealth Come." She lived with us for more than two years.

My husband's father was also with us. He tilled the family land and in the winter made baskets. When he was young he had been a servant in one of the yamen of the city.

I was but a child. We played games, the village children, Fats'ai, and I. We played knucklebones, hunting the tiger (hide and seek), kicking the shuttlecock, and coin throwing.

A Funeral

As was the custom, I went home every month to see my mother. But because my husband smoked opium and did not bring home food, I stayed longer with my mother than was the custom. Half of every month I stayed with my husband and half of every month I went home to my mother. My brother came with our neighbor's white horse or a borrowed donkey and took me home.

When I left home to go back to my husband's village I would not let my mother see me cry. I went to the latrine and wiped my eyes. Then I waited until I had turned the corner of the street before I cried again. That was because my older sister always cried and screamed when she had to go back to her mother-in-law. And so my father would scold her.

"What can we do?" he would say. "What is done is done. What good to make such an ado?" So I was always careful not to let them see me weep. My sister's husband was good and brought them money, but her mother-in-law was cruel. I had no mother-in-law but my husband did not bring in money.

When I left my mother she always sat with her face set and her eyes wide open. She did not smile but she did not weep. She held her eyes wide open and her face firm to keep from weeping.

I know now that there is no need to be angry with my parents for my marriage. They did the best they could for me. They thought they were getting a good home for me. Now I know that one's destiny is one's destiny. It was so decided for me. . . .

Across the west wall from us lived an old uncle and aunt. He was a cousin to my husband's father. They were an old couple with no children and they were very fond of me. They had land and houses. They wove baskets of willow withes and boiled sea water for salt.

This old uncle was over seventy, a strong old man who loved his wine. He was good to me and hated my husband. The old aunt was a little old woman, over fifty.

I often went to their house and they fed me many meals when my husband brought home nothing for me to eat.

When I was about twenty the old aunt died. I nursed her. She was ill for a month and very ill for half a month.

"I don't want Liu-Yi-tze to be my chief mourner." Liu-Yi-tze was my husband's baby name, the one his family knew him by. By rights he should have been the chief mourner as he was the nearest nephew. They asked me to be the chief mourner and carry the Heredity Jar. This is a small earthen jar into which all the members of the family, of the next generation, put food—rice, chiaotze, bread. They stuff the jar full that there may be many descendants and that there may be food for the person about to go on the long journey, also that there may be luck for those who put in the food. The child who stuffs in the most food will have the greatest fortune. The youngest son puts the round loaf of bread on the top of the jar and sticks a pair of chopsticks into it. I had to be all the children and stuff the jar, and also the youngest son and stick in the chopsticks, and the oldest son and carry the jar. Carrying the jar is the sign of the chief mourner. It is placed in the grave at the coffin head.

I was by the old aunt's side when she died. It is said that those who die alone, who die with no one beside them, will come back after transmigration as single people, people who have no descendants. The family must be there when anyone dies.

I made the little red bag which was to provide her with comforts for the journey and hung it on her buttonhole. I cut a piece of silver from an earring that she might have silver to buy what she needed, and put it in the bag with a pinch of tea and a piece of candy and a bit of salt vegetable to make her food more palatable. And, according to custom, as my old aunt died, as the breath left her body, I stuffed the little red bag into her mouth that she might have food to eat on her journey. I placed in her hand the small bundle of food which she needed to feed the dogs as she crossed the great Dog Mountain. I bound her feet together so that her body should not get up again. I did all the things for her that a son or a daughter-in-law or a daughter should do.

As soon as the breath had left her body we went to the Tu Ti Miao, the Temple of the Earth God. I pounded with my rolling pin three times on the ground to knock at the gate of Hades and pointed three times to the sky to knock at the gates of Heaven.

On the second morning all the family, male and female, went to the Cheng Huang Miao, the Temple of the City God, for by this time the Earth God had brought the spirit to this temple and we must feed it. We took a bowl of gruel and poured it in the court and we all kowtowed and wept. And on the third day all these things were done at the Temple of the Tien Chun Lao Yeh, the Master of the Hosts of Heaven. All the relatives and friends go there.

The funeral was on the fifth day. Old people should be kept at least seven days and young people at least three, but we buried her on the fifth day. All the night before we knelt around the coffin in our unbleached and unhemmed white clothes and wept, and the musicians played. This was to help the spirit start on its journey. It is natural that the spirit should linger by the body several days and find it difficult to leave and start on the unknown journey.

We put the ashes of all the paper money and clothes and the paper servants that had been burned for her into an earthen basin. As the coffin was lifted, to carry it away, the basin was thrown to the ground and broken and we all wailed.

I wore sackcloth and my head was bound with the rope of the chief mourner, and I walked in front of the coffin with the Heredity Jar in my arms. . . .

Secret Societies and Rebellions

Resentful of their meager lot in life, the young men of the villages sometimes turned to banditry against landlords and officials. Often they were organized in secret societies. In times of relative peace and plenty these societies were primarily religious groups, opposed to the Confucian beliefs of the gentry, and forming part of the peasant culture. When natural disasters or a particularly despotic official made conditions worse, the societies grew rapidly, and occasionally their "Robin Hood" banditry would flare into open rebellion. For all these reasons, the gentry and the government strongly opposed secret societies and took every opportunity to suppress them.

Despite their efforts, the societies flourished—Yellow Turbans, Red Eyebrows, White Lotus, Nien, and many others—and several times in Chinese history rebellions begun by the secret societies swept large parts of the country, ultimately bringing down the imperial house and placing some new peasant hero on the Dragon Throne. In this way the Mongols, who established the Yuan dynasty, were defeated and a member of the White Lotus sect founded the Ming dynasty.

In these readings there is a brief description of the nature of the secret societies by Chesneaux, a French scholar of Chinese secret societies, a passage from the novel *The Water Margin*, and the story of the overthrow of the Ming dynasty.

The Secret Societies
by Jean Chesneaux

The secret societies were diametrically opposed to the Confucian order and its social conventions (we shall see, for example, that they were feminist in outlook). But at the same time they set out to create, at least symbolically, a system of rules and political conventions as complete as the one they opposed.

In short, they mirrored established society while constituting—for hundreds of years—the principal force of political opposition and religious dissent.

Most of the sects went back a long way—the White Lotus, for example, to the twelfth century.

In traditional China, where the political power of the ruling class (the civil servants) and its economic power (feudal exploitation of the peasants) were intermingled, discontent with the established order was directed against both the rich and the state. This was the cause of the peasant revolts which punctuated the history of the great Chinese dynasties.

In earlier centuries the secret societies often took the initiative in these revolts. They provided them with a framework, strengthened with their rituals and magic formulae the ideological mobilisation of the peasants against Confucian orthodoxy, and offered them a means of retreat after the rebellion had collapsed.

This association between secret societies and peasant agitation continued into the nineteenth and even into the twentieth century with the Red Spears movement. . . .

The secret societies' refusal to recognise the established order was total: it was directed at both the social and political structures. Their lawless activities were never clearly differentiated from the politico-social struggle. To borrow a phrase which the historian Eric Hobsbawn uses of the "primitive rebels" of the West, it was "social banditry."

The secret societies practised armed robbery, the kidnapping of children for ransom, and piracy on exactly the same principle as that on which they attacked prisons, government convoys, or administrative buildings (*yamen*).

However, the banditry was aimed mainly at the rich, the merchants, the landowners, and the Mandarins. It claimed to be based on a higher justice than that of the imperial state.

Confucian tradition reduced women to a state of docile obedience towards their fathers and husbands. It declared them incapable of carrying on the ancestor cult, and saw something impure and despicable in the female element (*yin*) as opposed to the male (*yang*). The secret societies, on the other hand, by treating men and women on an equal footing, appeared as the earliest champions of the rights of Chinese women, well before the feminists of 1920.

Women, just as much as men, could be initiated and succeed to responsible positions. We shall see when we come to the Boxers how important women were in that organization.

· · · ·

Vicious sects (*Hsieh-chiao*), obscene sects (*yin-chiao*), pseudo-religions (*wei-chiao*), perverse sects (*yao-chiao*), brigand members of sects (*chiao-fei*)—such were the sort of names which the Mandarins used to denote the secret societies and their members. These designations reveal the double character which has already been stressed: these politico-social organisations of opposition were at the same time dissident religious groups.

About 1850 a Mandarin wrote an account of the foundation of the Golden Coins Society. His text reflects the same derogatory opinion and confirms the double aspect of this organization. Following a dream with a religious interpretation, an athletic restaurant proprietor who seems to step straight out of a medieval Chinese picaresque romance gathers round himself and his acolytes, vagabonds and law-breakers seeking to escape from justice, as well as "men who possess great wealth but are cut off from power." Such are the *chinfei*, the "brigands who quote gold as their authority."

The bandits of the Golden Coins Society began their activities in the early years of the reign of the emperor Hsien Feng. A man of about thirty named

Zhao Chi had a restaurant in his native village of Chian-cang, a district of Pingyi. He was thoroughly acquainted with the techniques of wrestling and boxing, and all his friends were boxers or athletes.

When his friends were in need, Zhao Chi gave them money or helped them with presents. On account of this, his name was known in North and South, as far as the boundaries of Fukien province. Many common criminals had come to him to take advantage of his protection. People called him *Zhao-da-ge* (big brother Zhao).

· · · ·

Behind all this was a vital tradition nourished by, and expressed through, folk literature. For example, the famous popular romance of the late Middle Ages, *Shui-hu-ch'uan* (The Water's Margin), which is extremely well known in China, presents 108 brigand-heroes from the Liang-shang-po Forest and exalts their prowess. The members of the secret societies were steeped in the *Shui-hu-ch'uan* and often borrowed titles and slogans from it.

From *The Water Margin*
by Shih Nai-an and Lo Kuan-chung

WITH AN INTRODUCTION BY CYRIL BIRCH

The Men of the Marshes (Shui hu chuan) *is a novel of massive size and scope which probably took shape in the years about 1368, when the Yüan dynasty yielded place to the native Chinese Ming. Little is known about the putative authors, Shih Naian and Lo Kuan-chung, although the latter (who lived from about 1330 to about 1400) is credited with several other lengthy historical novels. They had at their disposal a mass of material, part factual but mainly legendary, which storytellers for some two hundred years past had woven about the historical figures of Sung Chiang and his band of thirty-six. The novel Shih and Lo created continued to grow for another two centuries:*

the extract which follows is from chapters 14 to 16 of the most complete version, which appeared in 120 chapters toward the close of the Ming dynasty. Pearl S. Buck has translated, under the title All Men Are Brothers, *all of a later "truncated" version of the first 70 chapters only.*

The novel is rich in incident and in vivid portraits of hoa-han *or "bravos." These, from sneak-thieves to murderers, are presented as men of goodwill and generous heart driven outside the law by the injustices of the men in power over the land. The economic plight of the three fishermen brothers in our extract is a case in point. . . .*

It would be wrong to claim that The Men of the Marshes *was often taken seriously as a work of literature. Its popular origins, "vulgar" colloquial language and dangerous message all precluded the possibility. But Chinese scholars of modern times have recognized in it the first full masterpiece in that long line of novels which began with mass entertainment and progressed to include some of the finest literary products of later ages.*

Then Number Five broke in: "You don't realize, Schoolmaster—Liang-shan Marsh used to be a real ricebowl for us three brothers, but nowadays we don't dare go anywhere near."

"Don't tell me the government can manage to prohibit fishing over an area as great as that!" said Wu Yung.

"I'd like to see the government that would try to prohibit me from fishing!" cried Number Five. "I'd take no prohibition from the Lord of Hades himself!"

"Then if there's no government prohibition why are you afraid to go?"

"It's clear you don't realize what's behind all this," said Number Five. "Perhaps we'd better tell you all about it."

"Well, I certainly don't understand it at all," said Wu Yung.

At this point Juan Number Seven spoke up: "It's hard to describe what's happened at Liang-shan Marsh. The waterways have been taken over by a gang of scoundrels who have just arrived and won't let anyone fish there."

"I'd no idea of this," said Wu Yung. "I had heard

nothing in my part of the world about any gang of scoundrels arriving."

"The boss of the gang is one of those failed examination candidates," explained Juan Number Two. "His name is Wang Lun, and they call him the 'White-gowned Scholar.' His number two is the 'Skyscraper' Tu Ch'ien, and the third is the 'Cloud-wrapped Guardian God,' Sung Wan. Then there's a man called Chu Kuei, the 'Dry-land Sharpears,' who has opened a tavern now at the entrance to Li-chia-tao Village and spies out the land for the others, but he doesn't count for much. But there is a bravo just arrived, used to be an instructor in the imperial guard at the eastern capital, some fellow called Lin Ch'ung, the 'Leopard-headed,' a past master in the military arts. These bandits have gathered together with six or seven hundred people, men and women, and there they go robbing homes and plundering any traveller who passes. It's been more than a year since we went there to rob, and now that the waterways are closed to us our ricebowl is broken—that's why it's not easy to put it into a few words."

"I had really no idea of all this," said Wu Yung. "Why doesn't the government come and take them into custody?"

"Wherever they poke about nowadays," replied Number Five, "the government men only bring trouble. If they come out to a village they eat up innocent people's pigs and lambs and chickens and geese, and then they won't leave again until they've collected their 'travelling expenses'! And what help can you expect from them? The government thief-catchers daren't go near the villages! If one of the higher-ups orders them out to arrest somebody they daren't look him in the eye, they're so scared they mess their pants back and front!"

And Number Two added, "If we can't take any good-sized fish, at least we're spared a good number of taxes!"

"If that's the way things are," said Wu Yung, "those roughs of yours are well off."

"They fear neither heaven nor earth—nor the government," said Number Five. "I should think they *are* well off, measuring out their gold and silver, decking themselves out in the fanciest brocades, meat in thick slices and wine by the jar! Clever fishermen we might be, my brothers and me, but how could we ever hope to rival them? . . ."

"'A man has one lifetime as the grass has one summer,'" Juan Number Seven went on. "We stick to our fishing for our livelihood, but what a fine thing it would be to have one day of their life!"

"But why should you wish for their way?" asked Wu Yung. "How will they end up but as criminals sentenced to sixty or seventy strokes of a bamboo rod, all their might and majesty gone for good? And if the government does get its hands on them, they've only themselves to blame."

"The government!" said Number Two. "Rest upon it, they haven't a notion, plain stupid the whole lot of them. People get away with a thousand crimes that stink to high heaven and nothing happens to them. There's no getting rich for us brothers as we are, but if we could only find a contact with them, we'd be up there!"

"I've had this idea many a time," Number Five agreed. "We're as capable as anyone else, my brothers and me. But who there knows our worth?"

"Suppose someone did know your worth," said Wu Yung, "would you really go?"

"If someone were to recognize us," said Number Seven, "we'd go through water and we'd go through fire. One day of riches, and if we died for it we could smile in the next world."

The Fall of the Ming Dynasty
by Dun Li*

In 1628 when the last Ming emperor Ch'ung-chen ascended the throne, the regime had deteriorated to such an extent that nothing except a miracle could reverse the trend. Ch'ung-chen was one of the better emperors, conscientious and hard-working, but he could not stop the accelerating decline of the Ming regime. No sooner was he proclaimed emperor than he heard of a dreadful famine in Shensi province. One of the memorials he read described the situation as follows:

> Your humble servant was born in Anse subprefecture, Shensi province. I have read many memorials submit-

---

*Dun Li, *Ageless Chinese*.

ted by Your Majesty's officials in connection with the present state of affairs. They say that famine has caused fathers to desert their children and husbands to sell their wives. They also say that many people are so starved that they eat grass roots and white stones. But the real situation is worse than what they have described. Yenan, the prefecture from which your humble servant comes, has not had any rain for more than a year. Trees and grasses are all dried up. During the eighth and the ninth moon months of last year people went to the mountains to collect raspberries which were called grain but actually were no better than chaff. They tasted bitter and they could only postpone death for the time being. By the tenth moon month all raspberries were gone, and people peeled off tree bark for food. Among tree bark the best was that of the elm. This was so precious that to consume as little as possible people mixed it with the bark of other trees to feed themselves. Somehow they were able to prolong their lives. Towards the end of the year the supply of tree bark was exhausted, and they had to go to the mountains to dig up stones as food. Stones were cold and tasted musty. A little taken in would fill up the stomach. Those who took stones found their stomachs swollen and they dropped and died in a few days. Others who did not wish to eat stones gathered as bandits. They robbed the few who had some savings, and when they robbed, they took everything and left nothing behind. Their idea was that since they had to die either one way or another it was preferable to die as a bandit than to die from hunger and that to die as a bandit would enable them to enter the next world with a full stomach. . . .

While starved peasants in northern Shensi ravaged the countryside in search of food, garrison soldiers in South Manchuria and Shensi mutinied because they had not been paid for a long time. To make the situation worse, the government decided in 1629 to cut down some of its administrative expenses by reducing the number of coolie couriers in Shansi and Shensi provinces. These coolie couriers, employed by government posts in carrying mails, were suddenly without jobs, and they too decided to join the rebels. In the same year the Manchus moved southward to attack Peking. Responding to the call from the imperial government for help, the governors from Shansi, Suiyuan, and Kansu led their soldiers eastward, only to see them mutiny on the road before they could reach the capital. These soldiers, like those of the Shensi and Manchuria garrisons, had not been paid for some time and they refused to obey any more orders. Thus the rebellion, first started by bands of starved peasants, was quickly joined by unemployed coolie couriers and soldier mutineers. The number of rebels continued to grow as other dissatisfied elements joined them en masse.

Early in the 1630's Chang Hsien-chung and Li Tzu-ch'eng emerged as the two leaders of the rebel forces. Both were born in Shensi, had a common peasant background, and had received little or no education. Before the rebellion Chang was a mercenary soldier, and Li was first a coolie courier and then a Buddhist monk. Both had been once sentenced to death on account of crimes or alleged crimes and managed to escape through some devious methods. When the starving peasants began to revolt in 1628, Li was among the first to join them. Chang joined two years later after he had collected a small following. From 1628 to 1635 the rebels were most active in the Northwest, though occasionally they moved eastward to Honan and Hupeh and southward to Szechuan. In the latter year rebel forces had snowballed to more than 400,000 and at the suggestion of Li Tzu-ch'eng their leaders decided to move eastward to contend for all of China. Government troops that were sent against them retreated or otherwise dispersed before the marauding hordes. City after city surrendered without a fight, and others were captured after a brief engagement. To encourage surrender, the rebels announced that they would not take away a single life if a city surrendered the day they arrived. However, if it chose to defend itself for one day, 30 percent of the city's population would be put to death; 70 percent would be killed if it were defended for two days; and the entire city would be destroyed if it hesitated for more than three days before opening its gates. Among the things they looted they kept for themselves horses and arms; food, cloth, and money were generously distributed among starving peasants. They promised to abolish taxation forever if they won. And many peasants believed in them.

The rebel ranks soon split into two groups. One group led by Li Tzu-ch'eng ravaged the Yellow River basin; the other, led by Chang Hsien-chung, moved up and down the Yangtze River valley, killing and burning as it went. Chang Hsien-chung was one of the most bloodthirsty persons ever recorded in Chinese history and was said to have felt uncomfortable if he did not see somebody killed each day. His favorite targets were the Ming nobility, the bureaucrats, and the intellectuals. In one instance, he called students to take his civil service examinations, but when they arrived, he ordered all of them to be slaughtered in cold blood. His generals were rated according to the number of people they had killed; some of his generals were sentenced to death simply because they had not killed enough to meet the norm. In Chengtu, Szechuan province, there stands a monument believed to have been erected by Chang Hsien-chung. The monument bears the following inscriptions:

> Heaven produces myriads of things to nourish man;
> Man never does one good to recompense Heaven.
> Kill, kill, kill, kill, kill, kill, and kill!

It seems that he sought neither fame nor wealth, but the power to destroy. In one case, he dammed a river and placed millions of dollars' worth of gold, silver, and precious stones on the dried river bed, and then ordered the dam be broken so that all these valuables would be washed away towards the sea. Why did he do this? Because, said he, he wanted these valuables to be denied to posterity. From 1630 when he joined the rebels to 1646 when he was finally captured, millions of innocent people died victims of this psychopath. The most devastated area was Szechuan which at one time was said to have "few" people left. When the Manchus marched towards Szechuan, many people looked to them as their saviors. In 1646 one of Chang's generals deserted him and led the Manchus to his stronghold. Chang was wounded by a flying arrow and the pursuing Manchus found him hidden underneath a pile of firewood in a small village. He was captured and subsequently beheaded.

Equally ferocious but perhaps less brutal was Li Tzu-ch'eng, nicknamed "The Dashing King." In the beginning he was no better than other rebels; his hordes plundered, burned, and slaughtered wherever they went. After most of North China was brought under his control, he began to think seriously of being a contender for the Ming throne. He promised to abolish taxation to win the support of peasants and imposed some discipline on his marauding soldiers. His soldiers were no longer allowed to plunder and rape, while money, grain, and cloth which he stole from the rich were handed over to the very poor as relief. In 1643 he declared the establishment of a new regime at Sian (formerly Ch'angan) and organized his government according to the Ming pattern. In the same year his troops entered Peking without encountering much opposition. The last Ming emperor Ch'ung-chen hanged himself on the Coal Mountain behind the Forbidden City, after his wife the empress had committed suicide before him. Fearing that his beloved daughter, the First Princess, would be molested by the rebels if she fell into their hands, he proposed to kill her with a long sword. Sobbing audibly, he said to her: "Why did you have to be born a princess?"

Thus the Ming dynasty came to an end after an existence of 277 years.

Folk Culture

Throughout Chinese history two cultures existed side by side. We know a great deal about the literate and sophisticated culture of the leisured classes. We know far less of the culture of the rest of China, only what has been handed down through the generations, or what has been recorded by chance in some scholar's work, or parts which have survived in ceremonies like the wedding and funeral we read of in Little Tiger's story.

Because most peasants were illiterate, their culture was not based on written stories or poetry. Instead they sang, passed on legends and tales orally, performed dramas, embroidered and wove, and developed elaborate papercut decorations. At times the gentry would adopt one of their innovations, and it would become a part of the other culture; many scholars and retired officials collected folktales and parables as a hobby.

Tales with Morals

TRANSLATED BY LIN YU-TANG

Once a general was shot in the head with an arrow in battle, and he quickly ran home to have the arrow pulled out.

He asked a surgeon, which in Chinese is called "an external doctor," to treat him.

The surgeon examined it and, taking a pair of scissors, cut the arrow off as close to the skin as possible, and asked for his fee.

"Please take out the arrow for me, for it is inside my head, and I am going to die of it!" pleaded the general.

"I am an external doctor," replied the surgeon. "What has that got to do with me? I have done my part. You can ask a doctor of internal medicine to attend to the rest of it."

The general did not know what to do.

MORAL: *The authorities today who shirk their responsibilities and pass them on to the next official are of the opinion that the arrow inside should be left to the doctor of internal medicine.*

There was a quack doctor who advertised that he could cure the camel of his hump. Someone brought a camel to him to be cured.

The doctor placed a wooded board on the ground and made the camel lie on it. Then he placed another wooden board on top of the animal and made people go on top and stamp on it as hard as they could.

The camel died of it.

The owner of the camel went to sue him at court for killing the camel.

The camel doctor said: "I am a camel doctor. My business is to make humps straight. It is none of my business whether the animal remains alive."

MORAL: *The magistrates who see to it that the taxes are collected properly, but do not see to it that the people remain alive, are in no way different from the camel doctor.*

There was once a poor man who picked up a hen's egg. He brought the egg home and said to his wife:

"Look here, I have found a fortune!"

And he showed the egg to his wife, and said:

"This is my fortune, but you have to wait about ten years. I will have a neighbor's hen sit on this egg, and when the chicken grows up, I shall possess a hen. The hen will lay fifteen eggs a month, which means fifteen chickens. In two years' time, we shall have three hundred chickens, for which we shall get ten dollars. With these ten dollars, I will buy five calves, and when these grow up and bear other calves, I shall have twenty-five cows in three years. When these multiply, in another three years we shall have a hundred and fifty cows, which will sell for three hundred dollars. I will loan the three hundred dollars for interest, and in another three years, we shall have at least five hundred dollars. Then I shall spend two thirds of this sum on a house and farm, and one third of it for buying servants and a concubine, and live happily for life."

When his wife heard him mention the word "concubine," she became very angry and smashed the egg to pieces, shouting, "I will not tolerate this seed of all evil!"

The husband was also very angry, and he went to sue his wife at court, the charge being that she had broken up his fortune, and was consequently a bad wife. He asked that the wife be severely punished, and told the magistrate the whole story.

"But," said the magistrate, "your wife stopped you when you had come only to the concubine: you hadn't quite finished telling her what you were going to do yet."

"Indeed, I had finished, Your Honor," said the husband.

"But no," said the magistrate, "your concubine was going to have a son, who would pass the official examinations, become an official, and bring you great honor. Is all this nothing to you? To think that such a huge fortune should be smashed by the fist of a bad woman. She shall be killed!"

"But this was only a discussion; why should I be sentenced to death for it?" protested the wife.

"Your husband's buying a concubine was only a discussion also. Why should you be jealous?"

"That is right, too, Your Honor," said the woman. "But to forestall an evil, you have to nip it in the bud."

The magistrate was delighted and set her free.

MORAL: *To know that a thing does not exist is the best way to forget the desire for it*.

The Solicitor for Contributions

A robber and a monk met a tiger on a mountain path. The robber got ready his bow and arrow to attack the tiger, but that seemed to produce no effect on the tiger, who steadily advanced nearer in spite of the robber's threatening arrow. In that desperate situation, the monk, who held in his hand a book of receipts for soliciting contributions to his temple, threw the book at the tiger and the tiger ran away. Back in his cave, the tiger cub asked its father, "Why are you not afraid of the robber but of the monk?" And the old tiger replied, "Because I could fight with the robber when he came near, but what was I to do if the monk approached me for contributions?"

The Cuckoo

There was a fool whose wife had a lover. Once he came back at night, and as the lover was trying to leap through the window, he caught one of his shoes. This he put under his pillow thinking that he would use it as evidence and prosecute his wife at court the next day. During his sleep, however, his wife secretly exchanged it with one of the husband's own shoes. On waking up the next morning, the husband looked carefully at the shoe and finding it to be his own, apologized to his wife, "I am very sorry for last night. I didn't know it was I myself who jumped out of the window."

The Miser

There was a certain miser who, hearing about the reputation of a greater miser than himself, went to the other miser's home to become his disciple. As usual, he had to bring some present to his new master and brought with him a bowl of water with a piece of paper cut in the form of a fish. The great miser happened to be away from home and his wife received him. "Here is my fish as a humble present from your new pupil," remarked the visitor.

The miser's wife received it with thanks and brought up an empty cup and asked him to have tea. After the pupil had pretended to drink tea, the miser's wife again asked him to help himself to the cakes by drawing two circles in the air with her hand. In came the master miser and when he saw his wife drawing two circles, he shouted to her, "What extravagance! You are giving two cakes away! A semicircle should do!"

The story of Yingt'ai and Hsienpo is famous all over China. Like the other parables and stories, it tells us of the problems the common people of China faced, from monks and tax collectors to girls who desired an education.

Yingt'ai and Hsienpo

TRANSLATED BY WOLFRAM EBERHARD IN *FOLKTALES OF CHINA*

Faithful Even in Death

The village of the Liang family and that of the Chu family were close together. The inhabitants were well-to-do and content. Old excellency Liang and old excellency Chu were good friends. A son was born to the Liang family, who was given the name Hsienpo. Being an unusually quick and clever child, he was sent to the school in the same town.

At the same time a daughter was born to the Chu family, who, besides being very clever, was particularly beautiful. As a child she loved to read and study, and only needed to glance at a book to know a whole sentence by heart. Old Chu simply doted on her. When she grew up, she wanted to go away and study. Her father tried in vain to dissuade her, but eventually he arranged for her to dress as a boy and study with Hsienpo.

The two lived together, worked together, argued together, and were the best of friends. The eager and zealous Hsienpo did not notice that Yingt'ai was really a girl, and therefore he did not fall in love with her. Yingt'ai studied so hard and was so wrapped up in her work that her fellow students paid no attention to her. Being very modest, and never taking part in the children's jokes, she exercised a calming influence over even the most impudent. When she slept with Hsienpo, each lay on one side of the bed, and between them stood a bowl of water. They had arranged that whoever knocked over the bowl must pay a fine; but the serious little Hsienpo never touched it.

When Yingt'ai changed her clothes, she never stood about naked but pulled on her clean clothes under the old ones, which she then took off and finished dressing. Her fellow students could not understand why she did this, and asked her the reason. "Only peasants expose the body they have received from their parents," she said; "it should not be done." Then the boys began to copy her, not knowing her real reason was to prevent their noticing that she was a girl.

Then her father died, and her sister-in-law, who did not approve of Yingt'ai's studying, ordered her to come home and learn housework. But Yingt'ai refused and continued to study.

The sister-in-law, fearing that Yingt'ai had fallen in love with Hsienpo, used to send her from time to time babies' things, swaddling clothes, children's clothes and covers, and many other things. The students became curious when they saw the things, and Yingt'ai could tell them only that they were the things she herself had used as a child, which her sister-in-law was now sending her to keep.

The time passed quickly. Soon Yingt'ai and Hsienpo were grown up. Yingt'ai still dressed as a man, and being a well-brought-up girl, she did not dare to ask Hsienpo to marry her; but when she looked at him, her heart was filled with love. His delicate manner attracted her irresistibly, and she swore to marry him and none other.

She proposed the marriage to her sister-in-law, who did not consider it suitable, because after her father's death they had lost all their money. Against Yingt'ai's will the sister-in-law arranged a match with a Dr. Ma, of a newly rich family in the village. Yingt'ai objected strongly, but she could do nothing about it. Day after day she had to listen to complaints: she was without filial piety, she was a shameless, decadent girl, a disgrace to the family. Her sister-in-law still feared she might secretly marry Hsienpo, and she urged the Ma family to appoint a day for the wedding. Then she cut off Yingt'ai's school money, which forced her to return home.

Yingt'ai was obliged to hide her misery. Weeping bitterly, she said good-bye to Hsienpo, who accompanied her part of the way home. As they separated, Yingt'ai sang a song which revealed that she was a girl and that she wanted to marry him. But the good, dense Hsienpo did not understand her hints. He did not see into Yingt'ai's heart, and tried to comfort her by telling her that one must return home some time and that they would soon meet again. Yingt'ai saw that everything was hopeless, and went home in tears.

Hsienpo felt very lonely without his companion, with whom he had lived day and night for many years. He kept on writing letters to Yingt'ai, begging her to come back to school, but he never received a reply.

Finally he could bear it no longer, and went to visit her. "Is Mr. Yingt'ai at home?" he asked. "Please tell him his school friend, Hsienpo, has come and wants to see him."

The servant looked at him curiously, and then said curtly, "There is no Mr. Yingt'ai here—only a Miss Yingt'ai. She is to be married soon, and naturally she can't leave her room. How could she speak to a man? Please go away, sir, for if the master discovers you, he will make a complaint against you for improper behavior."

Suddenly everything was clear to Hsienpo. In a state of collapse he crept home. There he found, under Yingt'ai's books, a bundle of letters and essays which showed him clearly how deeply Yingt'ai loved him and also that she did not wish to marry any other man. Through his own stupidity, his lack of understanding, the dream had come to nought.

Overcome by remorse, he spent the days lost in tears. Yingt'ai was always before his eyes, and in his dreams he called her name, or cursed her sister-in-law and Dr. Ma, himself, and all the ways of society. Because he ceased to eat or drink, he fell ill and gradually sank into the grave.

Yingt'ai heard the sad news. Now she had nothing more to live for. If she had not been so carefully watched, she would have done herself some injury. In this state of despair the wedding day arrived. Listlessly she allowed herself to be pushed into the red bridal chair and set off for the house of her bridegroom, Dr. Ma. But when they passed the grave of Hsienpo, she begged her attendants to let her get out and visit it, to thank him for all his kindness. On the grave, overcome by grief, she flung herself down and sobbed. Her attendants urged her to return to her chair, but she refused. Finally, after great persuasion, she got up, dried her tears, and bowing several times in front of the grave, she prayed as follows: "You are Hsienpo, and I am Yingt'ai. If we were really intended to be man and wife, open your grave three feet wide."

Scarcely had she spoken when there came a clap like thunder and the grave opened. Yingt'ai leaped into the opening, which closed again before the maids could catch hold of her, leaving only two bits of her dress in their hands. When they let these go, they changed into two butterflies which flew up into the air.

Dr. Ma was furious when he heard that his wife had jumped into the grave of Hsienpo. He had the grave opened, but the coffin was empty except for two white stones. No one knew where Hsienpo and Yingt'ai had gone. In a rage the grave violators flung the two stones onto the road, where immediately a bamboo with two stems shot up. They were shimmering green, and swayed in the wind. The grave robbers knew that this was the result of magic, and cut down the bamboo with a knife; but as soon as they had cut down one, another shot up, until finally several people cut down the two stems at the same time. These then flew up to heaven and became rainbows.

Now the two lovers have become immortals. If they ever want to be together, undisturbed and unseen, so that no one on earth can see them or even talk about them, they wait until it is raining and the clouds are hiding the sky. The red in the rainbow is Hsienpo, and the blue is Yingt'ai.

Economic and Scientific Development

No history of Imperial China would be complete without a listing of the numerous scientific discoveries and technical inventions her people were responsible for. As in the West, technological progress stimulated economic development. By the time Marco Polo visited the northern cities (conquered by the Mongols) and Hangchow, capital of the defiant Southern Sung, China was a vast and highly sophisticated center of commercial and early industrial growth.

Discoveries and Inventions
by Maud Russell, in a review of
Science and Civilization in China
by Joseph Needham

The Chinese preceded the Greeks in many important scientific and technical discoveries; they kept pace with the Arabs who had access to all the treasures of the ancient Western world; they maintained between the third and thirteenth centuries a level of scientific knowledge unapproached in the West. The weakness of China in theory and geometrical systemization "did not prevent the emergence of technological discoveries and inventions often far in advance of contemporary Europe especially up to the 15th century," said Needham. And he points out that these technological inventions poured into Europe in a continuous stream during the first 13 centuries of the Christian era . . .

Some of the basic, every day things that have come to us in the West from China are rice, tea, porcelain, silk, the umbrella, eye-glasses, the printing press, the mariner's compass, paper, paper money, the finger print system of identification, water-tight compartments in ships, kites, etc.

Paper was invented in the first century A.D by Tsai Lun, but it was at least six hundred years before it passed to the West. And in China colored paper began to be used in the seventh century.

Printing had begun in China at least by the eighth century. The earliest block printing known is that of a Buddhist charm of 770. The Chinese had long used ink and paper and they knew how to make seals of metals, stone and clay; the time was ripe for such an invention as printing. Text books were needed by the thousands for the civil service system, and charms for warding off evil spirits and diseases were desired by the Buddhists and Taoists. In the tenth century Confucian classics were printed from wooden blocks in 130 volumes and were widely distributed throughout the country. By the end of the century Taoist books had become fairly common in the far western province of Szechuan.

China gets the credit for inventing gunpowder. "Cracking and exploding staves," say the chroniclers, were used in the Wei Dynasty (220–265 A.D) and fireworks were used in the Sui Dynasty (605–617 A.D.). Their use for war is not proven, though experiments along those lines were carried out. In 1161 "thunderbolt projectives" made of paper filled with lime and sulphur were used in battle; when they touched the water the fire leapt from them and the dense fumes that arose confused the enemy. And there were "fire-stones" thrown a considerable distance by a "fire-drug" made of nitre, sulphur and willow charcoal. Arab traders brought the secret of this combination to the West and it was adopted for warfare . . .

Chinese embassies made presents of *Chinese silk* to the Parthians in the first century, and it was they who introduced silk into Western Asia (though caravans from China to Iran date from 106 B.C.) and it was then that the trans-Asian silk trade was regularized. The event whereby the Roman Empire and thus ultimately Europe as a whole was rendered independent of China for a supply of raw silk took place in 552; someone guilefully smuggled silk moth-eggs in a hollow stick from Kashgaria. Domestication of the silk worm and the development of the silk industry had taken place at least as early as the Shang period, in the 14th century B.C.

True porcelain was not only made as early as the Tang Dynasty (618–907 A.D.) but had already become articles of overseas trade by that time. Proto-porcelain which is pottery with elements of porcelain had been made in Han times, just before the dawn of the Christian era. It was the 18th century before Europe was producing true porcelain.

Still extant writings (of Han Fei who died in 238 B.C.) tell of a "south pointer" which fixed the position of morning and evening; legend in China even puts the use of a guiding "south pointing contrivance" as far back as the 12th century B.C. The eastern deviation of the *magnetic needle* was already noted by a writer, Shen Kua, about

1068. The first mention in Europe of the deviation of the needle (by Pierre de Maricourt) in 1269 comes therefore two centuries later than the Chinese record...

It was not in 19th century Europe but in second century A.D. China that the *automatic clock-drive* of the astronomical telescope first appears; its equatorial mounting was made in Mongol Khanbaliq, not in the workshops of Uraniborg or Vienna. Fraunhofer invented his clock drive in 1824 and he certainly did not know that the Chinese had for many centuries caused their equatorial armillary sphere to rotate by water power. But Dr. Needham tells us that "One of the finest Chinese instruments was the armillary sphere of Su Sung, set up in 1088.... This was the first observational instrument in astronomical history to be provided with a clock-drive."

It was China, not Europe, that was responsible for the development of the *mechanical clock*. "Indeed," writes Dr. Needham, "the mechanical clocks of China built between A.D. 700 and 1300 have revealed at last the missing link between the very ancient water-receiving and water-giving vessels (clepsydras) of Babylonia and ancient Egypt and the purely mechanical clocks and watches of later ages."

Our *potato,* with its claim of American ancestry was known and eaten by the people of China in the Liang Dynasty (907–923). *Sugar* was already mentioned in records dating back to the 2nd century B.C. The Book of History (24th–8th century B.C.) mentions a fermented beverage of millet or rice; the straining of liquor from lees is mentioned in the Book of Odes (23rd–6th century B.C.). The first reference to *coal* in China was made about 100 B.C., called "ice charcoal," and was probably discovered about the same time in Europe, though Marco Polo (13th century A.D.) noticed its use in China and described it in such a manner that it seems it was utterly unknown to him or his contemporaries. The Chinese had perfectly developed *cooking stoves* by the time of the Han Dynasty and were also acquainted with the principle of the *chimney*. And it was the Chinese who introduced the washboard to the United States...

The most popularly known fact about the Chinese is that they use chopsticks. Westerners are often apt to look down on this as a crude method of eating; they should remember that the general use of the fork in Europe dates back no farther than the late 16th century, before which time our ancestors used only knives and their fingers.

European table-manners at the end of the 15th century indicate clearly that table forks were not then in general use in Europe. It was "manners" to reach for a piece of meat with only three fingers and not to leave the hand unduly long in the bowl. Another point of good behaviour was not to wipe the nose with the same hand you used in taking a piece of meat. The Chinese, on the other hand, had been using chopsticks for one thousand years—delicately and hygienically moving the food from the central bowls to their individual bowls, and easily and neatly "cutting" fish and fowl, not with knives or daggers, but with chopsticks. The Chinese people long antedate Europeans in refinement in eating!

This was China of the Southern Sung dynasty. Hangchow in the time of Marco Polo was the center of a culture and an economy far advanced in comparison with contemporary Europe. Yet only five centuries later, European capitalism was so much more vigorous and advanced that confrontations with China routinely resulted to the advantage of the westerners. The reasons for this great disparity in the development of classic capitalism have challenged historians and have been subjects of debate both in China and the west. Here Étienne Balazs, a French historian, discusses this question.

The Birth of Capitalism in China
by Étienne Balazs

... Why was it that, in spite of very favorable conditions—for China was technologically and scientifically ahead of the West until the time of the Renaissance—Chinese civilization never gave rise to capitalism? Were there ever the beginnings of capitalistic development—an embryonic capitalism that got strangled in the womb? Or did even such beginnings never occur? If they did, what prevented them from developing? Why did the buds never blossom? What are the main reasons for the failure? ...

The relations between the officials and the merchant class were stamped by the fact that the officials, in their capacity as the ruling class—endowed with learning that enabled them to supervise and coordinate the activities of an agrarian society, and thus to acquire their dominant position in the state—enjoyed an all-pervading power and prestige. In these relations, as seen from above, every means of keeping the merchant class down and holding it in subjection seemed permissible. Compromises, exceptions, favors, pardons—all were allowed so long as they were retracted at the earliest opportunity. Claims, titles, privileges, immunities, deeds, charters were never granted. Any sign of initiative in the other camp was usually strangled at birth, or if it had reached a stage when it could no longer be suppressed, the state laid hands on it, took it under control, and appropriated the resultant profits. As seen from below, there was, in these relations, no legal way of obtaining an immunity, a franchise, since the state and its representatives, the officials, were almighty. There remained only an indirect way of obtaining one's due: bribery.

The outstanding feature in these relations is the absence of pluck, the complete lack of a fighting spirit, on the part of the middle class. On the one hand, they felt impotent in the face of a competitor who seemed to hold all the advantages. On the other, they had no real desire to be different, to oppose their own way of life to that of the ruling class—and this inhibited them even more. Their ambition was limited: to find a position, if only a modest one, inside the ruling class, reflecting the social prestige attached to officialdom. Their consuming desire was that they, or their children, should become scholar-officials.

This is one of the secret springs accounting for China's particular course of development. The other is corruption. Corruption was, in fact, the main point of contact between the opposing classes. The merchants could not have operated their policy of bribery if it had not been for the practices of embezzlement and "squeeze" on the part of the officials. This kind of division of labor, while it may have been advantageous for a few individuals, not only was eventually to spell ruin for officialdom, but also was lethal so far as improvement of the status of the bourgeoisie is concerned. It prevented the middle classes from consolidating and extending momentary advantages, and prevented the bourgeoisie from achieving consciousness as a separate, autonomous body with its own interests. . . .

Another impediment to the development of capitalism was the traditionally preferred investment in land. Although the rent from land probably amounted to no more than 30 to 40 percent of the return from businesses such as pawnbroking, moneylending, and shopkeeping, we find that the laws of the Peking club of the townsmen from Hui-chou—the famous Hsin-an merchants—decreed that any unused public funds of the club "should be invested only in the purchase of real estate for receipt of rent, and should not be lent for interest, *in order to avoid risks.*" Small risk and high prestige were two major factors which had made investment in land attractive.

The history of the development of Chinese capitalism has an intermittent character and is full of leaps and bounds, regressions and relapses. I should like to give one example to illustrate this discontinuity. With the decline of the salt trade, the capital of the salt merchants was transferred to the more profitable business of pawnbroking. The chain of pawnshops founded as a state institution at the beginning of the eighteenth century was taken over by them, and the capital invested was called public funds "entrusted to merchants to produce interest."

The following points may serve as a summary of the arguments presented above.

First: I can give no exact date for the birth of capitalism in China. All I know is that the tendency will be to set this date further and further back, from the nineteenth to the eighteenth to the seventeenth century and so on, finally arriving at the Sung dynasty (tenth to thirteenth centuries), which in my opinion marks the beginning of modern times in China. Still, the discontinuity just mentioned distorts the steady, simple, ascending line so much favored by school textbooks.

Second: with regard to industrial capitalism, we must never forget that the purpose of machines is to economize labor or time. In China there was never any dearth of labor; on the contrary, China always had plenty of it. The superabundance of cheap labor certainly hampered the search for time-saving devices. Nevertheless, what was chiefly lacking in China for the further development of capitalism was not mechanical skill or scientific aptitude, nor a sufficient accumulation of wealth, but scope for individual enterprise. There was no individual freedom and no security for private enterprise, no legal foundation for rights other than those of the state, no alternative investment other than landed property, no guarantee against being penalized by arbitrary exactions from officials or against intervention by the state. But perhaps the supreme inhibiting factor was the overwhelming prestige of the state bureaucracy, which maimed from the start any attempt of the bourgeoisie to be different, to become aware of themselves as a class and fight for an autonomous position in society. Free enterprise, ready and proud to take risks, is therefore quite exceptional and abnormal in Chinese economic history.

Life in the Great Cities: Hangchow
by Jacques Gernet

The concentration of wealth in the town and the poverty in the countryside combined to promote a constant influx of peasants into the great urban centres. They quickly adapted to urban life, and it was they who formed the greater part of the population of Hangchow. Their numbers increased year by year until the phenomenon began to take on the aspect of a catastrophe. The existence of large towns in thirteenth-century China is in itself concrete proof of the malady from which the economy was suffering. Their overpopulation reflects the artificial overdevelopment of commercial activity and the immoderate growth of the luxury trades at the expense of the production of basic necessities.

All the ordinary people of Hangchow—whether poor devils who slaved all day long to satisfy the demands of their masters or employers, or porters, prostitutes, petty tradesmen with stalls set up at street corners, entertainers, pickpockets, thieves and beggars—had one thing in common: they had nothing to depend on for their living but the strength of their muscles or the sharpness of their wits. They had endless stores of patience and courage, of guile and cunning. The struggle was hard, because while capital was scarce and brought in a big return to its possessors, labour, on the contrary, was superabundant and wages always low.

The effect of the abundance and cheapness of labour was to produce an extraordinary degree of specialization. This was almost a kind of luxury not at all in keeping with the level of wealth and of techniques reached in China at that time. The labour market was remarkably well organized thanks to the guilds, who acted as employment exchanges. It was to them that both employers and employees applied, since no transaction was ever carried through without recourse to an intermediary (and it is probable that the guilds did not permit independent practice of any trade). It was through the heads of the guilds that merchants and members of the upper classes in Hangchow were able to procure managers for pawnshops and shops for selling rice-wine, for restaurants and pharmacies, or stewards for private mansions, gardeners, secretaries, accountants, cooks, specialists for heating and lighting. Some of these employment agencies even offered, on a short-term basis no doubt, concubines, dancers, young boy-singers (pederasty, let us note, was common and accepted), embroiderers, chair-porters, and escorts for people of rank proposing to travel, either in order to return to their native province or to make a tour for their education, or for officials travelling to take up their posts.

China's first contacts with the West began in the Middle Ages with the silk trade across the deserts of inner Asia, when Marco Polo and a few other hardy Europeans traveled with the caravans. Despite this, however, little was known of the Chinese empire, and Westerners had strange notions of the Chinese.

The first to systematically study China and to learn the Chinese language were Catholic Jesuit missionairies who took up residence in Peking in the late sixteenth century. Some of them had considerable influence in the Chinese court, where they taught the emperor's advisers about Western astronomy, history, and science. The Jesuits believed that in time, reasoned discourse would demonstrate the superiority of their culture and religion to these Imperial advisers, and it would then be easy to convert the rest of the Chinese. But eventually the Jesuits became embroiled in disputes with other missionary groups and lost their influence with the emperor. Though not officially suppressed, Christianity failed

to make further headway in gaining Chinese converts, and
the missionaries ultimately had little to show for their efforts.
Pat Barr is a British journalist and writer who has authored
books on both China and Japan.

Father Matteo Ricci (1552–1610)
by Pat Barr

Matteo Ricci, as the Chinese noted when they first met
him, "had a curly beard, blue eyes and a voice like a great
bell." Few Chinese had ever seen a man whose beard was
curly and whose eyes were blue and were not, therefore,
disposed to like him, for they are a conservative people
with a natural aversion to the unfamiliar. But Ricci won
many of them over in spite of his "odd" appearance. Wrote
one Chinese scholar, "I am very much delighted with his
ideas. . . . He is very polite when he talks to people and his
arguments, if challenged, can be inexhaustible. Thus,
even in foreign countries, there are also gentlemen."

Note that "even": the Chinese assumed that they were
the only well-mannered and civilized people on earth; it
was surprising indeed that a "barbarian from without"
could be a gentleman. Still, they conceded, this Italian
Jesuit missionary was "an extraordinarily impressive person,"
sympathetic, honest, intelligent, and many Chinese scholars liked and even admired him. This was an achievement
on Ricci's part, for it was not easy for a Westerner to make
a favorable impression on the self-sufficient, proud, wealthy
Ming Empire.

How did Ricci manage it? Well, he went to China as a
missionary in 1583 at a time when the Christian church
was vigorously expanding its frontiers, urged on by the
stimulation of the exciting explorations in the East and the
widening of intellectual horizons at home. He was thirty-
one years old then, geographer, astronomer and mathema-
tician as well as missionary, and, once settled near Canton,
he added to his talents a working knowledge of China's
language and social structure. In Ricci's view, the best
hope of spreading the gospel in China was first to gain the
confidence of its ruling literary and administrative class
(commonly known as "mandarins" in the West). To do this,

he had to make himself useful and interesting—to show these somewhat supercilious and narrow-minded mandarins that there were more things in heaven and earth than they had dreamed of in their philosophy.

So, in 1601, when Ricci and a few colleagues were allowed to go to Peking and set up a small mission, they took books on Western science, architecture, medicine, mathematics and also a clavicord, calendars, clocks and maps. But the maps caused difficulty, for, as Father Trigault, translator of Ricci's journals, explained, the Chinese thought that

> the heavens are round but the earth is flat and square, and they firmly believe that their Empire is right in the middle of it. They do not like the idea of our geographies pushing their China into one corner of the Orient. They could not comprehend the demonstrations proving that the earth is a globe, made up of land and water, and that a globe, of its very nature, has neither beginning nor end. The geographer [i.e. Ricci] was therefore obliged to change his design, and . . . he left a margin on either side of the map, making the Kingdom of China appear right in the center. This was more in keeping with their ideas and gave them a great deal of pleasure and satisfaction.

A coward's way out? Not in the circumstances. For, as Trigault continues, the Celestials felt that "only China among the nations is deserving of admiration. Relative to grandeur of empire, of public administration and of reputation for learning, they look upon all other people not only as barbarians, but as unreasoning animals. . . . The more their pride is inflated by this ignorance, the more humiliated they become when the truth is revealed." But Ricci had not come to humiliate the Chinese, rather to understand them and tell them about Christianity, so clearly the situation needed tact and patience—it was no good rushing about like a bull in a china shop expecting to change the Oriental mind at once.

Using his learning as an instrument to gain confidence, Ricci taught the Chinese scholars the rudiments of Western astronomy, mathematics and science and "this teaching," said Trigault, "was simply astounding and something beyond their imagination." So too in the matter of geography, Ricci eventually stretched the Chinese imagination. For though the mandarins had laughed when they first saw Ricci's map,

> when they learned of the symmetry of the five zones, and after reading of the customs of so many different peoples, and seeing the names of many places in perfect accord with those given by their own ancient writers, they admitted that the chart really *did* represent the size and figure of the world. From that time on, they had a much higher opinion of the European system of education.

Ricci, then, was a far-sighted tactician and by his methods converted a number of Chinese to Christianity. But the impact he made was upon the educated minority and was almost entirely through his own compelling personality and his writings in Chinese. . . .

Ricci was generally impressed by the quantity and quality of many Chinese products and concluded his list of them thus:

> Finally we shall say something about saltpetre which is quite plentiful but is not used extensively in the preparation of gunpowder because the Chinese are not expert in the use of guns and artillery and make but little use of these in warfare [though they had invented gunpowder]. Saltpetre however is used in lavish quantities in making fireworks for display at public games and on festival days. The Chinese take great pleasure in such exhibitions. . . . Their skill in the manufacturer of fireworks is really extraordinary and there is scarcely anything which they cannot cleverly imitate with them. They are especially adept at reproducing battles and making rotating spheres of fire, fiery trees, fruit and the like. . . . When I was in Nanking, I witnessed a pyrotechnic display for the celebration of the first month of the year, which is their great festival, and on this occasion I calculated that they consumed enough powder to carry on a sizeable war for a number of years.

So the men of the East had found a beautiful, joyous, harmless way of using saltpetre; the man of the West, a missionary, watched the procedure and calculated how many enemies the Chinese could have killed with that prodigal expenditure of explosive powder. And soon the Jesuits taught the Chinese how to cast more effective cannons for themselves. The Jesuits were not the barbarians of Chinese imagination, but when it came to gunpowder who were more civilized—the Chinese with their flowery fireworks or the Westerners with their warlike calculations?

PART III

CHINA AND THE WEST

1800–1937

Introduction

For the Chinese the nineteenth century and the first half of the twentieth century were a time of confusion and defeat. The first Westerners had come to admire her splendors and to trade for her valuable goods, but they were followed in the 1800s by others more avaricious and less awed by China's culture or might.

European confidence was based primarily upon their own strength, but they could not help observing that China was growing weaker under the Ching dynasty. Internally China faced increasing population pressure, disastrous floods, rebellions, and little incentive on the part of the Imperial government to try to solve her problems. At this low point the Westerners arrived and added to China's difficulties, and as a result of this combination of problems the Ching dynasty eventually fell. For the first time in Chinese history an external threat succeeded not only in overthrowing a dynasty but also in destroying the Imperial system itself. This Chinese-Western conflict from 1800 to 1937 is the subject of Part III, "China and the West."

What was this Western challenge? It took many forms: commercial competition, invasion, colonization, the sale of opium, and missionary work. All of these attacked the legitimacy of traditional Chinese customs and institutions. The Westerners were especially troublesome, for they did not behave like the Mongols or earlier "barbarians"—they refused to be "absorbed"—and by the beginning of the twentieth century they were firmly established in a number of enclaves along China's coast and major riverways. But the Ching government proved completely unable to enact reforms or deal with the foreign threat, and China's plight continued to worsen.

Finally, in 1911, unable to rally its people or energize the stagnant Imperial system, the Ching dynasty fell, ending three thousand years of Imperial rule. It was replaced by the new Chinese Republic under the direction of Sun Yat-sen and the Kuomintang party.

From 1920 on, two alternative paths to the solution of China's problems emerged: that of the Nationalist Kuomintang, led by Chiang Kai-shek, and that of the Chinese Communist party, which had been founded in 1921. The last half of these readings concentrate on the struggle between the two forces contending for political control over China. The narrative ends in 1937—before the outbreak of World War II—with the Communists' famous Long March from southern China to the desert provinces of northwestern China.

The First Modern "China Trade"— Opium

The first Western influence to make a lasting impact on the Chinese came in the form of an addictive drug—opium, an item of trade that produced impressive profits for Western merchants. In defiance of Chinese custom and law, British traders in the early part of the nineteenth century began selling large amounts of opium to Chinese smokers, as shown here by American sinologist Leonard Adams.

The Beginnings of the Opium Trade
by Leonard P. Adams

Although small amounts of opium were harvested in many parts of Asia, India was the chief producer of the drug for international trading. During the Mogul era, a number of her rulers attempted to tax opium sales for government profit. But as of the 1700s no single government possessed the will, the organization, or the political and naval power to foster new markets and to internationalize the Asian drug trade on a large scale.

Britain's move to colonize India changed this situation

dramatically. In 1772 Warren Hastings was appointed governor of the recently conquered territory of Bengal and faced the task of finding a dependable source of tax revenue. Given the Mogul precedent, he proceeded to sell the concession that granted the buyer the exclusive rights to oversee opium production, buy the harvest, and deliver the product to the British opium factory at the port of Calcutta, where it was auctioned off to wholesale merchants for export. The drug, Hastings piously delared, was not a consumer necessity "but a pernicious article of luxury, which ought not to be permitted but for purposes of foreign commerce only." And so it was. The British in India not only permitted but encouraged foreign sales of opium. The Indian opium concession, which later became a directly administered government monopoly, brought the government over half a million pounds sterling during Hastings' term in India alone. Opium exports, primarily to China, provided roughly *one-seventh* of the total revenue for British India. British officials and others objected to the trade, largely on moral grounds. But for policy makers from Hastings' era to the early part of the twentieth century, the morally questionable nature of the traffic was outweighed by the enormous profits it yielded....

Prior to about 1800 the British traded mainly their own and Indian goods, especially raw cotton, for Chinese tea and silk. But the relative self-sufficiency of China's economy, which perennially frustrated foreign traders, meant that China sold more than she bought, and Western merchants were forced to bring silver to China to make up the balance. After about 1800 the British increasingly substituted another currency: Indian opium. The Chinese paid for opium in silver at the port of entry. Merchants then exchanged this silver for Chinese goods to be sold elsewhere in Asia or in Europe. Opium shifted the balance of the China trade: the situation became economically as well as socially unfavorable to the Chinese.

Although the British gave the opium traffic their official blessing, the Chinese did not. Opium smoking was prohibited in 1729; smoking, cultivation, and importation of opium were specifically banned in 1800. But by the beginning of the nineteenth century the once powerful Ch'ing dynasty had been seriously weakened politically and financially by official corruption and domestic rebellion. As the century wore on, China's internal problems were aggravated by Western attempts to force open the country for trade and, later, for industrial development. Opium speeded up the decay, for Chinese officials and soldiers, underpaid, discontented and often idle, were among the first to take up opium smoking, weakening their government still further.

The edict of 1800 closed Canton, the only port at which foreigners were then officially allowed to trade, to opium. But this ban, like most later defensive gestures, merely helped move the opium traffic beyond the area where it might have been supervised, however ineffectively. The market near Canton rapidly became glutted, and with the connivance of corrupt officials and merchants, drug sales by Europeans spread along China's southeast coast beyond government control. . . .

The spectacular amount of opium entering China, the emperor's decision to take a strong stand against it, and British demands for free trade and diplomatic equality resulted in the Opium War of 1839–1842. Although the British resented the term "opium war," it seemed altogether appropriate to the defeated Chinese. Opium not only provoked the war, it helped China lose it, although given Britain's firepower the outcome was never in doubt.

When the Chinese tried to prevent the opium from entering China by confiscating shipments, the British government used this incident as an excuse to start the first Opium War. China's defeat forced her to allow opium imports and other trading rights to British merchants and to allow the creation of the "treaty ports" along her coast. This war was soon followed by a second conflict, from 1856 to 1860, known as the Arrow War, which pitted China against both England and France. For the Chinese, the Treaty of Nanking (1842), which ended the first Opium War, was not only the first of the Unequal Treaties, but also the first of a long series of indignities imposed upon her by the West. The major Chinese figure in the war was Commissioner Lin Tse-hsü, the customs inspector at Canton, who tried in vain to stem the tide of opium imports by seizing and destroying British supplies of the drug. McAleavy is a British historian.

An Effort to Stop the Opium Trade
by Henry McAleavy

Commissioner Lin at Canton

One man especially stood out in support of the proposal [to halt opium imports]. This was Lin Tse-hsü, the governor-general of the two central provinces of Hupei and Hunan, who had distinguished himself in this post by his zeal in confiscating opium and smoking equipment, and in supplying medicine to those who wished to overcome the addiction. . . .

Lin was informed that he himself had been chosen as the instrument to carry out the policy he had endorsed. In March 1839 he arrived at Canton as Imperial Commissioner.

He was fifty-four years of age and had never before had any dealings with foreigners, although he used to boast that as a native of the coastal province of Fukien he had heard all about the wildness of the barbarians.

A week after his arrival Lin sent a note to the Chinese middlemen and the foreigners, demanding that the latter should surrender all their existing stocks of opium and give a guarantee that for the future they would no longer import the drug to China. Although Lin ended his message by stating that he would never leave his post until the traffic had been stamped out, the foreigners had heard much the same kind of language before and imagined they were being treated to another puppet-show. Their amusement changed to outrage when Lin blockaded the "factories" in which they were living, so that there was no communication between them and their ships. They had sufficient food on the premises, but as their Chinese servants had been obliged to leave, it was not very entertaining for three hundred and fifty miscellaneous westerners, accustomed to being waited on hand and foot, suddenly to have to empty their own slops. Elliot, seeing that for the time being there was nothing for it but to give way, ordered his countrymen to hand over their stocks of the drug to him against his receipt, and when this transaction had been completed he in turn surrendered the hoard to the Chinese authorities. All told there were more than twenty thousand chests of opium.

Far off in Peking, the Emperor heard the news with delight, and wrote to Lin in the most flattering terms:

> Your loyalty to your prince and your love of your country are now revealed for all to see, both within the Empire and in the regions abroad outside the boundaries of civilization.

It was all that was needed to complete the triumph. The opium was thrown into pits, mixed with quicklime, salt and water and then flushed into the sea. The operation took twenty-three days to finish, and was watched throughout by admiring crowds.

Imagining that Lin's mission was accomplished, Peking signified that another governor-generalship was ready and waiting for him, that of Kiangsu, Anhwei and Kiangsi in the Lower Yangtze Valley, in many ways the most desirable appointment of all. But the Commissioner was well aware that the felicitations were premature and that the real trial of strength was yet to come. For Elliot and the British had refused to give an undertaking to discontinue the traffic and had withdrawn to Macao, where they were waiting to see what London would do. The latter half of 1839 and the first half of 1840 were thus taken up with preparations on both sides. Lin closed the approach to Canton by river, and saw to the strengthening of the fortifications.

Commissioner Lin's Advice to Queen Victoria, 1839

TRANSLATED BY SSU-YÜ TENG AND JOHN K. FAIRBANK

We find that your country is sixty or seventy thousand *li* [three *li* make one mile, ordinarily] from China. Yet there are barbarian ships that strive to come here for trade for the purpose of making a great profit. The wealth of China is used to profit the barbarians. That is to say, the great profit made by barbarians is all taken from the rightful share of China. By what right do they then in return use the poisonous drug to injure the Chinese people? Even though the barbarians may not necessarily intend to do us harm, yet in coveting profit to an extreme, they have no regard for injuring others. Let us ask, where is your conscience? I have heard that the smoking of opium is very strictly forbidden by your country; that is because the harm caused by opium is clearly understood. Since it is not permitted to do harm to your own country, then even less should you let it be passed on to the harm of other countries—how much less to China! Of all that China exports to foreign countries, there is not a single thing which is not beneficial to people: they are of benefit when eaten, or of benefit when used, or of benefit when resold: all are beneficial. Is there a single article from China which has done any harm to foreign countries? Take tea and rhubarb, for example; the foreign countries cannot get along for a single day without them. If China cuts off these benefits with no sympathy for those who are to suffer, then what can the barbarians rely upon to keep themselves alive? Moreover the woolens, camlets, and longells [i.e., textiles] of foreign countries cannot be woven unless they obtain Chinese silk. If China, again, cuts off this beneficial export, what profit can the barbarians expect to make? As for other foodstuffs, beginning with candy, ginger, cinnamon, and so forth, and articles for use; beginning with silk, satin, chinaware, and so on, all the things that must be had by foreign countries are innumerable. On the other hand, articles coming from the outside to China can only be used as toys. We can take them or get along without them. Since they are not needed by China, what difficulty would there be if we closed the frontier and stopped the trade? Nevertheless our Celestial Court lets tea, silk, and other goods be shipped without limit and circulated everywhere without begrudging it in the slightest. This is for no other reason but to share the benefit with the people of the whole world.

The goods from China carried away by your country not only supply your own consumption and use, but also can be divided up and sold to other countries, producing a triple profit. Even if you do not sell opium, you still have this threefold profit. How can you bear to go further, selling products injurious to others in order to fulfill your insatiable desire?

Suppose there were people from another country who carried opium for sale to England and seduced your people into buying and smoking it; certainly your honorable ruler would deeply hate it and be bitterly aroused. We have heard heretofore that your honorable ruler is kind and benevolent. Naturally you would not wish to give unto others what you yourself do not want. We have also heard that the ships coming to Canton have all had regulations promulgated and given to them in which it is stated that it is not permitted to carry contraband goods. This indicates that the administrative orders of your honorable rule have been originally strict and clear. Only because the trading ships are numerous, heretofore perhaps they have not been examined with care. Now after this communication has been dispatched and you have clearly understood the strictness of the prohibitory laws of the Celestial Court, certainly you will not let your subjects dare again to violate the law.

Commissioner Lin's seizure and destruction of foreign opium in Canton provided the excuse for Britain to begin a war against the troublesome Chinese, who refused to grant the British trading rights. The first Opium War (1840–1842), which resulted in a Chinese defeat, was the first of a series of foreign intrusions on Chinese sovereignty. Before Britain could attack China, however, the government approached Parliament for approval. The debates presented here took place after Lin's actions, as Lord Palmerston, British foreign minister, argued that British interests in China required war; meanwhile, his opponent, Gladstone, expressed strong opposition to a war waged over opium profits. Palmerston won, however, and after her defeat of China in 1842, Britain found other Western nations eager to share in the spoils of her victory. The "treaty ports" multiplied, and Americans as well as Europeans made their fortunes in opium. Trade in silks, tea, and ceramics was less profitable than the lucrative narcotic, and soon traders sailed directly between the Indian and Turkish ports and Chinese harbors without even returning home to Europe or North America.

Morality and the Opium Trade
by Maurice Collis

As Palmerston thought over what to do, he began to see that he had a golden opportunity of solving all the problems which had baffled generations of statesmen. Lin had played straight into his hands. He had been naïve enough in his headlong way to proceed against the whole foreign community in Canton, innocent and guilty, interning them, starving, constraining, insulting them, driving them on to their ships, sparing neither women nor children. And all this heated zeal in a mere custom's dispute! It was a godsend. The Chinese in their long years of intercourse with the West had never had so tactless an official as Lin, who had made the British Cabinet the present of a perfect case. It would be possible for him to go to the House with that story. He would appeal to the nation's honor and get his vote. The outcry of the moralists against the opium traffic would be smothered in patriotic huzzas for the flag. Nevertheless, he had no intention of rushing into the House. The less time given the public to think the better. He would say little or nothing until all the preparations were complete. Fortunately, the expedition could start from India. Ample troops were there, ample ships. Little should leak out at that distance. Only after the expedition was launched on its voyage to China, would he inform the Commons of what he had been doing. There were risks in such a policy, but it was the only way one could get an opium war through a Whig Parliament. . . .

On the debate being resumed next day, the House listened with wonderful patience to two long dull speeches by persons of little consequence, neither of whom clarified the issue by coming to essentials. In the third hour Mr. Gladstone rose to support the motion. . . .

". . . I will ask the noble Lord a question. Does he know that the opium smuggled into China comes exclusively from British ports, that is from Bengal and through Bombay? If that is a fact—and I defy the right honourable Gentleman to gainsay it—then we require no preventive service to put down this illegal traffic. We have only to stop the sailings of the smuggling vessels; it is a matter of certainty that if we stopped the exportation of opium from Bengal, and broke up the depôt at Lintin, and checked the cultivation of it in Malwa, and put a moral stigma upon it, that we should greatly cripple, if not extinguish, the trade in it. . . . The great principles of justice are involved in this matter. You will be called upon, even if you escape from comdemnation on this motion, to show cause for your present intention of making war upon the Chinese. They gave us notice to abandon the contraband trade. When they found that we would not, they had the right to drive us from their coasts on account of our obstinacy in persisting in this infamous and atrocious traffic. I am not competent to judge how long this war may last, but this I can say, that a war more unjust in its origin, a war more calculated in its progress to cover this country with permanent disgrace, I do not know, and I have not read of. The right honourable Gentleman opposite spoke last night in eloquent terms of the British flag waving in glory at Canton. We all know the animating effects produced when that flag has been unfurled on a field of battle. And how comes it to pass that the sight of that flag always raises the spirit of Englishmen? Because it has always been associated with the cause of justice, with opposition to oppression, with respect for national rights, with honourable commercial enterprise, but now, under the auspices of the noble Lord that flag is become a pirate flag to protect an infamous traffic."

American Involvement
by Chang Hsin-pao

At this time it was widely believed that Americans had very little to do with the opium traffic. This idea was refuted by a contemporary British journal, the *Quarterly Review:* "On the contrary, with one or two exceptions, every American house in China was engaged in the trade. There were American depot ships at Lintin, and on the coast . . . in fact, both in the act which originated the dispute [in 1839], and the insults and outrages consequent thereon, our transatlantic brethren have had their full share."

The Americans dealt in both Indian and Turkish opium, but they so monopolized the Turkish product that many Chinese concluded that Turkey must be a part of the United States....Although Turkish opium was quite negligible on the China market before 1828 and even in its good years (late 1820s and early 1830s) seldom amounted to more than 5 percent of the total opium shipments to China, American firms soon developed an interest in Indian opium. The Boston merchants began to deal in it after 1834, and in 1835 Russell and Company was able to report that its ventures in Indian opium for several American clients promised to yield a good profit. In 1839, the opium it surrendered to the Chinese was surpassed by only two firms, Dent and Jardine, Matheson; the amounts were 1500, 1700, and 7000 chests respectively....

Nationalities aside, the opium traffic was so lucrative that almost every foreign merchant in China was involved in it. Writing in 1839, the widow of Reverend Robert Morrison stated that D. W. C. Olyphant, an American merchant whom Morrison had regarded as a "pious, devoted servant of Christ, and a friend of China," was the *only* foreign trader in Canton who did not engage in the forbidden traffic. The *Chinese Repository*, with palpable uneasiness, summed up the rather anomalous commercial community at Canton:

> The most eminent merchants engaged freely in the traffic; and no man received a less ready welcome to the highest ranks of society because his eastern fortune had come from the sale of opium. And up to the present day, throughout India and in China, many of the most distinguished merchants—men who would be slow to engage in any other than what they regarded as just and honourable pursuits—have been foremost in this traffic.

The influx of opium into China on such a scale necessarily had far-reaching repercussions. It mobilized a large section of the population into active participation in law-defying pursuits: the grave social implications of this need no further comment. Economically, the most conspicuous effect of the opium trade was the drain of silver specie, then China's main currency. As a result, commerce and finance in China were seriously handicapped. Furthermore, it not only contributed to the corruption of local governments and police forces, but also sapped the energy of the army and made a useful and active life impossible for a great many merchants, sailors, laborers, and others in all occupations. More and more people were being drawn away from normal, socially productive careers.

China Versus the West

The period of the Unequal Treaties began after China was defeated by the Western powers in two wars (1842 and 1860) and was forced to make major economic and diplomatic concessions. She had to pay large cash indemnities to the victors, and a necklace of "treaty ports" was set up along China's coast. In the treaty ports, foreigners were permitted commercial and trading privileges, and eventually foreigners came to control most of China's overseas trade. Especially annoying was the right of "extraterritoriality" granted to foreigners. According to this doctrine, foreigners in China were not subject to Chinese law but to the laws of their home country. Thus they could not be arrested by Chinese police for any crimes committed in China, but were remanded to their own governments.

Treaty ports and extraterritoriality marked China's extreme weakness before the West—a situation that was terminated only with the collapse of the empire. How best to interpret and understand this period of the Unequal Treaties is still controversial among writers of China's history. The piece by Liu Ta-nien, a Communist historian, represents the view of most present-day Chinese—certainly those writing in the People's Republic.

How to Appraise the History of Asia?
by Liu Ta-nien

Histories of Asia, of the East, and of the various Asian countries written by such Western bourgeois scholars usually propagandize two concepts. Firstly, that Asia has been "barbarous," "backward," "immoral" and "uncivilized" in all its ages. Secondly, that the progress and civilization of Asia in modern times have been favours generously bestowed on her by the West. Deliberately distorting Chinese history in the U.S. White Paper of 1949, Dean Acheson, the former U.S. Secretary of State, wrote: "Then in the middle of the 19th century the heretofore impervious wall of Chinese isolation was breached by the West. These outsiders brought with them aggressiveness, the unparalleled development of Western technology, and a high order of culture which had not accompanied previous foreign incursions into China."

That is how the Western bourgeois scholars generally approached Chinese history as well as the history of Asia. Did the West brutally invade Asia? This is not apparently what happened; the West "brought...a high order of culture" with it to bestow on Asia. The second concept is stressed in dealing with the modern history of Asia while the first concept is stressed in regard to both ancient and modern times. It would be unfair to say that such historical writings on Asia by venal bourgeois scholars of the West possess no striking features. These works invariably fling mud at the peoples of Asia and their culture, while doing their best to ignore or whitewash the innumerable crimes committed by imperialism in Asia. This is their most striking feature....

The modern history of Asia (18th century to the present time) records many events and struggles. But the main current of that history can be summed up in one sentence: This was a period of criminal activities by colonialist marauders and imperialists, invading Asia and turning it into a colony or semi-colony, and of struggles waged by the Asian people to oppose and expel these invaders and their lackeys. This is the central theme of the modern history of Asia. All other struggles are inevitably subordinate to the struggle between these two opposites, and their course of advance inevitably hinges on circumstances in that developing struggle.

Invaded and dominated by Western colonialism, Asia lived through a dark period of history. This lasted for more than a century....

Colonialist penetration and conquest in Asia, and the reducing of Asian countries to colonies and semi-colonies was accompanied by crimes and tyranny unprecedented in history. The rule of the colonialists and their lackeys is more ruthless and terroristic than that of ancient Rome. More than 100 million Asians were killed. Whole populations were wiped out. Magnificent palaces, temples and other structures, some of the finest in the world, were destroyed or reduced to ruins. Historical records and valuable works of art were put to the flames. Production stagnated or declined, industry and agriculture remained backward, and social development was retarded.

In his 1834 report describing how the British machine-building industry had disrupted Indian social life, Lord Bentinck, the then British Governor-General of India, said that "the misery hardly finds a parallel in the history of commerce. The bones of the cotton-weavers are bleaching the plains of India." And this admitted crime was only one of those, uncountable as the sands in the Ganges River, committed by the colonialists. What part of the vast lands of Asia is not littered with the bones of Asian people murdered in modern times by the colonialists?...

Reactionary Western bourgeois scholars invariably refuse to admit that history other than that of Europe—to which North America is now added—has much importance in the history of world civilization. The golden rule followed by such Western bourgeois historical science is that history must be centred on Europe or West Europe. This "theory" is rotten to the core, but it is still being spread and still enjoys a certain audience.

Take the following lines from *Modern History* by two American authors for example:

From the time of the ancient Greeks and Romans down to the present day, the leading roles in the drama of human history have been taken by the white men of Europe. It was in Europe, the smallest of all the five continents, that what we call modern civilization arose; that the common people first dared wrest the sceptre of government from diademed autocrats; that nations learnt patriotism; that inventors harnessed nature's forces to drive machines of iron and steel or to move man's ships and cars; that bullets and explosives were first made deadly weapons of warfare; that scientists explored the heavens with their telescopes or learnt the secrets of chemistry, physics, biology, and medicine; that public schools and automatic printing presses opened to all the kingdom of knowledge.

It uses insulting labels for Asian and African peoples, speaking about the "retrogressive yellow race in the Far East" or the "illiterate African Negroes." This pernicious propaganda is widely spread in cheap editions.

The absurdity of this theory held by many Western historians manifests itself in teaching practice, which simply excludes Asia from world history. Chester Bowles states in his *Ambassador's Report* that lectures given at American schools on so-called "world history" start from Egypt and Mesopotamia, go on to Greece via the Island of Crete and then through Rome, to end in France and Britain. Students are asked to memorize one hundred of the most important dates in "world history." Only one of them concerns Asia—1857, when Commodore Perry, an American naval officer, "opened up" Japan.

The way the Western bourgeoisie looks at world history is just the way the ant, described in the fable, looks at the world. The ant thinks itself ruler and sole master of the world. In its eyes everyone else is insignificant.

———————

Those engaged in the colonizing of China were often quite honest about their motives. They boldly asserted their "right" to virtual occupation of China because of their greater strength and higher civilization, as J. Ross Brown claims here. Brown, an American in China, uses the straightforward language of the Westerners who believed that it was perfectly fair for the West to have economic concessions at China's expense. Felix Greene, on the other hand, an American journalist who has been to China many times, gives the perspective of a Chinese who finds this Western "right" hard to digest.

The word "imperialism" used here is one we will encounter frequently in later readings, and this article helps to define it. In China, imperialism is used to describe actions by other (usually more powerful) nations that interfered in internal Chinese affairs. The most obvious examples of imperialism in this period were the Opium War of 1840–1842 and the Arrow War of 1856–1860.

The Chinese refusal to accord the European powers equal status in the nineteenth century is often seen as simple arrogance and "irrationality." In a sense, this view is justified, because the same attitudes of the Imperial court which caused it to refuse to deal with the Westerners also prevented the court from recognizing the real threat posed by the West. The Chinese were thus unable to prepare against the Westerners when they arrived with guns and ships, unlike the Japanese, who knew the importance of the West's technology and tried to obtain it for themselves.

But it is important to remember that the concept of "equality among nations" is a modern phenomenon developed in Europe. Until modern times, every major civilization (Egypt, Greece, Rome, India) regarded itself as the center of the world, superior to all other states. When Imperial China faced the Europeans, the question of which ideology would win out was not decided by a greater "rationality" on the part of the Europeans, but by their vastly superior arms and technology.

A Western View

by J. R. Brown*

Believing our civilization to be superior to theirs we should endeavor to elevate the Chinese to our standard. But, surely, that can never be done by an unqualified acceptance of their claim to the independence enjoyed by Christian States. They do not possess it in point of fact, and there is no wisdom in proceeding upon false premises. If they were independent, they would cease to hold relations which give them perpetual trouble, and break down, one by one, the barriers of isolation which have so long enabled them to maintain their peculiar and degenerate form of national existence. Before they can hold a position of equality in the community of civilized nations, they must cease to cripple all intercourse; they must throw open the country; adopt the improved systems of industry and means of communication urged upon them by the Western world; and thus, by co-operation, strengthen and elevate themselves to an actual equality. Such an advance seems to me, to be an essential condition to friendly intercourse. We have no right to compel them to construct railroads or telegraphs, or to extend steam navigation, open coal mines, or accept any of our modern inventions

*in Hosea Morse, *International Relations* . . .

for saving time and developing material resources; but we have a perfect right to compel them to observe their treaty obligations, and, if in doing this all the rest becomes necessary to their continued existence as a nation, and their elevation as a people, it will be all the better for China. I question whether it is good policy to proclaim, in the solemn form of a treaty, that we will not interfere in the internal affairs of the Empire, when our very presence is an interference; or whether anything is to be gained by an unconditional admission of the right of the Chinese government to determine the time and manner of introducing improvements. . . .

Granted that China has shown unwillingness to accept foreign advice and act on foreign suggestions; to what is such unwillingness to be attributed? There are several causes in operation. First of all the Chinese are a very conceited people—they will hardly allow that their condition is to be improved upon; secondly, the Chinese are a very contented people—they dislike and fear change, and believe that the way of living that satisfied their forefathers for two or three thousand years will do well enough for themselves; thirdly, officials and people were alike ignorant on all foreign subjects, and did not for a moment imagine that there was anything better out of China than they already had in it; fourthly, people and officials, but more especially officials, have been suspicious of the foreigners' intentions, and still think every word must have some ulterior object, and every suggestion some sinister motive; these, one kindred reasons, have operated and are operating on all sides against foreign ideas and foreign ways, but, obstacles though they long have been and now are, they are nevertheless forces which must decrease in power in proportion as Chinese become better acquainted with foreigners and enlightenment becomes more general. At the same time their temporary potency will be rather increased than removed by any foreign pressure intended for their removal. But alongside of these there exists another set of opposing forces—forces which must increase in power in proportion as China increases in enlightenment, and whose removal China cannot effect till the foreigner himself wills it.

The Unequal Treaties

by Felix Greene

The result of this war [Opium War, 1840–1842], which ended in a Chinese defeat, was the humiliating Treaty of Nanking. Under its terms the Chinese government had to pay a large indemnity for the opium seized; the cities of Canton, Foochow, Amoy, Ningpo, and Shanghai, occupied by foreign troops, were to be opened to British trade, and residents were exempted from Chinese law. We had to give up our island of Hong Kong. This was the first of the humiliating "Unequal Treaties," imposing conditions which no country would ever have dared to offer a vanquished European nation.

Perhaps the cruelest of all the conditions imposed on us by this treaty was that the Chinese government was prevented from ever levying more than a 5 percent import tax on foreign goods. This opened up our country to a flood of cheap manufactured articles and prevented the development of our own industries. Countless thousands of our artisans and small traders were brought to ruin and starvation by this decree.

This, then, was our introduction to a century of exploitation by the "civilized" and "Christian" nations of the West. We submitted because we had to, for we were not a military power. But do you not suppose that our sense of justice was outraged?

China, still embittered after this defeat by the British, was forced to cede even wider extraterritorial privileges to America under the Treaty of Wanghsia and additional special rights for American ships on China's internal waterways. But the British were not to be outdone. Under the "most-favored-nation clause" they immediately claimed the extra benefits extorted by the Americans.

In 1853 the British, Americans, and French took over control of the Chinese customs. In 1856 a dispute about a flag (a dispute in which we still think we were in the right) was made the excuse by the British and the French to declare war on us again. Once more we were defeated; once more we were required to pay a war indemnity.

Under the Tientsin Treaties which followed, both the opium trade and missionary activities were legalized and the foreign control of our customs was made perpetual. Under this treaty foreign powers were permitted to export our very people to their colonial territories for use as cheap labor. When the Chinese Court, shocked by the harshness of the conditions, delayed ratification, the war was resumed and Western forces occupied Peking, looting and burning the famous Yuan Ming Yuan Summer Palace and committing barbarous outrages against our defenseless people. As the nineteenth century drew to a close, the Western powers grabbed further territorial footholds. It became a veritable scramble. In 1897 Germany seized the naval port of Tsingtao; in 1898 she took the Shantung peninsula. Three weeks after this treaty was signed, Tsarist Russia forced a lease on the naval base of Port Arthur and the commercial port of Dairen. Within five days Britain appropriated the naval base of Weihaiwei, and a few weeks after that France seized the South China bay of Kwangchowan. "Spheres of influence" were assumed by each of the powers.

And what about America? Did she protest? Did she attempt to curb the rapacity of her allies? Did she condemn the wanton sacking of Peking? No protests, no condemnations. In 1899 she pronounced the famous "Open Door" policy. This policy did not in any way dispute the advantages wrested from China by the others; all that it required was that the commerce within each "sphere of influence" be equally open to all. While able to assume a pose of "not wanting any of China's territory," America was able to reap all the financial and commercial advantages gained by the other nations by force. "Hitchhiking imperialism," one of your writers has called it!

How readily some Americans see themselves playing the heroic and magnanimous role in history—how rarely do they know the real facts! When our people, provoked beyond endurance, rose up in what is known to you as the "Boxer Rebellion" in 1901, a further infamous treaty was imposed upon us; foreign troops (including United States Marines) were stationed in our capital, the Chinese were excluded from parts of the city, and another huge indemnity was levied on our people.

Western Missionaries in China in the Nineteenth Century

Many missionaries in China were motivated by sincere desires to help the Chinese. Some, however, behaved like most other foreigners there at the time. Certainly the overall attitude of Christians living in China during the nineteenth century had changed radically from the open-eyed admiration of the first Jesuits for all things Chinese; it was now a general feeling of condescension.

The Chinese reaction to the missionaries, on the other hand, was often hostile or indifferent, and occasionally violent— reactions which may at first seem odd to Americans. It should be remembered that although many Chinese knew nothing about Christianity, the missionaries had arrived in China on the heels of opium-dealing merchants and avaricious foreign officials, in the midst of resentment fanned by China's defeats in a series of disastrous wars with the Western nations. The missionaries enjoyed unparalleled authority and freedom to preach and convert the Chinese, and they were often exempt from Chinese law as a result of the Unequal Treaties. Fitzgerald is an Australian sinologist.

China as the "Sick Man of Asia"
by C. P. Fitzgerald*

There is perhaps no greater example of a reversal of opinions than the contrast between the early Jesuit assessment of the Chinese Empire, made in the beginning of the eighteenth century, and the views which became universal among Europeans by the end of the nineteenth. To the first missionaries, and to their immediate successors, China was a magnificent spectacle: an empire far larger than any Europe had known since the fall of Rome, governed by a central administration through officers appointed, removed, transferred, or dismissed at the pleasure of the Throne, unhampered by feudal privileges or

---

*Fitzgerald, *Chinese View*.

local powers. It possessed a vast historical record far more accurate, better dated, and reaching back farther than any comparable achievement of the West. Commerce passed unrestricted over the huge territories of the Ch'ing dynasty. In arts and learning the Chinese at least equalled anything known to Europe. In one respect alone the Chinese were deficient. They were not Christians. . . .

By the middle of the nineteenth century totally different views prevailed. China was weak, corrupt, ill-governed, racked by rebellions, swept by famine, ignorant of science, indifferent to progress, and still pagan. Some things had indeed changed, on both sides. The Manchu dynasty declined rapidly after the death of Ch'ien Lung, for causes which were not wholly due to the failing abilities of the sovereigns, but were in part the result of the long peace established by the earlier great rulers. In this period of over a century the population had very rapidly increased, the area of free land had not been extended, and the consequent misery caused by crop failures, floods, and droughts was felt more widely and by many more people. K'ang Hsi and Ch'ien Lung had ended the nomad menace on the northern frontier, by the conquest of Mongolia. The result was that the military power of the state was allowed to decline, since the constant incentive of the northern border war was now removed. No attempt was made to keep pace with the advancing techniques of the West, developed as they had been by a long period of large-scale warfare. When the British went to war with China in 1839–42 it was found that the giant had feet of clay, the Manchu forces were medieval in equipment, no match for small numbers of European troops. This was made clearer still when the British and French in 1860 took Peking itself and forced the Emperor into flight.

It is a regrettable fact that the value of a nation's contribution to civilization, her place in the world, tends to be judged, from age to age, by the strength or weakness of her military power. When China under K'ang Hsi or Ch'ien Lung was manifestly too strong for any European encroachment to succeed, the real and serious weaknesses of the government and economy were not regarded; the achievements in art and literature were much respected. When China fell behind Europe, her military power becoming negligible, encroachment was continual, and the value of Chinese civilization fell sharply in Western eyes. Poverty and disease, now somewhat abated in Europe, were decried in China, art and literature, which had changed very little, were no longer admired or imitated. The pre-industrial outlook which all peoples had held in common a century before was now attributed to China as a local and peculiar failing of her people. The Europeans were more than ever convinced that China's only hope was in her conversion to Christianity and the adoption of the civilization of the West.

But the Chinese, both rulers and people, were by no means convinced of this. They held on the contrary to the view that as the barbarians were proving more dangerous than they had seemed to be at first, it was the more necessary to keep them out of China, and reduce contacts with them. Forced by defeat in war to admit the trader to more ports, to permit the missionary, Protestant now as well as Catholic, to preach at will throughout the land, the government continued to obstruct, delay, and when possible frustrate the provisions of the treaties. The people developed a dangerous xenophobia which broke out from time to time in riots, murders, and massacres. The Chinese government seemed to have reason on its side. The T'ai P'ing rebellion, which shook the dynasty in the mid-nineteenth century, was led by men strongly influenced by Christian teaching, men who believed themselves prophets of a new faith; they burnt Buddhist and Taoist temples, persecuted Confucian scholars, and showed no respect to the Sage. It was, therefore, obvious that here were the fruits of missionary endeavor.

Missionaries were under the protection of foreign powers: if they suffered injury the powers demanded reparation from the Chinese government, often far in excess of just compensation. The maltreatment or murder of missionaries was made the pretext for territorial and political exactions. As it was the xenophobia of the people, not the acts of the officials, which brought about these incidents, the government was placed in a humiliating position. By accepting the demands of the foreign powers they "lost face" in the eyes of the people; the officials who were dismissed for failing to protect a missionary, whose activities they disliked as much as did the populace that had injured him, were shown up as impotent, helpless victims of foreign pressure.

The Missionary as a Threat
by Paul A. Cohen

Around the time of Anot's arrival in Nanchang two inflammatory writings penned by the gentry of Chang-sha, Hunan, filtered into the Kiangsi capital. [In 1862 Antoine Anot arrived in the south China city of Nanchang to open a Catholic mission.] These pieces were reprinted again and again during the 1860's, enjoyed wider distribution perhaps than any other writings of the same genre, and were the subject of several angry communications from the British and French representatives. The first document, entitled "Public summons [*kung-hsi*] issued by the entire province of Hunan," commenced with a diatribe against the "English dogs," whose ruler was at times a man, at times a woman, and whose racial background was half-human, half-beast. Seven "absurdities" of the Christian religion were then subjected to scrutiny. If Jesus, merely by virtue of His power to heal the sick, could be classed as a god with infinite wisdom and spiritual force, did this not make Pien Ch'üeh (of the Warring States period), Hua T'o (eastern Han), and all the other famous doctors in Chinese history sages of the first rank? If Jesus was really heaven-sent, how could He have been crucified by a mortal ruler after having spent a scant thirty years on earth? The narration of these "absurdities" was mild in comparison with the catalogue of strange and harmful Christian practices that followed. The Christians violated the most sacred family relationships and ignored their ancestors. Christian men and women displayed their total indifference to evil by bathing together in communal tubs and revealed their complete lack of respect for the bodies given them by their parents by cutting out people's hearts and gouging out their eyes. Finally, they duped young lads in order to rob them of their vital powers and did untold harm to women by extracting their menstrual discharge. Whatever the Christians might say, their underlying intentions were crystal clear. If prompt action were not taken to defend China, this country which for several thousand years had been the home of civilized human beings would soon become transformed into a wasteland of uncultured savages. The proclamation closed with specific suggestions as to what should be done if the barbarians made their way into Hunan.

The second document was divided into ten sections, in each of which an example of the perverse and wayward behavior of the Christian missionary was recounted in lurid detail. . . . The document accused the missionaries of achieving ascendancy over the minds of converts by making them drink a mysterious potion, concocted by mixing the remains of dead priests with a stupefying drug. After consuming this, a tiny demon attached itself to the convert's heart, whereupon he became insane and was willing to die rather than change his convictions. The missionaries gave the female members of the religion pills which, though called "elixir of life," were in fact aphrodisiacs. Once these were taken, the fires of lust burned within, and the women, contrary to their usual inclination, chased after the missionaries. The latter than initiated them into the pleasures of sex, causing them henceforth to hold their husbands in very low regard. . . .

. . . Just as the missionary vied with the gentry for influence in the social and cultural spheres, so too in the political sphere he represented a significant threat to the authority of the local official. In some cases this threat was a simple consequence of the missionary's treaty rights. For example, when his life or property was endangered, he was empowered to seek the protection of the Chinese authorities. If this protection was not forthcoming and he suffered injury or damage as a result, he was further empowered to go over the head of the local authority and bring the matter to his government's attention. Invariably, his claims were then presented to the Chinese government, and he obtained material satisfaction for the wrong done him. If the case was sufficiently serious, moreover, the foreign government often proved powerful enough to see to it that punishment was inflicted upon the local Chinese authorities who had failed to carry out their treaty obligations. In such cases the missionary exercised an authority which, at bottom, was greater than that of the local official. . . .

Some Catholic missionaries, either to protect or to acquire converts, actually went so far as to use their political influence in clear contravention of Chinese law. In the early sixties, for example, a Christian woman of Kuan hsien, Szechwan, was charged with a long list of crimes including swindling and murder. According to the Chinese legal code, she was punishable by death. The French bishop, Eugène Desflèches, however, apparently spoke out in her favor, and Ch'ung-shih, in order to appease Desflèches, closed the case by sentencing her to banishment. . . .

Whatever short-term gains the Catholic missionary may have won by exercising political influence in local Chinese affairs, in the long run the damage done to his position in Chinese society was probably far in excess of any dubious benefits. Chinese subjects in trouble with the law frequently turned to the missionary for protection, causing more than a few Chinese officials to accuse the Church of being a refuge for the scum of society. Other subjects relied upon the Church's influence to act arrogantly toward their non-Christian neighbors, resist payment of taxes, trump up false legal charges, and commit all sorts of other unlawful acts. The extent to which the power of the Church was feared by the people is somewhat amusingly illustrated by an incident recounted by the Jesuits of Kiangnan. A blacksmith in the vicinity of Soochow, finding that his anvil was not bringing in enough cash, decided to supplement his income through more devious means. He traveled all about the area and, falsely claiming that he was Christian, fleeced numerous heathen families by threatening them with the wrath of the Catholic religion if they did not pay him a certain sum of money. It was not until after he had collected from 300,000 to 400,000 dollars cash in this manner that he was finally exposed.

The Western Impact

It is difficult to describe the effects of the Western presence on the daily life of the Chinese peasants, and a short story may illustrate this better than any analysis. In "The Story of a Peasant Family" Mao Tun, a famous writer of the twentieth century, deals with some of the difficulties faced by peasants in the nineteenth century. Chinese farmers trying to increase their family's income by growing silkworms for sale to foreign buyers were affected by the unpredictable fluctuations of the international silk market. Like the family in this story, many peasants were affected by the rising and falling prices of silk in Europe and the United States. They were unable to change the foreign system in which they were bound, and they had a sense that their misfortune was somehow linked to the presence of Western missionaries and opium traders. The second reading is more about the life of Little Tiger, of whom we read in Part II.

Spring Silkworms
by Mao Dun

The weather remained warm. The rays of the sun forced open the tender, finger-like, little buds. They had already grown to the size of a small hand. Around Old Tung Pao's village, the mulberry trees seemed to respond especially well. From a distance they gave the appearance of a low grey picket fence on top of which a long swath of green brocade had been spread. Bit by bit, day by day, hope grew in the hearts of the villagers. The unspoken mobilization order for the silkworm campaign reached everywhere and everyone. Silkworm rearing equipment that had been laid away for a year was again brought out to be scrubbed and mended. Beside the little stream which ran through the village, women and children, with much laughter and calling back and forth, washed the implements.

None of these women or children looked really healthy. Since the coming of spring, they had been eating only half their fill; their clothes were old and torn. As a matter of fact, they weren't much better off than beggars. Yet all were in quite good spirits, sustained by enormous patience and grand illusions. Burdened though they were by daily mounting debts, they had only one thought in their heads—If we get a good crop of silkworms, everything will be all right!... They could already visualize how, in a month, the shiny green leaves would be converted into snow-white cocoons, the cocoons exchanged for clinking silver dollars. Although their stomachs were growling with hunger, they couldn't refrain from smiling at this happy prospect....

Old Tung Pao's daughter-in-law examined their five sets of eggs. They looked bad. The tiny seed-like eggs were still pitch black, without even a hint of green. Her husband, Ah Sze, took them into the light to peer at them carefully. Even so, he could find hardly any ripening eggs. She was very worried.

"You incubate them anyhow. Maybe this variety is a little slow," her husband forced himself to say consolingly.

Her lips pressed tight, she made no reply.

Old Tung Pao's wrinkled face sagged with dejection. Though he said nothing, he thought their prospects were dim.

The next day, Ah Sze's wife again examined the eggs. Ha! Quite a few were turning green, and a very shiny green at that! Immediately, she told her husband, told Old Tung Pao, Ah To... she even told her son Little Pao. Now the incubating process could begin! She held the five pieces of cloth to which the eggs were adhered against her bare bosom. As if cuddling a nursing infant, she sat absolutely quiet, not daring to stir. At night, she took the five sets to bed with her. Her husband was routed out, and had to share Ah To's bed. The tiny silkworm eggs were very scratchy against her flesh. She felt happy and a little frightened, like the first time she was pregnant and the baby moved inside her. Exactly the same sensation!

Uneasy but eager, the whole family waited for the eggs to hatch. Ah To was the only exception. We're sure to hatch a good crop, he said, but anyone who thinks we're going to get rich in this life, is out of his head. Though the old man swore Ah To's big mouth would ruin their luck, the boy stuck to his guns.

A clean dry shed for the growing grubs was all prepared. The second day of incubation, Old Tung Pao smeared a garlic with earth and placed it at the foot of the wall inside the shed. If, in a few days, the garlic put out many sprouts, it meant the eggs would hatch well. He did this every year, but this year he was more reverential than usual and his hands trembled. Last year's divination had proved all too accurate. He didn't dare to think about that now.

Every family in the village was busy "incubating." For the time being there were few women's footprints on the threshing ground or the banks of the little stream. An unofficial "martial law" had been imposed. Even peasants normally on very good terms stopped visiting one another. For a guest to come and frighten away the spirits of the ripening eggs—that would be no laughing matter! At most, people exchanged a few words in low tones when they met, then quickly separated. This was the "sacred" season!

Old Tung Pao's family was on pins and needles. In the five sets of eggs a few grubs had begun wriggling. It was exactly one day before Grain Rain. Ah Sze's wife had calculated that most of the eggs wouldn't hatch until after that day. Before or after Grain Rain was all right, but for eggs to hatch on the day itself was considered highly unlucky. Incubation was no longer necessary, and the eggs were carefully placed in the special shed. Old Tung Pao stole a glance at his garlic at the foot of the wall. His heart dropped. There were still only the same two small green shoots the garlic had originally! He didn't dare to look any closer. He prayed silently that by noon the day after tomorrow the garlic would have many, many more shoots.

At last hatching day arrived. Ah Sze's wife set a pot of rice on to boil and nervously watched for the time when the steam from it would rise straight up. Old Tung Pao lit the incense and candles he had bought in anticipation of this event. Devoutly, he placed them before the idol of the Kitchen God. His two sons went into the fields to pick wild flowers. Little Pao chopped a lamp-wick into fine pieces and crushed the wild flowers the men brought back. Everything was ready. The sun was entering its zenith; steam from the rice pot puffed straight upwards. Ah Sze's wife immediately leaped to her feet, stuck a "sacred" paper flower and a pair of goose feathers into the knot of hair at the back of her head and went to the shed. Old Tung Pao carried a wooden scale-pole; Ah Sze followed with the chopped lamp-wick and the crushed wild flowers. Daughter-in-law uncovered the cloth pieces to which the grubs were adhered, and sprinkled them with the bits of wick and flowers Ah Sze was holding. Then she took the wooden scale-pole from Old Tung Pao and hung the cloth pieces over it. She next removed the pair of goose feathers from her hair. Moving them lightly across the cloth, she brushed the grubs, together with the crushed lamp-wick and wild flowers, on to a large tray. One set, two sets ... the last set contained the foreign breed. The grubs from this cloth were brushed on to a separate tray. Finally, she removed the "sacred" paper flower from her hair and pinned it, with the goose feathers, against the side of the tray.

A solemn ceremony! One that had been handed down through the ages! Like warriors taking an oath before going into battle! Old Tung Pao and family now had ahead of them a month of fierce combat, with no rest day or night, against bad weather, bad luck and anything else that might come along!

The grubs, wriggling in the trays, looked very healthy. They were all the proper black colour. Old Tung Pao and his daughter-in-law were able to relax a little. But when the old man secretly took another look at his garlic, he turned pale! It had grown only four measly shoots! Ah! Would this year be like last year all over again?

The first day after the Big Sleep, the "little darlings" ate seven loads of leaves. They were now a bright green, thick and healthy. Old Tung Pao and his family, on the contrary, were much thinner, their eyes bloodshot from lack of sleep.

No one could guess how much the "little darlings" would eat before they spun their cocoons. Old Tung Pao discussed the question of buying more leaves with Ah Sze.

"Master Chen won't lend us any more. Shall we try your father-in-law's boss again?"

"We've still got ten loads coming. That's enough for one more day," replied Ah Sze. He could barely hold himself erect. His eyelids weighed a thousand catties. They kept wanting to close.

"One more day? You're dreaming!" snapped the old man impatiently. "Not counting tomorrow, they still have to eat three more days. We'll need another thirty loads! Thirty loads, I say!"

Loud voices were heard outside on the threshing ground. Ah To had arrived with men delivering five loads of mulberry branches. Everyone went out to strip the leaves. Ah Sze's wife hurried from the shed. Across the stream,

Sixth Treasure and her family were raising only a small crop of silkworms; having spare time, she came over to help. Bright stars filled the sky. There was a slight wind. All up and down the village, gay shouts and laughter rang in the night. . . .

The next morning, Old Tung Pao went into town to borrow money for more leaves. Before leaving home, he had talked the matter over with daughter-in-law. They had decided to mortgage their grove of mulberries that produced fifteen loads of leaves a year as security for the loan. The grove was the last piece of property the family owned. . . .

The "little darlings" began spinning their cocoons, but Old Tung Pao's family was still in a sweat. Both their money and their energy were completely spent. They still had nothing to show for it; there was no guarantee of their earning any return. Nevertheless, they continued working at top speed. Beneath the racks on which the cocoons were being spun fires had to be kept going to supply warmth. Old Tung Pao and Ah Sze, his elder son, their backs bent, slowly squatted first on this side then on that. Hearing the small rustlings of the spinning silkworms, they wanted to smile, and if the sounds stopped for a moment their hearts stopped too. Yet worried as they were, they didn't dare to disturb the silkworms by looking inside. When the silkworms squirted fluid in their faces as they peered up from beneath the racks, they were happy in spite of the momentary discomfort. The bigger the shower, the better they liked it.*

Ah To had already peeked several times. Little Pao had caught him at it and demanded to know what was going on. Ah To made an ugly face at the child, but did not reply.

After three days of "spinning," the fires were extinguished. Ah Sze's wife could restrain herself no longer. She stole a look, her heart beating fast. Inside, all was white as snow. The brush that had been put in for the silkworms to spin on was completely covered over with cocoons. Ah Sze's wife had never seen so successful a "flowering"!

The whole family was wreathed in smiles. They were on

_____

*The emission of the fluid means the silkworm is about to spin its cocoon.

solid ground at last! The "little darlings" had proved they had a conscience; they hadn't consumed those mulberry leaves, at four dollars a load, in vain. The family could reap its reward for a month of hunger and sleepless nights. The Old Lord of the Sky had eyes!

Throughout the village, there were many similar scenes of rejoicing. The Silkworm Goddess had been beneficent to the tiny village this year. Most of the two dozen families garnered good crops of cocoons from their silkworms. The harvest of Old Tung Pao's family was well above average.

Again women and children crowded the threshing ground and the banks of the little stream. All were much thinner than the previous month, with eyes sunk in their sockets, throats rasping and hoarse. But everyone was excited, happy. As they chattered about the struggle of the past month, visions of piles of bright silver dollars shimmered before their eyes. Cheerful thoughts filled their minds— they would get their summer clothes out of the pawnshop; at Spring Festival perhaps they could eat a fat golden fish. . . .

Family after family was able to report a good harvest of cocoons. People visited one another to view the shining white gossamer. The father of Old Tung Pao's daughter-in-law came from town with his little son. They brought gifts of sweets and fruits and a salted fish. Little Pao was happy as a puppy frolicking in the snow.

The elderly visitor sat with Old Tung Pao beneath a willow beside the stream. He had the reputation in town of a "man who knew how to enjoy life." From hours of listening to the professional story-tellers in front of the temple, he had learned by heart many of the classic tales of ancient times. He was a great one for idle chatter, and often would say anything that came into his head. Old Tung Pao therefore didn't take him very seriously when he leaned close and queried softly:

"Are you selling your cocoons, or will you spin the silk yourself at home?"

"Selling them, of course," Old Tung Pao replied casually.

The elderly visitor slapped his thigh and sighed, then rose abruptly and pointed at the silk filature rearing up behind the row of mulberries, now quite bald of leaves.

"Tung Pao," he said, "the cocoons are being gathered, but the doors of the silk filatures are shut as tight as ever!

They're not buying this year! Ah, all the world is in turmoil! The silk houses are not going to open, I tell you!"

Old Tung Pao couldn't help smiling. He wouldn't believe it. How could he possibly believe it? There were dozens of silk filatures in this part of the country. Surely they couldn't all shut down? What's more, he had heard that they had made a deal with the Japanese; the Chinese soldiers who had been billeted in the silk houses had long since departed.

Changing the subject, the visitor related the latest town gossip, salting it freely with classical aphorisms and quotations from the ancient stories. Finally he got around to the thirty silver dollars borrowed through him as middleman. He said his boss was anxious to be repaid.

Old Tung Pao became uneasy after all. When his visitor had departed, he hurried from the village down the highway to look at the two nearest silk filatures. Their doors were indeed shut; not a soul was in sight. Business was in full swing this time last year, with whole rows of dark gleaming scales in operation.

He felt a little panicky as he returned home. But when he saw those snowy cocoons, thick and hard, pleasure made him smile. What beauties! No one wants them? —Impossible. He still had to hurry and finish gathering the cocoons; he hadn't thanked the gods properly yet. Gradually, he forgot about the silk houses.

But in the village, the atmosphere was changing day by day. People who had just begun to laugh were now all frowns. News was reaching them from town that none of the neighbouring silk filatures was opening its doors. It was the same with the houses along the highway. Last year at this time buyers of cocoons were streaming in and out of the village. This year there wasn't a sign of even half a one. In their place came dunning creditors and government tax collectors who promptly froze up if you asked them to take cocoons in payment.

Swearing, curses, disappointed sighs! With such a fine crop of cocoons the villagers had never dreamed that their lot would be even worse than usual! It was as if hailstones dropped out of a clear sky. People like Old Tung Pao, whose crop was especially good, took it hardest of all.

"What is the world coming to!" He beat his breast and stamped his feet in helpless frustration.

But the villagers had to think of something. The cocoons would spoil if kept too long. They either had to sell them or remove the silk themselves. Several families had already brought out and repaired silk reels they hadn't used for years. They would first remove the silk from the cocoons and then see about the next step. Old Tung Pao wanted to do the same.

"We won't sell our cocoons; we'll spin the silk ourselves!" said the old man. "Nobody ever heard of selling cocoons until the foreign devils' companies started the thing!"

Ah Sze's wife was the first to object. "We've got over five hundred catties of cocoons here," she retorted. "Where are you going to get enough reels?"

She was right. Five hundred catties was no small amount. They'd never get finished spinning the silk themselves. Hire outside help? That meant spending money. Ah Sze agreed with his wife. Ah To blamed his father for planning incorrectly.

"If you listened to me, we'd have raised only one tray of foreign breed and no locals. Then the fifteen loads of leaves from our own mulberry trees would have been enough, and we wouldn't have had to borrow!"

Old Tung Pao was so angry he couldn't speak.

At last a ray of hope appeared. Huang the Priest had heard somewhere that a silk house below the city of Wusih was doing business as usual. Actually an ordinary peasant, Huang was nicknamed "The Priest" because of the learned airs he affected and his interests in Taoist "magic." Old Tung Pao always got along with him fine. After learning the details from him, Old Tung Pao conferred with his elder son Ah Sze about going to Wusih.

"It's about 270 *li* by water, six days for the round trip," ranted the old man. "Son of a bitch! It's a goddam expedition! But what else can we do? We can't eat the cocoons, and our creditors are pressing hard!"

Ah Sze agreed. They borrowed a small boat and bought a few yards of matting to cover the cargo. It was decided that Ah To should go along. Taking advantage of the good weather, the cocoon selling "expeditionary force" set out.

Five days later, the men returned—but not with an empty hold. They still had one basket of cocoons. The silk filature, which they reached after a 270-*li* journey by water, offered extremely harsh terms—only thirty-five dollars a load for foreign breed, twenty for local; thin cocoons not wanted at any price. Although their cocoons were all first class, the people at the silk house picked and chose only enough to fill one basket; the rest were rejected. Old Tung Pao and his sons received a hundred and ten dollars for the sale, ten of which had to be spent as travel expenses. The hundred dollars remaining was not even enough to pay back what they had borrowed for that last thirty loads of mulberry leaves! On the return trip, Old Tung Pao became ill with rage. His sons carried him into the house.

Ah Sze's wife had no choice but to take the ninety odd catties they had brought back and reel the silk from the cocoons herself. She borrowed a few reels from Sixth Treasure's family and worked for six days. All their rice was gone now. Ah Sze took the silk into town, but no one would buy it. Even the pawnshop didn't want it. Only after much pleading was he able to persuade the pawnbroker to take it in exchange for a load of rice they had pawned before Clear and Bright.

That's the way it happened. Because they raised a crop of spring silkworms, the people in Old Tung Pao's village got deeper into debt. Old Tung Pao's family raised five trays and gathered a splendid harvest of cocoons. Yet they ended up owing another thirty silver dollars and losing their mortgaged mulberry trees—to say nothing of suffering a month of hunger and sleepless nights in vain!

A Child Is Sold

by Ida Pruitt

In the winter the rich of the city built mat sheds under which they gave out gruel to the poor. We went every day for one meal of hot gruel. We met there, for he begged in one part of the city, carrying Chinya, and I begged in another, leading Mantze.

One day when my husband handed the baby over to me as usual, saying, "Nurse her," one of the men in charge of the gruel station saw him do it.

"Is that your man?" said the man from the gruel station. I answered that he was.

"He is trying to sell the child. He tells people that her mother died last Seventh Month."

"Oh, that is the talk that he uses for begging," I said. But in my heart I wondered if it was true that he was trying to sell our child and to keep the knowledge from me.

One day, when the ground was wet with melting snow, I found that even with the three pairs of shoes my feet were not covered. The bare flesh showed through.

"You stay at home," he said, "and I will beg." He took the child in his arms as usual. "You wait at home," he said. "I will bring you food."

We waited, Mantze and I. The day passed; it got dark; and still he did not come. It was cold. I opened my clothes and took Mantze inside my garments to give her warmth, and still he did not come. We lay in the dark. We had no lights that winter; we had no money for oil. I heard the watchman beating the third watch and I knew the night was half over. Still he did not come.

Then I heard him push open the door and stumble as he crossed the threshold. He was opium sodden and uncertain in his movements. I waited for him to say as usual, "Here, take the child and nurse her." But there was no word. I heard him throwing something heavily on the bed.

"Now you have knocked the breath out of the child. Give her to me."

Still he said nothing.

"What is the matter? Give me the child." And he only grunted.

"Light the lamp and I will tell you," he said.

"It is not the custom to light lamps in this house. Do you not know me or do I not know you that we must have a light to talk by to each other? Tell me." Then he struck a match and I saw that there was no child, only a bundle, a bundle of sweet potatoes.

"I have sold her."

I jumped out of bed. I had no thought left for Mantze. I seized him by the queue. I wrapped it three times around my arm. I fought him for my child. We rolled fighting on the ground.

The neighbors came and talked to pacify us.

"If the child has not left the city and we can keep hold of this one, we will find her," they said.

So we searched. The night through we searched. We went to the south city through the Drum Tower and back to the examination halls. We walked a great circle inside the city, and always I walked with my hands on his queue. He could not get away.

We found a house. The father of the child knocked. Some men came to the door. It was the house of dealers who buy up girls and sell them to brothels in other cities. Their trade is illegal, and if they are caught they are put in prison and punished. They dared not let me make a noise. I had but to cry aloud and the neighbors would be there. So the dealer in little girls said soft words. My neighbors said, "What he says, he will do. Now that we have him we will find the child." But the child was not in that house.

"Take me to my child," I demanded. The man promised. So again we started out in the night, walking and stumbling through the streets. Then one of my neighbors who had more power to plan than the others said, "Why do you still hold on to him? He is now useless." I still had my arm twisted in my husband's queue. "Hold on to that one so he does not run away. He it is that knows where the child is."

So I let go of my husband's queue and in one jump was beside the man and had seized him by the slack of his coat. "Why do you seize me?" he said.

"So that you will not run away and I lose my child again." My husband was gone into the night, and still we walked. We came to the entrance of a narrow street.

"You stay here," said the man, "I will go in and call them."

"No," said I. "Where you go, I go. What kind of a place is this that I cannot go with you?"

And when he said that it was a residence, I said, "A residence! If you, a man, can go, surely I, a woman, can do so. If it was a bachelor's lair I still would go in to find my child." I held onto him by the slack of his coat as we went down the narrow street to a gate. He knocked and still I held to him.

The man who opened it held the two parts of the gate together with his hands to prevent anyone going in. But I ducked under his arm before he could stop me and ran into the passage. I went through the courts, calling, "Chinya, Chinya." The child heard my voice and knew me and answered, and so I found her. The woman of the house tried to hide the child behind her wide sleeves, but I pushed her aside and took the child into my arms. The man barred the door and said that I could not leave.

"Then," I said, "I will stay here. My child is in my bosom. Mother and child, we will die here together." I sat on the floor with my child in my arms.

The neighbors gathered and talked. A child, they said, could not be sold without the mother's consent. He had, they said, got another five hundred cash from them by saying that I had not at first consented. They had first paid him three thousand. He had sold my child for a mere three thousand and five hundred cash.

They tried to frighten me. They said they would sell us both to get their money back. I was young then, and salable. But I said, "No. I have another child at home. I must go to that child also." The neighbors all began to talk and said that I had another child and that I must go home to her, and the dealers talked of their money that they must have back.

"You stay here until we go and get the money back," they said. But at last we all started out together. I was carrying the child and they came along to get their money. They lighted a lantern and let it shine under my feet.

Then a neighbor who thought more quickly than others said, "It is cold tonight and the way is long. We have walked far. Let me carry the child."

I said that I was well and strong and could carry her myself.

But again she said, "My coat is bigger than yours. I can carry the child inside and protect her from the cold." So I gave the child to her. She walked ahead, and gradually as they lighted the way for me she disappeared into the night. When we got home she was there with the child, but my old opium sot was gone. She knew that he would have spent all the money and would have been unable to pay, and that when they had found this out they would have taken him out and beaten him. So she had gone ahead and warned him and he had slipped away into the night. And she also had the child safely at home.

So that passed over.

He promised not to sell her again and I believed him.

The old people tell us that her husband is more important to a woman than her parents. A woman is with her parents only part of her life, they say, but she is with her husband forever. He also feels that he is the most important. If a wife is not good to her husband, there is retribution in heaven.

My husband would sit on the k'ang with his legs drawn up under his chin and his head hanging. He would raise his head suddenly and peer at me from under his lids.

"Ha! Why don't you make a plan? Why don't you think of a way for us to eat?"

I would answer, "What can I do? My family have no money. I know no one."

Then, at last, he would get up and go out to beg. People urged me to leave him and follow another man, to become a thief or a prostitute. But my parents had left me a good name, though they had left me nothing else. I could not spoil that for them.

In those years it was not as it is now. There was no freedom then for women. I stayed with him.

For another year we lived, begging and eating gruel from the public kitchen.

The father of my children was good for a while, and I thought he had learned his lesson. He promised never to sell the child again and I believed him. Then one day he sold her again and I could not get her back that time. . . .

Discrimination and Narrow-Mindedness: Who's the Real Barbarian?

Chinese views of the West were sharply affected by the reception given to the Chinese who immigrated to the United States. Chinese immigrants to America faced harsh discrimination. They were brought to the United States to work on the railroads, but their treatment at the hands of American pioneers was vicious and brutal, and word of it soon got back to China. Eventually most Chinese immigrants were driven out of the western United States, and further immigration was sharply restricted. Such experiences confirmed a widespread Chinese view of foreigners as violent and unjust.

The Heathen Chinee
by Robert McClellan

The presence of the Chinese in the country in increasing numbers stimulated a growing concern over the effect which they might have on economic and social institutions. The result was that exclusion legislation was suggested as a means of curbing the threat which they were thought to represent. It was through the debates over exclusion that the rest of the country outside of the West Coast became aware of the Chinese. The question of excluding the Chinese expanded into a consideration of all things Chinese, and in the process Americans were exposed to some rather narrow interpretations of oriental institutions. A book by a missionary in China, Arthur Smith, contained one of the most influential and at the same time most distorted descriptions of Chinese life and culture ever to appear in the United States. The author's conclusion that the Chinese could endure greater amounts of pain because of a less highly developed nervous system was commonly accepted at the turn of the century.

First contacts of Americans in San Francisco with the Chinese were typical. Fresh from the Far East with its consignment of freight and coolies, a ship from the Orient would tie up at a San Francisco wharf to disgorge its human cargo. Herded down the gangplank into the frantic melee on the dock, the Chinese were identified and gathered into groups around the wagons which would carry them to the waiting flatcars and boxcars. They had been invited to come by the railroads because they were needed as construction workers to help accomplish the vast project of connecting the West Coast with Chicago and points east. Railroad agents had gone to China to describe the need for laborers, the high wages, and plentiful work, and to arrange for passage, sometimes with the assistance of a United States consul. Other agents met them in San Francisco and hurried them to the construction sites where the shortage of white laborers made their presence so desirable. Some Chinese also came to work in the mines, to help develop the barren regions of the west, and to pick the fruit.

The Chinese had been told that they were needed; they came; and then in a few years they were told to leave. For twenty years the Chinese worked alongside European immigrants and native Americans. They marched in the Fourth of July parades, and the Chinese display was often the most elaborate and vigorously applauded. In 1868 the Chinese merchants of San Francisco were present at a banquet honoring their contributions to the life and well-being of that city. Occasionally instances of persecution of the Chinese by members of other minorities occurred, but they were of a minor nature. In the same year that the Chinese merchants were banqueted in San Francisco, the Burlingame Treaty was applauded in that city as the keystone of a new era of prosperity based on Chinese immigration. In 1869 the Central Pacific met the Union Pacific in Utah. Nine years later the Nevada mines collapsed. In between these dates the presence of the Chinese had changed from a blessing to a curse in the minds of most Californians.

Hostility toward the Chinese was increased by agitators like Dennis Kearny. When the overflow crowd from an anti-Chinese mass meeting gathered on the large sandy lot adjacent to San Francisco's city hall, he exhorted them in excited tones to defend their jobs and homes from the Chinese peril. These "sandlotters" became the nucleus for the agitation which culminated in the first exclusion act of 1882. In the presidential campaign of 1879–80 California and Oregon were doubtful states. The Republicans were the first to seek the support of the anti-Chinese sentiment in those areas by sending a commission to China to "investigate" the immigration problem and discuss changes in the treaty of 1868. The instructions to the commissioners were vague, but the mission accomplished its main purpose when California and Oregon voted Republican in the election. In 1881 the terms of the Burlingame Treaty were modified with the consent of China, and the following year a restrictive act suspended immigration from China for ten years. In 1888 a new treaty strengthening the restrictions on immigration was drawn up and presented to China; but she debated "too slowly," and Congress rushed through a new exclusion act, with the Scott Act, which, with the exceptions of merchants and diplomats, even barred Chinese then on leave from the country.

The people who lived on the West Coast, particularly in California, were the first to come into contact with the Chinese in America, and their attitude had a formative influence on the rest of the nation. "John Chinaman" (or even just "John") soon became the derisive epithet for the Chinese immigrant, indicating the facelessness and anonymity attributed to him by his American hosts. "Only John!" warned one author on the West Coast in 1896, "yet in a few years he has overrun the coast. . . ."

Americans who traveled in the Orient and the far greater number who stayed home denigrated the Chinese largely because they were not American. Unfamiliar with Eastern ways, quick to criticize and deprecate customs which seemed strange, Americans were unable to appreciate the merits of a radically dissimilar way of life. Not a little of this feeling was based upon a fear of the unknown during a period when the nation's relationship to the rest of the world was being expanded in ways which required the restatement of national values. .,. [EDITOR'S NOTE: *Such attitudes were held not only by Americans at home but also by Americans working in China.*]

The [American] consul at Hankow revealed the same attitude. Shortly after the diplomats had been rescued from the besieged legations at Peking, he wrote to the assistant secretary of state. "The only way to deal with Chinese is with a club, and they will settle at once most graciously, and respect you above all men." Most American officials were only mildly disturbed over the use of force against the Chinese. When an American missionary shot and killed a Chinese, the consul indicated concern over the appropriateness of his action but made no attempt to bring him under court jurisdiction. Acts of violence against Chinese by Americans in China were common enough so as to attract little notice. When an American seaman on shore leave wrecked the British consulate, threw several Chinese in the river, and beat up two Chinese police who tried to control him, he was fined ten dollars. Because Americans were not subject to trial in Chinese courts, the protests of the local police were to no avail. Consuls worked hard to protect the interests of American citizens but rarely gave much thought to the rights of the Chinese.

On another occasion a young American who was employed as a bank teller in one of the port cities described the manner in which he traveled the streets outside the compound. "If a Chinaman does not at once make room for me in the street I would strike him forcibly with my cane in the face." When questioned as to whether that sort of an act would go unpunished, the young man replied, "Should I break his nose or kill him, the worst that can happen would be that he or his people would make complaints to the Consul, who might impose the fine of a dollar for the misdemeanor, but I could always prove that I had just cause to beat him." Americans in China resorted to force as a means of expressing their contempt for the Chinese with enough frequency to fix in the minds of many Chinese a strong resentment against their caucasian visitors. In many instances the root of this resentment traced back not to any particularly highhanded act but simply to the common practice employed by almost all Americans in China of referring to the Chinese as "boy" or "Chinaman." Their resentment was heightened because they felt that they were being treated as inferiors by people whom they in turn classified as barbarians.

Memorial of the Chinese Six Companies to U. S. Grant, President of the U.S.A.

Unable to appeal to their own government for help, the Chinese Six Companies wrote to President Ulysses S. Grant to ask for protection against the atrocities then being committed against them. This Memorial recounts the many prejudices held by the whites and the Chinese answers to them. The Chinese even suggest limiting their own immigration as a means of mitigating such prejudices.

Sir: In the absence of any Consular representative, we, the undersigned, in the name and in behalf of the Chinese people now in America, would most respectfully present for your consideration the following statements regarding the subject of Chinese emigration to this country:

We understand that it has always been the settled policy of your honorable Government to welcome emigration to your shores from all countries, without let or hindrance. The Chinese are not the only people who have crossed the ocean to seek a residence in this land. . . .

American steamers, subsidized by your honorable Government, have visited the ports of China, and invited our people to come to this country to find employment and improve their condition. Our people have been coming to this country for the last twenty-five years, but up to the present time there are only 150,000 Chinese in all these United States, 60,000 of whom are in California, and 30,000 in the city of San Francisco.

Our people in this country, for the most part, have been peaceable, law-abiding, and industrious. They performed the largest part of the unskilled labor in the construction of the Central Pacific Railroad, and also of all other railroads on this coast. They have found useful and remunerative employment in all the manufacturing establishments of this coast, in agricultural pursuits, and in family service. While benefiting themselves with the honest reward of their daily toil, they have given satisfaction to their employers and have left all the results of their industry to enrich the State. They have not displaced white laborers from these positions, but have simply multiplied the industrial enterprises of the country.

The Chinese have neither attempted nor desired to interfere with the established order of things in this country, either of politics or religion. They have opened no whiskey saloons for the purpose of dealing out poison and degrading their fellow-men. They have promptly paid their duties, their taxes, their rents, and their debts.

It has often occurred, about the time of the State and general elections, that political agitators have stirred up the minds of the people in hostility to the Chinese, but formerly the hostility has usually subsided after the elections were over.

At the present time an intense excitement and bitter hostility against the Chinese in this land, and against further Chinese emigration, has been created in the minds of the people, led on by His Honor the Mayor of San

Francisco and his associates in office, and approved by His Excellency the Governor, and other great men of the State. These great men gathered some 20,000 of the people of this city together on the evening of April 5, and adopted an address and resolutions against Chinese emigration. . . .

It is charged against us that we eat rice, fish, and vegetables. It is true that our diet is slightly different from the people of this honorable country; our tastes in these matters are not exactly alike, and cannot be forced. But is that a sin on our part of sufficient gravity to be brought before the President and Congress of the United States?

It is charged that the Chinese are no benefit to this country. Are the railroads built by Chinese labor no benefit to the country? Are the manufacturing establishments, largely worked by Chinese, no benefit to this country? Do not the results of the daily toil of a hundred thousand men increase the riches of this country? Is it no benefit to this country that the Chinese annually pay over $2,000,000 duties at the Custom house of San Francisco? Is not the $200,000 annual poll-tax paid by the Chinese any benefit? And are not the hundreds of thousands of dollars taxes on personal property, and the foreign miners' tax, annually paid to the revenues of this country, any benefit?

Rebellion and Restoration

The Western incursions created internal political instability and tumult which greatly weakened the reigning Ching dynasty. (The Ching rulers were descendants of tribal Manchus who had invaded China two centuries before; during their rule they became increasingly "Sinified," or Chinese.) But the greatest threat to the Ching dynasty in the mid-nineteenth century came from the huge Taiping Rebellion from 1850 to 1856. Led by a Chinese claiming to be Christian, the Taiping rebels at their height controlled much of south-central China, and they left the Chinese empire even weaker in its dealings with the Western powers.

The Taiping Rebellion

by Dun Li*

In the 1840's all evidence seemed to indicate that the Manchu dynasty had lost the mandate of Heaven. There were foreign invasions, domestic disturbances, natural disasters, famines, and a discredited, incompetent government which was unable to cope with them. The sequence was incomplete without a rebellion, and a rebellion there was. The Taiping Rebellion was the greatest social upheaval of nineteenth-century China and the most serious challenge to the Manchu government before 1911. It was generated by indigenous forces, and it was suppressed by native resources. The professed Christianity of the rebels, however, was an indication of the Western influence.

From 1847 to 1849 natural disasters struck China repeatedly, and famines were reported in practically every province. The region most adversely affected was Kwangtung and Kwangsi where many peasants, driven by hunger, had appeared as organized bandits as early as 1847. Local officials were unable to maintain peace and order, and lawlessness spread over a large section of this region. The factors that had historically nourished a rebellion were present, and only a capable leader was required to organize it. In Hung Hsiu-ch'üan the dissatisfied peasants found their leader.

Hung Hsiu-ch'üan was born in 1812 near Canton to a small farmer. As the brightest member of the family, he was given the opportunity to study, while his two elder brothers continued to work on the family farm. He left school at the age of eighteen and, as was normally expected, went to take the lowest level of the civil service examination in Canton. He failed, and when he tried again in 1836, he did not fare any better. It was then that he was exposed to the teaching of Christianity for the first time, having read a pamphlet entitled *Good Advice to the World* (Ch'üan-shih liang-yen) handed to him by a street evangelist.

---

*Dun Li, *Ageless Chinese*.

He took the examination again the following year and failed for the third time. He then became seriously ill and was in a state of coma for forty days. When he woke up, he told an astonished audience that he had met God the Father and Jesus in his dream and that Jesus was God's elder son, whereas he, Hung, was His younger son. He was instructed by God the Father to kill the "demons," who later turned out to be the Manchus. It did not seem then that he had decided to lead a revolt, because as late as 1843 he took and failed the civil service examination for the fourth time. His bitterness could well be imagined, since he was an ambitious man. Of course, he had to bide his time until the opportune moment arrived. The moment did arrive when famine struck a wide area in his native province.

The base of his operation was a secret society called the Society of God Worshippers, efficiently organized under his command. It recruited its followers from poor peasants, and being looked down upon by Confucian scholars as another form of superstition, it was boycotted by the leaders of each community. . . . From time to time its members clashed with local militia men who were organized by the gentry leaders to combat the society as well as the widespread banditry. In the winter of 1850–1851, Hung raised the standard of revolt, calling for the overthrow of the Manchu dynasty.

The weakness of the Ch'ing regime had been shown in the Opium War. Now it could not even cope with the ill-trained, ill-equipped peasant rebels. The regular army collapsed before the rebels, and city after city fell into their hands. After each city was captured, the rebels singled out two groups for persecution: Ch'ing officials and Buddhist and Taoist priests. The persecution of the first group was to be expected; the persecution of the second group was unusual and was done on religious grounds, as the Buddhist and Taoist priests had allegedly worshipped "idols." A sizable number of these Buddhist and Taoist priests were killed, and their temples and monasteries were confiscated to provide homes for the homeless and the very poor. The discipline of the Taiping soldiers was generally good; a household only needed to paste the word "obedience" (shun) on its front door to assure that it would not be disturbed by the Taiping soldiers. In 1853 Nanking fell into the hands of the rebels. Hung proclaimed himself as *T'ien Wang*, or Prince of Heaven, and called his kingdom *T'ai-p'ing T'ien-kuo*, or Heavenly Kingdom of Great Peace. But there was to be no peace, not even an earthly one.

In retrospect, what made the Taiping regime unique was its attempted reforms. It decreed that all land belonged to the nation as a whole and that private property was forever abolished. Every household was to receive from the state a certain amount of land in proportion to its size. Since women were declared equals of men, they were entitled to an equal share. After a harvest, a household kept what it needed for its sustenance and handed over to the government the surplus. "Areas that suffer from famine shall receive help from areas that have had bumper harvests," said a Taiping decree, "so that everyone will enjoy the blessing of God, the Supreme Lord." "We shall till together and enjoy the fruits of our work in common. Food and clothing shall be shared; so shall money. No one shall have more than his neighbor has, and no one shall ever suffer from cold or hunger." Thus, four years after the *Communist Manifesto* (which nobody in China had then heard of) and one century before Mao Tse-tung's communes, a communistic society was established in China under the doctrine of Christian love.

The social reforms of the Taiping regime were equally drastic. Every twenty-five households were organized as a comradeship (*wu*), the basic administrative unit of the nation. Each comradeship was headed by a comrade leader (*wu-chang*), the military as well as the administrative chief. He was responsible for the training of the twenty-five soldiers (one from each household) under his command as well as the supervision of farming; he led his soldiers in police and war activities whenever the necessity arose. In carrying out his administrative duties he was assisted by a teacher-priest called *liang-ssu-ma* who was also the judge and treasurer of the comradeship. All children were required to go to the church school where they were taught the *Old* and *New Testaments*, together with the decrees of the Prince of Heaven....

The Taipings' communistic and collectivistic life may not appeal to us; some of their other reforms, however, were progressive and modern. They deplored the inferior role women had played in Chinese society and tried to elevate their position to the same level as that of men. Women were entitled to land distribution as has been said before, and were encouraged to attend school. In the Taiping government many talented women served as officials, and some of them even distinguished themselves on the battlefield. In the Taiping army women were a common sight. Civil service examinations were open to women as well as men, and candidates were asked to write an essay on such a topic as the refutation of Confucius' assertion that "Women and small people are the most difficult to deal with." Moreover, the Taiping law forbade concubinage, foot-binding, and prostitution. The transportation and smoking of opium were punishable by death. . . .

Face to face with the Taiping regime and what it stood for were an ancient culture, the landed interests, some of the best brains of contemporary China, and finally, the Western interests in China. The odds against the Taipings were overwhelming. Their appeal to Chinese nationalism against "barbarian" Manchus fell on deaf ears because first, the Manchu regime had been Sinicized and had long been accepted by most, if not all Chinese; and second, whatever nationalist appeal the Taipings might have had was more than offset by the alien institutions and beliefs which they proposed for their new regime. . . .

At the beginning of the rebellion Christian missionaries showed considerable interest in the rebels who professed Christianity. A careful study of the Taiping beliefs soon disillusioned them because what Hung advocated could not be characterized in any way other than as outright heresy. The Taiping regime's prohibition of the opium traffic affected adversely the interests of Western traders who, together with their Chinese counterparts, had profited enormously by the spread of this vice. Moreover, the Western powers had only recently obtained many treaty concessions from the Ch'ing government, and there was no guarantee that the Taipings would honor these obligations if they replaced the Manchu regime. The feuds among the Taiping leaders and their inability to organize a real, respectable government dispelled whatever illusions some Westerners might once have had. When the showdown arrived, the Western interests sided with the Manchu government. . . .

In the summer of 1864, the Ch'ing forces, led by Tseng Kuo-ch'üan, a younger brother of Tseng Kuo-fan, made the final assault on Nanking. The city fell after a bloody battle which lasted fifteen days. Hung Hsiu-ch'üan, the Prince of Heaven, had committed suicide one month before, and his son and successor escaped from the city, only to be captured afterwards. "Not a single man of the 100,000 bandits in the city responded to the order of surrender," reported Tseng Kuo-fan to the imperial government, "and they burned themselves alive in groups as if they had no regret."

Shortly after the Taiping Rebellion and after China's defeat in the second Opium War (which resulted in more concessions to the Western powers), the Ching government attempted a number of wide-ranging reforms. During this brief period, konwn as the Tung-chih Restoration, the Imperial rulers of China tried to find new ways to deal with both the internal unrest and the increasingly ominous foreign threat. Li Hung-chang and Prince Kung were the principal figures advocating such reforms. Li's 1872 memorial (a statement of advice directed at the emperor) reflects his awareness of the need to arm China militarily and economically against further Western penetration. If he had succeeded in instituting some of his ideas, China might have begun to industrialize and to establish her independence instead of becoming increasingly subjugated by the West.

Problems of Industrialization
by Li Hung-chang

TRANSLATED BY SSU-YÜ TENG AND JOHN K. FAIRBANK

The Westerners particularly rely upon the excellence and efficacy of their guns, cannon, and steamships, and so they can overrun China. The bow and spear, small guns, and native-made cannon which have hitherto been used by China cannot resist their rifles, which have their bullets fed from the rear opening. The sailing boats, rowboats, and the gunboats which have been hitherto employed cannot oppose their steam-engined warships. Therefore, we are controlled by the Westerners.

To live today and still say "reject the barbarians" and "drive them out of our territory" is certainly superficial and absurd talk. Even though we wish to preserve the peace and to protect our territory, we cannot preserve and protect them unless we have the right weapons. They are daily producing their weapons to strive with us for supremacy and victory, pitting their superior techniques against our inadequacies, to wrangle with and to affront us. Then how can we get along for one day without weapons and techniques?

The method of self-strengthening lies in learning what they can do, and in taking over what they rely upon. Moreover, their possession of guns, cannon, and steamships began only within the last hundred years or so, and their progress has been so fast that their influence has spread into China. If we can really and thoroughly understand their methods—and the more we learn, the more improve—and promote them further and further, can we not expect that after a century or so we can reject the barbarians and stand on our own feet? Japan is just a small nation. Recently she has begun to trade with Europe; she has instituted iron factories and built many steamships. She has changed to the use of Western weapons. Does she have the ambition to plot to invade the Western nations? Perhaps she is merely planning for self-protection. But if Japan seeks only self-protection, she is nevertheless oppressing and looking down on our China. Should not China plan for herself? Our scholars and officials have confined themselves to the study of stanzas and sentences and are ignorant of the greatest change of the last several thousand years; they are accustomed to the temporary security of the present, and so they forget why we received the heavy blow and deep suffering of twenty or thirty years ago [the Opium War], and how we can obtain domestic security and control the foreigners within several centuries. That is how this talk of stopping steamship construction has originated.

Your minister humbly thinks that all other expenditures of our nation can be economized, but the expenses for supporting the army, establishing defense measures, drilling in guns and cannon, and building warships should by all means never be economized. If we try to save funds, then we shall be obliged to neglect all these defense measures, the nation will never have anything to stand upon, and we shall never be strong. . . . The amount which has already been spent will, in turn, become a sheer waste. Not only will we be a laughing stock to foreigners, but we will also strengthen their aggressive ambitions . . .

[The rest of the memorial explains why the expenditure has surpassed the original estimate—because it was roughly estimated by Frenchmen who were not experts, and because the price of machinery subsequently and unexpectedly rose. The progress of English and French warships is described, and a small type of warship for defense purposes is suggested. According to Li, China has "more land than water; it is more urgent to train an army than a navy." Li also discusses the difficulty of converting warships to commercial use, but he recognizes the need of commercial vessels for grain transportation and commercial competition with foreigners. Then he continues:]

Furthermore, the building of ships, cannon, and machinery will be impossible without iron, and then we shall be helpless without coal. The reason for England's power and influence over the Western lands is only her possession of these two items (iron and coal). The various arsenals in Foochow and Shanghai daily need a huge amount of imported coal and iron, because the Chinese product is most unsuitable. Even foreign ships coming to our ports have to carry foreign coal. Suppose there is a time when the points of entry to China are closed by boycott; then not only all our iron factories would have to suspend work and stand distressingly in idleness, but also the steamships which have been built would be unable to move a single inch without coal. What deserves more anxious thought than this! . . .
Recently Westerners have frequently requested permission to open coal and iron mines in the Chinese interior, pointing out that it is a great pity that China's natural resources cannot be developed by herself. We have heard that now Japan is adopting Western methods of opening coal and iron mines to gain a great profit,

and this has also helped her shipbuilding and machinery.
... If we can really make plans to persuade the people,
by means of the system of "government-supervision and
merchant-operation" [*kuan-tu shang-pan*], to borrow and
use foreign machines and foreign methods only, but not
allow foreigners to do the whole job on our behalf, then
these articles of daily necessity, when produced and
processed by proper methods, must have a good market.
A source of profit will naturally be opened. Taking the
surplus funds from the new source we can even use it to
maintain our ships and train our soldiers.

[In 1880, through military necessity, Li Hung-chang
also recognized the importance of the telegraph: "In
mobilizing troops," he writes, "speed is of the essence.
... A telegram from Russia to Shanghai takes only one
day, whereas from Shanghai to Peking ... a Chinese mail
steamer requires six or seven days. ... In 1874, when
Japan invaded Taiwan, Shen Pao-chen and others
repeatedly spoke of the advantage of the telegraph and
an Imperial decree was issued to institute it, but the
matter was only perfunctorily carried out and thus far
there has been no achievement." Accordingly, Li urged
the construction of two telegraph lines: from Nanking to
Peking, and from Hankow to Peking. Trunk railroad
construction still remained suspect, however, partly on
the ground that it would enable foreign invaders to
penetrate the interior too easily—as the Japanese were
to demonstrate in a later generation.

[Textile production had less obvious strategic value
and moved more slowly. Tso Tsung-t'ang had set up a
woolen mill in Lanchow, Kansu, in 1878 with the help of
German technicians and machinery, but it did not flourish after his death. In 1882, Li Hung-chang planned to
establish a cotton mill at Shanghai, and called for merchants' share-capital to help finance it. He proposed to
exempt its products from transit or *likin* taxes en route
from Shanghai to other parts of the country, which would
have set a precedent for giving special protection to
"national goods." His plan, however, was not carried
through until 1891, and the new Shanghai cotton mill,
the first in China, burned down in 1893 after one year of
successful operation. Li soon reorganized it on a larger

scale. At Wuchang, Chang Chih-tung also established a cotton mill in 1891, and another one in 1894. Li set up a paper mill in Shanghai in 1891; a cement factory was attached to the Kaiping coal mine; and a match factory and flour mill were also opened.

[Heavy industry got started even more slowly. Chang Chih-tung opened the Ta-yeh iron mine and the Hanyang Iron Works in Hupei in 1890, employing German technicians, but these projects never developed into the big industrial complex that their founder had hoped for.

[The variety and yet the ineffectiveness and slow development of some of these projects, many of them sponsored by Li Hung-chang, may be indicated in a list:

1863 A foreign language school was established at Shanghai.

1865 The Kiangnan Arsenal was established at Shanghai, with a translation bureau attached.

1867 The Nanking Arsenal was established.

1870 A machine factory, first established by Ch'ung-hou in 1867 at Tientsin, was enlarged.

1871 A foreign-style fort was planned for Taku, outside Tientsin.

1872 Students were sent to study in America.
Officers were sent to Germany to learn military sciences.
The China Merchants Steam Navigation Company was organized.
The opening of coal and iron mines was requested.

1875 A plan was made to build steel warships.

1876 A request was made to open a bureau to study foreign sciences in all provinces; also to add a new subject on foreign affairs in the civil service examinations.
Students and apprentices from the Foochow shipyard were sent to study in England and France.
Seven army officers were sent to Germany for advanced training.

1878 The Kaiping coal mine was opened.

1879 A telegraph line was opened from Taku to Tientsin.

1880 A plan for a modern navy was launched, beginning with a program to purchase warships from foreign countries.

A naval school was established at Tientsin.

Telegraph land lines were requested and sanctioned.

1881 Li supported Liu Ming-ch'uan's request to build railways.

North of Tientsin the T'angshan railroad (about six miles) was completed.

The first telegraph line, Shanghai-Tientsin, was opened and merchants were invited to develop the telegraph service in all provinces.

1882 A dockyard was built at Port Arthur (completed in 1891).

A cotton mill was planned at Shanghai.]

The "100 Days" and the Boxer Rebellion

The thirty years from the 1860's—when the West began actively to occupy China—up to the turn of the century saw serious attempts by Western-oriented Chinese to begin building industrial enterprises, railways, and mines. Yet compared with neighboring Japan, which during this same period successfully laid the base for later industrial growth, Chinese efforts were a failure. Why did this early Chinese attempt to industrialize fail, and what did that failure mean?

Three reasons partially explain China's lack of progress in the nineteenth century. First, China, unlike Japan, was continually besieged by the Western powers after the Opium Wars of the 1850's: she did not have Japan's "breathing space" to strengthen herself before the Westerners had seized commercial rights and colonies. Second, floods, famines, and droughts plagued the Imperial government during the latter half of the century and created chaos and political confusion internally. Third, there was never the firm commitment to large-scale Western reforms in China as there was in Meiji Japan. Conservative bureaucrats sabotaged modernizing efforts, and so projects proposed by Li Hung-chang and others were never fully carried out.

China's stunning defeat at the hands of Japan in the war of 1894–1895 came as even more of a shock. That the vast Chinese empire could be handily beaten by the small island nation of Japan—referred to by the Chinese contemptuously as the land of "dwarfs"—was unbelievable to most Chinese.

Yet Japan had overcome China precisely through industrial and military reforms based on Western models.

The first two selections below explore China's situation at the turn of the century. T'an Ssu-t'ung, one of the leading advocates of Western reforms in the 1890s, was also aware that along with necessary technical innovations in industry and mining, China's social and institutional structure also needed to be changed.

America at this time finally joined the European powers and Japan in claiming a share of the China market, although she did not seek a colony in China, as the other powers did; the third selection examines the American "open-door" policy toward China. Eberhard is a famous American scholar, and Bastid-Brugière, Bergère, and Chesneaux are French specialists of modern Chinese history.

Excerpts from a Letter Urging Complete Westernization
by T'an Ssu-t'ung

TRANSLATED BY SSU-YÜ TENG AND JOHN K. FAIRBANK

Your letter says that during the last several decades Chinese scholars and officials have been trying to talk about "foreign matters" (*yang-wu*), but that they have achieved absolutely nothing and, on the contrary, they have been driving the men of ability in the empire into foolishness, greed, and cheating. Ssu-t'ung thinks that not only do you not know what is meant by "foreign matters," but also that you are ignorant of the meaning of discussion. In China, during the last several decades, where have we had genuine understanding of foreign culture? When have we had scholars or officials who could discuss them? If they had been able to discuss foreign matters, there would have been no such incident as we have today [the defeat of China by Japan]. What you mean by foreign matters are things you have seen, such as steamships, telegraph lines, trains, guns, cannon, torpedoes, and machines for weaving and for metallurgy; that's all. You have never dreamed of or seen the beauty and perfection of Western legal systems and political institutions. . . . All that you speak of are the branches and foliage of foreign matters, not the root. . . .

We have more than one arsenal, and those at Tientsin, Shanghai, and Nanking are the oldest; but at the time when we need guns and cannon, there are no guns and cannon. We have more than one shipyard, and those at Port Arthur and Foochow are the largest; but at the time when we need ships, there are no ships. Helplessly we have to purchase these things from foreign countries. But the foreigners know that China has no machinery to test the quality of ships and weapons, and no way to distinguish between good and bad, so they sell to China, for an exorbitant price, weapons which have already been abandoned. . . . And Chinese diplomatic envoys in foreign countries seek a share of the profit. When they receive a remittance and dispatch the officers to make the purchase, they ask for a fee. Consequently, the higher the price, the poorer the weapons. . . . In this way China has wasted several decades. Yet you still consider Chinese scholar-officials to be learning about foreign matters. Are you not overestimating the various authorities and wishing to wash off their blame? . . .

We should extend the telegraph lines, establish post offices to take charge of postal administration, supply water, and burn electric or gas lamps for the use of the people. When the streets are well kept, the sources of pestilence will be cut off; when hospitals are numerous, the medical treatment will be excellent. We should have parks for public recreation and health. We should have a holiday once every seven days to enable civil and military officials to follow the policy of (alternation between) pressure and relaxation. We should thoroughly learn the written and spoken languages of all countries so as to translate Western books and newspapers, in order to know what other countries are doing all around us, and also to train men of ability as diplomats. We should send people to travel to all countries in order to enlarge their points of view and enrich their store of information, to observe the strengths and weaknesses, the rise and fall, of other countries; to adopt all the good points of other nations and to avoid their bad points from the start. As a result there will be none of the ships and weapons of any nation which we shall not be able to make, and none of the machines or implements which we shall not be able to improve.

The Boxer Rising
by Wolfram Eberhard*

China had lost the war with Japan because she was entirely without modern armament. While Japan went to work at once with all her energy to emulate Western industrialization, the ruling class in China had shown a marked repugnance to any modernization; and the center of this conservatism was the dowager empress Tzǔ Hsi. She was a woman of strong personality, but too uneducated—in the modern sense—to be able to realize that modernization was an absolute necessity for China if it was to remain an independent state. The empress failed to realize that the Europeans were fundamentally different from the neighbouring tribes or the pirates of the past; she had not the capacity to acquire a general grasp of the realities of world politics. She felt instinctively that Europeanization would wreck the foundations of the power of the Manchus and the gentry, and would bring another class, the middle class and the merchants, into power.

There were reasonable men, however, who had seen the necessity of reform—especially Li Hung-chang [the Governor General of the province in which Peking is situated]. In 1896 he went on a mission to Moscow, and then toured Europe. The reformers were, however, divided into two groups. One group advocated the acquisition of a certain amount of technical knowledge from abroad and its introduction by slow reforms, without altering the social structure of the state or the composition of the government. The others held that the state needed fundamental changes, and that superficial loans from Europe were not enough. The failure in the war with Japan made the general desire for reform more and more insistent not only in the country but in Peking. Until now Japan had been despised as a barbarian state; now Japan had won! The Europeans had been despised; now they were all cutting bits out of China for themselves, extracting from the government one privilege after another, and quite openly dividing China into

---

*Eberhard, *History of China*.

"spheres of interest," obviously as the prelude to annexation of the whole country.

In Europe at that time the question was being discussed over and over again, why Japan had so quickly succeeded in making herself a modern power, and why China was not succeeding in doing so; the Japanese were praised for their capacity and the Chinese blamed for their lassitude. Both in Europe and in Chinese circles it was overlooked that there were fundamental differences in the social structures of the two countries. The basis of the modern capitalist states of the West is the middle class. . . . In China there was only a weak middle class, vegetating under the dominance of the gentry; the middle class had still to gain the strength to liberate itself before it could become the support for a capitalistic state. And the gentry were still strong enough to maintain their dominance and so to prevent a radical reconstruction; all they would agree to were a few reforms from which they might hope to secure an increase of power for their own ends.

In 1895 and in 1898 a scholar, K'ang Yo-wei, who was admitted into the presence of the emperor, submitted to him memoranda in which he called for radical reform. . . . He was a man of strong and persuasive personality, and had such an influence on the emperor that in 1898 the emperor issued several edicts ordering the fundamental reorganization of education, law, trade, communications, and the army. These laws were not at all bad in themselves; they would have paved the way for a liberalization of Chinese society. But they aroused the utmost hatred in the conservative gentry and also in the moderate reformers among the gentry. K'ang Yo-wei and his followers, to whom a number of well-known modern scholars belonged, had strong support in South China. We have already mentioned that owing to the increased penetration of European goods and ideas, South China had become more progressive than the north; this had added to the tension already existing for other reasons between north and south. In foreign policy the north was more favourable to Russia and radically opposed to Japan and Great Britain; the south was in favour of co-operation with Britain and Japan, in order to learn from those two states how reform could be carried through. In the north the men of the south were suspected of being anti-Manchu and revolutionary in feeling. This was to some extent true, though K'ang Yo-wei and his friends were as yet largely unconscious of it.

When the empress Tzŭ Hsi saw that the emperor was actually thinking about reforms, she went to work with lightning speed. Very soon the reformers had to flee; those who failed to make good their escape were arrested and executed. The emperor was made a prisoner in a palace near Peking, and remained a captive until his death; the empress resumed her regency on his behalf. The period of reforms lasted only for a few months of 1898. . . .

There now began, from 1898, a thoroughly reactionary rule of the dowager empress. But China's general situation permitted no breathing-space. In 1900 came the so-called Boxer Rising, a new popular movement against the gentry and the Manchus similar to the many that had preceded it. The Peking government succeeded, however, in negotiations that brought the movement into the service of the government and directed it against the foreigners. This removed the danger to the government and at the same time helped it against the hated foreigners. But incidents resulted which the Peking government had not anticipated. An international army was sent to China, and marched from Tientsin against Peking, to liberate the besieged European legations and to punish the government. The Europeans captured Peking (1900); the dowager empress and her prisoner, the emperor, had to flee; some of the palaces were looted. The peace treaty that followed exacted further concessions from China to the Europeans and enormous war indemnities, the payment of which continued into the 1940's, though most of the states placed the money at China's disposal for educational purposes. When in 1902 the dowager empress returned to Peking and put the emperor back into his palace-prison, she was forced by what had happened to realize that at all events a certain measure of reform was necessary. The reforms, however, which she decreed, mainly in 1904, were very modest and were never fully carried out. They were only intended to make an impression on the outer world and to appease the continually growing body of supporters of the reform party, especially numerous in South China. The south remained, nevertheless, a focus of hostility to the Manchus. After his failure in 1898, K'ang Yo-wei went to Europe, and no longer played any important political part. His place was soon taken by a young Chinese physician who had been living abroad, Sun Yat-sen (1866–1925), who turned the reform party into a middle-class revolutionary party.

The American "Open Door" Policy
by Marianne Bastid-Brugière, Marie-Claire Bergère, and Jean Chesneaux

Through a series of agreements among themselves, the European powers mutually recognized the privileges extorted from China and agreed upon the size of their respective zones of influence. This division of spoils appeared to be the prelude to a political partition. But one of the powers was left out. Occupied in its war against Spain, the United States did not enter into the fray at the time the European states each took their portions. A solitary American company in 1898 had obtained the railroad concession to build the Hankow-Canton line. However, American leaders soon became worried, afraid of seeing the Chinese market cornered by the Europeans, while the annexation of Hawaii and the Philippines encouraged and made easier the expansion of American interests in the Pacific. In September, 1899, Secretary of State John Hay addressed to England, Germany, Russia, France, Italy, and Japan a note requesting that commercial equality, the statute of open ports, and the customs administration be respected and that those nations possessing areas of influence, leased territories, or railroad concessions in China renounce the establishment of preferential tariffs for their own citizens. The powers concerned gave their assent to this.

It is often said that this "Open Door" policy, evidence of the "friendship" of the United States toward China, helped her avoid territorial dismemberment. Actually, the American note—about which the Chinese government was not even informed—did not call into question either the spheres of influence or the encroachments upon Chinese sovereignty. It was confined to limiting their annoying consequences for the United States, while claiming her own participation in the benefits obtained by the others. In the eyes of the other imperialist powers—none of whom felt strong enough to seize all of the immense empire, and who each feared being evicted by its rivals—the principles proposed by the United States implied recognition of the spheres of influence and amounted to a mutual guaranty of their collective domination over China.

Translated from the French by Jon Livingston

The shock of Japanese victory over China compounded the growing sense of crisis as the twentieth century began. The Chinese leaders were apparently unable to deal with the multiple threats, Western and Japanese, and finally the people rose in an abortive revolt against the foreigners; this was the Boxer Rebellion of 1900, which led to the famous siege of the foreign legations in Peking.

The Boxers were in fact a curious mixture; on the one hand they were a traditional Chinese secret society, with strange rituals and a mistaken belief in immunity to Western bullets; on the other hand, they expressed the nearly universal desire of the Chinese to be rid of the Western imperialists. But their failure to accomplish this was not due to their odd religious beliefs. Rather, they failed because the Imperial government was too disorganized and weakened to aid them. The Boxers attempted to drive out the foreigners without an effective and modern military force and without rousing the majority of Chinese to fight with them. The Boxers were thus similar to many of the other desperate but unsuccessful peasant rebellions occurring in times of extreme distress in China.

The Boxers: A Secret Society
by Jean Chesneaux

The Boxer movement drew its support mainly from the poor peasantry of North China, particularly the agricultural workers who had been victims of the drought of the preceding years. It had an equally strong appeal among the boatmen who had been ruined by the recent falling-off of traffic on the Imperial Canal now that goods were transported by sea; and among disbanded soldiers, of whom there were many in the area.

Of the two principal Boxer leaders, one, Chang Techeng, was a former boatman, and the other, Ch'ao Fu-tien, was a former soldier. Thus the Boxers were no exception to the rule we have already observed; their administrators came from marginal elements of rural society, not directly engaged in agricultural production.

The place held by women in the movement is equally significant. Special units of young girls from 12 to 18 years old, the Red Lanterns and the Blue Lanterns, operated alongside the male units. They were led by a woman named Huang-lian Sheng-mu, the "Sacred Mother of the Yellow Lotus," who was claimed to possess great magical powers; she, too, came from a family of boatmen.... [EDITORS' NOTE: *The following is a Boxer exhortation against the blue-eyed barbarians.*]

To Expel the Blue-Eyed Devils

When the devils* troubled our country, the gods came to the aid of the Boxers of *I Ho Tuan*. To be converted to Christianity is to disobey Heaven, to refuse to worship our gods and Buddhas, and to forget our ancestors.

If people act in this way, the morality of men and the chastity of women will disappear. To be convinced of this, one has only to look at their eyes, which are completely blue. If the rain does not fall and the land dries up, it is because the churches stand in the way of Heaven. The gods are angry and they come down from the mountains to preach *Tao*.... †

Our military strategy is simple: boxing must be learned so that we can expel the devils effortlessly; the railways must be destroyed, the electric wires severed, and the ships demolished. All this will frighten France and demoralise Britain and Russia. The devils must be suppressed so that the Ch'ing empire may unite and celebrate peace.

---

*I.e., Westerners.
†The Sacred Way, the basis of the Taoist religion.

Chinese Response to the Boxer Treaty as Imagined by a Westerner
by Goldsworthy L. Dickinson
("John Chinaman")

Consider for a moment the conditions you have imposed on a proud and ancient empire, an empire which for centuries has believed itself to be at the head of civilization. You have compelled us, against our will, to open our ports to your trade; you have forced us to permit the introduction of a drug which we believe is ruining our people; you have exempted your subjects residing among us from the operation of our laws; you have appropriated our coasting traffic; you claim the traffic of our inland waters. Every attempt on our part to resist your demands has been followed by new claims and new aggressions. And yet all this time you have posed as civilized peoples dealing with barbarians. You have compelled us to receive your missionaries, and when they by their ignorant zeal have provoked our people to rise in mass against them, that again you have made an excuse for new depredations, till we, not unnaturally, have come to believe that the cross is the pioneer of the sword, and that the only use you have for your religion is to use it as a weapon of war. Conceive for a moment the feelings of an Englishman subjected to similar treatment; conceive that we had permanently occupied Liverpool, Bristol, Plymouth; that we had planted on your territory thousands of men whom we had exempted from your laws; that along your coasts and navigable rivers our vessels were driving out yours; that we had insisted on your admitting spirits duty free to the manifest ruin of your population; and that we had planted in all your principal towns agents to counteract the teachings of your Church and undermine the whole fabric of habitual belief on which the stability of your society depends. Imagine that you had to submit to all this. Would you be so greatly surprised, would you really even be indignant, if you found one day the Chinese Legation surrounded by a howling mob and Confucian missionaries everywhere hunted to death? What right then have you to be surprised, what right have you to be indignant at even the worst that has taken place in China? What is there so strange or monstrous in our conduct? A Legation, you say, is sacrosanct by the law of nations. Yes; but remember that it was at the point of the sword that you forced us to receive Embassies whose presence we have always regarded as a sign of national humiliation. But our mobs were barbarous and cruel. Alas! Yes. And your troops? And your troops, nations of Christendom? Ask the once fertile land from Peking to the coast; ask the corpses of murdered men and outraged women and children; ask the innocent mingled indiscriminately with the guilty; ask the Christ, the lover of men, whom you profess to serve, to judge between us who rose in mad despair to save our country and you who, avenging crime with crime, did not pause to reflect that the crime you avenged was the fruit of your own iniquity!

Well, it is over—over, at least, for the moment. I do not wish to dwell upon the past.

The 1911 Revolution and the End of Imperial China

Despite the disastrous defeat suffered by the Chinese empire in the Sino-Japanese War and the embarrassing occupation by foreign troops during the Boxer Rebellion, the last Chinese dynasty managed to survive through the first decade of the twentieth century. Then, on October 10, 1911, after numerous unsuccessful attempts, a revolution succeeded in putting an end to three thousand years of Imperial rule, and a republic was proclaimed under the leadership of Sun Yat-sen.

The events leading up to this event are outlined below in a selection by Chin-tung Liang. It should be remembered that the revolt of 1911 was not only anti-Western, but also strongly anti-Manchu, and Sun's secret society, the T'ung Meng Hui, was organized against the Manchu dynasty. Many Chinese at the time blamed China's crisis on the fact that the ruling Manchus were an "alien" dynasty. The Manchus were originally a tribal people who had conquered China and then become culturally Chinese while they governed in Peking. Also included is an explanation of Sun Yat-sen's "Three

People's Principles," the main political text associated with the early republic.

The date 1911 was a highly symbolic turning point for China, signifying both the end of the traditional society and the beginning of a new and untested form of government. It was shortly after this date that the Kuomintang, or Nationalist party, the Republic's principal political party, was set up. The proclamation of the Chinese republic, however, was followed by several more decades of turmoil and civil war before a satisfactory solution was found for dealing with the foreigners and with China's internal problems. White and Jacoby were American journalists in China; Liang teaches Chinese history.

The Chinese Revolution of 1911
by Chin-tung Liang

On October 10, 1911, Hsiung Ping-k'un, a soldier of the Engineering Battalion of the New Army stationed in Wu-ch'ang, shot and killed his commander, T'ao Ch'i-sheng. This was the first shot of the Revolution. The whole Battalion rose in revolt. In 48 days, it spread to fourteen provinces. In 81 days, the Chinese Republic was established and Dr. Sun Yat-sen was elected the provisional president. Forty-two days later, the Manchu Emperor issued an edict abdicating his throne, thus marking the end of two hundred and sixty-seven years of Manchu rule as well as the end of the system of monarchy in China. Following the Manchu abdication, Dr. Sun gave up the presidency in favor of Yuan Shih-k'ai, a position Dr. Sun had acquired after more than twenty years of revolutionary effort. . . .

The oath of the T'ung Meng Hui contained the following stirring words: "Expel the Tartars, revive China, establish a republic and equalize the land." The latter oath was an expression of Sun Yat-sen's ideas of the Three People's Principles. It also symbolized the beginning of the idea of the Chinese Republic. This idea was formed in Brussels, Berlin, Paris, and Tokyo in the same year (1905). It was not until this time that Dr. Sun began to feel that students were qualified to take part in the revolution and that the revolution could be achieved during his lifetime.

In addition to the ten revolutionary attempts, there were six independent uprisings. This shows that Dr. Sun Yat-sen was not the only person who laid the groundwork for the 1911 Revolution. The Revolution was the result of various forces.

Sun Yat-sen
by Theodore H. White and Annalee Jacoby

Sun Yat-sen was a Cantonese who had been educated in Hawaii; he participated in almost every unsuccessful revolt against the Manchu dynasty in the last decade of its existence, and he had lived the life of a hunted exile in Japan, America, and Europe. Almost every war lord who verbally espoused unity adorned his ambition with quotations from Sun Yat-sen; almost all ended by betraying him. The wretchedness of China, the burning eloquence of Sun Yat-sen's cause within him, the examples of Western civilization in the countries of his exile, were all finally synthesized in his book *San Min Chu I*, or *Three Principles of the People.* . . .

Sun's theory started by examining China. Why was she so humiliated in the family of nations? Why were her people so miserable? His answer was simple—China was weak, uneducated, and divided. To solve the problem, he advanced three principles.

The first was the Principle of Nationalism. China must win back her sovereignty and unity. The foreigners must be forced out of their concessions; they must be made to disgorge the spoils they had seized from the Manchus. China must have all the powers and dignities that any foreign nation had; she must be disciplined and the war lords purged. The second was the Principle of People's Democracy. China must be a nation in which the government serves the people and is responsible to them. The people must be taught how to read and write and eventually to vote. A system must be erected whereby their authority runs upward from the village to command the highest authority in the nation. The third was the Principle of People's Livelihood. The basic industries of China must be socialized; the government alone should assume responsibility for vast industrialization and reconstruction. Concurrently with the erection of the superstructure of a modern economic system, the foundation had to be strengthened. The peasant's lot was to be alleviated; those who tilled the soil should own it.

The founding of the republic was the beginning both of China's modern era and also of the era of the warlords—a period when China was divided into dozens of territories under the control of military chieftains, each with his own private army. This period of confusion, described here by Fitzgerald and Li, lasted well into the 1920s. While it made the final unification of China much more difficult, the warlord period also dashed Chinese hopes that the overthrow of the Imperial regime would lead to a new democratic and powerful China able to deal effectively with her own problems.

The Warlord Era
*by C. P. Fitzgerald**

Not far from Peking, in the western hills, there is an ancient temple, where grew a strange and rare plant. This plant flowered at long intervals, and then only at the accession of a new emperor. Then it put forth a single blossom. When the Empire fell the plant flowered again, but this time was covered with a multitude of small flowers. So, at least, the Peking people will tell you. The monks were asked to explain this strange phenomenon. To republican officials, visiting foreigners and other persons of modern cut, they said that the crowd of little flowers symbolized the rule of the many, the people of China. To the more old-fashioned inquirers the monks would say that perhaps the explanation of the miracle was that in place of one sovereign, the Empire would now suffer the oppression of many small despots.

It was under the dreary and disastrous rule of the

---

*Fitzgerald, *Birth of Communist China*.

warlords that this story became popular in Peking; at the fall of the Empire, even in the ancient capital, there was perhaps a less cynical outlook. The Republic which was established early in 1912 following the abdication of the Manchu Dynasty was, the revolutionaries hoped, to be a democracy modelled closely on those of the United States and France, the two republican countries which were most familiar to the Chinese intellectuals. In the intention of its other chief founder, the former Imperial commander-in-chief and first president of the Republic, Yuan Shih-k'ai, it was to be a brief interregnum ending in the foundation of his own imperial dynasty. The event proved that both were wrong; the Republic was destined to end neither in democracy nor in a new dynasty, but in chaos.

Between the republicans, who were led by men long out of touch with their own country, exiles who had worked for years abroad, and the vast mass of the Chinese people, there was only one idea in common: that the Manchu Dynasty was beyond reform and must go. It had been in full decline for many years, and that decline had involved the decay of China as a power, the invasion of her sovereignty at home, and mounting economic distress in the countryside. Already in 1840 the ancient pattern of dynastic decline had begun to show its well-known symptoms. The failure of the Empire to defend itself against the English in the Opium War revealed its weakness; the T'ai P'ing rebellion was the first great peasant rising caused by oppression and corruption and inspired, like many of its predecessors, by an esoteric creed. It was suppressed only after years of devastation by new armies which the court could but imperfectly control.

Further disastrous foreign wars, the Anglo-French attack which took Peking in 1860, the war with France in 1884 which lost China her suzerainty over Indo-China, and finally the war with Japan in 1895 which lost Korea and Formosa had ruined the prestige of the dynasty. The Empress Dowager Tz'u Hsi, a familiar type in history, the forceful woman of few scruples who dominates a decadent court, had arrested the fall of the dynasty at the expense of paralysing every tendency to reform. She had virtually dethroned, and actually imprisoned, the Emperor Kuang Hsu for his part in the sudden wave of reforms which were initiated in 1898 in a last attempt to imitate the Japanese restoration movement and modernize the Empire. The Empress Dowager by the force of her personality and the support of the conservatives had held China stiff and rigid in the old hierarchic pattern; beneath that mask the corpse of the Empire was fast decaying, and when she died in 1908 the swift crumbling of the Imperial power brought all to ruin.

Yuan Shih-k'ai had been the instrument which the Empress Dowager had used to overthrow the reformers and the Emperor Kuang Hsu. He had also been the last Chinese viceroy in Korea and he was the commander and creator of the modernized army, armed at least with rifles and artillery instead of bows and arrows and spears, which had been formed after the T'ai P'ing rebellion and the war with Japan. He was disliked by the Regent who took power in the name of the child Emperor when Tz'u Hsi and the Emperor Kuang Hsu died, on the same day, in 1908. Yuan was then dismissed from all his posts. Four years later the revolt of the garrison of Wu Chang, on the Yang Tze, following the accidental discovery of a republican conspiracy which involved officers of that garrison, brought the dynasty face to face with a vast insurrection. The southern provinces, always anti-Manchu, and more affected by foreign contacts, rose without resistance and joined the republican cause. The north, nearer to the throne, less interested in foreign ideas, remained passive. The only hope which remained to the dynasty was the modern army, which Yuan had created. Unless he also commanded it, it would most probably join the rebels. Yuan was recalled, given supreme command, and took the field.

Yuan certainly did not intend to save the dynasty which was in any case beyond rescue. But he was able and intended to defeat the rebels and then, the saviour of the monarchy, to usurp the throne. His chance had come, following the pattern of past history....

Under the Empire there had been few troops in the countryside. The landlords lived in their villages, the peasants paid them rent. When times were bad, the landlords remitted rent, to alleviate the distress around them. If they did not they were in danger of being burnt out or slain. The magistrate and the governor were careful not to overtax the people, lest revolt occur. Revolt might mean calling upon the court for troops. The court would also inquire into the disorder and probably execute the over-covetous officials.

There was a natural balance; the poor were oppressed, but not too far; they could react with success, or at least with danger to the oppressor. The troops were armed with sword and spear, so were the peasants. Rifles did not exist, machine-guns were unknown. Jack was as good as his master on the battlefield. Or nearly as good; trained troops could of course easily rout a peasant rabble, but trained troops were few.

Now the general balance of the countryside was upset. There was no court to rebuke or decapitate a greedy official; there was, instead, a horde of soldiers, vagabonds in uniform, without discipline or pay, who fattened on the land. They were allowed to pillage, to rob granaries and slay without punishment. The landlords fled to the cities from these disorders. They left bailiffs behind to collect their rents. The bailiffs found that the only way to live, and to grow rich at the same time, was to go into partnership with the military. If both agreed to collect from some village, good times or bad, all opposition could be overcome. Those who resisted would be shot. The soldier with his rifle and machine-gun could lord it over thousands of peasants.

Throughout the period of warlord rule, from 1916 to 1925, conditions steadily deteriorated. Little was heard of the distress of the countryside in the cities or abroad. Missionaries might report what they saw, but few realized how great the change was, nor what storms were brewing. The Chinese Revolution had become an incomprehensible confusion. No principles appeared to be in conflict; no contest between democracy and tyranny was visible, no climax and no conclusion. The western world, when it gave any attention to this scene, either despaired of China and foresaw Japanese conquest or clung to the belief that a strong man would emerge to restore some kind of order. Japan, well pleased at the rapid decline of China, continued her slow penetration and prepared for swifter and more decisive strokes.

The warlord period was, however, not without lasting importance. It consummated the destruction of two main pillars of the old order. The civil service, still more or less intact when the Empire fell, perished in the Age of Confusion. The older officials withdrew to retirement. The younger either joined the hangers-on of some general for a brief period of spoliation or, leaving politics aside, endeavoured to obtain a post at one of the many new universities. In the warlord period the scholar class, at least the best elements of it, withdrew from government into academic life. Government and administration were left to ignorant soldiers and self-seeking careerists.

The flight of the rich from the countryside, the prevalence of banditry hardly differing from the exactions of the military destroyed the balanced economy of the countryside, drove the peasants down further into misery, drained money away to the coast, and left the great irrigation and drainage works uncared for and in decay. Disastrous floods, famine for which no relief, unless from foreign sources, was available, the decline of inland trade, the dislocation of communications, all contributed to the ruin of the older order of society. The military rule had alienated both scholars and peasants; it had defied every moral restraint and outraged every hope of improvement; it was the direct cause of the second phase of the Chinese Revolution.

It was not generally realized in the West, which continued to proffer good advice to China and still made no sustained attempt to comprehend her problems, that in this sad period of disorder democracy and with it all that the West had hoped to see flourish in China had been discredited and cast aside. It is true, of course, that democracy had never had any trial at all; had never taken root in this alien soil, and that the pitiful travesty of the early Republic was neither an example of democracy nor a proof of its failure. Yet that is how it appeared to the Chinese people. In the name of Parliament they had seen gross and shameless corruption; in the name of democracy they had seen nothing but weak and bad government, military usurpation, violation of law, every kind of oppression and national decline. By the end of the second decade of the twentieth century the Chinese people were completely disillusioned with the false gods imported from the West. They turned restlessly to some other solution.

The May Fourth Movement of 1919

The republican government which followed the Imperial Manchu regime proved in fact to be helpless and ineffective and so politically divided that it could neither agree on nor implement new policies. Sun Yat-sen's term as president of the republic lasted only a little more than a year. He was followed by the dictator Yuan Shi-kai, who seized power, declared himself the emperor of a new dynasty, and then found that he was unable to hold the nation together. Indeed, for most of the decade 1911–1919, no one seemed to rule China at all, as feuding warlords and a weak central government fought over territory.

The end of World War I brought dramatic developments in Chinese politics. The Treaty of Versailles, which concluded the war, contained provisions highly unfavorable to China. A wave of public outrage arose spontaneously in China to protest the Versailles conference's decision to give to Japan the former German concessions in Shantung province. These protests came to be called the May Fourth Movement. It was sparked by students at Peking University and grew rapidly, expanding into boycotts of Japanese goods and heightening Chinese awareness of their helplessness before the West. This important movement also led to the beginning of the Chinese Communist movement, and the Chinese Communist party was formed in 1921.

Perhaps even more than the formal date of the republic's establishment, the year 1919 marks the real beginning of China's modern era. In addition to a selection describing the events of 1919, we have included one of the few pieces of dependable information about Mao Tse-tung's childhood. John Israel teaches Chinese history at the University of Virginia. Edgar Snow was among the first Americans to visit the Communist base areas in the 1930's. The story below was told to Snow by Mao Tse-tung during a visit to Yenan.

May 4, 1919

by John Israel

Historians date the modern Chinese student movement from the demonstration of May 4, 1919, which was staged to protest this injustice [the Versailles conference's decision to give former German possessions to Japan] and to denounce the pro-Japanese warlords and politicians who had acquiesced in it. The ensuing nationwide indignation culminated in China's refusal to sign the treaty, and more important, made student opinion a thing to be reckoned with. The salient features of the student movement in subsequent years—the countrywide unity, the slogans denouncing Japanese imperialists and Chinese traitors, the demonstrations, the use of modern propaganda methods, the crusades to educate and indoctrinate workers and peasants—all can be traced back to May Fourth.

Thus in 1919 a pattern was set for a generation of student uprisings. During the next three decades it became common to see thousands of high school and college youths surging through the streets demanding resistance to imperialists insults or an end to unpopular policies in their own government. Police suppression usually failed to end these disturbances and in fact often won the demonstrators wide support both from fellow students and from the public at large. Sympathy was especially prevalent among writers and journalists. Professors also applauded the students' aims, though not always their means; administrators in government schools were torn between their obligation to enforce the law and their desire to defend students from police oppression. Movements spread rapidly to cities with large collegiate populations. Regional and national student organizations were quickly formed. . . .

The nature of student commitment was radically altered between 1919 and 1949. The May Fourth generation was in revolt against all authority: family, school, and state alike seemed decadent, venal, and hopelessly encrusted with worn-out ways of thought. From about 1915 through the early 1920's, the accent was on liberating the individual from the old order. Anti-Confucianism, the family revolution, and the "literary renaissance" were foremost in students' minds. But though the family revolution continued, after the May Fourth demonstration the battleground began to shift from the home to society and the nation. The new student generation acquired new loyalties.

Mao Tse-tung's School Days
by Edgar Snow*

"My scholastic adventure was in the First Provincial Middle School. I registered for a dollar, took the entrance examination, and passed at the head of the list of candidates. It was a big school, with many students, and its graduates were numerous. A Chinese teacher there helped me very much; he was attracted to me because of my literary tendency. . . .

"I did not like the First Middle School. Its curriculum was limited and its regulations were objectionable. After reading *Chronicles with Imperial Commentaries*, I had also come to the conclusion that it would be better for me to read and study alone. After six months I left the school, and arranged a schedule of education of my own, which consisted of reading every day in the Hunan Provincial Library. I was very regular and conscientious about it, and the half-year I spent in this way I consider to have been extremely valuable to me. I went to the library in the morning when it opened. At noon I paused only long enough to buy and consume two rice cakes, which were my daily lunch. I stayed in the library every day reading until it closed.

"During this period of self-education I read many books, studied world geography and world history. There for the first time I saw and studied with great interest a map of the world. I read Adam Smith's *The Wealth of Nations*, and Darwin's *Origin of Species*, and a book on ethics by John Stuart Mill. I read the works of Rousseau, Spencer's *Logic*, and a book on law written by Montesquieu. I mixed poetry and romances, and the tales of ancient Greece, with serious study of history and geography of Russia, America, England, France and other countries.

"I was then living in a guild house for natives of Hsiang Hsiang district. Many soldiers were there also—'retired' or disbanded men from the district, who had no work to do and little money. Students and soldiers were always

---

*Snow, *Red Star Over China*.

quarrelling in the guild house, and one night this hostility between them broke out in physical violence. The soldiers attacked and tried to kill the students. I escaped by fleeing to the toilet, where I hid until the fight was over.

"I had no money then, my family refusing to support me unless I entered school, and since I could no longer live in the guild house I began looking for a new place to lodge. Meanwhile, I had been thinking seriously of my 'career' and had about decided that I was best suited for teaching. I had begun reading advertisements again. An attractive announcement of the Hunan Normal School now came to my attention, and I read with interest of its advantages: no tuition required, and cheap board and cheap lodging. Two of my friends were also urging me to enter. They wanted my help in preparing entrance essays. I wrote of my intention to my family and received their consent. I composed essays for my two friends, and wrote one of my own. All were accepted—in reality, therefore, I was accepted three times. I did not then think my act of substituting for my friends an immoral one; it was merely a matter of friendship.

"I was a student in the Normal School for five years, and managed to resist the appeals of all future advertising. Finally I actually got my degree. Incidents in my life here, in the Hunan Provincial First Normal School, were many, and during this period my political ideas began to take shape. Here also I acquired my first experience in social action. . . .

"A teacher named T'ang used to give me old copies of the *People's Paper (Min Pao)*, and I read them with keen interest. I learned from them about the activities and programme of the T'ung Meng Hui.* One day I read a copy of the *Min Pao* containing a story about two Chinese students who were travelling across China and had reached Tatsienlu, on the edge of Tibet. This inspired me very much. I wanted to follow their example; but I had no money, and thought I should first try out travelling in Hunan.

---

*The T'ung Meng Hui, a revolutionary secret society, was founded by Dr. Sun Yat-sen, and was forerunner of the Kuomintang, which now has power in Nanking. Most of its members were exiles in Japan, where they carried on a vigorous "brush-war" against Liang Ch'i-ch'ao and K'ang Yu-wei, leaders of the "reformed monarchist" party.

"The next summer I set out across the province by foot, and journeyed through five counties. I was accompanied by a student named Hsiao Yü. We walked through these five counties without using a single copper. The peasants fed us and gave us a place to sleep; wherever we went we were kindly treated and welcomed. . . .

"Feeling expansive and the need for a few intimate companions, I one day inserted an advertisement in the Changsha paper, inviting young men interested in patriotic work to make a contact with me. I specified youths who were hardened and determined, and ready to make sacrifices for their country. To this advertisement I received three and one-half replies. One was from Liu Chiang-lung, who later was to join the Communist Party and afterwards to betray it. Two others were from young men who later were to become ultra-reactionaries. . . .

"But gradually I did build up a group of students around myself, and the nucleus was formed of what later was to become a society that was to have a widespread influence on the affairs and destiny of China. It was a serious-minded little group of men and they had no time to discuss trivialities. Everything they did or said must have a purpose. They had no time for love or 'romance' and considered the times too critical and the need for knowledge too urgent to discuss women or personal matters. I was not interested in women. My parents had married me when I was fourteen to a girl of twenty, but I had never lived with her—and never subsequently did. I did not consider her my wife and at this time gave little thought to her. Quite aside from the discussions of feminine charm, which usually play an important rôle in the lives of young men of this age, my companions even rejected talk of ordinary matters of daily life. . . .

"I built up a wide correspondence with many students and friends in other towns and cities. Gradually I began to realize the necessity for a more closely knit organization. In 1917, with some other friends, I helped to found the Hsin Min Hsüeh Hui ('New People's Study Society'). It had from seventy to eighty members, and of these many were later to become famous names in Chinese Communism, and in the history of the Chinese Revolution. . . .

"At this time my mind was a curious mixture of ideas of

liberalism, democratic reformism, and Utopian Socialism. I had somewhat vague passions about 'nineteenth-century democracy,' Utopianism and old-fashioned liberalism, and I was definitely anti-militarist and anti-imperialist.

"I had entered the normal college in 1912. I was graduated in 1918."

Chiang Kai-shek

Until the Nationalist Kuomintang party managed to gain control over and partially unify China in 1927, the government of the republic maintained very weak control over its territory, and much of China lay in chaos. The attempt by Yuan Shi-kai to resurrect the empire and have himself declared emperor failed miserably. Instead, the political weaknesses of the central government were further aggravated, and the republic floundered. It was during this period of political divisions and social turmoil that China's future leaders, both Nationalist and Communist, emerged. Included is a brief sketch of Chiang Kai-shek, leader of the Kuomintang from this time on.

Chiang Kai-shek
by Theodore H. White and
Annalee Jacoby

While he was in Japan, he was stirred, like other student thinkers, by Sun Yat-sen's vision of a new China, strong and great. In 1911 he returned to China to join the uprising that overthrew the Manchus and established the Chinese Republic. When the first republic proved a mockery, he went to Shanghai; what he did there is a matter of gossip and guess, for official biographies skip hastily over this period. It is known, though, that he was helped by a revolutionary named Ch'en Chi-mei, uncle of the CC brothers. In 1915 Chiang participated in another military coup aimed at seizing the Kiangnan arsenal near Shanghai. His comrades of that adventure, who are still among his intimate associates, fled the country, but Chiang disappeared somewhere into Shanghai's murky underworld. He lived a fast, hard life of personal danger, hunger, and abandon; then for a while he was an inconspicuous clerk on the Shanghai stock exchange. At that time, the underworld of Shanghai was dominated by the notorious Green Gang that controlled the city's rackets of opium, prostitution, and extortion. The Green Gang was an urban outgrowth of one of the many secret societies that have flourished in China for centuries. Such a gang has no counterpart in western life; it sank its roots into all the filth and misery of the great lawless city, disposed of its gunmen as it saw fit, protected its clients by violence, was an organized force perhaps more powerful than the police. . . .

Out from the mists of Shanghai, Chiang Kai-shek strode forth into the full blaze of Chinese national politics at Canton in the summer of 1924. Precisely how he arrived at this eminence from his previous estate of penniless dependency on the Shanghai publicans is obscure. He served briefly with a Fukienese war lord after Shanghai; he had been brought to Sun Yat-sen's attention by his Shanghai friends, and Sun sent him to study Russian military techniques at Moscow in 1923. He had returned to China and Canton with a huge distrust of the Russians but a shrewd appreciation of the methods of the one-party state. Canton in those days was bursting with fresh energy and new ideas. Kuomintang leaders argued and competed; intrigue dissolved and remade political alliances. During the two years of Chiang's stay in Canton he was never beaten in a quarrel. He staged his first successful armed coup in the spring of 1926 against the left wing of his own party; it was a masterful piece of timing, and after Sun Yat-sen's death he succeeded to the post of party leader.

During the next twenty years both China and Chiang changed, but his dominance in the Kuomintang was never once seriously threatened. His one passion now became and remained an overriding lust for power. All his politics revolved about the concept of force. He had grown up in a time of treachery and violence. There were few standards of human decency his early warlord contemporaries did not violate; they obeyed no law but power, and Chiang outwitted them at their own game. His false starts in insurrection had taught him that he should show no mercy to the vanquished and that the victor remains victor only as long as his armies are intact. When he started north from Canton in 1926 to seize the Yangtze Valley, he was an accomplished student in all the arts of buying men or killing them.

Birth of Communism in China: End of First United Front

Amid the chaos of the warlord period, the two parties that were to determine China's twentieth-century development were maturing. Following the May Fourth Movement of 1919, Chinese politics were a unique mixture of domestic elements and foreign inspiration, in large part a reaction to the Bolshevik victory in Russia. At this stage, both the Kuomintang (KMT) and the Chinese Communist party (CCP) were inspired by the Russian Revolution and adopted some Russian ideas and models of political organization. Both also maintained links with the Russian foreign-policy body, Comintern, which controlled many Communist movements around the world. For much of this period, the Nationalists and the Communists were allied politically in support of the common goal of national unification of China, although they remained far apart in long-range purposes.

The high point of this first united front between the KMT and the CCP was the Northern Expedition of 1926–1927, led by Chiang Kai-shek, a military venture which successfully unified most of China for the first time since the fall of the Manchus. Many of the warlords were brought under military control, and Chiang established himself in Nanking, the capital of the republic. Yet shortly after the Northern Expedition, in April, 1927, Chiang turned on his Communist allies and massacred large numbers of CCP members and labor organizers in Shanghai and other cities. The Communists had been establishing themselves in labor unions and political organizations in Shanghai, and they turned out to welcome Chiang's troops when they arrived; their work in China's cities was largely destroyed in the reign of terror that followed. Chou En-lai, for example, barely managed to escape from Shanghai alive.

The year 1927 thus marks both the partial reunification of China and the end of the KMT-CCP alliance. From then on, the Communists and the Kuomintang struggled for control of China. Civil war between the two parties lasted until the Japanese invasion of the 1930's forced a second temporary

United Front on the contending parties in order to fight the common enemy. Formerly a *Newsweek* war correspondent in China, Harold Isaacs teaches at MIT.

KMT–Communist Split
by Congressional Quarterly Service

In the early twenties, Dr. Sun established contact with Lenin. In 1923, a Soviet political mission arrived in Canton, which was the capital of the newly established Republic of South China, and by now "the seat of an incandescent revolutionary movement." A Russian agent, Michael Borodin, became Sun's political adviser. . . .

In August 1923, Sun sent Chiang, who was now Chief of Staff, to the Soviet Union to study its political and social system. He remained in Moscow for six months and returned in early 1924. Unlike Dr. Sun, however, Chiang was never attracted by the Communist ideology.

On his return, Chiang organized and became the first commandant of the Whampoa Military Academy. The Academy was to produce men who would wield force, not for its own sake, but for a new China. Chiang told his cadets—who included Chou En-lai and Lin Piao—that the great common bond between the revolutionary Kuomintang and Soviet Russia was their mutual determination "to vanquish imperialism and liberate the peoples enslaved by it."

A Soviet marshal, Vassily Blucher, was assigned as Chiang's chief adviser. . . .

Dissension had begun to overtake the Kuomintang leaders, but Sun was able to keep the party together during his lifetime. When he died on March 12, 1925, the Kuomintang was under a Central Executive Committee composed of right-wing leader Hu Man-min, the Borodin-supported Wang Ching-wei, and Chiang, who was also chairman of the Military Affairs Commission. . . .

In 1925, Chiang staged a military coup, which was followed by the flight of Wang, and the naming of Chiang as Commander-in-Chief, Northern Expeditionary Force.

The Northern Expedition—1926–1927

The "Northern Expedition" was a campaign of the revolutionary armies of the Kuomintang to march from Canton to the Yangtze Valley with the goal of reclaiming China from the warlords. It was the dream of Sun Yat-sen since 1917 and was adopted as the objective of the Kuomintang. The expedition was finally launched in the summer of 1926, with the plan of attack devised by the chief Russian military adviser, Gen. Blucher.

Chiang was given dictatorial powers by the Kuomintang for the duration of the Northern expedition. He declared that the party "would follow the program that Sun had laid down: a phase of military supervision first, then a period of political tutelage, and finally a constitutional government."

From his march to the Yangtze Valley, Chiang became aware that certain groups, principally wealthy Chinese in Shanghai, were looking to him to give the Kuomintang a more conservative leadership. In return they could offer him a base of support for his armies and his party. Chiang discovered he no longer needed to be dependent on Russian aid.

As Chiang prepared to enter Shanghai in March 1927, he was aided by a Communist-led union, which first disarmed and then expelled the warlord garrison. Chiang, a month later, turned on the union and suppressed it in a ruthless massacre. Similar massacres of workers belonging to radical labor movements followed, deflecting the Kuomintang from its leftward orientation.

The Communists' Move to the Countryside

by Harold Isaacs

The defeat of 1927 was nearly one of annihilation. The Communist party had been founded only seven years before and had been led to disaster mainly because it was so totally dependent upon Russian guidance and subject to

Russian control. After the defeat, the Chinese Communists did not cease to be subject to Russian pressure and dictation, but they were not and did not become merely an alien graft. In the remote hinterlands of Central China they found their own means of survival and new paths to power. . . .

Survivors and stubborn dissenters had a broad and remote and mountainous hinterland in which to seek refuge. They had, too, a tradition in which they could take shelter and find moral and psychological support for their persistence. Defeat and frustration were, after all, far more common than success in the long history of peasant struggle. From time almost immemorial those who would not accept such defeats had lived on in the mountains, in shadowy secret societies, in small bands, half-outlaw, half-insurgent. The Communist survivors of the defeated revolution in 1927 made themselves part of this tradition in Chinese life.

In twos and threes and in scattered bands, these survivors made their way to the mountainous border regions of Kiangsi, where they formed into small guerrilla bands which slowly enlarged into armies. Gradually they established a measure of control over scattered rural districts in the regions bordering on Hunan and Fukien and in several neighboring provinces. In the tiny Kiangsi village of Juichin on November 7, 1931, they proclaimed the "Chinese Soviet Republic." Its largest single piece of territory was the "central Soviet district," an area covering some seventeen counties astride the Kiangsi-Fukien border with a total population of about three million. The Communist armies and partisan forces of this period learned to become, in the old Chinese phrase, like "flowing water and moving clouds," constantly changing in size and location. For nearly five years, they successfully outwitted Chiang Kai-shek and his best generals and foreign advisers, evading or successfully parrying the repeated attacks of incomparably larger and better-armed Kuomintang forces. They developed a superb mastery of guerrilla tactics based upon the assistance and friendly support of the local population—an experience which prepared them for their future, more spectacular achievements.

With the end of the first united front between the Communists and the Nationalist Kuomintang party in 1927, a new and independent Communist movement developed. In contrast to its early concentration on labor organizing in cities like Shanghai, the Communist movement after 1927 developed rural roots and a new political outlook based in the countryside. Chiang Kai-shek had made China's urban areas unlivable for the Communists, so they established guerrilla bases in the mountainous parts of South China during the late 1920's and early 1930's. Centered in Kiangsi province, this phase of the Communist movement is named after the "Kiangsi Soviets" (Communist local governments) set up there.

Although these early bases were eventually engulfed and destroyed by Chiang Kai-shek in a series of military campaigns, it was here that the distinctive Communist approach to politics in China was formulated. It was here, for example, that the "fish-in-the-ocean" idea was worked out in practice. This roughly meant that the Communists—or "fish"—would be politically effective only if they worked from a secure base of support in China's vast peasant population, which provided the "sea" in which the Communist guerrillas could "swim." Thus they gave up their initial notion of organizing China's relatively few industrial workers and moved permanently to the rural areas, where the overwhelming majority of China's population lived.

The origins of this dramatic change can be felt in Mao Tse-tung's report on the peasant situation in Hunan province. Based on a trip to get firsthand information for the party, this famous report shows Mao's insistence on relying on popular support in the countryside. Since this went against the conventional Russian ideas of how to organize the Chinese Communist party or conduct a revolution, his ideas took several years and much painful experience to gain approval.

Chiang's "Bandit-Suppression" campaigns against the Communists led to another near-disaster in 1934, when the mountain bases in Kiangsi were encircled and their supply routes cut. Once again the Communists faced a major turning point. They decided to leave South China and embarked on their "Long March" to the Northwest. The events of 1927 to 1934 leading up to this important decision are described below by Issacs, who traveled in China during this period.

The Chinese Soviet Republic
by Harold Isaacs

Shanghai, Wuhan, Tientsin, Canton, and all other centers of industrial and proletarian concentration had become, in effect, the "rear" of the mountains of southern Kiangsi.... Deep in the hills of south Kiangsi in the village of Juichin the Red armies established their capital and there, on November 7, 1931, they proclaimed the creation of the "Chinese Soviet Republic" and set up a Provisional Soviet Government.

The "Chinese Soviet Republic" consisted in 1932–33, the years of its maximum development, of six widely separated areas scattered along the border regions of the Central China provinces....

Because the Red armies and partisan forces were for the most part, to use a favorite Chinese phrase, "like flowing water and moving clouds," the territory they occupied expanded and contracted according to the fortunes of war. At various times the Red Army, led by Chu Tê, undoubtedly crossed or temporarily occupied at least sixty or seventy of Kiangsi's eighty-one hsien (counties); but there is ample authority for the statement that the most important and most stable Red Army area, the so-called "central Soviet district," held more or less permanently from 1930 to the end of 1934, comprised about seventeen hsien astride the Kiangsi-Fukien border, with a total population of three million....

The Red armies themselves varied no less in size and strength, both in their more or less regular formations and in the auxiliary corps of peasant Red Guards who functioned with them in the incessant civil war against Chiang Kaishek's Kuomintang forces. In 1932 one quite carefully checked estimate based on Communist records put the grand total of all armies operating in all districts at 151,000, of whom only 97,500 had rifles....

That these forces and the territory they permanently occupied were in reality so small sharpens into all the bolder relief the quality of their achievements. No more brilliant pages have ever been written in the history of peasant wars than those which must record the exploits of the Chinese Red armies engaged in a civl war against enemies five, six, and seven times their number and a thousand times their superior in armaments. For more than five years, the Red armies out-maneuvered and defeated five successive Kuomintang campaigns against them. Because of the incomparable advantage of the support of the population, their superior mobility and generalship, their knowledge of the terrain, the Reds cut off and defeated division after division of Chiang Kai-shek's best troops and armed themselves exclusively with the weapons they captured. The slogans of land to the peasants and freedom from the rapacity of the Kuomintang regime plowed like tanks through the columns of Chiang's hired soldiers.

Report on an Investigation of the Peasant Movement in Hunan: March 1927

by Mao Tse-tung

During my recent visit to Hunan I made a first-hand investigation of conditions in the five counties of Hsiangtan, Hsianghsiang, Hengshan, Liling and Changsha. In the thirty-two days from January 4 to February 5, I called together fact-finding conferences in villages and county towns, which were attended by experienced peasants and by comrades working in the peasant movement, and I listened attentively to their reports and collected a great deal of material. Many of the hows and whys of the peasant movement were the exact opposite of what the gentry in Hankow and Changsha are saying. I saw and heard of many strange things of which I had hitherto been unaware. I believe the same is true of many other places, too. All talk directed against the peasant movement must be speedily set right. All the wrong measures taken by the revolutionary authorities concerning the peasant movement must be speedily changed. Only thus can the future of the revolution be benefited. For the present upsurge of the peasant movement is a colossal event. In a very short time, in China's cental, southern and northern provinces, several hundred million peasants will rise like a mighty storm, like a hurricane, a force so swift and violent that no power, however great, will be able to hold it back. They will smash all the trammels that bind them and rush foward along the road to liberation. They will sweep all the imperialists, warlords, corrupt officials, local tyrants and evil gentry into their graves. Every revolutionary party and every revolutionary comrade will be put to the test, to be accepted or rejected as they decide. There are three alternatives. To march at their head and lead them? To trail behind them, gesticulating and criticizing? Or to stand in their way and oppose them? Every Chinese is free to choose, but events will force you to make the choice quickly. . . .

The main targets of attack by the peasants are the local tyrants, the evil gentry and the lawless landlords, but in passing they also hit out against patriarchal ideas and institutions, against the corrupt officials in the cities and against bad practices and customs in the rural areas. In force and momentum the attack is tempestuous; those who bow before it survive and those who resist perish. As a result, the privileges which the feudal landlords enjoyed for thousands of years are being shattered to pieces. Every bit of the dignity and prestige built up by the landlords is being swept into the dust. With the collapse of the power of the landlords, the peasant associations have now become the sole organs of authority and the popular slogan "All power to the peasant associations" has become a reality. . . . The local tyrants, evil gentry and lawless landlords have been deprived of all right to speak, and none of them dares even mutter dissent. In the face of the peasant associations' power and pressure, the top local tyrants and evil gentry have fled to Shanghai, those of the second rank ot Hankow, those of the third to Changsha and those of the fourth to the county towns, while the fifth rank and the still lesser fry surrender to the peasant associations in the villages.

"Here's ten yuan. Please let me join the peasant association," one of the smaller of the evil gentry will say.

"Ugh! Who wants your filthy money?" the peasants reply. . . .

* * *

The peasants' revolt disturbed the gentry's sweet dreams. When the news from the countryside reached the cities, it caused immediate uproar among the gentry. Soon after my arrival in Changsha, I met all sorts of people and picked up a good deal of gossip. From the middle social strata upwards to the Kuomintang right-wingers, there was not a single person who did not sum up the whole business in the phrase, "It's terrible!" Under the impact of the views of the "It's terrible!" school then flooding the city, even quite revolutionary-minded people became down-hearted as they pictured the events in the countryside in their mind's eye; and they were unable to deny the word "terrible." Even quite progressive people said, "Though terrible, it is inevitable in a revolution." In short, nobody could altogether deny the word "terrible." But, as already mentioned, the fact is that the great peasant masses have risen to fulfill their historic mission and that the forces of rural democracy have risen to overthrow the forces of rural feudalism. The patriarchal-feudal class of local tyrants, evil gentry and lawless landlords has formed the basis of autocratic government for thousands of years and is the cornerstone of imperialism, warlordism and corrupt officialdom. To overthrow these feudal forces is the real objective of the national revolution. In a few months the peasants have accomplished what Dr. Sun Yat-sen wanted, but failed, to accomplish in the forty years he devoted to the national revolution. This is a marvellous feat never before achieved, not just in forty, but in thousands of years. It's fine. It is not "terrible" at all. It is anything but "terrible." "It's terrible!" is obviously a theory for combating the rise of the peasants in the interests of the landlords; it is obviously a theory of the landlord class for preserving the old order of feudalism and obstructing the establishment of the new order of democracy, it is obviously a counterrevolutionary theory. No revolutionary comrade should echo this nonsense. If your revolutionary viewpoint is firmly established and if you have been to the villages and looked around, you will undoubtedly feel thrilled as never before. Countless thousands of the enslaved—the peasants—are striking down the enemies who battened on their flesh. What the peasants are doing is absolutely right; what they are doing is fine! "It's fine!" is the theory of the peasants and of all other revolutionaries. Every revolutionary comrade should know that the national revolution requires a great change in the countryside. The Revolution of 1911 did not bring about this change, hence its failure. This change is now taking place, and it is an important factor for the completion of the revolution. Every revolutionary comrade must support it, or he will be taking the stand of counterrevolution.

Then there is another section of people who say, "Yes, peasant associations are necessary, but they are going rather too far." This is the opinion of the middle-of-the-roaders. But what is the actual situation? True, the peasants are in a sense "unruly" in the countryside. Supreme in authority, the peasant association allows the landlord no say and sweeps away his prestige. This amounts to striking the landlord down to the dust and keeping him there. . . . People swarm into the houses of local tyrants and evil gentry who are against the peasant association, slaughter their pigs and consume their grain. They even loll for a minute or two on the ivory-inlaid beds belonging to the young ladies in the households of the local tyrants and evil gentry. At the slightest provocation they make arrests, crown the arrested with tall paper-hats, and parade them through the villages, saying, "You dirty landlords, now you know who we are!" Doing whatever they like and turning everything upside down, they have created a kind of terror in the countryside. This is what some people call "going too far," or "exceeding the proper limits in righting a wrong," or "really too much." Such talk may seem plausible, but in fact it is wrong. First, the local tyrants, evil gentry and lawless landlords have themselves driven the peasants to this. For ages they have used their power to tyrannize over the peasants and trample them underfoot; that is why the peasants have reacted so strongly. The most violent revolts and the most serious disorders have invariably occurred in places where the local tyrants, evil gentry and lawless landlords perpetrated the worst outrages. The peasants are clear-sighted. Who is bad and who is not, who is the worst and who is not quite so vicious, who deserves severe punishment and who deserves to be let off lightly—the peasants keep clear accounts, and very seldom has the punishment exceeded the crime. Secondly, a revolution is not a dinner party, or writing an essay, or painting a picture, or doing embroidery; it cannot be so refined, so leisurely and gentle, so temperate, kind, courteous, restrained and magnanimous. A revolution is an insurrection, an act of violence by which one class overthrows another. A rural revolution is a revolution by which the peasantry overthrows the power of the feudal landlord class. Without using the greatest force, the peasants cannot possibly overthrow the deep-rooted authority of the landlords which has lasted for thousands of years. The rural areas need a mighty revolutionary upsurge, for it alone can rouse the people in their millions to become a powerful force. All the actions mentioned here which have been labelled as "going too far" flow from the power of the peasants, which has been called forth by the mighty revolutionary upsurge in the countryside. It was highly necessary for such things to be done in the second period of the peasant movement, the period of revolutionary action. In this period it was necessary to establish the absolute authority of the peasants. It was necessary to forbid malicious criticism of the peasant associations. It was necessary to overthrow the whole authority of the gentry, to strike them to the ground and keep them there. There is revolutionary significance in all the actions which were labelled as "going too far" in this period. To put it bluntly, it is necessary to create terror for a while in every rural area, or otherwise it would be impossible to suppress the activities of the counterrevolutionaries in the countryside or overthrow the authority of the gentry. Proper limits have to be exceeded in order to right a wrong, or else the wrong cannot be righted.

Chiang and the Kuomintang

During the early 1930's Japanese incursions began in the northeast, and Manchuria was surrendered to Japan as a colony. Communist guerrilla bands roamed the mountains of several southern China provinces, establishing Communist administrations in the larger "liberated" areas. Despite the nominal unification of China achieved in 1927, warlords still held important pieces of real estate and maintained feudal rule over much of China.

Amid this confusion, Chiang Kai-shek and the Kuomintang

party in Nanking attempted to provide China with central administration and simultaneously to reform some of her most archaic institutions. One of the groups set up by Chiang in this period was the Blue Shirt corps, modeled on the Italian Brown Shirts, which was intended to organize China's youth into military groups. Another aspect was the scramble for power among the Kuomintang politicians in Nanking. Chiang Kai-shek has come to symbolize for many Chinese the excesses of Nationalist politics in this period. Despite the attempts of "Third Force" political groups (so-called because they were neither Communist nor Nationalist) to gain a share of power, Chiang held an iron grip over the Republic of China.

Fascism in Kuomintang China: The Blue Shirts
by Lloyd E. Eastman

The Blue Shirts during the 1930s became one of the most influential and feared political movements in China. To both contemporaries and historians, however, the Blue Shirt movement has been a shadowy force, known mostly through hearsay, with little solid information regarding its doctrine or its activities. Now, on the basis of memoirs, interviews, and especially Japanese intelligence reports of the 1930s, a rough picture of this secret organization can be pieced together. And the image that emerges is not simply a terrorist organization, but a political faction that reflected the concerns and ideals of many Chinese during the troubled Nanking decade. . . .

The Blue Shirt organization was formed in early 1932 at a time when Chinese of virtually every political hue felt disillusionment and frustration at the seemingly irreversible decline of the nation. Only four years earlier, in 1927 and 1928, there had been a brief period of optimism, for many had thought that the new government established under the aegis of the Kuomintang would cope with the nation's problems. But the Kuomintang failed to create an effective administration or to restore political stability. Corruption seeped through the bureaucracy; factional struggles erupted repeatedly into civil wars; and political repression replaced popular support as the keystone of nationalist rule. By November 1931, Chiang Kai-shek himself confessed that "the revolution is in danger of failing, and the entire nation has gradually lost confidence in the Party." In December 1931, he bowed to political pressures, and resigned all of his governmental offices....

Chiang Kai-shek returned to Nanking on 21 January 1932, and he became a member of the newly formed Military Affairs Commission on the 29th—the day after the Japanese assault on Shanghai. It was during this last week of January that Chiang convoked a secret meeting in the offices of the Officers' Moral Endeavour Corps (*Li-chih she*), and the organization that became known as the Blue Shirts was instituted....

The appeal of fascism to the Blue Shirts was that it seemed to provide a proven and unambiguous method of attaining the goal of national salvation. "Fascism," read an editorial in the Blue Shirt organ, *She-hui hsin-wen,* "is the only tool of self-salvation of nations on the brink of destruction. It saved Italy and Germany.... Therefore, there is no other road than imitating the fascist spirit of violent struggle as in Italy and Germany." Chiang Kai-shek shared this enthusiasm for fascism. Addressing a gathering of Blue Shirts, he proclaimed that "fascism is...a stimulant for a declining, stagnant society. Can fascism save China? We answer: Yes! Fascism is what China now most needs. At the present stage of China's critical situation," Chiang continued, "fascism is a wonderful medicine exactly suited to China, and the only spirit that can save it."

The Blue Shirts' total exaltation of the nation was matched by their total abnegation of the individual. Ho Chung-han, who was perhaps the dominant figure in the Blue Shirt oligarchy beneath Chiang Kai-shek, called for the people to relinquish their freedom and even their lives so that the nation might be free. Only then, he said, could one speak of "true freedom...." The Blue Shirt goal was the totalitarian one of the individual's unqualified submission to the nation. He was to "perform his duties without speaking of his rights." Naturally, he would benefit if the nation became rich and strong. "But the individual definitely cannot impose conditions on society before serving."

The fascist principle of obedience to a supreme leader was an integral part of the Blue Shirt ideology. The Blue Shirt "Programme" read: "Chiang Kai-shek is the Kuomintang's only supreme leader and also China's only great leader; therefore, members must absolutely support him, follow his orders only, and make his will their own...."

Regardless of who conceived the original idea, the New Life Movement as it took form meshed precisely with the spirit and program of the Blue Shirts....

The New Life Movement was one means that Chiang Kai-shek and the Blue Shirts would use to implant this spirit—this fascist spirit—among the Chinese people. But it was a means that disguised the goal, for Chiang Kai-shek would use Confucianism, and even Christianity, in realizing his desired transformation of the nation.

It was an attenuated Confucianism that Chiang Kai-shek brought to the New Life Movement. It was a Confucianism for the masses, devoid of philosophical subtleties, stripped to its ethical essentials. It was a sloganized Confucianism, encapsulated for popular consumption in four vague virtues: *li-i-lien-ch'ih* (rendered loosely as "propriety, justice, honesty, and sense of self-respect")....

The models for this social movement were the fascist regimes of the West and the Japanese military academy. Chiang recalled his student days in Japan, convinced that the moral fibre of the cadets had been strengthened by the rigorous observance of barracks regulations. And he now hoped to recreate the entire Chinese nation in the image of a Japanese military academy. "In fascism, the organization, the spirit, and the activities must all be militarized.... In the home, the factory, and the government office, regardless of place, time, or situation, everyone's activities must be the same as in the army.... In other words, there must be obedience, sacrifice, strictness, cleanliness, accuracy, speed, diligence, secrecy... and everyone together must firmly and bravely sacrifice everything for the group and for the nation."

This vision of the whole of Chinese society performing with the discipline, obedience, and efficiency of a military academy was central to the New Life Movement. "What is the New Life Movement that I now propose?" Chiang inquired rhetorically. "Stated simply, it is to thoroughly militarize the lives of the citizens of the entire nation so that they can cultivate courage and swiftness, the endurance of suffering and a tolerance for hard work, and especially the habit and ability of unified action, so that they will at any time sacrifice for the nation."

The KMT Regime
by Theodore H. White and Annalee Jacoby

Chiang K'ai-shek was the chief architect of the new China that emerged. Occasionally, in fits of sulkiness, he would withdraw from the government for a few months to prove that only he could hold its diverse elements together; he always returned with greater prestige and strength than before. The new Kuomintang government was a dictatorship. It glossed itself with the phrases of Sun Yat-sen and claimed that it was the "trustee" of the people, who were in a state of "political tutelage." Its secret police were ubiquitous, while its censorship closed down like a vacuum pack over the Chinese press and Chinese universities. It held elections nowhere, for its conception of strengthening China was to strengthen itself, and it governed by fiat. This government rested on a four-legged stool—an army, a bureaucracy, the urban businessmen, the rural gentry.

The army was the darling of Chiang K'ai-shek. Chiang imported a corps of Prussian advisers to forge it into a powerful striking weapon. Its soldiers learned to goose-step, to use German rifles and artillery. Within the army was a praetorian guard consisting of the original group of Whampoa cadets. The young students of the military academy had been decimated in the early revolutionary battles, but those who survived were loyal to the Kuomintang before all else and faithful to Chiang as the symbol of the new China. As succeeding classes of students entered, the cadets rose in rank from captain to major to colonel. By the time the war against Japan broke out, an estimated forty of the Whampoa cadets were divisional commanders. About Chiang clustered a number of senior military men who shared his own background of war-lord education; they were men who belonged to no coherent group. They commanded the campaigns Chiang wished to fight, but never did they have any such affection or loyalty as he gave to the youths he trained himself. Chiang's army was the strongest ever seen in China. From 1929 to 1937 there was not a year when he was not engaged in civil war. The base of his strength was the lower Yangtze Valley, while all about him lay the provinces controlled by war lords. These individually and then in coalition challenged his rule, and one by one he would either buy them off or destroy them. He gradually brought central China as far as the gorges of the Yangtze under his control, until all China south of the Yellow River had acknowledged him as its overlord by the time the Japanese struck. . . .

As for Chiang, he hated the Japanese with the stubborn fury that is his greatest strength and his greatest fault. His armies, he felt, were unable to stop the Japanese army; China's industry could not match the modernized power of Japan's industry; China was disunited. He wanted to wipe out the Communists first, establish unity, and then face Japan. The new Communist slogan forced him into an intolerable position. Its logic was irrefutable; why should Chinese kill each other when a foreign enemy was seeking to kill all Chinese? The Kuomintang explained in whispers that it was only biding its time against the Japanese—that when it was ready it would turn and defend China. At the same time students were arrested and jailed for anti-Japanese parades and demonstrations. Chinese journalists and intellectuals stood aghast at what they saw. The threat of national annihilation from without became graver with every passing day; within, the government spent its resources not on resistance to Japan but on a Communist witch-hunt.

Both during the KMT-CCP civil war and during the national war against Japan, soldiers often had to be forcibly drafted to fight for the government side, as this sketch by journalist Graham Peck shows. Writing about the early 1940s, Peck describes a typical press-gang of Chinese peasants being marched through a small village to fight the Japanese—or perhaps the Communists.

KMT Soldiers
by Graham Peck

The human cost of this cruel joke of a government could be seen most clearly in the military traffic which passed through Shuangshihpu on foot. Armies on the move came over the mountains often while I was living there. Every time, their order of march was the same.

First came the commander on horseback, with his tasseled sash and ornamental sword. Next came his higher officers, afoot or on horseback, with their gear carried by orderlies. Then, between an armed guard of junior officers or trusted enlisted men, came a long line of peasants kidnaped to carry the field ovens and other heavy equipment.

The enlisted men followed the carriers, sometimes walking in step, sometimes just slogging ahead in the uneven, rolling motion of a mob. They were always burdened with field equipment, plus whatever bedding or furniture or food they personally owned, but I never saw them carrying their guns. The weapons followed in conscripted farm carts, safely out of reach of the men. The escape of any enlisted men was guarded against by as large an escort of armed officers and trusties as watched the peasant carriers.

It was easy to see that they might want to escape. Except for a sprinkling of lean, leathery veterans who would boast they had been campaigning since the years of the warlords and were satisfied with the only life they knew, almost all passed with faces marked by pain or worry. Usually their limbs were emaciated, thickened at wrist and ankle by undernourishment. Their eyes were mattered or feverish, their swollen feet often bound with bloody rags.

Behind the last of the armed guards followed the scarecrow march of the very weak, sick, or dying soldiers. They need not be guarded. Unless they had the strength to catch up with the others, they would be no use to the army. And the more hopeless their condition, the less likely their attempt to escape, since there was less chance that they could ever make their way back to their distant families or anyone else who would care for them. It was a well-established Kuomintang policy to send new conscripts into armies so far from their homes that they could not desert with much hope of getting back. For miles after the main column, the road would be littered with wretched men, tottering and even crawling along, in the effort to keep up with the field kitchens which were their only source of food.

These were seldom troops who were suffering their way to the front to throw their last strength against the invaders. They were more often provincial armies who never had faced the Japanese, and probably never would. They were pawns juggled back and forth in the Kuomintang's dreary game of internal power-politics, and the purpose of their suffering was to reduce the strength of this or that regional nabob, to build up a garrison of outsiders in some rear area, to increase the national weakness and disunity from which the Kuomintang drew its strength. The guns carted along with them were to awe and quiet the peasants where they were sent.

Several times that spring, batches of new conscripts were herded through Shuangshihpu, and since they had not the training which gave a soldier's life a minimum value to his masters, they were treated with a more casual brutality. The worst group I saw was about one hundred and fifty men who had already been goaded up several hundred miles of highway from Chengtu and had another hundred or more ahead of them before they reached their "training camp" in Sian.

I shall never forget the afternoon they were herded into the village. It was splendid sunny weather, the hills burning red and green, the sky like peacock glass, snow rimming the highest summits. Slowly around a bend in the yellow road staggered the long line of spectres, their flapping black rags thick with dust, their faces gleaming pale as the distant snow. They were roped together, of course, and they cruelly jerked and cut each other as they lurched about. Many seemed delirious, staring wildly and talking to themselves. Some inhumanity toward conscripts was usual enough to go unremarked but this was a surpassing case, and there was a startled hush on the busy Shuangshihpu street as their guards drove the groaning, panting, gibbering creatures into the barns which had been requisitioned as their night's lodging.

That evening there was much gossip, interested if not indignant, and the stories of those who had talked to the conscripts or their guards were widely circulated. It was said they were opium smokers, beggars, and other riffraff cleaned off the streets of Chengtu for the New Life Movement. They had been sent on this walking trip with the idea that most of them would die and the rest of them become real conscripts. The villagers who lived near the requisitioned barns reported they were given no bedding. Coming from frostless Chengtu, dressed in thin cotton, many had already become sick during the freezing mountain nights. It was also reported they were fed nothing but a little porridge made chiefly of water. Some said the guards had admitted to underfeeding them by policy, to make them so weak they would not try to escape.

But the conscripts still had one way out. Next morning, before the party was whipped off again, the guards laid out on the riverbank, then thriftily stripped, the frail bony corpses of four starved and exhausted men.

The Long March

When Chiang Kai'shek's fifth "Bandit Suppression" campaign in 1934 convinced the Communists to leave their mountain bases in southern China, some believed that this was the end. Chiang's claim to have eradicated Communism was certainly credible in view of the short history of the Chinese Communist party from 1927 to 1934. The Communists had been caught unprepared in Shanghai, Canton, and many other cities, and had been driven out with high losses. They retreated to the mountains after failing to capture a single city. Finally they had been surrounded and nearly destroyed in the mountains in 1934. Their chances for survival looked grim indeed.

Yet their retreat from southern China, known as the Long March, proved to be a crucial event in the Communists' path to eventual victory. At the end of their trek, they were able at last to establish a firm base against the Kuomintang military forces. The Long March itself contributed to the growing reputation of the Communists and the People's Liberation Army as just, courageous, and truly nationalist. The Long March also marked the consolidation of Mao's leadership of the party. Many others who made and survived

THE LONG MARCH
1934-35

≡≡≡ Communist areas in South
▓▓▓ Communist area in Shensi
⟶ Route of main Communist force
   from Juichin area
--▸ Route of subordinate Communist
   forces from other areas

Miles
100   300   500
   200   400

the Long March became leaders of People's China after 1949: Chou En-lai, Chu Teh, Lin Piao. Included here are descriptions of the course of the march and some of its most dramatic episodes, as well as the "Eight Rules" followed by the PLA.

Retreat from Kiangsi
by Edgar Snow*

It was not until the seventh year of the fighting against the Reds that any notable success crowned the attempts to destroy them. The Reds then had actual administrative control over a great part of Kiangsi, and large areas of Fukien and Hunan. There were other Soviet districts, not physically connected with the Kiangsi territory, located in the provinces of Hunan, Hupeh, Honan, Anhui, Szechuan, and Shensi.

Against the Reds, in the Fifth Campaign, Chiang Kai-shek mobilized about 900,000 troops, of whom perhaps 400,000—some 360 regiments—actively took part in the warfare in the Kiangsi-Fukien area, and against the Red Army in the Anhui-Honan-Hupeh (Oyüwan) area. But Kiangsi was the pivot of the whole campaign. Here the regular Red Army was able to mobilize a combined strength of 180,000 men, including all reserve divisions, and it had perhaps 200,000 partisan and Red Guards, but altogether could muster a firing power of somewhat less than 100,000 rifles, no heavy artillery, and a very limited supply of grenades, shells, and ammunition, all of which were now being made in the Red arsenal at Juichin.

Chiang adopted a new strategy to make the fullest use of his greatest assets—superior resources, technical equipment, access to unlimited supplies from the outside world (to which the Reds had no outlet), mechanized warfare, and a modern air force that had come to comprise nearly 400 navigable war planes. The Reds had captured a few of Chiang's aeroplanes, and they had three or four pilots, but they lacked petrol, bombs, and mechanics. Instead of an invasion of the Red districts and an attempt to take them

---

*Snow, *Red Star Over China*.

by storm of superior force, which had in the past proved disastrous, Chiang now used the majority of his troops to surround the "bandits" and impose on them a strict economic blockade. It was, therefore, primarily a war of exhaustion.

And it was very costly. Chiang Kai-shek built hundreds of miles of military roads and thousands of small fortifications, which were made connectable by machine-gun or artillery fire. His defensive-offensive strategy and tactics tended to diminish the Reds' superiority in manoeuvring, and emphasized the disadvantages of their smaller numbers and lack of resources. In effect, in his famous Fifth Campaign, the Generalissimo built a kind of Great Wall round the Soviet districts, which gradually moved inward. Its ultimate aim was to encompass and crush the Red Army in a stone vise. . . .

The Fifth Campaign is said to have been planned largely by Chiang Kai-shek's German advisers, notably General Von Falkenhausen, of the German army, and for a while the Generalissimo's chief adviser. The new tactics were thorough, but they were also very slow and expensive. Operations dragged on for months and still Nanking had not struck a decisive blow at the main forces of its enemy. The effect of the blockade, however, was seriously felt in the Red districts, and especially the total absence of salt. The little Red base was becoming inadequate to repel the combined military and economic pressure being applied against it. The Reds deny it, but I suspect that considerable exploitation of the peasantry must have been necessary to maintain the astonishing year of resistance which was put up during the campaign. At the same time, it must be remembered that their fighters were mostly enfranchised peasants and proud owners of newly acquired land. For land alone, most peasants in China will fight to the death. The Kiangsi people knew that return of the Kuomintang meant return of the landlords.

Nanking believed that its efforts at annihilation were about to succeed. The enemy was caged and could not escape. Thousands of peasants had been killed in the daily bombing and machine-gunning from the air, as well as by "purgations" in districts reoccupied by the Kuomintang. The Red Army itself, according to Chou En-lai, suffered over 60,000 casualties in this one siege, and sacrifice of life among the civilian population was terrific. Whole areas were depopulated, sometimes by forced mass migrations, sometimes by the simpler expedient of mass executions. The Kuomintang itself admitted that about 1,000,000 people were killed or starved to death in the process of recovering Soviet Kiangsi.

Nevertheless, the Fifth Campaign proved inconclusive. It failed in its objective, which was to destroy the living forces of the Red Army. A Red military conference was called at Juichin, and it was decided to withdraw, transferring the main Red strength to a new base. The plans for this great expedition, which was to last a whole year, were complete and efficient. They perhaps revealed a certain military genius that the Reds had not shown during their periods of offensive. For it is one thing to command a victorious advancing army, and quite another to carry through to success a plan calling for retreat under such handicaps as those which lay ahead in the now famous Long March to the North-west.

The retreat from Kiangsi evidently was so swiftly and secretly managed that the main forces of the Red troops, estimated at about 90,000 men, had already been marching for several days before the enemy headquarters became aware of what was taking place. They had mobilized in southern Kiangsi, withdrawing most of their regular troops from the northern front, and replacing them with partisans. Those movements occurred always at night. When practically the whole Red Army was concentrated near Yütu, in southern Kiangsi, the order was given for the Great March, which began on October 16, 1934.

For three nights the Reds pressed in two columns to the west and to the south. On the fourth they advanced, totally unexpectedly, almost simultaneously attacking the Hunan and Kwangtung lines of fortifications. They took these by assault, put their astonished enemy on the run, and never stopped until they had occupied the ribbon of blockading forts and entrenchments on the southern front. This gave them roads to the south and to the west, along which their vanguard began its sensational trek.

Besides the main strength of the army, thousands of Red peasants began this march—old and young, men, women, children, Communists and non-Communists. The arsenal was stripped, the factories were dismantled, machinery was loaded onto mules and donkeys—everything that was portable and of value went with this strange cavalcade. As the march lengthened out, much of this burden had to be discarded, and the Reds tell you today that thousands of rifles and machine-guns, much machinery, much ammunition, even much silver, lies buried on their long trail from the south. Some day in the future, they say, Red peasants, now surrounded by thousands of policing troops, will dig it up again. They await only the signal—and the war with Japan may prove to be that beacon.

After the main forces of the Red Army evacuated Kiangsi, it was still many weeks before Nanking troops succeeded in occupying the chief Red cities. Thousands of peasant guards and partisans, held together and led by a few Red regulars, put up a stiff resistance till the end. The heroism of many of these Red leaders, who volunteered to stay behind for self-immolation, is memorialized in many ways by the Reds today. They provided the rearguard action which enabled the main forces to get well under way before Nanking could mobilize sufficient forces to surround and annihilate them on the march.

Tibor Mende works for the United Nations in Europe and is a well-known journalist.

North to Shensi

by Tibor Mende

The Communists realized that the ring was closing around them. Their hope that from Kiangsi they could spread out all over China, lay shattered. To avoid annihilation, and after much deliberation, they decided to abandon Kiangsi, to try to break through the tight blockade, and so to carry with them the Soviet Republic to a new and more secure base.

Their choice fell on the Northern province of Shensi. There, in the great bend of the Yellow River, they knew of the existence of another Communist group. But to get there by the direct route, about twelve hundred miles long, would have been impossible. It led across regions where the Kuomintang was in full control. Instead, it was decided to try a roundabout way which would lead through areas where, owing to distance and the difficulty of the terrain, the Kuomintang's control was partial only.

Once the Communists were dislodged from Kiangsi, however, the Kuomintang was triumphant. As in 1927, so in 1934 again, its press and radio announced the final annihilation of the Communists and the end of the danger they represented for the Nationalist regime.

What really had happened was rather different.

The evacuation of the Kiangsi region began in October 1934. At the cost of some hard fighting the bulk of the Red Army managed to break through the concentric lines of besieging troops. They had to move southwest before they could head westward in the direction of the Tibetan borderlands. Thrown back toward the South, they changed direction and crossed the upper Yangtze. Continuing their northward advance, they again had to fight hard battles in order to cross the Tatu River. Beyond it, following the Szechwan border over difficult mountainous country, the trek led through the northwestern Moslem areas and from there over some of the most desolate regions of Kansu province. Finally, about a year after their departure from Kiangsi, the tattered remnants of the Communist armies reached the remote northern part of Shensi. There, at last, they could join up with the guerrilla forces in control of the region.

This prodigious feat of endurance became known as the Long March. It involved an organized trek of some eight thousand miles within a year. It led across eleven provinces, over remote regions inhabited by suspicious peoples, through murderous marshy lands overgrown by grass, and in face of continuous danger from local and governmental forces. It is claimed that the three Communist armies who participated in the march crossed eighteen mountain chains and twenty-four large rivers, broke through the armies of ten warlords, defeated dozens of Kuomintang regiments, and took temporarily sixty-two cities.

The basic aim, to save the Revolution, was thus achieved. But the price was heavy. Of the 130,000 men who had left Kiangsi and Hunan, fewer than 30,000 arrived in north Shensi. Some deserted on the way, intimidated by hardship. Many more perished in battle or succumbed to fatigue, frost, or to the other rigors of a hostile nature. Of several hundred women, no more than thirty survived. Among those who perished was Mao Tse-tung's wife. But those who reached Shensi constituted a hard core of tempered steel, a reliable and disciplined force with which to build the new Soviet Republic.

Three factors connected with the Long March were to help that task.

The first concerned Communist prestige. The Kuomintang continued to claim that the Communists had succumbed and ceased to represent any threat. Its press was tightly controlled and public opinion was preoccupied with Japan's moves so that few people were aware of the historic events in the remote interior of the country. Yet the epic story of the Long March was fast growing into a legend. Its incidents became the themes of songs and stories. Slowly what really had happened became known and the heroes of such a performance could hardly be described any longer as the unprincipled bandits of the Kuomintang's propaganda. On the contrary, a new prestige, springing from the admiration due to national heroes, was beginning to surround the Communists' enterprise.

The second factor was the new, total cohesion of the Communist party. Next to the Kiangsi Soviet there had existed other Communist-controlled areas and not all of them had been unconditional in their acceptance of Mao's leadership. As the various groups had joined up with the Long March, a number of political meetings had been held on the way which gradually helped to eliminate existing differences. By the time the Communists reached their destination, the military and political leaders had won unanimous support and Mao Tse-tung's "line" and leadership of the Party emerged uncontested.

The third factor was the human experience the Long March had provided. Like an involuntary and monumental study tour, it splendidly completed the Communists' already unrivaled knowledge of the Chinese peasant's psychology. It brought them into contact with new regions and different peoples. Disseminating their ideas among them on their way, they also learned a great deal about the problems and the attitudes of masses they were destined to govern later on. As a significant by-product of the experience, for the first time, the Long March brought the

Communists into direct contact with the "national minorities" of the Southwest and of the Western regions and rendered both sides conscious of their ideas and aims.

Thus, with their moral stature grown but physically and numerically weakened, the Communists began to organize their new base.

The Red Army Crosses the Tatu River
by Edgar Snow*

Moving rapidly northward from the Gold Sand River (as the Yangtze there is known) into Szechuan, they soon entered the tribal country of warlike aborigines, the White and Black Lolos of Independent Lololand. Never conquered, never absorbed by the Chinese who dwell all round them, the turbulent Lolos have for centuries occupied that densely forested and mountainous spur of Szechuan whose borders are marked by the great southward arc described by the Yangtze just east of Tibet. Chiang Kai-shek confidently counted on a long delay and weakening of the Reds here which would enable him to concentrate north of the Tatu. Lolo hatred of the Chinese is traditional, and rarely has any Chinese army crossed their borders without heavy losses or extermination.

But the Reds had a method. They had already safely passed through the tribal districts of the Miao and the Shan peoples, aborigines of Kweichow and Yunnan, and had won their friendship and even enlisted some tribesmen in their army. Now they sent envoys ahead to parley with the Lolos. *En route,* they captured several towns on the borders of Independent Lololand, where they found a number of Lolo chieftains who had been imprisoned as hostages by the Chinese militarists. Freed and sent back to their people, these men naturally praised the Reds.

In the vanguard of the Red Army was Commander Liu Pei-ch'eng, who had once been an officer in a warlord army of Szechuan. Liu knew the tribal people, and their inner feuds and discontent. Especially he knew their hatred of Chinese, and he could speak something of the

---

*Snow, *Red Star Over China*.

Lolo tongue. Assigned the task of negotiating a friendly alliance, he entered their territory and went into conference with the chieftains. The Lolos, he said, opposed Warlords Liu Hsiang and Liu Wen-hui and the Kuomintang; so did the Reds. The Lolos wanted to preserve their independence; Red policies favoured autonomy for all the national minorities of China. The Lolos hated the Chinese because they had been oppressed by them; but there were "White Chinese" and "Red Chinese," just as there were White Lolos and Black Lolos, and it was the White Chinese who had always slain and oppressed the Lolos. Should not the Red Chinese and the Black Lolos unite against their common enemies, the White Chinese? The Lolos listened interestedly. Slyly they asked for arms and bullets to guard their independence and help Red Chinese fight the Whites. To their astonishment, the Reds gave them both.

And so it happened that not only a speedy but a safe and pleasant passage was accomplished. Hundreds of Lolos enlisted with the "Red Chinese" to march to the Tatu River and fight the common enemy. Some of those Lolos were to trek clear to the North-west. Liu Pei-ch'eng drank the blood of a newly killed chicken before the high chieftain of the Lolos, who drank also, and they swore blood brotherhood in the tribal manner. By this vow the Reds declared that whosoever should violate the terms of their alliance would be even as weak and cowardly as the fowl that they had killed.

Thus a vanguard division of the First Army Corps. led by Lin Piao, reached the Tatu Ho. On the last day of the march they emerged from the forests of Lololand (in the thick foliage of which Nanking pilots had completely lost track of them), to descend suddenly on the river town of An Jen Ch'ang—just as unheralded as they had come into Chou P'ing Fort. Guided over narrow mountain trails by the Lolos, the vanguard crept quietly up to the little town, and from the heights looked down to the river-bank, and saw with amazement and delight one of the three ferry-boats made fast on the *south* bank of the river! Once more an act of fate had befriended them.

How did it happen? Now, on the opposite shore, there was only one regiment of the troops of General Liu Wen-hui, the co-dictator of Szechuan province. Other

Szechuan troops, as well as reinforcements from Nanking, were leisurely proceeding towards the Tatu, but the single regiment meanwhile was enough. A squad should have been ample, indeed, with all boats moored to the north. But the commander of the regiment was a native of the district; he knew the country the Reds must pass through, and how long it would take them to penetrate to the river. They would be many days yet, he told his men. And his wife, you see, had been a native of An Jen Ch'ang, so he must cross to the south bank to visit his relatives and his friends and to feast with them. Thus it happened that the Reds, taking the town by surprise, captured the commander, his boat, and secured their passage to the north.

Sixteen men from each of five companies volunteered to cross in the first boat and bring back the others, while on the south bank the Reds set up machine-guns on the mountain-sides and over the river spread a screen of protective fire concentrated on the enemy's exposed positions. It was May. Floods poured down the mountains, and the river was swift and even wider than the Yangtze. Starting far upstream, the ferry took two hours to cross and land just opposite the town. From the south bank the villagers of An Jen Ch'ang watched breathlessly. They would be wiped out! But wait. They saw the voyagers land almost beneath the guns of the enemy. Now, surely, they would be finished. And yet . . . From the south bank the Red machine guns barked on. The onlookers saw the little party climb ashore, hurriedly take cover, then slowly work their way up a steep cliff overhanging the enemy's positions. There they set up their own light machine-guns, and sent a downpour of lead and hand grenades into the enemy redoubts along the river.

Suddenly the White troops ceased firing, broke from their redoubts, and fled to a second and then a third line of defence. A great murmur went up from the south bank, and shouts of *"Hao!"* drifted across the river to the little band who had captured the ferry landing. Meanwhile the first boat returned, towing two others, and on the second trip each carried eighty men. The enemy had fled. That day and night, and the next, and the next, those three ferries of An Jen Ch'ang worked back and forth, until at last nearly a division had been transferred to the northern bank.

But the river flowed faster and faster. The crossing became more and more difficult. On the third day it took four hours to shift a boatload of men from shore to shore! At this rate it would be weeks before the whole army and its animals and supplies could be moved. Long before the operation was completed they would be encirled. The First Army Corps had now crowded into An Jen Ch'ang, and behind were the flanking columns, and the transport and rear-guard. Chiang Kai-shek's aeroplanes had found the spot, and heavily bombed it. Enemy troops were racing up from the south-east; others approached from the north. A hurried military conference was summoned by Lin Piao. Chu Teh, Mao Tse-tung, Chou En-lai, and Peng Teh-huai had by now reached the river. They took a decision, and began to carry it out at once.

Some 400 *li* to the west of An Jen Ch'ang, where the gorges rise very high and the river flows narrow, deep, and swift, there is a famous iron-chain suspension bridge called the Liu Ting Chiao—the Bridge Fixed by Liu. It is the last possible crossing of the Tatu east of Tibet. Towards this the barefoot Reds now set out along a trail that wound through the gorges, at times climbing several thousand feet, again dropping low to the level of the swollen stream itself, and wallowing through waist-deep mud. If they captured the Liu Ting Chiao the whole army could enter central Szechuan. And if they failed? If they failed they would have to retrace their steps through Lololand, re-enter Yunnan, and fight their way westward towards Likiang, on the Tibetan border—a detour of more than a thousand *li*, which few might hope to survive.

As their main forces pushed westward along the southern bank, the Red division already on the northern bank moved also. Sometimes the gorges between them closed so narrowly that the two lines of Reds could shout to each other across the stream; sometimes that gulf between them measured their fear that the Tatu might separate them for ever, and they stepped more swiftly. As they wound in long dragon files along the cliffs at night their 10,000 torches sent arrows of light slanting down the dark, inscrutable face of the imprisoning river. Day and night these vanguards moved at double-quick, pausing only for brief ten-minute rests and meals, when the soldiers listened to lectures by their weary political workers, who over and over again explained the importance of this one action, exhorting each to give his last breath, his last urgent strength, for victory in the test ahead of them. There could be no slackening of pace, no half-heartedness, no fatigue. Victory was life; defeat, certain death.

On the second day the vanguard on the right bank fell behind. Szechuan troops had set up positions in the road and skirmishes took place. Those on the southern bank pressed on more grimly. Presently new troops appeared on the opposite bank, and through their field-glasses the Reds saw that they were White reinforcements, hurrying to the Bridge Fixed by Liu! For a whole day these troops raced each other along the stream, but gradually the Red vanguard, the pick of all the Red Army, pulled away from the enemy's tired soldiers, whose rests were longer and more frequent, whose energy seemed more spent, and who after all were none to anxious to die over a bridge.

The Bridge Fixed by Liu was built centuries ago, and in the manner of all bridges of the deep rivers of Western China. Sixteen heavy iron chains, with a span of some 100 yards or more, were stretched across the river, their ends inbedded on each side under great piles of cemented rock, beneath the stone bridgeheads. Thick boards lashed over the chains made the road of the bridge, but upon their arrival the Reds found that half this wooden flooring had been removed, and before them only the bare iron chains swung to a point midway in the stream. At the northern bridgehead an enemy machine-gun nest faced them, and behind it were positions held by a regiment of White troops. Now that bridge should, of course, have been destroyed. But the Szechuanese are sentimental about their few bridges; it is not easy to rebuild them, and they are costly. Of Liu Ting it was said that "the wealth of the eighteen provinces contributed to build it." And, anyway, who should have thought the Reds would insanely try to cross on the chains alone? But that is just what they did.

No time was to be lost. The bridge must be captured before enemy reinforcements arrived. Once more volunteers were called for. One by one Red soldiers stepped forward to risk their lives, and, of those who offered themselves, thirty were chosen. Hand grenades and Mausers were strapped to their backs, and soon they were swinging out above the boiling river, moving hand over hand, clinging to the iron chains. Red machine-guns barked at the enemy redoubts and spattered the bridgehead with bullets. The enemy replied with machine-gunning of its own, and snipers shot at the Reds tossing high above the water, working slowly towards them. The first warrior was hit, and dropped into the current below; a second fell, and then a third. But as they drew nearer the chains, the bridge flooring somewhat protected these dare-to-dies, and most of the enemy bullets glanced off, or ended in the cliffs on the opposite bank.

Never before had the Szechuanese seen Chinese fighters like these—men for whom soldiering was not just a rice-bowl, but youths ready to commit suicide to win! Were they human beings or madmen or gods? wondered the superstitious Szechuanese. Their own morale was affected; perhaps they did not shoot to kill; perhaps some of them secretly prayed that they would succeed in their attempt! At last one Red crawled up over the bridge flooring, uncapped a grenade, and tossed it with perfect aim into the enemy redoubt. Desperate, the officers ordered the rest of the planking to be torn up. It was already too late. More Reds were crawling into sight. Paraffin was thrown on the planking, and it began to burn. By then about twenty Reds were moving forward on their hands and knees, tossing grenade after grenade into the enemy machine-gun nest.

Suddenly, on the southern shore, their comrades began to scream with joy. "Long live the Red Army! Long live the Revolution! Long live the thirty heroes of Tatu Ho!" For the Whites were withdrawing, were in pell-mell flight! Running full speed over the remaining planks of the bridge, right through the flames licking towards them, the assailants nimbly hopped into the enemy's redoubt and turned the abandoned machine-gun against the shore.

More Reds now swarmed over the chains, and arrived to help put out the fire and replace the boards. And soon afterwards the Red division that had crossed at An Jen Ch'ang came into sight, opening a flank attack on the remaining enemy positions, so that in a little while the White troops were wholly in flight—either in flight, that is, or with the Reds, for about a hundred Szechuan soldiers here threw down their rifles and turned to join their pursuers. In an hour or two the whole army was joyously tramping and singing its way across the River Tatu into Szechuan. Far overhead angrily and impotently roared the planes of Chiang Kai-shek, and the Reds cried out in delirious challenge to them. As the Communist troops poured over the river, these planes tried to hit the bridge, but their bombs only made pretty splashes in the river.

Eight Points of the People's Liberation Army
by Anne C. Fremantle

In its severe mountain isolation, the Red Army grew in discipline, though Mao wrote sadly at least once of their loneliness. He enforced three rules on all Red soldiers: prompt obedience to every order; no confiscation from peasants; prompt delivery to headquarters of all goods confiscated from landlords. To these three were added the Eight Points, which still have to be memorized by every Red soldier, and repeated daily, as well as being frequently sung as a Red Army song. These Eight Points were (and are):

1. Replace all doors when you leave a house (the wooden doors of the Chinese houses are easily detachable and are often taken down at night, set on blocks, and used as beds). Later this became simply: Replace any article used.
2. Roll up and return the straw matting on which you sleep.
3. Be courteous and help out when you can.
4. Return all borrowed articles.
5. Replace all damaged articles.
6. Be honest in all transactions with the peasants.
7. Pay for all articles purchased.
8. Be sanitary, and especially establish latrines at a distance from people's houses.

NEW CHINA

1937 to the Present

Introduction

From the moment the Communists arrived in Yenan in 1935, all their energies went into two closely related tasks: defeating Japan and uniting the Chinese people around their leadership. The first half of Part IV covers the years from the Long March to Liberation, 1937–1949, in which both these goals were accomplished and the People's Republic was born. The selections were chosen primarily because they help in understanding a very basic question: why did the Communists win?

Seen in hindsight, the Communist victory sometimes seems almost inevitable—as though the Red leaders in Yenan had drawn up a blueprint and then confidently proceeded to carry it through. Mao Tse-tung and the Communists certainly believed firmly that socialism was the correct path for China and that they would eventually win against both the invading Japanese and the Kuomintang. But when World War II ended and the civil war began again, the Communists were prepared to fight for many years. In fact, they were surprised at the speed of their victory; after less than four years of further fighting, the Nationalist government collapsed in 1948–1949 and Chiang Kai-shek fled to Taiwan. On October 1, 1949, Mao stood on Tien An Men square in Peking to announce the establishment of the People's Republic.

The Communist victory came as a shock to many foreign nations, and especially to the United States, which had given large amounts of aid to Chiang's government. Chiang's defeat sparked a bitter debate inside America over why the Communists had won. In the "witch-hunting" years of the anti-Communist McCarthy era, some Americans were blamed for having permitted China to "go Red." Yet it is now clear that the success of the Chinese Communist party was due to their own programs of socialist revolution, mobilization, and organization of the Chinese people—all internal factors over which Americans had little or no effect. Nonetheless, following 1949 the U.S. attitude hardened into an anti-Chinese stand that continued until the 1970s.

With Liberation in 1949 China began the immense task of rebuilding a land devastated by decades of foreign and civil war. Farmland was distributed to millions of poor peasants and basic social reforms begun in the areas of women's rights, mass education, medicine, housing. Economically, large efforts were directed toward building an industrial base, which was begun in the 1950s, with Russian aid. Since the Great Leap Forward, China's continuing progress has provided a decent and equal standard of living for her people. The three major campaigns—the Great Leap Forward, the Cultural Revolution, and the smashing of the Gang of Four—are discussed in the later section of Part IV, together with the foreign policy developments which have seen China's emergence as an independent and influential power.

Life in the Liberated Areas of the Northwest

In late 1935, an exhausted and nearly decimated band of Communists ended the Long March in the northwestern province of Shensi. For most of the next thirteen years the city of Yenan was their capital, and this "Yenan period" saw the shaping of the Chinese Communist party; here ideas were developed which later became the basis of New China. The story of these years was recorded not only by the Communists themselves but also by a number of American journalists who traveled and lived in both the Red and KMT territories. In these selections Edgar Snow writes of the men, women, and children he met in the Red Army and recalls his impressions on first meeting in Yenan with Mao Tse-tung; then Li Yiu-hua and Mau Ke-yeh, two peasants from the northwest, recall the roles played by the landlords and the KMT in their village. At the end we have included some of Mao Tse-tung's poems from these years. In China Mao is rightly famed for his literary talent as well as for his political leadership.

Little Red Devils

by Edgar Snow*

Half-way round the crenellated battlement I came upon a squad of buglers—at rest for once, I was glad to observe, for their plangent calls had been ringing incessantly for days. They were all Young Vanguards, mere children, and I assumed a somewhat fatherly air towards one to whom I stopped and talked. He wore tennis shoes, grey shorts, and a faded grey cap with a dim red star on it. But there was nothing faded about the bugler under the cap: he was rosy-faced and had bright shining eyes, a lad towards whom your heart naturally warmed as towards a plucky waif in need of affection and a friend. How homesick he must be! I thought. I was soon disillusioned. He was no mama's boy, but already a veteran Red. He told me he was fifteen, and that he had joined the Reds in the South four years ago.

"Four years!" I exclaimed incredulously. "Then you must have been only eleven when you became a Red? And you made the Long March?"

"Right," he responded with comical swagger. "I have been a *hung-chun* for four years."

"Why did you join?" I asked.

"My family lived near Changchow, in Fukien. I used to cut wood in the mountains, and in the winter I went there to collect bark. I often heard the villagers talk about the Red Army. They said it helped the poor people, and I liked that. Our house was very poor. We were six people, my parents and three brothers, older than I. We owned no land. Rent ate more than half our crop, so we never had enough. In the winter we cooked bark for soup and saved our grain for planting in the spring. I was always hungry.

"One year the Reds came very close to Changchow. I climbed over the mountains and went to ask them to help our house because we were very poor. They were good to me. They sent me to school for a while, and I had plenty

---

*Snow, *Red Star Over China*.

to eat. After a few months the Red Army captured Changchow, and went to my village. All the landlords and money-lenders and officials were driven out. My family was given land and did not have to pay the tax-collectors and landlords any more. They were happy and they were proud of me. Two of my brothers joined the Red Army."

"Where are they now?"

"Now? I don't know. When we left Kiangsi they were with the Red Army in Fukien; they were with Fang Chih-min. Now, I don't know."

"Did the peasants like the Red Army?"

"Like the Red Army, eh? Of course they liked it. The Red Army gave them land and drove away the landlords, the tax-collectors, and the exploiters." (These "little devils" all had their Marxist vocabulary.)

"But, really, how do you *know* they liked the Reds?"

"They made us a thousand, ten thousands, of shoes, with their own hands. The women made uniforms for us, and the men spied on the enemy. Every home sent sons to our Red Army. That is how the *lao-pai-hsing* treated us!"

No need to ask him whether *he* liked his comrades: no lad of thirteen would tramp 6,000 miles with an army he hated.

Scores of youngsters like him were with the Reds. The Young Vanguards were organized by the Communist Youth League, and altogether, according to the claims of Fang Wen-ping, secretary of the C.Y.L., there were then some 40,000 in the North-west Soviet districts. There must have been several hundred with the Red Army alone: a "model company" of them was in every Red encampment. They were youths between twelve and seventeen (really eleven to sixteen by foreign count), and they came from all over China. Many of them, like this little bugler, survived the hardships of the march from the South. Many joined the Red Army during its expedition to Shansi.

The young Vanguards worked as orderlies, messboys, buglers, spies, radio-operators, water-carriers, propagandists, actors, *mafoos*, nurses, secretaries, and even teachers! I once saw such a youngster, before a big map, lecturing a class of new recruits on world geography. Two of the most graceful child dancers I have ever seen were Young Vanguards in the dramatic society of the First Army Corps, and had marched from Kiangsi.

You might wonder how they stood such a life. Hundreds must have died or been killed. There were over 200 of them in the filthy jail in Sianfu, who had been captured doing espionage or propaganda, or as stragglers unable to keep up with the army on its march. But their fortitude was amazing, and their loyalty to the Red Army was the intense and unquestioning loyalty of the very young.

Most of them wore uniforms too big for them, with sleeves dangling to their knees and coats dragging nearly to the ground. They washed their hands and faces three times a day, they claimed, but they were always dirty, their noses were usually running, and they were often wiping them with a sleeve, and grinning. The world nevertheless was theirs: they had enough to eat, they had a blanket each, the leaders even had pistols, and they wore red bars, and broken-peaked caps a size or more too large, but with the red star on it. They were often of uncertain origin: many could not remember their parents, many were escaped apprentices, some had been slaves, most of them were runaways from huts with too many mouths to feed, and all of them had made their own decisions to join, sometimes a whole group of youngsters running off to the Reds together.

Many stories of courage were told of them. They gave and asked no quarter as children, and many had actually participated in battles. They say that in Kiangsi, after the main Red Army left, hundreds of Young Vanguards and Young Communists fought with the partisans, and even made bayonet charges—so that the White soldiers laughingly said they could grab their bayonets and pull them into their trenches, they were so small and light. Many of the captured "Reds" in Chiang's reform schools for bandits in Kiangsi were youths from ten to fifteen years old.

Perhaps the Vanguards liked the Reds because among them they were treated like human beings probably for the first time. They ate and lived like men; they seemed to take part in everything; they considered themselves any man's equal. I never saw one of them struck or bullied. They were certainly "exploited" as orderlies and messboys (and it was surprising how many orders starting at the top were eventually passed on to some Young Vanguard), but they had their own freedom of activity, too, and their own organization to protect them. They learned games and sports, they were given a crude schooling, and they acquired a faith in simple Marxist slogans—which in most cases meant to them simply helping to shoot a gun against the landlords and masters of apprentices. Obviously it was better than working fourteen hours a day at the master's bench, and feeding him, and emptying his "defile-mother" night-bowl!

I remember one such escaped apprentice I met in Kansu who was nicknamed the Shansi Wa-wa—the Shansi Baby. He had been sold to a shop in a town near Hung T'ung, in Shansi, and when the Red Army came he had stolen over the city wall, with three other apprentices, to join it. How he had decided that he belonged with the Reds I do not know, but evidently all of Yen Hsi-shan's anti-Communist propaganda, all the writings of his elders, had produced exactly the opposite effect from that intended. He was a fat roly-poly lad with the face of a baby, and only twelve, but he was quite able to take care of himself, as he had proved during the march across Shansi and Shensi and into Kansu. When I asked him why he had become a Red he said: "The Red Army fights for the poor. The Red Army is anti-Japanese. Why should any man not want to become a Red soldier?"

Another time I met a bony youngster of fifteen, who was head of the Young Vanguards and Young Communists working in the hospital near Holienwan, Kansu. His home had been in Hsing Kuo, the Reds' model *hsien* in Kiangsi, and he said that one of his brothers was still in a partisan army there, and that his sister had been a nurse. He did not know what had become of his family. Yes, they all liked the Reds. Why? Because they "all understood that the Red Army was our army—fighting for the *wu-ch'an chieh-chi*" —the proletariat. I wondered what impressions the great trek to the North-west had left upon his young mind, but I was not to find out. The whole thing was a minor event to this serious-minded boy, a little matter of a hike over a distance about twice the width of America.

"It was pretty bitter going, eh?" I ventured.

"Not bitter, not bitter. No march is bitter if your comrades are with you. We revolutionary youths can't think about whether a thing is hard or bitter; we can only think of the task before us. If it is to walk 10,000 *li*, we walk it, or if it is to walk 20,000 *li*, we walk it!"

"How do you like Kansu, then? Is it better or worse than Kiangsi? Was life better in the South?"

"Kiangsi was good. Kansu is also good. Wherever the revolution is, that place is good. What we eat and where we sleep is not important. What is important is the revolution.

Copy-book replies, I thought. Here was one lad who had learned his answers well from some Red propagandist. Next day I was quite surprised when at a mass meeting of Red soldiers I saw that he was one of the principal speakers, and a "propagandist" in his own right. He was one of the best speakers in the army, I was told, and in that meeting he gave a simple but competent explanation of the present political situation, and the reasons why the Red Army wanted to stop civil war and form a "united front" with all anti-Japanese armies.

I met a youth of fourteen who had been an apprentice in a Shanghai machine-shop, and with three companions had found his way, through various adventures, to the North-west. He was a student in the radio school in Pao An when I saw him. I asked whether he missed Shanghai, but he said no, he had left nothing in Shanghai, and that the only fun he had ever had there was looking into the shop-windows at good things to eat—which he could not buy.

But best of all I liked the "little devil" in Pao An, who served as orderly to Li Ko-nung, chief of the communications department of the Foreign Office. This *hsiao-kuei* was a Shansi lad of about thirteen or fourteen, and he had joined the Reds I know not how. He was the Beau Brummell of the Vanguards, and he took his rôle with utmost gravity. He had inherited a Sam Browne belt from somebody, he had a neat little uniform tailored to a good fit, and a cap whose peak he regularly refilled with new cardboard whenever it broke. Underneath the collar of his well-brushed coat he always managed to have a strip of white linen showing. He was easily the snappiest-looking soldier in town. Beside him Mao Tse-tung looked a tramp. . . .

One of the duties of the Young Vanguards in the Soviets was to examine travellers on roads behind the front, and see that they had their road passes. They executed this duty quite determinedly, and marched anyone without his papers to the local Soviet for examination. P'eng Teh-huai told me of being stopped once and being asked for his *lu-t'iao* by some Young Vanguards, who threatened to arrest him.

"But I am P'eng Teh-huai," he said. "I write those passes myself."

"We don't care if you are Commander Chu Teh," said the young sceptics; "you must have a road pass." They signalled for assistance, and several boys came running from the fields to reinforce them.

P'eng had to write out his *lu-t'iao* and sign it himself before they allowed him to proceed.

Altogether, as you may have gathered, the "little devils" were one thing in Red China with which it was hard to find anything seriously wrong. Their spirit was superb. I suspect that more than once an older man, looking at them, forgot his pessimism and was heartened to think that he was fighting for the future of lads like those. They were invariably cheerful and optimistic, and they had a ready *"hao!"* for every how-are-you, regardless of the weariness of the day's march. They were patient, hard-working, bright, and eager to learn, and seeing them made you feel that China was not hopeless, that no nation was more hopeless than its youth. Here in the Vanguards was the future of China, if only this youth could be freed, shaped, made aware, and given a rôle to perform in the building of a new world. It sounds somewhat evangelical, I suppose, but nobody could see these heroic young lives without feeling that man in China is not born rotten, but with infinite possibilities of personality.

Li Yiu-hua's Story

by Jan Myrdal

The women too were liberated. The three mountains may have weighed heavily on the people of China, but they had weighed most heavily on the women. A woman's sufferings were unspeakable. When she was fourteen or fifteen she was married off to someone twenty years her senior. Many girls committed suicide then. Their feet were bound. No one would marry a "big foot." None dared cut her hair. They all wore theirs in a bun on the nape of their necks, as my wife still does today. When a young girl's feet were bound, the bindings were pulled so tight that she could not walk. It hurt to much that she could not stand. But she was forced to get up and walk; she was hit with a broom till she did so. And this was not done because people were evil. They only wanted what was best for the girl. Nobody wanted to hit their child, but if her feet weren't bound, she would have such an unhappy life that one was compelled to be hard for her own sake. At first, after having their feet bound, girls just stumbled about.

Now, after our revolution, all the women's feet were to be freed. We removed the bindings from the feet of all the little girls. Many women took part in our discussions and meetings. Women were elected to different committees and different posts in the villages. The women also formed their own propaganda groups. Then we sang about women's emancipation. I can still remember many of the songs of those days about women's rights. We made propaganda for the equality of women and free choice in marriage. There were lots of divorces in those days, for most people's marriages had been arranged for them and they did not care for each other. We held meetings about love then. Most did not go back to their former marriage partners, but looked for new ones with whom they would be happier. The class enemy then slandered us and flung mud at us, saying that we had no morals. But we wanted everyone to be free and equal, and the new marriages were both happier and more enduring than the old. The upper classes still tell lies about us.

But this new equality certainly was a problem. Li Hai-fu's first wife left him in 1935. She went off with a troupe of women propagandists. She was going to make propaganda for the revolution. Her father-in-law was still very feudal in his attitude. He said: "Do you want to run away? Then I'll break your leg so that you won't be able even to limp along." Then I told him: "If you break her leg, you will regret it. How could you even think of such a thing?" "She wants to run away from us," he said. "She isn't running away," I said. "She's transferring to different work." He had to give in. The power of the people would not let him break her leg and she went with her propaganda troupe. She did a good job for the revolution. Later, when the K.M.T. came, she was taken prisoner and badly tortured. We succeeded in freeing her in the end, but she died soon afterwards. Her son is grown-up now.

In July 1935, I joined the party. It was very simple. The party was holding a meeting in the old temple above the village. There were four people there. Two party members came and fetched me and took me to the meeting. There we discussed revolutionary work, after which they said to me: "Are you prepared to become a member of the Communist Party of China?" "Yes, I am," I said. That was how I became a party member.

Right up to the end of May 1937, when the enemy attacked us from Hengshan, we had no idea that they were going to launch an attack. The enemy's troops reached our village in September. They rounded up us farmers and made us build fortifications in the hills. There had been many fights in the years before this, but in the great attack of 1937 the Red Guard could not do much against the enemy's troops. We had knives and spears and muzzle-loaders, but they came with machine-guns and cannon and modern weapons. There were many enemy troops. They were advancing the whole time. They advanced ten li, then they compelled the villagers to build them a fort, and, when it was finished, they advanced another ten li. . . .

Now, too, the owner of the land, Yang Kung-shan, returned. The year before, 1936, when we still were in power, he had led an enemy force to the village of Shiwan, forty li away, and there had stolen goats and corn and plundered us, but on that occasion we had been able to drive him off. . . .

So, when Yang Kung-shan came back and took me prisoner and hauled me before the K.M.T. court in Shiwan in 1937, he said: "He has eaten up my corn and divided up my possessions." Then I replied: "I was not the only one to make revolution. We all did so and it was your own fault. You weren't worth anything better." Yang Kung-shan wanted them to cut my head off, but they didn't. They just beat me till I lost consciousness and then poured water over me to bring me round and then beat me again. They kept on with that for a bit. The enemy had a special committee called "Committee for Quelling the Revolution," and after being thus tortured, I was brought before their committee. There they interrogated me to find out if I was a communist. Then they tortured me again. I never told them anything, and they got nothing out of me, and in the end they put me in prison and left me there. Then friends in Shiwan stood guarantee for me and so got me out of prison. I had been tortured so much that I was unable to walk, and they had to hire a donkey to transport me home. There I lay on my kang for three months unable to get up.

But Yang Kung-shan did not like my being released. He would have liked to have me condemned to death and my head cut off. Not only because he disliked me, but because he would then have been able to sell my widow and my children and in that way get his money back. He never forgave me for having helped to divide up his property. I had scarcely got on my feet again before he had me in prison a second time. Then people in the villages round about said that they had all helped to make the revolution, and not just me, and that it was unfair to treat me in that way.

A Meeting with Mao

by Edgar Snow*

I met Mao soon after my arrival [1936]: a gaunt, rather Lincolnesque figure, above average height for a Chinese, somewhat stooped, with a head of thick black hair grown very long, and with large, searching eyes, a high-bridged nose and prominent cheekbones. My fleeting impression was of an intellectual face of great shrewdness, but I had no opportunity to verify this for several days. Next time I saw him, Mao was walking hatless along the street at dusk, talking with two young peasants, and gesticulating earnestly. I did not recognize him until he was pointed out to me—moving along unconcernedly with the rest of the strollers, despite the $250,000 which Nanking had hung over his head. . . .

*Snow, *Red Star Over China.*

Mao has the reputation of a charmed life. He has been repeatedly pronounced dead by his enemies, only to return to the news columns a few days later, as active as ever. The Kuomintang has also officially "killed" and buried Chu Teh many times, assisted by occasional corroborations from clairvoyant missionaries. Numerous deaths of the two famous men, nevertheless, did not prevent them from being involved in many spectacular exploits, including the Long March. Mao was indeed in one of his periods of newspaper demise when I visited Red China, but I found him quite substantially alive. There seems to be some basis for the legend of his charmed life, however, in the fact that, although he has been in scores of battles, was once captured by enemy troops and escaped, and has had the world's highest reward on his head, during all these years he has never once been wounded. . . .

Mao seemed to me a very interesting and complex man. He had the simplicity and naturalness of the Chinese peasant, with a lively sense of humour and a love of rustic laughter. His laughter was even active on the subject of himself and the shortcomings of the Soviets—a boyish sort of laughter which never in the least shook his inner faith in his purpose. He is plain-speaking and plain-living, and some people might think him rather coarse and vulgar. Yet he combines curious qualities of naïveté with the most incisive wit and worldly sophistication.

I think my first impression—dominantly one of native shrewdness—was probably correct. And yet Mao is an accomplished scholar of Classical Chinese, an omnivorous reader, a deep student of philosophy and history, a good speaker, a man with an unusual memory and extraordinary powers of concentration, an able writer, careless in his personal habits and appearance but astonishingly meticulous about details of duty, a man of tireless energy, and a military and political strategist of considerable genius. It is an interesting fact that many Japanese regard him as the ablest Chinese strategist alive.

The Reds were putting up some new buildings in Pao An, but accommodations were very primitive while I was there. Mao lived with his wife in a two-roomed *yao-fang* with bare, poor, map-covered walls. He had known much worse, and as the son of a "rich" peasant in Hunan he had also known better. The chief luxury they boasted was a mosquito net. Otherwise Mao lived very much like the rank and file of the Red Army. After ten years of leadership of the Reds, after hundreds of confiscations of property of landlords, officials and tax-collectors, he owned only his blankets, and a few personal belongings, including two cotton uniforms. Although he was a Red Army commander as well as chairman, he wore on his coat collar only the two red bars that are the insignia of the ordinary Red soldier.

I went with Mao several times to mass meetings of the villagers and the Red cadets, and to the Red theatre. He sat inconspicuously in the midst of the crowd and enjoyed himself hugely. I remember once, between acts at the Anti-Japanese Theatre, there was a general demand for a duet by Mao Tse-tung and Lin Piao, the twenty-eight-year-old president of the Red Academy, and formerly a famed young cadet on Chiang Kai-shek's staff. Lin blushed like a schoolboy, and got them out of the "command performance" by a graceful speech, calling upon the women Communists for a song instead.

Mao's food was the same as everybody's, but being a Hunanese he had the southerner's *ai-la*, or "love of pepper." He even had pepper cooked into his bread. Except for this passion, he scarcely seemed to notice what he ate. One night at dinner I heard him expand on a theory of pepper-loving peoples being revolutionaries. He first submitted his own province, Hunan, famous for the revolutionaries it has produced. Then he listed Spain, Mexico, Russia and France to support his contention, but laughingly had to admit defeat when somebody mentioned the well-known Italian love of red pepper and garlic, in refutation of his theory. One of the most amusing songs of the "bandits," incidentally, is a ditty called "The Hot Red Pepper." It tells of the disgust of the pepper with his pointless vegetable existence, waiting to be eaten, and how he ridicules the contentment of the cabbages, spinach and beans with their invertebrate careers. He ends up by leading a vegetable insurrection. "The Hot Red Pepper" was a great favorite with Chairman Mao.

He appears to be quite free from symptoms of megalomania, but he has a deep sense of personal dignity, and something about him suggests a power of ruthless decision when he deems it necessary. I never saw him angry, but I heard from others that on occasions he has been roused to an intense and withering fury. At such times his command of irony and invective is said to be classic and lethal.

I found him surprisingly well-informed on current world politics. Even on the Long March, it seems, the Reds received news broadcasts by radio, and in the North-west they published their own newspapers. Mao is exceptionally well-read in world history and has a realistic conception of European social and political conditions. He was very interested in the Labour Party of England, and questioned me intensely about its present policies, soon exhausting all my information. It seemed to me that he found it difficult fully to understand why, in a country where workers are enfranchised, there is still no workers' government. I am afraid my answers did not satisfy him.

Three Poems
by Mao Tse-tung
TRANSLATED BY WILLIS BARNSTONE

Warlords

Wind and clouds suddenly rip the sky
and warlords clash.
    War again.
Rancor rains down on men who dream of a Pillow
of Yellow Barley.

Yet our red banners leap over the calm Ting River
    on our way
to Shanghang and to Lungyen the dragon cliff.
The golden vase of China is shattered.
    We mend it,
happy as we give away its meadows.

September or October 1929

Kunlun Mountain

Over the earth
the greenblue monster Kunlun who has seen

all spring color and passion of men.
Three million dragons of white jade
    soar
and freeze the whole sky with snow.
When a summer sun heats the globe
rivers flood
and men turn into fish and turtles.
Who can judge
a thousand years of accomplishments or failures?
Kunlun,
you don't need all that height or snow.
If I could lean on heaven, grab my sword,
    and cut you in three parts,
I would send one to Europe, one to America,
    and keep one part here
    in China
that the world have peace
and the globe share the same heat and ice.

October 1935

Liupan, The Mountain of Six Circles

Dazzling sky to the far cirrus clouds.
I gaze at wild geese vanishing into the south.
If we cannot reach the Long Wall
    we are not true men.
On my fingers I count the twenty thousand li we have
    already marched.

On the summit of Liupan
the west wind lazily ripples our red banner.
Today we have the long rope in our hands.
When will we tie up the gray dragon of the seven
    stars?

October 1935

The KMT and the Second United Front

As the Japanese continued their invasion in the late 1930s, Chiang Kai-shek faced mounting pressure to come to an agreement with the Communists and turn his full attention to the defense of China. These pressures came most directly from the non-Communist politicians and intellectuals who formed the "third force"—urban and educated Chinese so named because they could not support the KMT, yet still hoped their country might be able to solve its problems without becoming Communist. But this third force was pitifully small and wielded very little power.

In the end it was the more powerful military who forced Chiang into a compromise with the Communists. In December, 1936, Chiang flew to the Northern city of Sian to meet with the "Young Marshal" Chang Hsueh-liang. The Young Marshal and his troops (the Tungbei, or Northeast, Army made up of Manchurians) had been driven out of Manchuria by the Japanese; because of this, they especially resented Chiang's orders to fight fellow Chinese instead of the invaders. When Chiang arrived, they captured him and held him prisoner until finally he agreed to form the second united front. The first reading of this section tells the story of the Sian incident.

The Generalissimo Is Arrested
*by Edgar Snow**

I emerged from Red China to find a sharpening tension between the Tungpei (ex-Manchurian) troops of Young Marshal Chang Hsueh-liang, and Generalissimo Chiang Kai-shek. The latter was now not only Commander-in-Chief of China's armed forces, but also chairman of the Executive Yuan—a position comparable to that of Premier.

. . . the Tungpei troops were gradually being transformed, militarily and politically, from mercenaries who had been shipped to half a dozen different provinces to fight the

---

*Snow, *Red Star Over China.*

Reds, into an army infected by the national revolutionary anti-Japanese slogans of its enemy, convinced of the futility of continued civil war, stirred by only one exhortation, loyal to but one central idea—the hope of "fighting back to the old homeland," of recovering Manchuria from the Japanese who had driven them from their homes, and abused and murdered their families. These notions being directly opposed to the maxims then held by Nanking, it has been told how the Tungpei troops, naturally enough, had found themselves with a growing fellow feeling for the anti-Japanese Red Army. . . .

A flame of strong nationalist feeling swept through the country, and the Japanese demanded the suppression of the National Salvation Movement, which they held responsible for the anti-Japanese agitation. Nanking obliged. Seven of the most prominent leaders of the organization, all respectable citizens, including a prominent banker, a lawyer, educators, and writers, were arrested. At the same time the Government suppressed fourteen nationally popular magazines at one stroke. Strikes in the Japanese mills of Shanghai, partly in patriotic protest against the Japanese invasion of Suiyuan, were also broken up with considerable violence by the Japanese, in co-operation with the Kuomintang. When other patriotic strikes occurred in Tsingtao, the Japanese landed their own marines, arrested the strikers, occupied the city. The marines were withdrawn only after Nanking had agreed virtually to prohibit all strikes in Japanese mills of Tsingtao in the future.

All these happenings had further repercussions in the North-west. In November, under pressure from his own officers, Chang Hsueh-liang dispatched his famous appeal to be sent to the Suiyuan front. "In order to control our troops," this missive concluded, "we should keep our promise to them that whenever the chance comes they will be allowed to carry out their desire of fighting the enemy. Otherwise, they will regard not only myself, but also Your Excellency, as a cheat, and thus will no longer obey us. Please give us the order to mobilize at least a part, if not the whole, of the Tungpei Army, to march immediately to Suiyuan as enforcements to those who are fulfilling their sacred mission of fighting Japanese imperialism there. If so, I, as well as my troops, of more than 100,000, shall follow Your Excellency's leadership to the end." The earnest tone of this whole letter, the hope of restoring an army's lost prestige, were overwhelmingly evident. But Chiang rejected the suggestion. He still wanted the Tungpei Army to fight the Reds. . . .

Meanwhile, important things had happened on both the right and left wings of the stage. Among the Tungpei commanders an agreement had been reached to present a common request for cancellation of civil war, and resistance to Japan. . . .

All this must have been known in a general way to the Premier-Generalissimo. Although he had no regular troops in Sian, a few months earlier some 1,500 of the Third Gendarmes, a so-called "special service" regiment of the Blueshirts, commanded by his nephew, General Chiang Hsiao-hsien, who was credited with the abduction, imprisonment, and killing of hundreds of radicals, had arrived in the city. They had established espionage headquarters throughout the province, and begun arrests and kidnapping of alleged "Communist" students, political workers, and soldiers. . . .

The Generalissimo's whole staff, together with his personal bodyguards, were with him in Sianfu. Chiang refused to see the Tungpei and Hsipei commanders in a group, as they wished, but talked to them separately, and attempted, by various inducements, to break their solidarity. In this effort he failed. One and all acknowledged him as Commander-in-Chief, but each expressed his displeasure with the new campaign, and all asked to be sent to the anti-Japanese front in Suiyuan. For them all Chiang had but one command: *"Destroy the Reds."* "I told them," said Chiang in his own diary, "that the bandit-suppression campaign had been prosecuted to such a stage that it would require only the last five minutes to achieve the final success."

So, despite all the objections and warnings, the Generalissimo summoned a General Staff Congress on the 10th, when final plans were formally adopted to push ahead with the Sixth Campaign. A general mobilization order was prepared for the Hsipei, Tungpei, and Nanking troops already in Kansu and Shensi, together with the Nanking troops waiting at T'ungkuan. It was announced that the order would be published on the 12th. It was openly stated that if Marshal Chang refused these orders his troops would be disarmed by Nanking forces, and he himself would be dismissed from his command. General Chiang Ting-wen had already been appointed to replace Chiang Hsueh-liang as head of the Bandit Suppression Commission. At the same time reports reached both Chang and Yang that the Blueshirts, together with the police, had prepared a "black list" of Communist sympathizers in their armies, who were to be arrested immediately after publication of the mobilization order.

Thus it was at the culmination of this complicated and historic chain of events that Chang Hsueh-liang called a joint meeting of the division commanders of the Tungpei and Hsipei armies at ten o'clock on the night of December 11. Orders had been secretly given on the previous day for a division of Tungpei troops, and a regiment of Yang Hu-cheng's army to move into the environs of Sianfu. The decision was now taken to use these forces to "arrest" the Generalissimo and his staff. The mutiny of 170,000 troops had become a fact.

Whatever we may say against its motives, or the political energies behind them, it must be admitted that the *coup de théâtre* enacted at Sian was brilliantly timed and brilliantly executed. It was infinitely less bloody and clumsy than Chiang Kai-shek's *coup d'état* at Nanking or Shanghai, or the Communists' seizure of Canton. No word of the rebels' plans reached their enemies until too late. By six o'clock on the morning of December 12 the whole affair was over. Tungpei and Hsipei troops were in control at Sian. The Blueshirts, surprised in their sleep, had been disarmed and arrested; practically the whole General Staff had been surrounded in its quarters at the Sian Guest House, and was imprisoned; Governor Shao Li-tzu and the chief of police were also prisoners; the city police force had surrendered to the mutineers, and the fifty Nanking bombers and their pilots had been seized at the aerodrome.

But the arrest of the Generalissimo was a bloodier affair. Chiang Kai-shek was staying ten miles from the city, at Lintung, a famous hot-springs resort, which had been cleared of all other guests. To Lintung, at midnight, went twenty-six-year-old Captain Sun Ming-chiu, commander of the Young Marshal's bodyguard. Halfway there he picked up two hundred Tungpei troops, and at 3 A.M. drove to the outskirts of Lintung. There they waited till five o'clock, when the first lorry, with about fifteen men, roared up to the hotel, was challenged by sentries, and opened fire.

Reinforcements soon arrived for the Tungpei vanguard, and Captain Sun led an assault on the Generalissimo's residence. Taken by complete surprise, the bodyguards put up a short fight—long enough, however, to permit the astounded Generalissimo to escape. When Captain Sun reached his bedroom he had already fled. Sun took a search party up the side of the rocky, snow-covered hill behind the resort and conducted his manhunt. Presently they found the Generalissimo's personal servant, and not long afterwards came upon the man himself. Clad only in a loose robe thrown over his nightshirt, his bare feet and hands cut in his nimble flight up the mountain, shaking in the bitter cold, and minus his false teeth, he was crouching in a cave beside a great rock.

Sun Ming-chiu hailed him, and the Generalissimo's first words were, "If you are my comrade, shoot me and finish it all." To which Sun replied, "We will not shoot. We only ask you to lead our country against Japan."

Chiang remained seated on his rock, and said with difficulty, "Call Marshall Chang here, and I will come down."

"Marshal Chang isn't here. The troops are rising in the city; we came to protect you."

At this the Generalissimo seemed much relieved, and called for a horse to take him down the mountain. "There is no horse here," said Sun, "but I will carry you down the mountain on my back." And he knelt at Chiang's feet. After some hesitation, Chiang accepted and climbed painfully on to the broad back of the young officer. They proceeded solemnly down the slope in this fashion, escorted by troops, until a servant arrived with Chiang's shoes. The little group got into a car at the foot of the hill, and set off for Sian.

"The past is past," Sun said to him. "From now on there must be a new policy for China. What are you going to do? . . . The one urgent task for China is to fight Japan. This is the special demand of the men of the North-east.

Why do you not fight Japan, but instead give the order to fight the Red Army?"

"I am the leader of the Chinese people," Chiang shouted. "I represent the nation. I think my policy is correct."

In this way, a little bloody but unbowed, the Generalissimo arrived in the city, where he became the involuntary guest of General Yang Hu-cheng and the Young Marshal.

On the day of the *coup* all division commanders of the Tungpei and Hsipei armies signed and issued a circular telegram addressed to the central Government, to various provincial leaders, and to the people at large. The brief missive explained that "in order to stimulate his awakening" the Generalissimo had been "requested to remain for the time being in Sianfu." Meanwhile, his personal safety was guaranteed. The demands of "national salvation" submitted to the Generalissimo were broadcast to the nation—but everywhere suppressed. Here are the famous eight points:

1. Reorganize the Nanking Government and admit all parties to share the joint responsibility of national salvation.

2. End all civil war immediately *and adopt the policy of armed resistance against Japan*.

3. Release the (seven) leaders of the patriotic movement in Shanghai.

4. Pardon all political prisoners.

5. Guarantee the people liberty of assembly.

6. Safeguard the people's rights of patriotic organization and political liberty.

7. Put into effect the will of Dr. Sun Yat-Sen.

8. Immediately convene a National Salvation conference.

To this programme the Chinese Red Army, the Soviet Government and the Communist Party of China immediately offered their support.

Following the December, 1936, Sian incident, the year 1937 marked the opening of full-scale war in northern and central China between Chiang's forces and the Japanese. In July at Marco Polo Bridge near Peking the Japanese Army attacked

Chinese forces and began its occupation of northern China. In August Chiang threw his troops into the first serious KMT counterattack against the Japanese at Shanghai, a bloody battle described here. The Japanese successfully defended their position in Shanghai and then proceeded to push their way up the Yangtze River into KMT-held territory. Chiang fled the capital at Nanking, which was moved farther upstream on the Yangtze to Hankow, and finally to Chungking, a mountain-girt city that remained KMT China's wartime capital until 1945.

Chiang and the Japanese
by Theodore H. White and Annalee Jacoby

Japanese calculations, which had been upset in northern China by partisan resistance, were even more thoroughly upset by what happened in the lower Yangtze Valley. Long before the Communists rooted themselves in the north, the attention of the Japanese staff and the interest of the entire world had concentrated on the battle that was suffusing the entire Shanghai delta in flame and blood. This was Chiang K'ai-shek's war.

Chiang watched the preliminary moves of the Japanese in northern China with indecision. For a month he seesawed back and forth between the decision to fight and the knowledge of China's weakness. When he did decide to resist, he struck in a way that wrecked the smooth political-military structure of Japan's ambitions. The Japanese had hoped to fight in the north and to negotiate in the south. Chiang chose to precipitate a war of the entire people against the enemy by throwing down the gage of battle in his own bailiwick of the lower Yangtze, closest to his own internal bases, where his best troops were marshaled and ready. On August 13, 1937, he flung the best units of his German-trained army into action against the Japanese marine garrison in Shanghai. For a few days Chinese flesh and numbers compressed the Japanese into a narrow strip by the banks of the Whangpoo River. The Japanese realized that they were confronted not with an isolated incident in northern China but with a war against the Chinese people. To win this war would require full mobilization of

Japan's resources. The Japanese moved their fleet to off-shore anchorages, marshaled their air force at Formosa, and proceeded to pump steel at the massed Chinese troops in overwhelming tonnages. Not even today is there any accurate estimate of the carnage at Shanghai; Chinese casualties mounted to the hundreds of thousands as the blood and courage of the soldiers absorbed the shock of Japan's barrages.

Chiang's decision to hold at Shanghai is now, as it was then, one of the most bitterly debated episodes of the entire war. It was symbolic, almost with the symbolism of caricature, of the personality of the man. There was no hope of success in matching Chinese flesh against Japanese metal; a withdrawal might have salvaged some of the good units of the Chinese army for later operations in the hinterland, where they could meet the Japanese on more nearly even terms. These, however, were factual considerations, and Chiang's stubbornness refused to submit to them. The soldiers standing in the wet trenches and fed endlessly into the slaughter were a projection of an inflexible will to resist. Since Chiang had accepted war with Japan, he meant to fight it out his own way—yielding no foot of ground that was not taken from him by force.

The resistance at Shanghai was futile in a military sense; in a political sense it was one of the great demonstrations of the war. It astounded the most world-weary of old China hands, and it proved beyond further question in the record of history how much suffering and heroism the Chinese people could display in the face of hopeless odds. The demonstration at Shanghai was even more valuable internally. The tale of the battle, carried into the interior by word of mouth, kindled a spreading bonfire of patriotic fervor. The line at the Yangtze gave time to mobilize the nation. For two months the Japanese battered at Shanghai. Then, by a clever outflanking movement to the south, they unpinned the Chinese line and swept it away in utter confusion to Nanking. . . .

The winter of '37–'38 worked a miracle in China. The seat of government was transferred to the upriver port of Hankow, 800 miles from the sea, and the most complete unity of spirit and motive that China had ever known existed there for a few months. The Hankow spirit could never be quite precisely defined by those who experienced it there and then. All China was on the move—drifting back from the coast into the interior and swirling in confusion about the temporary capital. War-lord armies from the south and southwest were marching to join the battle. The Communists were speeding their partisans deeper into the tangled communications that supported Japan's front. In Hankow the government and the Communists sat in common council, made common plans for the prosecution of the war. The government authorized the creation of a second Communist army—the New Fourth—on the lower Yangtze behind the Japanese lines; the Communists participated in the meetings of the Military Council.

The elite of China's writers, engineers, and journalists converged on Hankow to sew together the frayed strands of resistance. By spring of 1938, when the Japanese resumed the campaign, with Hankow as their ultimate objective, the new armies and the new spirit had crystallized. In April 1938, for the first time in the history of Japan, her armies suffered a frontal defeat at the battle of Taierchwang. The setback was only temporary. Moving in two great arms, the Japanese forces closed on Hankow from the north and the east to pinch it off in the following fall. Almost simultaneously their landing parties seized Canton, the great port city of the south, and the Japanese rested on their arms a second time.

On paper the Japanese strategy was perfect. China falls into a simple geographical pattern. Western China is a rocky, mountainous land; eastern China is flat and alluvial, with scarcely a hill to break the paddies for miles on end. Both western and eastern China are drained by three great rivers that flow down from the mountains across the flatlands to the Pacific Ocean. The Japanese army now controlled the entire coast and all the centers of industry. It also controlled the outlets of the three great rivers. In the north it held the Peking-Tientsin area and the outlet of the Yellow river. In central China it garrisoned both banks of the Yangtze, from Shanghai through Nanking to Hankow. In southern China it held Canton and dominated the West River. With the cities, railways, and rivers under control, the Japanese felt that they could wait until a paralysis of all economic and transport functions brought Chinese resistance to a halt, and they waited. They were still waiting seven years later, when the Japanese army surrendered a ruined homeland to the Allies.

The Japanese blundered in China. Why they blundered was best explained later by one of the shrewder statesmen of the Chungking government, General Wu Te-chen, who said, "The Japanese think they know China too much." Japanese political and military intelligence in China was far and away the finest in the world, but it had concentrated on schisms and rifts, on personalities and feuds, on guns and factories. Its dossiers on each province, each general, each army, contained so much of the wickedness and corruption of China that the accumulated knowledge was blinding. The one fact that was obscure to them was that China was a nation. They had seen a revolution proceeding in China for thirteen years, but only its scum, its abortions, its internal tensions; they had not measured its results. They were fighting more than a coalition of armies; they were fighting an entire people. They had watched the infant growth of Chinese industries on the coast, had marked the new railways on the map. But the strength of the Chinese was not in their cities; it was in the hearts of the people. China was primitive, so primitive that the destruction of her industries and cities, her railways and machinery, did not upset her as similar disaster disrupted Europe in later days. China was rooted in the soil. As long as the rain fell and the sun shone, the crops would grow; no blockade of the Japanese navy could interpose itself between the peasant and his land. China had just emerged from chaos, but she was still so close to it that the disruption of war could be fitted into the normal routine of her life; if, for example, it was necessary to move government, industry, people, and army into the interior, it could be done. There was an enormous elasticity in the system that Japan meant to wreck—when it was struck, it yielded, but it did not break.

Through the long months of 1938, as the Chinese armies were pressed slowly back toward the interior, they found their way clogged by moving people. The breathing space of winter had given hundreds of thousands time to make their decision, and China was on the move in one of the greatest mass migrations in human history....

The migrations of factories and universities were the most spectacular. How many more millions of peasants and city folk were set adrift by the Japanese invasion no one can guess—estimates run all the way from three to twenty-five million. The peasants fled from the Japanese; they fled from the great flood of the Yellow River, whose dikes had been opened to halt the Japanese armies; they fled out of fear of the unknown. The workers who accompanied the factories numbered perhaps no more than 10,000; they came because without them the machines would be useless. The restaurant keepers, singsong girls, adventurers, the little merchants who packed their cartons of cigarettes or folded their bolts of cloth to come on the march, probably numbered hundreds of thousands. The little people who accompanied the great organized movements traveled by foot, sampan, junk, railway, and ricksha. Thousands crusted the junks moving through the gorges; hundreds of thousands strung out over the mountain roads like files of ants winding endlessly westward. There is no estimate of the number who died of disease, exposure, or hunger on the way; their bones are still whitening on the routes of march. . . . [EDITOR'S NOTE: *In the Communist areas, meanwhile, the campaign against the Japanese continued.*]

The tremendous energy behind the Communist drive was co-ordinated from Yenan. A radio and courier network linked all Communist centers from Hainan in the south to the outskirts of Manchuria. The radios were an amateur patchwork of broken Japanese sets, secondhand tubes, and makeshift materials. But the codes, which were excellent, baffled both the Kuomintang and the Japanese, and these communications bound together with iron cords of discipline the eighteen local governments in a coalition that seemed at times a shadow government and at times the most effective fighting instrument of the Chinese people. . . .

The entire Communist political thesis could be reduced to a single paragraph: If you take a peasant who has been swindled, beaten, and kicked about for all his waking days and whose father has transmitted to him an emotion of bitterness reaching back for generations—if you take such a peasant, treat him like a man, ask his opinion, let him vote for a local government, let him organize his own police and gendarmes, decide on his own taxes, and vote himself a reduction in rent and interest—if you do all that, the peasant becomes a man who has something to fight for, and he will fight to preserve it against any enemy, Japanese or Chinese. If in addition you present the peasant with an army and a government that help him harvest, teach him to read and write, and fight off the Japanese who raped his wife and tortured his mother, he develops a loyalty to the army and the government and to the party that controls them. He votes for that party, thinks the way that party wants him to think, and in many cases becomes an active participant. . . .

The party set out to teach the peasants self-government. In all of Chinese history the peasants had had no such experience, and they were putty in the hands of their Communist mentors. Village and county councils were created, and in them were lodged the powers that touched the peasants' life most closely. Their problems were such as the peasants had been exposed to since childhood. Swept into the machinery of government for the first time, the peasants found that they possessed unknown talents and unsuspected abilities. No village council needed a classical education to decide who should pay more taxes and who less, for the common good. The villagers knew who collected how much grain and from what fields; they were the best fitted to apportion the burden of war. Scholars and bureaucrats with college degrees were not needed to organize village self-defense corps. The crude talents that were called forth by the new responsibilities were skillfully developed by far-seeing Communist leadership.

To the Kuomintang what the Communists were doing seemed devilishly clever. The Communists took the laws that Kuomintang liberals had written into sterile statute books, and they taught the peasants to apply them. Nanking, in 1930, had passed an abortive law limiting rent on land to 37.5 per cent of the crop yield. The law had never been implemented. But now, in Communist areas, the village and county councils chosen from among the people voted these laws into effect. The voting may have been illegal, but it could not be assailed as undemocratic. Who would vote against cutting his rent rates by half? Peasants participating in such meetings and belonging to such governments learned that government is a lever that can be applied for their interests as well as against them. Democracy meant more grain in the harvest basket of the man who tilled the soil. In Communist areas where the Japanese could not penetrate, the peasants actually lived better during the war than they had before.

By 1938 it was obvious to Chiang that because the Communists were more effectively organizing the people for guerrilla warfare against the Japanese they were winning the loyalty of the people. The united front began to crumble, and Chiang turned his troops in a blockade against the Red territories. Third-force leaders in Chungking tried to patch up the split and to convince Chiang to change his policies. In response he created the Peoples Political Council as a form of elected congress, but gave it only advisory powers; he reinstituted the traditional *pao-chia* system of "collective responsibility," but allowed it to become a tool of repression against the peasants. The author Edgar Snow was traveling through the "Red areas" of northwestern China and describes a local variety of *pao-chia* organization.

The *Pao-Chia* System Revived
by Edgar Snow*

When I opened my eyes again dawn was just breaking. The chairman was standing over me, shaking my shoulder. Of course I was startled and I sat up at once, fully awake.

"What is it?" I demanded.

"You had better leave a little early. There are bandits near here, and you ought to get to An Tsai quickly."

"Bandits? It was on my tongue to reply that I had in fact come precisely to meet these so-called bandits, when I suddenly realized what he meant. He was not talking about Reds, he meant "White-bandits." I got up without further persuasion. I did not want anything to happen to me so ridiculous as being kidnapped by White-bandits in Soviet China.

The reader is entitled to some explanation. White-bandits were in the Kuomintang's terminology called *min-*

---

*Snow, *Red Star Over China*.

t'uan, or "people's corps," just as Red-bandits were in Soviet terminology called *Yu-chi-tui*, or "Red partisans." In an effort to combat peasant uprisings, these *min-t'uan* forces had increasingly been organized by the Kuomintang. They functioned as an organic part of the *pao-chia* system, an ancient method of controlling the peasantry which is now being widely imposed both by the Kuomintang in China and the Japanese in Manchukuo.

Pao-chia literally means "guaranteed armour." The system thus known requires that every ten peasant families must have a headman, through whom their respectability is established to the satisfaction of the local magistrate. It is a mutual-guarantee system, so that for any offence committed by one member of a *pao-chia* the whole or any part of the group can be held responsible. This was also the way the Mongols and Manchus ruled China as their empire.

As a measure for preventing the organization of peasant opposition it is almost unbeatable. Since headmen of the *pao-chia* are nearly always rich farmers, landlords, pawnbrokers, or money-lenders—most zealous of subjects—it is natural that they are not inclined to "guarantee" any tenant or debtor peasants of a rebellious turn of mind. Yet not to be guaranteed is a serious matter. An unguaranteed man can be thrown in jail on any pretext, as a "suspicious character."

The following is a selection from the book *China's Destiny*, which Chiang Kai-shek wrote in 1943 to explain his understanding of China's needs. Although engaged in a fight for survival against Japanese fascism, Chiang's own political theories were a blend of the traditional feudal and more modern fascist ideas. Chiang's Blue Shirts have already been described in Part III, and his San Min Chu I Youth Corps in particular bore a striking resemblance to youth groups set up in Germany and Italy in the 1930s.

As KMT support eroded in the cities and the urban "third force" increasingly looked to the Communists for programs and leadership, Chiang incorporated part of the language used by Mao and the Party. Here he writes, ". . . youths throughout the country, if you really wish to fulfill your great *revolutionary* ambitions and carry out the great enterprise of national reconstruction, you must join the Youth Corps. . . ."

But because he adopted only the language and not the content, Chiang never was able to recover the confidence and faith he needed to maintain KMT control.

China's Destiny
by Chiang Kai-shek

With regard to the relation between the people of the entire country and the Kuomintang, Sun Yat-sen clearly stated: "Every citizen of the country not only has the privilege of joining the Party, but also the duty to join it." The youth of the country also has a similar privilege and similar duty to join the *San Min Chu I* Youth Corps. We must recognize that revolutionary reconstruction is a great task that must be jointly shouldered by all citizens. The Kuomintang and the *San Min Chu I* Youth Corps are the general directing agencies for the carrying out of revolutionary reconstruction. Adult citizens must join the Kuomintang and youthful citizens must join the Youth Corps—only then will the happiness of the entire nation be safeguarded, the interest of the state protected, and permanent security for the nation and the state be assured. Therefore, joining the Party and the Corps is both a privilege and a duty. At the same time, the Kuomintang and the *San Min Chu I* Youth Corps have the power to demand and the duty to urge all ambitious and zealous adult citizens and youth to join the Party and the Corps. The heritage left us by our ancestors through hundreds and thousands of generations will be reformed and administered by the Party and the Corps. The foundation upon which our descendants for countless years to come will depend must also be created and enriched by the Party and the Corps. Our Party and our Corps, in order to fulfill their responsibility for preserving the past and building for the future, therefore have the power to demand that all our citizens come forward and unitedly take up the task, and also have the duty to permit them to come forward and unitedly carry on the Revolution. . . .

This is the turning point in China's destiny; the decision will be made during the present War of Resistance within the next two years. But China's revival has already become a predestined fact; it cannot be shaken by any reactionary force....

Furthermore, all our country's youth should especially have a correct understanding of the *San Min Chu I* Youth Corps. Hereafter, youths throughout the country, if you really wish to fulfill your great revolutionary ambitions and carry out the great enterprise of national reconstruction, you must join the Youth Corps as the only course and the absolutely essential road to establish your careers and serve your country....

In summary, the Kuomintang and the *San Min Chu I* Youth Corps are the organizations to solidify the state and the nation into one body—a fact that is shown by history and does not require further explanation. But there is another point that ought to be repeated to our citizens, namely that the Kuomintang is the principal organization for the building of the state, to be shared and enjoyed by the citizens of the entire country.

So long as the Kuomintang remains in existence, so long will China continue to exist. If China today did not have the Kuomintang, there would be no China. Had the Revolution of the Kuomintang been defeated, it would have meant the complete defeat of the Chinese state. Briefly speaking, China's destiny rests entirely with the Kuomintang. If there was no Kuomintang, or if the Kuomintang should fail in its task, China would have nothing on which to depend. [In the revised edition, the passage from "So long as" to "depend" has been rewritten to read: "If the Kuomintang Revolution is brought to a successful conclusion, then and only then can China be independent. If China no longer had the Kuomintang there would be no more China. Briefly speaking, the destiny of China rests entirely with the Kuomintang. If by any mischance the Kuomintang Revolution should fail, the Chinese nation would have nothing on which it could depend."]

Under the Kuomintang, the prosecution of the war against the Japanese was marked by widespread corruption, war profiteering, starvation—and KMT efforts to prevent knowledge of this situation from leaking out. By and large, these efforts were successful, since wartime censorship of the Chinese government could stop dispatches by foreign correspondents that were unfavorable, while allowing "positive" news to get out. One of the most famous of the unreported wartime episodes was the 1943 Honan famine, in which uncounted thousands or millions died, in large part because the government failed to act. The report here is by two *Time* magazine correspondents stationed in China, Theodore H. White and Annalee Jacoby.

The Honan Famine
by Theodore H. White and Annalee Jacoby

Famine and flood are China's sorrow. From time out of mind Chinese chronicles have recorded these recurrent disasters with the beating, persistent note of doom. Always in their chronicles Chinese historians have judged the great dynasties of the past by their ability to meet and master such tragic emergencies. In the concluding years of the war against Japan such a famine ravaged the north and tested the government of Chiang K'ai-shek. The story of the Honan famine rolled into Chungking like tumbleweed blown by the wind. You clutched at facts, and they dissolved into fragments of gossip: "I heard from a man who was there . . ." "I saw in a letter from Loyang . . ." "In Sian they say that . . ." But there was no substance—merely that ominous tone of Chinese conversation that runs before disaster like darkness before a thundercloud. In February 1943 the *Ta Kung Pao*, the most independent Chinese paper in Chungking, published the first real report of the almost unendurable suffering of the people of Honan under one of the most terrible famines in Chinese history. The government retaliated by suppressing the *Ta Kung Pao* for three days.

The suppression of the *Ta Kung Pao* acted like a barb on the foreign press. I decided to go to Honan; Harrison Forman of the London *Times* came to the same decision at the same time. . . .

Each large town along the way had at least one restaurant open for those whose purses were still full. Once we ordered a meal in such a restaurant, but for us the spicy food was tasteless. Hungry people, standing about the open kitchen, inhaled the smell with shuddering greed; their eyes traced each steaming morsel from bowl to lips and back. When we walked down the street, children followed crying, "*K'o lien, k'o lien* (mercy, mercy)." If we pulled peanuts or dried dates from out pockets, tiny ragamuffins whipped by to snatch them from our fingers. The tear-stained faces, smudgy and forlorn in the cold, shamed us. Chinese children are beautiful in health; their hair glows then with the gloss of fine natural oil, and their almond eyes sparkle. But these shrunken scarecrows had pus-filled slits where eyes should be; malnutrition had made their hair dry and brittle; hunger had bloated their bellies; weather had chapped their skins. Their voices had withered into a thin whine that called only for food.

The smaller villages were even worse than the market towns. The silence was frightening. People fled the impersonal cruelty of hunger as if a barbarian army were upon them. The villages echoed with emptiness; streets were deserted, compost piles untended waiting for spring, doors and windows boarded up. The abandoned houses amplified the slightest sound. A baby crying in a hidden room in a village sounded louder than the pounding of our horses' hooves. Two lone women quarreled in a haunted street, and their shrieking rang louder than the hurly-burly of a village fair.

There were corpses on the road. A girl no more than seventeen, slim and pretty, lay on the damp earth, her lips blue with death; her eyes were open, and the rain fell on them. People chipped at bark, pounded it by the roadside for food; venders sold leaves at a dollar a bundle. A dog digging at a mound was exposing a human body. Ghostlike men were skimming the stagnant pools to eat the green slime of the waters. We whipped our horses to the quickest possible pace in the effort to make Chengchow by evening of the third day. As dusk closed, snow began to fall, light and powdery. Once our horses stumbled in a field and sheered off violently from two people lying side by side in the night, sobbing aloud in their desolation. By the time we entered the city, the snow was heavy enough to muffle the thudding of our horses' hooves.

When we awoke in the morning, the city was a white sepulcher peopled with gray ghosts. Death ruled Chengchow, for the famine centered there. Before the war it had held

120,000 people; now it had less than 40,000. The city had been bombed, shelled, and occupied by the Japanese, so that it had the half-destroyed air of all battlefront cities. Rubble was stacked along the gutters, and the great buildings, roofless, were open to the sky. Over the rubble and ruins the snow spread a mantle that deadened every sound. We stood at the head of the main street, looked down the deserted way for all its length—and saw nothing. Occasionally someone in fluttering, wind-blown rags would totter out of a doorway. Those who noticed us clustered round; spreading their hands in supplication, they cried *"K'o lien, k'o lien,"* till our ears rang with it. . . .

Letters of the Protestant missionaries recorded the early stages of the crisis, when the trek started in the fall. Mobs of hungry peasants, their women and children with them, had forced their way into wealthy homes and stripped them of anything that could be carried off. They had rushed into irrigated grain fields to seize the standing crops. In some cases hunger had burned out the most basic human emotions; two maddened parents had tied six children to trees so they could not follow them as they left in search of food. When a group of mother, baby, and two older children became tired from the long hunt for food, the mother, sitting down to nurse the infant, sent the older children on to look for food at the next village; when they returned the baby was still sucking at the breast of the dead mother. In a fit of frenzy the parents of two little children had murdered them rather than hear them beg for something to eat. Some families sold all they had for one last big meal, then committed suicide. Armed assaults and robberies were epidemic all through the countryside. The missionaries did what they could to pick up waifs along the road, but they had to do it by stealth, for a report that the missionaries were caring for starving children would have overwhelmed them at once with orphans abandoned on their doorsteps. . . .

The Chinese government failed to foresee the famine; when it came, it failed to act until too late. As early as October, reports of the situation were arriving in Chungking. In November two government inspectors visited Honan, traveled the main motor roads, and returned to say that the crisis was desperate and something must be done immediately. The Central Government dismissed the matter by appropriating $200,000,000—paper money—for famine relief and sending a mandate to provincial authorities to remit taxes. The banks in Chungking loaded the bales of paper currency on trucks and sent a convoy northward bearing paper, not food, to the stricken. It would indeed have been hopeless to try to move heavy tonnages of grain from central China over the broken, mountainous communications to northern China and Honan. Yet just across the provincial border from Honan was the province of Shensi, whose grain stores were more than ample. A vigorous government would have ordered grain from Shensi into neighboring Honan immediately in order to avert disaster. But cracking down on Shensi in favor of Honan would have upset the delicate balance of power the government found so essential to its functioning. Grain might also have been moved to Honan from Hupeh, but the war area commander in Hupeh would not permit it.

———————

Some Americans stationed in China had relatively realistic views of the corrupt KMT and its prospects in a post-war contest with the Communists for control of China. The two authors, John S. Service and John Paton Davies, reporting for the U.S. State Department from Chungking, were attacked after the war for their views, which were seen as unnecessarily unfavorable to Chiang and the KMT. Today, however, it is generally recognized that Service and Davies were correct. Many of Service's wartime reports are now available in *Lost Chance in China* (New York: Random House, 1974), edited by Joseph Esherick.

U.S. Foreign Service Officer Reports
by John S. Service and John Paton Davies

June 20, 1944 (Service)
The position of the Kuomintang and the Generalissimo is weaker than it has been for the past ten years.
China faces economic collapse. This is causing disintegration of the army and the government's administrative apparatus. It is one of the chief causes of growing political unrest. The Generalissimo is losing the support of a China

which, by unity in the face of violent aggression, found a new and unexpected strength during the first two years of the war with Japan. Internal weaknesses are becoming accentuated and there is taking place a reversal of the process of unification.

1. Morale is low and discouragement widespread. There is a general feeling of hopelessness.

2. The authority of the Central Government is weakening in the areas away from the larger cities. Government mandates and measures of control cannot be enforced and remain ineffective. It is becoming difficult for the Government to collect enough food for its huge army and bureaucracy.

3. The governmental and military structure is being permeated and demoralized from top to bottom by corruption, unprecedented in scale and openness.

4. The intellectual and salaried classes, who have suffered the most heavily from inflation, are in danger of liquidation. The academic groups suffer not only the attrition and demoralization of economic stress; the weight of years of political control and repression is robbing them of the intellectual vigor and leadership they once had.

5. Peasant resentment of the abuses of conscription, tax collection and other arbitrary impositions has been widespread and is growing. The danger is ever-increasing that past sporadic outbreaks of banditry and agrarian unrest may increase in scale and find political motivation. . . .

9. The Kuomintang is losing the respect and support of the people by its school policies and its refusal to heed progressive criticism. It seems unable to revivify itself with fresh blood, and its unchanging leadership shows a growing ossification and loss of a sense of reality. To combat the dissensions and cliquism within the Party, which grow more rather than less acute, the leadership is turning toward the reactionary and unpopular Chen brothers clique.

10. The Generalissimo shows a similar loss of realistic flexibility and a hardening of narrowly conservative views. His growing megalomania and his unfortunate attempts to be "sage" as well as leader—shown, for instance, by "China's Destiny" and his book on economics—have forfeited the respect of many intellectuals, who enjoy in China a

position of unique influence. Criticism of his dictatorship is becoming outspoken.

In the face of the grave crisis with which it is confronted, the Kuomintang is ceasing to be the unifying and progressive force in Chinese society, the role in which it made its greatest contribution to modern China. . . .

On the internal political front the desire of the Kuomintang leaders to perpetuate their own power overrides all other considerations. The result is the enthronement of reaction.

The Kuomintang continues to ignore the great political drive within the country for democratic reform. The writings of the Generalissimo and the Party press show that they have no real understanding of that term. Constitutionalism remains an empty promise for which the only "preparation" is a halfhearted attempt to establish an unpopular and undemocratic system of local self-government based on collective responsibility and given odium by Japanese utilization in Manchuria and other areas under their control.

Questions basic to the future of democracy such as the form of the Constitution and the composition and election of the National Congress remain the dictation of the Kuomintang. There is no progress toward the fundamental conditions of freedom of expression and recognition of non-Kuomintang groups. Even the educational and political advantages of giving power and democratic character to the existing but impotent Peoples Political Council are ignored.

The Kuomintang shows no intention of relaxing the authoritarian controls on which its present power depends. Far from discarding or reducing the paraphernalia of a police state—the multiple and omnipresent secret police organizations, the Gendarmerie, and so forth—it continues to strengthen them as its last resort for internal security. . . .

These apparently suicidal policies of the Kuomintang have their roots in the composition and nature of the Party.

In view of the above it becomes pertinent to ask *why* the Kuomintang has lost its power of leadership; *why* it neither wishes actively to wage war against Japan itself nor to cooperate whole-heartedly with the American Army in China; and *why* it has ceased to be capable of unifying the country.

The answer to all these questions is to be found in the present composition and nature of the Party. Politically, a classical and definitive American description becomes ever more true; the Kuomintang is a congerie of conservative political cliques interested primarily in the preservation of their own power against all outsiders and in jockeying for position among themselves. Economically, the Kuomintang rests on the narrow base of the rural-gentry-landlords and militarists, the higher ranks of the government bureaucracy, and merchant bankers having intimate connections with the government bureaucrats. This base has actually contracted during the war. The Kuomintang no longer commands, as it once did, the unequivocal support of China's industrialists, who as a group have been much weakened economically, and hence politically, by the Japanese seizure of the coastal cities. . . .

December 9, 1944 (Davies)

. . . The Generalissimo realizes that if he accedes to the Communist terms for a coalition government, they will sooner or later dispossess him and his Kuomintang of power. He will therefore not, unless driven to an extremity, form a genuine coalition government. He will seek to retain his present government, passively wait out the war and conserve his strength, knowing that the Communist issue must eventually be joined.

The Communists, on their part, have no interest in reaching an agreement with the Generalissimo short of a genuine coalition government. They recognize that Chiang's position is crumbling, that they may before long receive substantial Russian support and that if they have patience they will succeed to authority in at least North China. . . .

The Communists would, inevitably, win such a war because the foreign powers, including the United States, which would support the Government, could not feasibly supply enough aid to compensate for the organic weaknesses of the Government.

January 23, 1943 (Service)

. . . Assuming that open hostilities are for the time being averted, the eventual defeat and withdrawal of the Japanese will leave the Kuomintang still confronted with the

Communists solidly entrenched in most of North China (East Kansu, North Shensi, Shansi, South Chahar, Hopei, Shantung, North Kiangsu and North Anhwei). In addition the Communists will be in a position to move into the vacuum created by the Japanese withdrawal from Suiyan, Jehol and Manchuria, in all of which areas there is already some Communist activity. In the rest of China they will have the sympathy of elements among the liberals, intellectuals, and students.

. . . There is undoubtedly a strong revulsion in the mind of the average, non-party Chinese to the idea of renewed civil war and the Kuomintang may indeed have difficulty with the loyalty and effectiveness of its conscript troops. *October 9, 1944 (Service)*

Just as the Japanese Army cannot crush these militant people now, so also will Kuomintang force fail in the future. With their new arms and organization, knowledge of their own strength, and determination to keep what they have been fighting for, these people—now some 90 million and certain to be many more before the Kuomintang can reach them—will resist oppression. They are not Communists. They do not want separation or independence. But at present they regard the Kuomintang—from their own experience—as oppressors; and the Communists as their leaders and benefactors.

With this great popular base, the Communists likewise cannot be eliminated. Kuomintang attempts to do so by force must mean a complete denial of democracy. This will strengthen the ties of the Communists with the people: a Communist victory will be inevitable. . . .

From the basic fact that the Communists have built up popular support of a magnitude and depth which makes their elimination impossible, *we must draw the conclusion that the Communists will have a certain and important share in China's future* . . . I suggest the future conclusion that unless the Kuomintang goes as far as the Communists in political and economic reform, and otherwise proves itself able to contest this leadership of the people (none of which it yet shows signs of being willing or able to do), the Communists will be the dominant force in China within a comparatively few years.

The End of World War II and the Beginning of the Civil War

In 1945 World War II ended and the Japanese returned home. At that point even Mao believed the struggle to determine China's fate would last for many years. In troops, equipment, finances, and foreign aid, Chiang's position was far superior; the Communists of necessity relied almost solely on their wide popular support in the countryside.

Yet the KMT-Communist civil war that ensued after Japan's defeat lasted only four years and ended with the Communists' victory. This four-year struggle is described by Franz Schurmann, a noted modern China scholar, and Orville Schell, co-editor of *The China Reader*.

The Strategy and Ideology of Communist Victory
by Franz Schurmann and Orville Schell

The years 1945 to 1949 witnessed one of the greatest events of the twentieth century: the triumph of Communism in China. Communism not only altered the lives of six hundred million Chinese, but radically affected the world balance of power. The entire Eurasian heartland from Berlin to Pyongyang was under the red flag. The victory of Communism in China raised fears that a wave of Communist Revolution might begin to break out in the underdeveloped world and engulf the advanced West as Lenin and Mao Tse-tung predicted.

It was well known that Kuomintang China was corrupt, disorganized, and opposed by a large segment of its people. Yet as late as 1947 most people could not envisage the possibility of a Communist triumph. . . .

The war against Japan only delayed the inevitable mortal confrontation between the two foes, and almost as soon as Japan surrendered, Nationalists and Communists poured into the occupied areas, each trying to gain as much territory as possible. One of the main targets for both was

Manchuria, which was to become the heartland of the Civil War struggle.

In February 1945 the United States, Britain, and the Soviet Union signed the controversial Yalta Pact in which Stalin was granted concessions in Manchuria in return for a pledge to enter the war against Japan shortly after the defeat of Germany. We will not debate the political wisdom of the Yalta Pact except to observe that it paved the way for Soviet occupation of Manchuria in the immediate postwar period.

Shortly after the Japanese surrender in August 1945 the Russians occupied Manchuria, where, by Allied agreement, they were to remain for only three months, until the arrival of Nationalist military units. (The Soviet Union was still technically allied to the Nationalist government by wartime treaty.) But by November 1945 it was obvious that the Nationalist takeover of Manchuria could not possibly be completed in the projected time, since Chiang was hampered by insufficient transport. As improbable as it may sound today, the Nationalists finally requested that the Russians remain in Manchuria longer than originally outlined, obviously fearing that the Chinese Red Army would take over if some foreign power did not fill the vacuum. In view of later statements accusing Stalin of conspiring with Mao, it is difficult to see how the Nationalists hoped to protect Manchuria from one Red Army with another Red Army.

What actually transpired between the Japanese surrender in August 1945 and the final Soviet withdrawal in March 1946 is still a source of much contention. There are, however, some known facts: the Soviets looted most of Manchuria's industrial plant equipment; Nationalist forces at this time totaled about three million, while the Communists had less than one million; it is also common knowledge that the United States supplied Chiang with large quantities of aid and the vital air transport required to move troops from Burma, India, and Central China to Manchuria. What has not been firmly established is the extent to which the Soviet Union collaborated with the Chinese Communists prior to the arrival of Chiang's troops in early 1946. . . .

The race to reoccupy China brought the subterranean Civil War out into the open. While the Americans were rushing Nationalist troops northward by air, the Communists were being marched by Lin Piao through North China into Southern Manchuria. As Lin's army moved, they expended great efforts to mobilize the countryside, thereby laying the foundations for future isolation of Manchuria from Central China. At the same time they constantly harassed the tenuous rail lines linking Manchuria to the main body of Chiang's forces.

Nationalist-Communist relations deteriorated rapidly. By the end of 1945 Chou En-lai had given up negotiating in the Nationalist capital and had flown back to Yenan. Clashes increased as troops from both sides poured into Manchuria. Tension had reached a high point by December 1945, when the Marshall Peace Mission arrived in China. [General George C. Marshall was sent to China by President Truman to arrange an alliance between the Communists and the KMT.] Marshall made a heroic attempt to end the hostilities, and for a while it looked as though he might succeed. But in retrospect it is obvious that the shaky coalition he patched together was little more than a veneer of unity beneath which the desperate struggle continued. Intransigence on both sides moved the dispute from the conference table to the battlefield. Chiang refused anything short of complete Nationalist control over all of Manchuria. Unfortunately for him, the Communists were in far too strong a position in Manchuria to consider acquiescing so completely. Marshall's terms were finally unacceptable to both sides, for each wanted nothing less than total victory. By the spring of 1946 full-scale civil war was inevitable.

Actually Chiang appeared to be in a relatively strong position at this time. Having availed himself of the American air-lift, he held over half of Manchuria's larger cities. He had received promises of considerable American aid, and his American-trained and -equipped army outnumbered anything that the Communists could put in the field. What is more, in early 1946 the Nationalists won a series of engagements with the Communists which gave them cause for optimism. In March 1947 Chiang's troops even took Yenan, the Communist capital. But these victories were deceptive. Still mustering their forces and avoiding a showdown, the Communists had not yet begun to go on the offensive. Before moving decisively, they deliberately allowed the Nationalists to overextend themselves, a mistake for which the Nationalists would pay dearly.

In the winter of 1947 Chiang's commanders, deluded by a false sense of confidence, ordered their men to dig in in the cities to wait out the cold Manchurian winter—a tactic referred to as "sitting the enemy to death."

In the spring of 1947 the People's Liberation Army (PLA), which had been formally constituted in March under Lin Piao's command, exploded in a series of quick offensives which left the citybound Nationalists dazed and confused. Lin swept town after town under his control until he had almost completely isolated the big Manchurian cities of Mukden, Kirin, and Changchun. This was the turning point in the Civil War, and except for the cities, Manchuria was lost. Initiative was clearly in the PLA's hands. Each Communist victory made Nationalist defeat more certain. Crippled from within by poor morale, corruption, poor strategy, and weak leadership, and battered from without by one of the world's finest fighting forces, the Nationalists disintegrated.

Chiang stubbornly chose to play his all-or-nothing game to its final conclusion, and as the situation grew more hopeless, his regime became more authoritarian and repressive in tactics, which resulted in mass disaffection among student and intellectual groups. Chiang's last crutch was American aid, but even Washington was becoming skeptical about pouring countless millions into China without any positive returns. They looked on critically as North China fell into Communist hands, leaving the Nationalist-held Manchurian cities isolated islands in a Red sea.

Mao had declared in December 1947 that "the Chinese people's revolutionary war has now reached a turning point." The PLA, whose ranks had been swelled with large numbers of defectors from the Nationalist armies, launched the final phase of its Mainland conquest in the beginning of 1948 with the siege of Mukden. By November the Nationalists had been cut to ribbons and Manchuria had fallen. The struggle then shifted to China proper as the Communists closed in for the kill. By April, P'eng Te-huai had retaken Yenan, reversing one of the few much-heralded Nationalist victories. In June, Chen Yi and Liu Po-cheng took the old city of Kaifeng in Honan. Defeat followed defeat, severing the last threads of hope which held the shattered Nationalist cause together. In November 1948 the United States Embassy in Nanking reported that in the four battles of Tsinan, the Liaoning Corridor, Changchun, and Mukden alone, the Nationalists had lost 33 divisions and over 320,000 men, 85 percent equipped by the United States. The situation was so bad that in November 1948 General David Barr reported the following to the Department of the Army:

> I am convinced that the military situation has deteriorated to the point where only active participation of U.S. troops could effect a remedy. . . . Military matériel and economic aid in my opinion is less important to the salvation of China than other factors. No battle has been lost since my arrival due to the lack of ammunition or equipment. [The Nationalists'] debacles in my opinion can all be attributed to the world's worst leadership and many other morale-destroying factors that can lead to a complete loss of will to fight. The complete ineptness of high military leaders and the widespread corruption and dishonesty throughout the armed forces, could, in some measure, have been controlled and directed had the above authority and facilities been available. Chinese leaders lack the moral courage to issue and enforce an unpopular decision.

General Barr went on to recommend the withdrawal of the Joint United States Military Advisory Group from China.

Disaster followed disaster for the Nationalists, as the fighting moved into China's heartland. In November and December 1948 the Communists delivered the *coup de grâce* to the Nationalists at the epic battle of Huai-Hai. The battle lasted sixty-five days during which time a million troops maneuvered back and forth across the huge battlefield in a bloody slaughter. Once again the Communists, led by Ch'en Yi, used the strategy which had been so successful in Manchuria: the PLA concentrated on systematically cutting Nationalist communication lines until Chiang no longer had any means of resupplying or reinforcing his troops. The Nationalists' defeat at Huai-Hai was a crushing

blow, from which they never even began to recover.
Military chaos was accompanied by economic collapse and
political disintegration. The Nationalists pleaded for American intervention, but there was little interest in Washington.

The Nationalists' final year on the Mainland was marked
by a series of disorganized and humiliating retreats to the
South, leading to their final flight to Taiwan. The Mandate
of Heaven had clearly passed. By the fall of 1949 China
was "lost."

Why did the Communists win and the Nationalists lose?
Ever since the defeat of Chiang and the Kuomintang and the
establishment of the People's Republic, there has been a
great debate around this issue. The United States gave
massive amounts of aid to Chiang—including military equipment and air support—and then withdrew. The Communists,
in contrast, were without the benefit of foreign assistance,
and relied on themselves and on popular support among the
Chinese peasantry for their ultimate victory.

The Civil War
from Sociological Resources for the Social Sciences

In 1949, the civil war between the Nationalists and the
Communists came to an end. The Communists won, but
not because they started with superior weapons or more
soldiers. In fact when the final phase of the civil war began
in 1946, the Nationalists far outnumbered the Communists
and held vastly superior fire power. The crucial difference
lay in the morale of the Communists and their ability to
win more support and compliance from the millions of
Chinese peasants. . . .

Why did the Communists win and the Nationalists lose?
There are several reasons. One was that the Nationalists
did not have enough power to overcome the warlords and
introduce many of the social changes which they advocated.

Another reason for the Nationalist defeat was the war
with Japan from 1936 to 1945. Weak China was no match
for Japan's aggressive and powerful invasion of the Chinese
mainland. The weakness of the government, the inflation-
ary economy, and the misery caused by the war undermined

confidence in the Nationalists and made the people receptive and eager for change. The Communists on the other hand, with high morale and a keen sense of organization, confidently enlarged their following among the Chinese people by leading and publicizing their guerrilla activity against the Japanese.

Still another reason for the Nationalist defeat was the difference between Nationalist and Communist soldiers. Mao Tse-tung worked hard to give his soldiers a sense of purpose and deliberately trained them to help the peasants, to pay for the food they ate, and not to loot in the villages. The Nationalist soldiers were far less disciplined and were often feared by the villages they passed through.

A final and extremely important reason for the Communist victory was the differences between the two parties in rural policies. The Nationalist leaders relied on the support of the wealthy strata of Chinese society, the successful businessmen in the cities, and the landlords in the countryside. They did not encourage change in the countryside for fear the peasantry would get out of control and turn against the government. The Nationalists were not unaware of the peasant problem and drew up excellent rural plans, including a land reform. But the pressure of events and lack of conviction kept them from putting these plans into action.

The Communists, on the other hand, had a completely different approach to the problems of rural China. They sought a broader base of political support. The Communist leaders more than the Nationalists were able to capture the support of more peasants who longed for improvement in their daily lives. The Communists built up a stronger organization and were able to carry out plans for agrarian reform. If the Nationalists had been able to carry out their agrarian plans, the Communists might never have come into power. The Nationalists feared fanning the flames of peasant discontent against their allies, the landlords and the cultivated gentlemen in the countryside. The Communists fed the fires and exploited the peasant discontent to begin shaping a new society.

Mao has used this tale, based on an old Taoist version, to put across the idea that when sufficiently organized, people can indeed accomplish "miracles." The political moral of this story is that average people (in this case Chinese peasants) can make their own history.

The Foolish Old Man
Who Removed the Mountains
by Mao Tse-tung

There is an ancient Chinese fable called "The Foolish Old Man Who Removed the Mountains." It tells of an old man who lived in northern China long, long ago and was known as the Foolish Old Man of North Mountain. His house faced south, and beyond his doorway stood the two great peaks, Taihang and Wangwu, obstructing the way. With great determination, he led his sons in digging up these mountains, hoe in hand. Another graybeard, known as the Wise Old Man, saw them and said derisively, "How silly of you to do this! It is quite impossible for you few to dig up these two huge mountains." The Foolish Old Man replied: "When I die, my sons will carry on; when they die, there will be my grandsons, and then their sons and grandsons, and so on to infinity. High as they are, the mountains cannot grow any higher and with ever bit we dig, they will be that much lower. Why can't we clear them away?" Having refuted the Wise Old Man's wrong view, he went on digging every day, unshaken in his conviction. God was moved by this, and he sent down two angels, who carried the mountains away on their backs. Today, two big mountains lie like a dead weight on the Chinese people. One is imperialism, the other is feudalism. The Chinese Communist Party has long made up its mind to dig them up. We must persevere and work unceasingly, and we too will touch God's heart. Our God is none other than the masses of the Chinese people. If they stand up and dig together, with us, why can't these two mountains be cleared away?

Jack Belden was an American correspondent in China during the closing years of the civil war who traveled through the rural areas of the north then being fought over by Communist and KMT armies. An adventuresome traveler, he made his way through dangerous countryside and personally witnessed the collapse of the old rural society under the blows of the civil war. Through his portrayal of the struggle to overthrow landlords in Stone Wall Village, Belden describes events happening in the late 1940's throughout the liberated regions of northern China as the Communists consolidated their control. Thus, although this is the story of only a single village, thousands of similar Chinese villages also "overturned" as revolution swept away the established social order.

Stone Wall Village
by Jack Belden

I think I can best illustrate the difficulty of making this type of revolution and incidentally reveal some of the techniques of the Communist party by telling the story of how a single village revolted against its landlord. It is a story rather reminiscent of a Greek tragedy in its plot and it concerns Stone Wall Village—a hamlet of five hundred people located in the southern part of Shansi Province, amid a range of hills, old and redolent of Chinese legend, that are known as the Taiyueh Mountains.

The land in this region is rocky, bare of forest and grudging in it fertility so that the hard-pressed farmers have been forced to build terraces and cultivate the hill slopes nearly to the top of every peak. For many centuries, the peasants have been struggling not only against the parsimonious nature of these mountains, but against the brutal exactions and dark superstitions of a civilization probably very much like that which Christ knew. These people, however, believed in no Supreme God, but rather knew many gods, including the God of Fate who made them poor, and ghosts, devils and evil spirits whom they believed lurked in the rocks, trees and the bodies of the animals which roamed their hills. As a consequence, they were easy prey for the intrigues of village witches who called down spirits to their incense tables and frightened peasants into doing the bidding of the landlords.

The common farmers, always hungry and always in debt, had a verse about their bitter lot which ran like this:

Harvest every year; but yearly—nothing
Borrow money yearly; yearly still in debt.
Broken huts, small basins, crooked pots;
Half an acre of land; five graves.

About one hundred families lived in Stone Wall Village, many of them in caves hollowed out of the side of the mountain at the base of which the village was situated. South of the town ran a river, overhung with willows and cedars, on the banks of which was a mill where the people ground their wheat and Indian corn—the two crops raised yearly by Stone Wall Village. The barren aspect of the place was somewhat relieved by small orchards of peach, apricot and pear trees.

Stone Wall Village had one peculiarity that set it apart from most Chinese villages: its women did not raise many children. The reason for this were manifold. In the first place, many of the farmers were too poor to support a wife and did not marry. Secondly, girl babies were often strangled by their parents at birth because of poverty. Thirdly, the Japanese, who had occupied a strong point on the opposite bank of the river for six years, had raped many of the women, venereal disease had become widespread and many of the women had become sterile.

Politically, Stone Wall Village was in the hands of its village chief, a landlord named Wang Chang-ying. Although his personal characteristics are not germane to this story, it may be mentioned in passing that Landlord Wang was fifty years old, that he wore a small goatee and smoked a long-handled water pipe. In fair weather, it was said that he promenaded on the streets and beat any child who was unfortunate enough to bump into him. At sight of him, many of the village poor would immediately run indoors.

Wang's possessions included sixty-five acres (no one else owned more than three acres) of irrigated land, the riverside mill, a large store of grain, one wife, one son, one daughter, one daughter-in-law and a vengeful nature. . . .

Twenty-five years old, tall, handsome and with a proud manner, Wang's son used to stride about the village in the daytime in a long black gown and a clean white towel on his head. At night, however, he was a tiger on the prowl, peremptorily knocking on doors and forcing himself on whatever woman took his fancy. If any were bold enough to object, he would threaten them with the Japanese.

Wang's chief friend in the village was a rich farmer named Shih Ping-hua, who acted as the landlord's clerk and assistant. There were two or three other small landlords in the village, but none of them owned more than two acres of land and none had power.

The chief personal enemy of Wang was a tenant farmer named Lee Tien-shang, or Original Fortune Lee. Sixty years old, with a beard down to his chest, his forehead wrinkled like a washboard, his mouth half emptied of teeth, and his eyes radiating crow's-feet, Lee walked around the village, summer and winter, in filthy white rags, his back bent at a forty-five degree angle and his head inclined toward the ground. Lee rented seven mow of land from Wang, but since he had to give half of his crops to the landlord, he was barely able to support his wife and ten-year-old son. There had been another son, but he had died, and the manner of his dying was the principal cause for the enmity between the landlord and the tenant.

During the Japanese war, the landlord used to feast the Japanese platoon leader at frequent intervals, exacting from his tenants all the food necessary for such entertainments. The peasants became incensed at the continued extortions and Lee's son and two militiamen decided to kill the platoon leader, but unfortunately a grenade they threw at him from an overhead cave did not explode. Learning who was behind the plot, the landlord informed the lieutenant who dragged Lee's son and the two militiamen from the fields and slowly bayoneted them to death inside the Three Sects Temple. Thus Lee had come to hate Wang, but he was too afraid and had been too long suppressed to take any action of his own. There were other enemies of the landlord in the village, but here it is not necessary to do any more than note their existence.

In 1945, the Japanese Empire surrendered to the United States, but this meant little to the people of Stone Wall Village. True, they saw the Japanese across the river pack up and leave, and no longer did the platoon leader come to feast with Wang and sleep with his daughter and wife, but the landlord remained the power in the village, his son still blackjacked women into sleeping with him, land rents remained as high as ever and everyone was always in debt.

Such was the condition of Stone Wall Village when the Chinese Revolution suddenly descended on it. There had been vague stories of this revolution in the village; there had been murmurings about the 8th Route Army, about a thing called democracy and about villages where there were no landlords and everyone had an equal amount of land. But the people had listened to these rumors with only half an ear; they were poor and fated to be poor; they did not want to fight anybody, they only wanted to be left alone.

Landlord Wang had also heard these rumors; he did not take them seriously either. But as a precaution, he used to tell the people: "Flesh cut from others won't stick to your own body." The people, however, did not need this warning: they had no intention of moving against Landlord Wang.

Nevertheless, the Revolution came to Stone Wall Village.

It did not come like a flash of swift lightning; for a revolution like everything else moves slowly in China. Nor did it announce itself like a clap of thunder, with the beat of drums, the sound of rifle fire or hot slogans shouted on the country air.

To be more exact, five men brought the revolution to Stone Wall Village. They were not soldiers nor were they Communist party members. One had been a schoolteacher, another a student, a third a waiter, a fourth a shop assistant and a fifth a farmer. They were all members of the Hohsien County Salvation Association and their job was to "overturn" Stone Wall Village.

"Overturn" is a term of the Chinese Revolution that came into being after the surrender of the Japanese. In Communist terminology it means to turn over the social, political and economic life of every village, to overturn feudalism and establish democracy, to overturn superstition and establish reason. The first step of the overturning movement is to "struggle" against the landlords and divide the land.

To do this sounds easy. You have the guns and the power and you just tell the landlord to give a share of his land to the people. But it is never that easy. In Stone Wall Village, there was no army, there was no militia. The 8th Route

Army was far to the south. Even the guerrillas had gone elsewhere. Landlord Wang was the power and the people were afraid of him.

The leader of the Hohsien Salvation team was a thirty-one-year-old cadre, the son of a bankrupt rich farmer, named Chou Yu-chuan. When Chou and his fellow-workers arrived in Stone Wall Village they posted proclamations of the Shansi-Hopei-Honan-Shantung Border Region government, announcing that every village had the right to elect their own officials and that land rents and rates of interest should be reduced. Then they called a meeting to explain these proclamations, but the people listened only half-heartedly, kept their mouths tightly shut and went home without speaking further to the cadres.

For several days, the cadres went individually among the people asking them about local conditions and their own lives, but no one would talk. Whenever a cadre approached groups of people, they would break apart and move away. One or two men cornered alone admitted they were afraid of the landlord.

Under these conditions, the cadres could not carry on their work, so they decided to seek out one of the poorer men in the village and talk to him alone and in secret.

At this time, Chou and another cadre were living in a cave next door to one occupied by a tenant farmer, named Ma Chiu-tze. Ma had bought his cave before the Japanese war with six dollars earned by his wife in spinning thread. Now, his wife was sick and Ma often came to the cadre's cave and slept on the same kang with them. During the night, the three men always talked.

Ever since the Ching dynasty, Ma revealed, his family had been poor tenants, renting land and never having any of their own. Every year, he raised eight piculs of millet and every year he had to give four of these piculs to Landlord Wang. He could afford no medicine for his wife whom he feared was dying. Two years before, his father had died and he had not been able to buy the old man a coffin, but had to wrap him in straw. Now he was thirty-five and he was still poor and it looked as if he would always be poor. "I guess I have a bad brain," he would say in summing up the reasons for his poverty.

Then the cadres would ask: "Are you poor because you

have a bad brain or because your father left you no property."

"I guess that's the reason; my father left me no property."

"Really is that the reason?" asked the cadres. "Let us make an account. You pay four piculs of grain every year to the landlord. Your family has rented land for sixty years. That's 240 piculs of grain. If you had not given this to the landlord, you would be rich. The reason you are poor, then, is because you have been exploited by the landlord."

They would talk like this for hours and Ma would finally acknowledge that he was exploited by the landlord. Then he would say: "What can I do? Everyone looks down on me. When it's mealtime, the landlord eats inside the house, but I must eat outside, standing up. I am not good enough. Everyone looks down on me."

"And why is that?" said the cadres. "That is because you have no money and because you have no money you have no position. That is why we must overturn so that everyone can have an equal position and no man will look down on another."

Ma agreed that the landlords had to be overthrown before there could be any happiness for the poor, but he was only half convinced of his own statements. There was yet a long distance between words and action and the weight of two thousand years of tradition lay very heavily on Ma as on most Chinese peasants.

For fifteen days, the cadres talked with Ma. In this period they had twenty-three formal talks with him besides the numerous evening talks. They conversed with other farmers in the village, but Ma was the most "active" element. From this it can be seen it is not easy to stir a Chinese peasant.

At last Ma was ready to "struggle" and "settle"—two terms of the Revolution that mean to struggle against the landlord and to settle accounts with him. Still, Ma was a little frightened.

"If we go to work," he said to the cadres, "you must not leave us."

"We will stay until the whole village has turned over," the cadres promised.

Ma Chiu-tze became the Revolution in Stone Wall

Village. But one man is not enough to overturn feudalism. More help was needed. So on the sixteenth night of the cadre's stay in the village, Ma brought three of his friends into the cave, including the old farmer Original Fortune Lee.

After offering the farmers cigarettes, the cadres announced they had come to Stone Wall Village to help the people establish a government of their own choosing. "We know you people of Stone Wall Village are eating bitterness," they said. "We, too, in our turn have been oppressed. All the oppressed are from one home. Tell us your sufferings and we shall try to settle them for you. If you don't want to tell us tonight—why—think them over and come and tell us in three or four days."

Under the influence of this talk, the four men began to tell their own private sufferings, sometimes all speaking at once. One of them, a twenty-year-old boy named Liu Kwang, told how Wang had ordered him to go to work in the Japanese labor corps. When he refused, the landlord and his son had lowered him into a well in water up to his neck. When pulled up he was more dead than alive and could neither work for the Japanese or in his own fields.

A long-term worker named Second Jewel Pao told how the landlord had forced him to dig up grain from a secret hiding place. Finally, Original Fortune Lee told how his son had been bayoneted to death. At this time, the four peasants became so emotional they began to cry. Toward midnight, they reached the conclusion that the time had at last come for their revenge. They swore a solemn oath. "If the Japanese come back tomorrow or if the troops of Chiang Kai-shek come, we will turn over. Even if only for a day, we will turn."

The meeting then broke up with the decision to mobilize more farmers. On the following night, a second meeting was attended by thirteen peasants. It was to prove an unlucky number. In this meeting after the usual "reveal bitterness" talk, it was decided to mobilize more farmers and then hold a mass meeting in which all the villagers could reveal their sufferings.

During the meeting, one or two farmers expressed the fear that Landlord Wang had heard about their talks. Since an ex-puppet militiaman knew of the meeting and since he was sleeping with the landlord's daughter, they surmised the landlord must by now be informed of everything. The cadres made light of the peasant's fears and told them not to worry.

That night, Original Fortune Lee did not come home. As he was an old man and never stayed out at night his wife was worried. When a whole day and then another passed without his appearing, she became frantic and inquired of everyone in the village if they had seen her husband, but no one could give her any information. He had last been seen leaving the meeting and heading for home. His path, it was known, led along a cliff that overhung the river. Whether he had slipped in the darkness and fallen in the water or had just continued walking by his home and left the village was a mystery which no one in the town could answer.

On the third day, a man grinding flour in the water mill beside the river noticed that his water wheel was not turning properly and on investigation he found the body of Original Fortune Lee riding amid the spokes. The old man's mouth was gagged with a cloth, his hands were tied behind him and he had been some time dead.

As no one else would touch him, the cadres extricated the body from the water wheel and carried it up to the Three Sects Temple. Since there is an ancient law in China that the body of a murdered man may not be brought to his home, they left him there and called his wife. Then she came and dressed Original Fortune Lee in funeral white and shed tears on his pock-marked face and moaned over his body. The people saw and they felt sorry, but they went off home and they whispered among themselves: "Better keep quiet, we may be next."

The revolution in Stone Wall Village had been dealt a blow. The counterrevolution had struck first.

After the murder of Original Fortune Lee the people went about in terror and shut up again like clams. Even those who had attended the second meeting now said: "We haven't begun to struggle with the landlord, but one of us is gone already."

The cadres were very much surprised by the murder. They thought they had been too careless and had not placed enough belief in the peasants' fears. They also thought a hand grenade might be thrown at any time into their meeting cave. Their biggest fear, however, was that the peasants would give up the overturning movement altogether. Therefore they decided to hold a memorial meeting in honor of Original Fortune Lee, and by this meeting to mobilize the people.

On the stage opposite the Three Sects Temple, where semireligious plays were held during festival times, the cadres placed pictures of Mao Tze-tung, chairman of the Chinese Communist party and General Chu Teh, commander in chief of the Communist-led 18th Group Army. Beside these pictures they placed strips of paper saying: WE SHALL TAKE REVENGE FOR THIS PEASANT.

One hundred people of Stone Wall Village attended this meeting, but Landlord Wang did not come. The county magistrate came especially to make a speech and announced: "The government intends to clear up all murders. The people should continue to overturn and to establish a democratic government of their own."

The memorial meeting lasted four hours. After it was over, another meeting was called to decide how to continue "overturning." Only six farmers came to this meeting. No one said directly that he was afraid to attend, but weakly gave the excuse: "I have a little work to do."

These six men, however, decided that because of the murder they would have to "settle" with Landlord Wang immediately.

At the end of five days, thirty farmers mobilized by the other six gathered in the cave for another meeting. Until nearly midnight, they told stories of how they had suffered at the landlord's hands.

Suddenly, someone said: "Maybe Wang will run away."

"Let's get him tonight," said several farmers at once.

After some discussion, they all trooped out of the cave and started a march on Landlord Wang's home. Among the thirty men, there was one rifle and three hand grenades.

The marching farmers separated into two groups. One climbed on top of the cliffs and worked along the cave roofs until they were over the courtyard. They others marched directly to the gate, knocked loudly and commanded the landlord to open up.

Wang's wife answered the door and announced that her husband was not at home. Refusing to believe her, the peasants made a search and discovered a secret passage behind a cupboard. Descending through an underground tunnel, they found Wang cowering in a subterranean cave. They took him away and locked him up overnight.

That night Wang's son fled to the county seat of Hohsien, ten miles away. Here landlords from other villages had organized bandits, former puppet troops, and some of the soldiers of Warlord Yen Hsi-shan into a "Revenge Corps." When the people learned of the flight of Wang's son, they grew anxious and said among themselves: "It is easy to catch a tiger, but it is dangerous to let him go back to the forest."

Nevertheless, they decided to go ahead with the struggle against Landlord Wang. That same day a mass meeting was called in a great square field south of the town, not far from the river. About eighty people came to complain against Wang, while the rest of the village watched—among them Wang's wife and daughter.

In the course of the morning and afternoon, the crowd accused the landlord of many crimes, including betrayal of resistance members to the Japanese, robbing them of grain, forcing them into labor gangs. At last, he asked if he admitted the accusations.

"All these things I have done," he said, "but really it was not myself who did it, but the Japanese."

He could not have chosen worse words. Over the fields now sounded an angry roar, as of the sea, and the crowd broke into a wild fury. Everybody shouted at once, proclaiming against the landlords words. Even the nonparticipating bystanders warmed to something akin to anger.

Then above the tumult of the crowd came a voice louder than the rest, shouting: "Hang him up!"

The chairman of the meeting and the cadres were disregarded. For all that the crowd noticed they did not exist.

The crowd boiled around Wang, and somewhere a rope went swishing over a tree. Willing hands slung one end of the rope around Wang's waist. Other eager hands gave the rope a jerk. Wang rose suddenly and came to a halt in mid-air about three feet above the earth. And there he hung, his head down, his stomach horizontal and his legs stretched out—a perfect illustration of what the Chinese call a "duck's swimming form."

About his floating body, the crowd foamed, anger wrinkling their foreheads and curses filling their mouths. Some bent down and spit in the landlord's eyes and others howled into his ears.

As he rose from the ground, the landlord felt a terror which mounted higher as his position became more uncomfortable. Finally, he could bear it no longer and shouted: "Put me down. I know my wrongs. I admit everything."

The spite of the crowd, however, was not so easily assuaged and they only answered the landlord's pleas with shouts: "Pull him up! He's too low! Higher! Higher!"

After a while the anger of the people abated and cooler heads counseled. "If we let him die now, we won't be able to settle accounts with him." Then they allowed him to come down for a rest.

At this point, the wife of Original Fortune Lee came up close to Wang and said in a plaintive voice: "Somebody killed my husband. Was it you?"

Wang's face which had grown red from hanging in the air slowly was drained of all color. "No, I did not do it," he said.

"Tell the truth," said the crowd. "You can admit everything to us and nothing will happen. But if you don't tell us the truth, we will hang you up again."

"No, it was not me."

These words were hardly out of his mouth before someone jerked on the rope and the landlord flew into the air again. This time the crowd let him hang for a long while. Unable to bear the pain, Wang finally said: "Let me down. I'll speak."

Then, between sobs and sighs, he told how he and his son had seized Original Fortune Lee as he was walking home from the meeting, tied his hands together, held his head under water until he was dead and then had thrown him in the river, thinking he would float away.

A cry of rage went up as Wang finished speaking.

"You've already killed three of our men in the war," said Liu Kwang. "That could be excused. But now your own life can never repay us for the crimes you've done."

Again Wang was hung up and this time many shouted: "Let him hang until he is dead." But others said: "That is too quick; he must first have a taste of the suffering we've had."

At dusk, they let Wang down once more and put him in a cave under guard again.

As soon as the meeting was over, twenty or thirty men went to the landlord's house, drove the wife and daughter out of doors and sealed the house. The two women went to a nearby village to stay with relatives.

That evening the five cadres and those who had taken an active part in the struggle against the landlord walked around the village to listen to the gossip and sample public opinion. Such words were heard as: "Serves him right; he's so wicked. This is too light for him. Just count his sins."

Later that night another meeting of those of the village who wanted to struggle against the landlord was held in a courtyard. This time 120 people attended.

When the cadres asked: "How do you feel? Have you done well?" the answer came back: "Oh fine! Fine!"

But exactly what to do with the landlord was a problem for which the people at first had no solution. Half of these in the meeting thought he should be beaten to death. A few said: "He is too old." Some had no ideas at all. Others thought that his clerk, the rich farmer Shih Tseng-hua, should be bound up with him at the same time in the struggle. This suggestion, however, was voted down when someone pointed out: "You should always collect the big melons in the field first. So we should cut off the big head first."

It was decided that Wang must die for his murders. . . .

When the struggle against the landlords of Stone Wall Village ended, an immediate settlement of accounts was begun. According to Communist terminology, this involved the division of the "fruits of struggle." A man who could write was located and established in a cave where he wrote down all the things that were to be divided. Amont other things, this included furniture, grain, cotton and cloth, but principally land.

Naturally, this was a complicated process and not everyone at first was satisfied, but after several meetings, all the land taken from Wang Chang-ying was split up in a fashion that satisfied most of the people. When all the land was divided, everyone owned on the average two-thirds of an acre of water land; not much it is true, but far more than the poor had had before. Those whose bitterness had been especially heavy in the past were favored where an exactly equal division was impossible. The families of the four murdered farmers received half an acre more than the others.

Ma Chiu-tze, who previously had owned only one-sixth of an acre of land, now had about an acre and a half for himself and his wife. As soon as the land was his, he gave a feast for his relatives, for those who made out the land credentials, for the county cadres and for those who had helped to turn over Stone Wall Village. Every day, he went out to look at his land and in autumn he weeded, cut grass and plowed the whole day long.

Liu Kwang, no longer afraid of being lowered into a well by the landlord, received a new house from the settlement. Early every morning, his wife got up and swept out the courtyard, she was so happy to be living in a house instead of a cave.

Even stranger things happened which the reader may believe or not, as he likes. In the village, there was an old man who was deaf in one ear. Once he had borrowed four cents from the landlord and he had not been able to repay it, so Wang had boxed him on the ear and he had been deaf ever since. In the overturning movement he acquired two-thirds of an acre of land and he became very happy. One day he remarked to his son: "In the past, I was deaf because I was oppressed by the landlord, but now I am in such high spirits that I can hear with my bad ear again." Shortly after this, the old man looked at the pictures of the Earth and Heaven gods on his wall and angrily said: "I worshipped you for many years, but you did me no good. Now I am going to get rid of you all." So saying, he tore the gods from the wall and threw them in the latrine.

After the struggle against the landlords, the cadres urged the village to organize a Farmers Association and then to elect officers from among the 155 members of whom thirty were women.

Election day proved to be a gala event. The mountains had seen nothing like it in years and people gathered from neighboring villages in a holiday spirit. There had been long and heated discussion in the villages on just how the voting should take place. No one had ever voted before; most could not write. If voting were done by raising hands, there would be no dignity in the first election and it would not be secret. Therefore, it was decided to vote by putting beans in a bowl. Five officers were elected, among them Old Legality Ma, Liu Kwang and Second Jewel Pao. So, with the exception of the murdered Original Fortune Lee, every one of the four members who had attended the original secret meeting was elected.

1949: Liberation

On October 1, 1949, Mao Tse-tung, Chairman of the Chinese Communist Party, proclaimed the establishment of the People's Republic of China. The actual victory of the Red Army, however, is not so easy to date. Parts of the north had been liberated since 1936; parts of southern China were not liberated until 1950. For this reason 1949 has a dual significance. It stands for the whole time span of 1948–1951, during which the People's government slowly consolidated their control over all of China, and thus October 1 is primarily a symbolic date. But there is another significance that also makes it a day of great celebration and unique importance all over China; on that day the people of China claimed power over their own fate. In rapid succession laws were passed ending oppressive traditional practices and freeing women, children, peasants, and soldiers—everyone in China who had suffered under the old system. These laws, together with the constitution, became the basis of organization and government in what her people call New China.

Derk Bodde was studying Chinese literature in Peking in 1949, and we have included his story of a play performed by a troupe of the new "people's artists" at the time of liberation. An article by Mao Tse-tung, "On People's Democratic Dictatorship," declares bluntly that China's new government is a special form of dictatorship, and explains why; this is followed by several sections from the marriage law with which Chinese women won their freedom.

The White-haired Girl
by Derk Bodde*

Yesterday I attended a performance of the most famous of the new plays, *The White-haired Girl*, beautifully produced and expertly acted by the Artist Workers Group of the (Communist) North China University. This semi-operatic drama is an elaborate production, written by four persons and requiring a cast of twenty and an orchestra of twelve. Seeing it was an exciting and memorable experience, despite its length of four hours and the fact that, as all tickets were unreserved, I had to come more than an hour early to insure getting a seat.

The plot, laid in a small farming village near the mountains of northwestern Hopei between 1935 and 1939, is said to be based on actual fact. Its theme is the struggle of the farmers against landlord oppression, and their final liberation. Happy One, the seventeen-year-old daughter of a widowed farmer, is sold by her father, under compulsion, into the service of the landlord as payment for debt. The father then commits suicide. In the landlord's family, Happy One, after constant abuse, is raped and made pregnant by the landlord. Seven months later her master, having decided to marry someone else, plans to sell her into a brothel. Her attempted suicide is prevented by another servant, who helps her escape. From that day onward her one aim is to gain revenge for herself and her father. She finds refuge in a mountain cave, where she gives birth to her child and maintains a precarious existence during the next several years by making nightly forays to steal the offerings from a lonely mountain temple. Diet deficiency, coupled with the fact that she never sees the light of day, causes her hair to turn white, so that to the people of the locality who occasionally glimpse her she becomes known as the "white-haired immortal fairy." Then comes the Sino-Japanese War and the landlord turns into a Japanese puppet official. But the Eighth Route Army guerrillas arrive at the village, and with them Happy One's

*Bodde, *Peking Diary*.

farmer lover. The guerrillas organize the farmers, and the lover rescues Happy One and her child from the mountain cave. The last scene is the public trial of the landlord by the enraged farmers—an enactment of what has actually happened innumerable times in rural China during the past few years. Happy One appears at the trial to give her testimony, and, as the curtain falls, the trussed-up landlord and his emissary are dragged away to their execution. . . .

Ideologically speaking, there is nothing subtle about this drama. Mood is suggested by certain obvious stage tricks. The bleakness of the farmer's home, for example, is heightened by the raging snow storm which we see without; the joy and hope of Happy One as she is rescued from the cave by her lover, by the crowing of a cock and flooding the cave entrance with rosy light—symbol of the dawning of China's New Day. The characters remain types rather than fully rounded individuals. Happy One's old, bent father is the symbol of the passive despair of China's peasants under millennia of oppression. The sly landlord is a monster of heartless cruelty, meanness, and corruption. Happy One herself symbolizes the will to live and gain revenge. The Eighth Route guerrillas typify the purposeful, organized, idealistic activity which can bring to the old China new life and hope. . . .

As I watched the sobbing heroine being dragged away from her father's corpse to serve the landlord, I could not help wondering: Is this artistically true to life? Granted that such scenes do happen in China and that there are thousands of landlords whose underlying motives, in the final analysis, are as heartless as this one's, would it be typical of many to act with such complete disregard for at least the external appearances of decency? These thoughts prevented me from full satisfaction at the triumph of good over evil in the final trial scene. On the contrary, its mob violence unpleasantly suggested the Communes of the French revolution, and this despite the fact that the scene has been toned down for urban audiences: in its original version it showed the farmers mobbing and killing the landlord; in the revised play, the curtain falls as he is being led to execution.

It is obvious, however, that no such considerations disturbed the minds of the audience (among whom I was probably the only foreigner). Emotionally, they were completely one with the play and, during tense moments, roared their disapproval of the landlord, shouted advice to the heroine, and cheered the arrival of the Eighth Route Army. "Let her get him!" shouted my neighbor—a mild-looking youth two seats away, who before the play had been reading a pamphlet entitled *The Chinese Revolution and Chinese Communist Party*—during one exciting episode in which the heroine is restrained by her comrade from attacking the landlord.

The behavior of the spectators, in fact, was in some ways almost as interesting as the play itself. They filled every seat and overflowed into the aisles. During the hour or so of waiting before the play began, some groups passed the time by singing the new revolutionary songs at the top of their voices. True, the audience was predominantly youthful and contained many students and soldiers; yet there were many older people. The man to my right, for example, was an oldish worker—apparently illiterate, judging from the fact that he barely glanced at the program I gave him. A good part of the row in front of me was occupied by a respectable old gentleman, his wife, and their several grown-up daughters, complete with teapot and melon seeds. The theater is a good-sized one (seating perhaps 2,000), and the play has been running for over a month— an exceptionally long time for Peking. Though slated to close tomorrow, it could easily run for an additional month, judging from the capacity houses. The whole experience of seeing it, in fact, gave overwhelming proof of the strength of the new ideas in revolutionary China. Let any man beware who glibly assumes that these ideas are the monopoly of but a few visionary fanatics beneath whom lies a sea of "growing discontent."

On People's Democratic Dictatorship
by Mao Tse-tung

"You are dictorial." My dear sirs, what you say is correct. That is just what we are. All the experiences of the Chinese people, accumulated in the course of successive decades, tell us to carry out a people's democratic dictatorship.

This means that the reactionaries must be deprived of the right to voice their opinions; only the people have that right.

Who are the "people"? At the present stage in China, they are the working class, the peasantry, the petty bourgeoisie, and the national bourgeoisie.

Under the leadership of the working class and the Communist Party, these classes unite to create their own state and elect their own government so as to enforce their dictatorship over the henchmen of imperialism—the landlord class and bureaucratic capitalist class, as well as the reactionary clique of the Kuomintang, which represents these classes, and their accomplices. The people's government will suppress such persons. It will only permit them to behave themselves properly. It will not allow them to speak or act wildly. Should they do so, they will be instantly curbed and punished. The democratic system is to be carried out within the ranks of the people, giving them freedom of speech, assembly, and association. The right to vote is given only to the people, not to the reactionaries.

These two things, democracy for the people and dictatorship for the reactionaries, when combined, constitute the people's democratic dictatorship.

Why must things be done in this way? Everyone is very clear on this point. If things were not done like this, the revolution would fail, and people would suffer, and the state would perish.

"Don't you want to abolish state power?" Yes, we want to, but not at the present time. We cannot afford to abolish state power just now. Why not? Because imperialism still exists. Because, internally, reactionaries still exist and classes still exist.

Our present task is to strengthen the people's state apparatus—meaning principally the people's army, the people's police, and the people's courts—thereby safeguarding national defense and protecting the people's interests. Given these conditions, China, under the leadership of the working class and the Communist Party, can develop steadily from an agricultural into an industrial country and from a New Democratic into a Socialist and, eventually, Communist society, eliminating classes and realizing universal harmony.

Such state apparatus as the army, the police, and the courts are instruments with which one class oppresses another. As far as the hostile classes are concerned, these are instruments of oppression. They are violent and certainly not "benevolent" things.

"You are not benevolent." Exactly. We definitely have no benevolent policies toward the reactionaries or the counterrevolutionary activities of the reactionary classes. Our benevolent policy does not apply to such deeds or such persons, who are outside the ranks of the people; it applies only to the people.

The people's state is for the protection of the people. Once they have a people's state, the people then have the possibility of applying democratic methods on a nationwide and comprehensive scale to educate and reform themselves, so that they may get rid of the influences of domestic and foreign reactionaries. (These influences are still very strong at present and will remain for a long time to come; they cannot be eradicated quickly.) Thus the people can reform their bad habits and thoughts derived from the old society, so that they will not take the wrong road pointed out to them by the reactionaries, but will continue to advance and develop toward a Socialist and then Communist society.

The methods we use in this respect are democratic, that is, methods of persuasion and not of compulsion. If people break the law, they will be punished, imprisoned, or even sentence to death. But these will be individual cases, differing in principle from the dictatorship imposed against the reactionaries as a class.

As for those belonging to reactionary classes or groups, after their political power has been overthrown, we will also give them land and work, permitting them to make a living and to reform themselves through labor into new persons—but only on condition that they do not rebel, sabotage, or create disturbances. If they do not want to work, the people's state will force them to do so. Furthermore, the propaganda and educational work directed toward them will be carried out with the same care and thoroughness as the work already conducted among captured army officers. This may also be spoken of as a "benevolent policy," but it will be compulsorily imposed upon those originally from enemy classes. This can in no way be compared to our work along self-educational lines among the ranks of the revolutionary people.

This job of reforming the reactionary classes can be handled only by a state having a people's democratic dictatorship. When the work has been completed, China's major exploiting classes—the landlord class and the bureaucratic capitalist class, that is, the monopoly capitalist class—will have been finally eliminated.

Then there will remain only the national bourgeoisie. In the present stage a great deal of suitable educational work can be done among them. When the time comes to realize Socialism, that is, to nationalize private enterprise, we will go a step further in our work of educating and reforming them. The people have a strong state apparatus in their hands, and they do not fear rebellion on the part of the national bourgeoisie.

The education of the peasantry presents a serious problem. Peasant economy is dispersed. According to the Soviet Union's experience, it takes a long time and much painstaking work before agriculture can be socialized. Without the socialization of agriculture, there can be no complete and consolidated socialism.

If we wish to socialize agriculture, we must develop a strong industry having state-operated enterprises as its main component.

The Marriage Law of the People's Republic of China

Chapter 1
General Principles

The feudal marriage system which is based on arbitrary and compulsory arrangements and the superiority of man over woman and ignores the children's interests shall be abolished.

Article 2. Bigamy, concubinage, child betrothal, interference with the remarriage of widows, and the exaction of money or gifts in connection with marriages shall be prohibited.

Chapter 2
The Marriage Contract

Article 3. Marriage shall be based on the complete willingness of the two parties. Neither party shall use compulsion and no third party shall be allowed to interfere.

Article 4. A marriage can be contracted only after the man has reached 20 years of age and the woman 18 years of age. . . .

Chapter 3
Rights and Duties of Husband and Wife

Article 7. Husband and wife are companions living together and shall enjoy equal status in the home.

Article 8. Husband and wife are in duty bound to love, respect, assist and look after each other, to live in harmony, to engage in productive work, to care for the children and to strive jointly for the welfare of the family and for the building up of the new society.

Article 9. Both husband and wife shall have the right to free choice of occupation and free participation in work or in social activities.

Article 10. Both husband and wife shall have equal rights in the possession and management of family property. . . .

Chapter 4
Relations Between Parents and Children

Article 13. Parents have the duty to rear and to educate their children; the children have the duty to support and to assist their parents. Neither the parents nor the children shall maltreat or desert one another.

The foregoing provision also applies to foster-parents and foster-children. Infanticide by drowning and similar criminal acts are strictly prohibited.

Article 14. Parents and children shall have the right to inherit one another's property. . . .

Chapter 5
Divorce

Article 17. Divorce shall be granted when the husband and wife both desire it. In the event of either the husband or wife alone insisting on divorce, it may be granted only when mediation by the district people's government and the judicial organ has failed to bring about a reconciliation....

Chapter 6
Maintenance and Education of Children After Divorce

Article 20. The blood ties between parents and children do not end with the divorce of the parents. No matter whether the father or the mother acts as guardian of the children, they still remain the children of both parents.

After divorce both parents still have the duty to support and educate their children.

After divorce, the guiding principle is to allow the mother to have custody of a baby still being breast-fed. After the weaning of the child, if a dispute arises between the two parties over the guardianship and an agreement cannot be reached, the people's court shall render a decision in accordance with the interests of the child....

———————————

The fledgling People's Republic faced grave internal problems in the wake of almost twenty years of continuous war, but immediately two new threats arose beyond her borders. In 1950 the United States obtained UN consent to intervene in the Korean civil war, and American military and civilian leaders spoke openly of going all the way to China's Manchurian border and of taking this opportunity to attack the Chinese Communists. At the same time, President Truman sent the American Seventh Fleet to patrol the Taiwan Strait, renewing U.S. intervention in China's civil conflict. When U.S. troops crossed the 38th parallel in Korea, Chinese troops entered the war. The fighting did not end until 1953.

The Korean War

by Felix Greene

Fighting in Korea started on June 25th, 1950. No Chinese forces were involved at the time. Indeed, the Indian ambassador to Peking, Mr. K. N. Pannikar, reported in his book *In Two Chinas*, "that United Nations intervention in Korea caused no particular reaction in China. . . . During the first three months of the Korean War, there was hardly any noticeable military activity. . . ."

Upon the outbreak of hostilities in Korea that June, the American Seventh Fleet was ordered to "protect" Taiwan, and has been so engaged ever since, thus providing Chiang Kai-shek with a shield from the shelter of which he has carried on an endless series of raids and nuisance attacks against coastal shipping and against the mainland. Deployment of the Seventh Fleet constituted a direct intervention by the United States in the Chinese civil war. Had it not been for this intervention, the civil war might have ended in that summer of 1950—with the removal of Chiang from his last foothold on Chinese soil. This in turn would have terminated Chiang's claim to a seat in the United Nations.

In October 1950, American forces began their drive north to the 38th Parallel, which had been established by the Allies after Japan's surrender as the dividing line between North and South Korea. Certain American generals spoke publicly of going all the way to the "Manchurian border."

On October 2nd, Premier Chou En-lai called in the Indian Ambassador to inform him that "if the Americans crossed the 38th Parallel, China would be forced to intervene in Korea." Mr. Pannikar records how he then asked Premier Chou whether China would intervene if only the South Koreans crossed. The Premier was emphatic: the South Koreans did not matter, but American intrusion into North Korea would encounter Chinese resistance.

This warning was passed on to the British Minister in Peking, and was relayed to Washington. It was ignored. There were many who believed the Chinese government was bluffing. The 38th Parallel was crossed, and a week later Chinese troops entered North Korea.

Early Reforms: The 1950s

The question facing the Chinese leaders in the early 1950s was how best to resolve these vast and complex difficulties. China was a Communist country (in the "stage of socialism," that is, everyone was paid—in Karl Marx's famous words—according to how much they worked rather than according to need; and there was still a good deal of private property), but being Communist was not a blueprint for development. In every area the leaders and the people had to try new ideas and methods, learn from their mistakes, and try again. In organizing these readings about the early period of development in the People's Republic, we have created several categories, such as agriculture, industry, family life, the role of women, health care, and language reform. The first readings are about the economic situation at Liberation in 1949 and the revolutionary changes that followed in the agricultural countryside (remember that more than 80 percent of China's people are farmers even today) and the industrializing cities.

The Economic Situation
by E. L. Wheelwright and Bruce McFarlane

The economy inherited by the new regime was a shambles. Since the fall of the Manchu dynasty in 1911, extensive areas of China had been wracked by revolution, war lordism, civil war, foreign invasion, and flood and famine. Industry and commerce had almost come to a standstill in major urban centers. The industrial base in Manchuria had been looted by the U.S.S.R. of more than $2 billion worth of machinery and equipment. Dams, irrigation systems, and canals were in a state of disrepair. Railroad lines had been cut and recut by the contending armies. Inflation had ruined confidence in the money system. And finally, the population had suffered enormous casualties from both man made and natural disasters and was disorganized, half starved, and exhausted.

In 1949 China was a poor and backward country. The modern industrial sector was small and predominantly foreign-owned. It was concentrated along the Eastern seaboard and in Manchuria, in a few large cities such as Shenyang, Harbin, Tientsin, and Shanghai, where foreigners had been able to obtain special privileges. It was mainly light industry, although the beginnings of heavy industry existed. Steel output never exceeded one million tons, and machine-building industries were almost non-existent. A few modern power stations supplied electricity to the large cities, but in the countryside electricity was virtually unknown. The transport system was inadequate—only about 12,000 miles of railway existed, mostly in Manchuria and linking the cities on the Eastern seaboard. Vast areas of the country were inaccessible to motor vehicles.

Most manufactured goods in everyday use still were made by traditional methods, either in the home or in very small handicraft industries, especially in the remote interior where the products of the Western commerical enterprises could not penetrate. About four-fifths of the population was employed in agriculture, which provided the bulk of the national income, and most were poor peasants. It was found, at the time of the land reform of 1949–1952, that landlords and rich peasants, constituting less than ten percent of the total population, owned seventy percent of the land. . . .

The Chinese economy was thus predominantly feudal, with enclaves of foreign capitalist industry in the coastal cities. The industrial base and infrastructure was smaller than that possessed by Russia in 1914, and smaller than that of India when it became independent. In addition, much of what industry existed had been run down, agricultural production drastically reduced, and the primitive transport system severely disrupted by decades of war— culminating in the worst inflation of modern times. . . .

The immediate strategic objective clearly had to be the rehabilitation of the national economy, in a way which would lay the groundwork for the future socialist transformation of the economy and society. During this period economic control was secured over the "commanding heights" of the economy, such as banking, trade, railways, steel, and other key industries; and land reform redistributed the estates of landlords and rich peasants. But neither in agriculture nor in industry was there any large scale nationalization, with the exception of industrial assets belonging to supporters of the Kuomintang, who were allied to foreign interests, and characterized as "bureaucrat capitalists," as opposed to "national capitalists," whom the government tolerated. The latter were smaller businessmen who had tried to build up independent industry. They were looked on as a progressive force, and possessed valuable skills which the regime could not do without; policy was not to expropriate them but gradually to assimilate them into the socialist sector. They continued to receive interest on their investments, and were paid fairly high salaries to continue managing their enterprises. Many produced under contract to the state, and by 1952, twenty-two percent of industry by value was in this position. Simultaneously the government was setting up joint State-private enterprises, and creating completely State-owned industry in the capital goods sector.

Land reform was begun before 1949 in the liberated areas, and was completed by 1952. Over 300 million peasants benefited from the redistribution, but the equalization of land holdings was not complete; rich peasants were treated relatively lightly, and middle peasants also shared in the distribution, so that after the reform, although the number of middle peasants greatly increased, rich and poor peasants still remained. Most landlords were allowed to retain sufficient land to support themselves. A completely egalitarian land reform would have alienated the middle peasants and disrupted production.

Thus, at this stage, China became a country of small owner-cultivators. The ultimate aim of the regime in respect to agriculture was stated from the first to be its full socialization, yet neither the material nor the political conditions for this existed during this period.

In the Cities
by Ruth Sidel*

Cities faced severe disorganization during the civil war that followed Japanese occupation. When the Communists

---

* Sidel, *Families of Fengsheng*.

occupied the urban areas in 1949, they found chaos—inflation was rampant, food was in short supply, and human services had broken down. Ezra Vogel writes of the situation in Guangzhou.

> When the Communist troops entered Canton, they found the city in turmoil. The main Kuomintang forces had departed hastily toward Hainan Island and high Kuomintang officials and businessmen had flown to Szechwan or Hong Kong. Some underlings remained in hiding to assess the possibility of staying on. Some of the lower elements of society, taking advantage of the hasty departure of "bourgeois opportunists," were looting deserted homes and the stores and gathering goods abandoned in the streets. Some remnants of the Kuomintang army and the civil defense forces continued minor sabotage and sniping, and the targets were the Communist cadres who walked the streets with their eight-cornered hats or their green uniforms. Inflation was rampant, the city was filled with transients, and both armies had sorely taxed the local food supply.

During the first decade after Liberation, the assumption of power by the Chinese Communists in 1949, the Chinese government faced severe problems in its attempt to govern the cities. These included the need to cope with ever-increasing rural to urban migration, to deliver human services to large numbers of people, to develop successful methods of social control over the urban population, to stem the anomie that seems to be endemic to modern industrial cities, and to involve people politically in their own governing. . . .

In 1951 the first residents' committees were established in Tientsin and Shanghai . . . One of the earliest was established in Hsueht'ang Street, Tientsin, in October, 1951. According to Schurmann,

> Hsueht'ang was a working-class quarter, consisting of 114 households or 531 persons. Most were workers in state-owned factories. Sometime in 1951, the city government dispatched an "experimental work team for administrative construction" into the neighborhood to organize the residents. The 114 households

were divided into fifteen residents groups. These groups, after suitable education, elected 19 residents representatives of which 16 were housewives. In October 1951 a delegates meeting was held, and the urban residents committee was formally established.

In addition to the central task of mediating disputes, the representatives of the new residents' committees organized literacy classes and sanitation work and dealt with some welfare problems. In 1952 residents' committees and neighborhood committees were established in Tientsin; both were set up in residential districts only and were basically a device for organizing the unorganized, the unemployed women, and the elderly.

The tasks of the new residents' committees were (1) to serve as a transmitter of government policies from higher urban authority to the people; (2) to perform public security functions and organize fire prevention, sanitation work, welfare work, mediation, and cultural and recreational activities; and (3) to serve as an intermediary for the transmission of ideas and requests from the people to the government level. (It is startling how closely descriptions of the tasks of residents' committees today resemble the description of tasks outined in 1952.) The residents' committee was directly responsible to the neighborhood committee, which in turn was the administrative level the city administration used to relate to the people. . . .

Eventually the residents' committees moved into such areas as food rationing and the granting of certificates to people who wished to leave China. They therefore became the local branch of urban government closest to the people and were run by members of the masses themselves. From the start, women played an important role in the workings of the residents' committee, often gaining power at that level when they had little at higher levels. . . .

Although China's urban neighborhoods today may seem to us in the West to be far more integrated than anything that we know, they are organized around the residential areas rather than around production. As Schurmann states, "The Chinese city remains today what it has been for a century, an area of concentrated human residence. . . ."

The lanes and courtyards of the Fengsheng Neighborhood are quiet on a weekday morning. Children are in school, most of their parents at work, leaving only a few older women, retired workers, and small children around the courtyards. Just before noon children stream out of the nearby schools and start home for lunch, some walking two-by-two, some running and shouting, others talking in small groups. . . . Midafternoon is once again quiet, sleepy, but starting at four o'clock, children and adults begin streaming home, bicycle riders stirring up the dust of the narrow lanes, ringing their bells insistently to warn pedestrians out of the way. The streets become jammed with shoppers buying food. But by midevening dinner is over, and by nine or ten the courtyards are quiet once again.

The Liu family and six other families live together in their courtyard; these seven families are part of the fourteen thousand families who make up the Fengsheng Neighborhood in Peking.

The Sung Family
by Ruth Sidel*

Sung Kwang-chen is a fifty-four-year-old woman with a long thin oval face. She and her husband, her seventy-six-year-old mother-in-law, her seventeen-year-old daughter, her married daughter, son-in-law, and three-and-a-half-year-old grandson live in their small three-room house in a courtyard of the Fengsheng Neighborhood. The front room of the house is decorated with plants and lace curtains at the windows, a map of China on one wall, pictures of the family on another. Sitting in this simple room with its white-washed walls and stone floors, a few toys scattered around—a helicopter, a doll, a car—a tiny black and white kitten playing outside the door, Comrade Sung tells about her life. "Before Liberation we were very poor. My husband's father worked for a landlord in Hupei province. He died at the age of twenty-six, leaving two children both very young, one a year old and the other, my husband, just a few months old. My mother-in-law took care of the two children, but when they became thirteen, they had to find

* Sidel, *Families of Fengsheng*. (Mrs. Sidel conducted this interview with the Sung family in the early 1970s.)

work. It was very difficult to find work at that time, and my husband did not have enough to eat.

"After Liberation people were able to get work regularly, and my husband started working in a factory here in Peking twenty-three years ago. I came to Peking to be with him eighteen years ago and worked in a factory until recently when I stopped because of ill health. In the past there was no medical care or medicine when people were ill; now the lane health station is there to help the people, and the Red Medical Workers come to the house to take care of you if you are sick. Before we were so very poor, and now we have a sewing machine, a radio, and every member of the family who works has a watch."

The family is crowded in its small house: Comrade Sung's mother-in-law, her small grandson, and her seventeen-year-old daughter, a teacher in a primary school, share one bedroom; she and her husband share a second bedroom; and her daughter, thirty, a saleswoman in a local shop, and her son-in-law, a factory worker in another district of Peking, share the third bedroom. They have two other children who are not living at home, a son, twenty-six, a factory worker in another city, and a daughter, twenty-one, who is also a factory worker and lives in a dormitory here in Peking.

Comrade Sung proudly told of how the family is now able to save money in the bank. The total family income is 206 yuan per month, food costs 150 yuan for the entire family, and rent, electricity, and water together come to 12 yuan per month. But what seemed even more important to Comrade Sung was that if she became ill, the residents' committee would arrange a car to bring her to the neighborhood hospital, and if she needed to, she could even go to a higher-level hospital. . . .

A large red-brick building houses the Fengsheng Neighborhood Insulation Material Factory. The factory, established as part of the Great Leap Forward in 1958, produces insulation material for electrical machines. In a large conference room with a television set in one corner but without a picture of Mao Tse-tung on the walls (something that would have been unthinkable just one year earlier) Chang Liang, the chairman of the revolutionary committee, a tall man in his mid-thirties who, like many other Chinese men, smokes his cigarettes down to his fingertips, told about the history of the factory: "In the old society housewives didn't work, but after Liberation women's lives began to change. When this factory was started in nineteen fifty-eight, all of the workers were housewives, but since the Cultural Revolution we have a hundred and ninety workers—thirty-four men and a hundred fifty-six women. Eighty-three middle-school graduates have also come to work here as apprentices to learn their jobs from more experienced workers." Comrade Chang pointed out that the apprentice system existed before Liberation, too, but then apprentices earned hardly any money. Today an apprentice earns sixteen yuan the first year (really only a subsistence wage, but they are all young people, still living at home, and therefore have minimal expenses), eighteen yuan the second year, and the third year they earn a regular worker's salary. To supplement their income, they are given bus fare and medical care, haircuts, and admission to films as well as a yearly clothing allowance of twenty-five yuan. These apprentices are treated much the same as university students, who receive a stipend of nineteen yuan per month in addition to many free services. Regular workers at the insulation factory earn between forty and sixty yuan per month, still a relatively low salary by Chinese standards. . . .

The factory personnel are divided into groups, some of which test components made by other groups. Most of the workers are simultaneously working and studying in order to increase their knowledge of transistor production. For example, Wang Chin-tsai is a housewife and mother of three children who lives near the factory. She has been working here for ten years, and although she had only two years of primary-school education, she was one of the original workers who went to Tsinghua University for special training. She was also one of the workers who developed headaches when she needed to read blueprints. According to Comrade Wang, "After several years of practice I have mastered some of the techniques but still have a lack of knowledge of theory and will continue to study."

The factory provides a small nursery and kindergarten for the children of the workers and also provides medical care for the workers. A young woman wearing a yellow and gray plaid shirt and pigtails and looking ten years younger than her thirty-one years is one of the two worker-doctors at the factory. She has been interested in medical work since she was a child, she explained, and when the doctor from the district hospital came to the factory to recruit worker-doctors, she expressed her interest. The factory's revolutionary committee subsequently chose her to be a medical worker. She then spent three months part-time in early 1970 in a training course given in the factory by a doctor from a local hospital. Later she spent two months in the neighborhood hospital learning acupuncture and the technique of giving injections. Worker-doctors, like their rural counterparts, the barefoot doctors, spend part of their time doing their regular jobs in the factory and part of the time doing medical work. And like the neighborhood medical workers, they treat only "minor illnesses"—bronchitis, diarrhea, headaches, fever, colds.

Perhaps the most deeply entrenched form of oppression in traditional China was that against women. The next selection is about the life of Li Kuei-ying, a young woman from the village of Liu Ling in northwest China, who saw the first great changes in the status of women in the 1950s.

Li Kuei-ying's Story

by Jan Myrdal

In 1951, we were told that the party school in Yenan was having a training course for female ganbus [ganbu: cadre, a leader or party representative]. It was said that as half of the population consisted of women, trained women were needed as well. Our labour group for mutual help was now to be turned into a farmer's cooperative. It was Father who forced that through. It was the first of its kind and it was an experiment. The labour group for mutual help took the party school about me, and I was accepted and sent off to attend the course and study for six months. Ever since I had been small, I had dreamed of being able to learn to read and write. I had dreamed day-dreams of becoming a student. Yet when they talked with me and told me that I had got permission to go to the party school, I became worried. Because what could a farm girl learn at school? I was worried about the housework too: the spring sowing was about to start and there was so much that ought to be seen to at home.

When I got to the school, I met a lot of women and men there. After a couple of weeks, I had got accustomed to being in school. The main object was for us to learn to read and write. To begin with, it was rather difficult for me to live a collective life, but afterwards it went quite all right. I decided to learn all that I could. Now that I had managed to get to a school I was not going to lose a minute. I thought of how things were in the new society and how they had been under Hu Tsung-nan's occupation and I promised myself that, when I was finished with the school, I would organize all the women in the village for this new life, and I read seriously.

At the school, I got up as early as in the village. First, we had a lesson of forty minutes, when our homework was corrected. Then, after a short break, we had another lesson, which was either arithmetic or Chinese. At eight o'clock we had breakfast. We usually got steam bread and vegetables. Then we had three lessons of arithmetic and Chinese. We had fifteen minutes' interval between each lesson. Then we had a rest period of one and a half hours. After that a further three lessons of arithmetic and Chinese. Then we had dinner. We used to get steamed millet and vegetables. Once a week we had a meat dish. This, of course, was better food than we were accustomed to at home, but we needed it, because we were working hard and had to learn everything at once. After dinner, we had ninety minutes' prep. After that we did different kinds of personal activities. We did not have any political studies. This was a course at which we were to learn to read. In the evenings we used to sing and discuss things. We learned lots of songs and talked a lot about our home villages and all the things that could be done. We all knew that we must learn to read as soon as possible. Six of us women shared a room. I still see a lot of two of them; they live near by; but I have lost touch with the others. We were free on Sundays. I used to go home to the village then and help in the fields. I was needed there too.

That time at the party school was the decisive time of my life. It was then I realized what I must do with my life.

I came back to Liu Ling in July 1951. I could then read and write, and I took part in the autumn harvest and, in the winter, I began organizing the women to study. When I got back, the women said: "We didn't think grown-ups could learn to read and write, but you have." Because of that, the younger women now wanted to learn to read too, and I told them all how good it was to be able to read and write; that she who could read could see; and she who couldn't was blind.

That winter I taught ten women to read and write a hundred characters each. That isn't enough to be able to write simple accounts and receipts and to keep notes. They have gone on with it since, but it has been difficult for them. They can't read much more now after ten years, though I have been working with them the whole time.

I continued studying on my own. I got hold of old books of legends which I read. I swotted up more characters; I read newspapers and began reading simple news stories. In 1952, I married. That was in August and I was very happy. It was a marriage of free will. We had met at the party school and fallen in love with each other. He was attending a different course. When I told Mother that I was in love and wanted to get married, she said nothing at all, but Father said: "If it's so that you really want to, then I don't intend to oppose it."

There were three labour groups in the farmers' cooperative in 1953. Two of men and one of women. I was chosen leader of the women's group. At the meeting, the women said: "She is young and hard-working and she can read." So I thought that, if they had such faith in me, I must show that I was worthy of their opinion of me. That I must work much harder than before. I wanted to get the women as a group moving. I wanted to get them to break away from the past. I was thinking of the time when Hu Tsung-nan had occupied the area. There was a cavalry regiment quartered here in Liu Ling then. Its duties were to track down and capture deserters. They shot the deserters in our potato plot. Every day I used to stand by my cooking stove in the cave and see them shoot deserters down there. I thought then that that must never be allowed to happen again. That we women must all get together to see that it never happened again.

That winter I opened a winter school. We had lessons in

the school and in the homes of Shi Yü-chieh and Li Hai-kuei, who had large caves. We helped the women to make shoes and clothes and to improve their agricultural tools. We gave them lessons in feeding poultry and in spinning. We had discussions after the lessons. We tried to get the women to tell us themselves what things had been like before, and how it was now, and how it ought to be in the future. For example, they said: "My feet were bound so that I could not walk. In the old society, a woman was not supposed to go beyond the threshold of her home for the first three years of her marriage. We weren't allowed to eat on the *kang* [bed platform], but had to sit on a stool when we ate, and if my parents had decided to marry me off with a cur, then I had to be content with a cur. But now you are allowed to see your husband before you marry, and you can refuse to marry him if you don't like the look of him. The old society was bad and the new is good." We discussed whether women are men's equals or not, and most said: "Within the family, man and woman are equal. We help the men when they work in the fields and they should help us in the house." But many of the older women said: "Women are born to attend to the household. A woman cannot work in the fields. That can't be helped. It is just that men and women are born different. A person is born either a man or a woman. To work in the fields or in the house." We had long discussions. The young ones were all on the side of equality and freedom. It had now become quite usual with our generation for husband and wife to discuss the family's problems and decide about them together. Women now no longer work just in the house; they also work in the fields and earn their own money. But the men of the older generations still say: "What does a woman know? Women know nothing! What's a woman worth? Women are worth nothing!" In such families the men decide everything and their wives say: "We are just women. We are not allowed to say anything."

The first time we women took part as a group in an open discussion was at the meeting about whether or not we should turn Liu Ling Farmers' Co-operative into the East Shines Red Higher Agricultural Co-operative. Officially, we had the same political and economic rights as the men. We were citizens too, so She Shiu-ying and Li Yang-ching asked to speak and stood up in the middle of the meeting and said: "The old women still say that they don't under-stand things and are just women, and that it is the men's business to decide. But we say that we do understand. We are women and we know what this discussion is about. Everything has to progress. We must increase production. It isn't fair to pay a dividend on land. That can mean that a person who works a lot can be paid less than one who works less well. That is not right. We must increase our investment instead, so that we can all increase production and be better off by doing more work. Therefore we must join forces and do away with land interest. That is progress and we stand for that."

Li Ying-teh, who is an old man and Li Hsin-chen's father, then said: "We should not listen to women when it is a question of serious business. They understand nothing. After all, they are only women and ought not to disturb our discussions. We do not need to concern ourselves with what they have said." But my brother, Li Hai-tsai, replied to this: "Why shouldn't we listen to the women? Every other Chinese is a woman. There is a lot of sense in what they've just said about investment and production and land interest and joint effort. I am entirely with them."

We won. Gradually the others were voted down and persuaded and got to agree. I was elected a member of the committee of the East Shines Red Higher Agricultural Co-operative.

Today in China almost everyone above school age can read enough to enjoy a newspaper. This is quite an accomplishment; in 1949, the illiteracy rate was around 85 percent.

How did the Chinese achieve this? The first steps were in the Red Army, where schoolchildren would tutor the troops. After 1949, public schools were established and night classes for adults were organized. Later the most common written characters were simplified. Finally the widespread reading of newspapers and Chairman Mao's writings (especially of the "Little Red Book") helped accustom many older people to using their new skills.

The next two selections cover the problems involved in learning to read the difficult Chinese characters and the new system of romanization adopted in 1979 by the Chinese government. Since the Greene piece was written, more simplified characters have been added and the total in common use is now more than 2000. Overly complex charac-ters for most common words have been simplified with fewer strokes. In addition, new computer technology promises that some form of typewriter will be soon be available for Chinese.

Language Reform

by Felix Greene

Among the real problems confronting the Chinese people as they move into the modern world is the complexity of their language, written and spoken.

Unlike our own language, Chinese has no alphabet. Written Chinese was originally ideographs, or pictures, or the object denoted; and though these ideographs, known as characters, today are no longer recognizable as such, they are a cumbersome way of expression.

With our alphabet of twenty-six symbols we can make tens of thousands of words with comparative ease; in Chinese each word requires its own character to be laboriously memorized. Many of them are highly complex. The word for "I" in Chinese requires seven strokes. "Salt" calls for no less than twenty-four.

I

Salt
(Traditional)

Salt
(Simplified)

The Chinese have estimated, for example, that it takes a child at least two years longer to master the rudiments of reading and writing in China than it does his counterpart in a country where an alphabet is used.

The handicaps of written Chinese are obvious. Typewriters in China—there are very few—need several hundred keys; typesetting of books, magazines and newspapers is enormously complicated; telegrams have to be encoded and decoded, with each character given a four-number code; and the work required to learn even a minimum of one thousand to fifteen hundred characters—enough to be able to read a newspaper—is extremely arduous. A scholar is required to know characters in the thousands. Experts are divided on the total number of characters in the language—between forty and fifty thousand.

Another complication that confronts the Chinese is the great variety of their dialects. Although more than 70 percent of the people speak various forms of *putonghua* (known in the West as Mandarin), the remainder speak dialects quite different from this, as well as different from each other. While the written language is the same throughout the country, the dialects often are so different that people from one area cannot understand those from another. For example, "Mandarin" pronunciation for cabbage, *bai tsai*, is pronounced *bak choi* in Cantonese. Wu dialect, which is spoken in and around Chekiang province and Shanghai, pronounces the word for foreigner *na ge ning;* in "Mandarin" it is *wai gwo ren.*

Many urban Chinese speak "Mandarin" and one other dialect, and it is not uncommon to hear a conversation going on between two people in two "languages." It is also not uncommon, as I have witnessed, to see men from different areas trying to communicate by writing out a word in mid-air, or one dipping a chopstick into the soy sauce and making himself understood on a restaurant table.

The complicated task of language reform was tackled almost immediately after the present government came to power. A committee for reforming the Chinese written language was set up. There were three main objectives: to simplify the written characters; to popularize *putonghua* ("common speech"); to draw up and put into practice a scheme for a Chinese phonetic alphabet to annotate the characters by sound symbols.

The task has not been finished, but a start has been made. . . . To popularize the "common speech," it is being taught in all public schools and emphasized in films and radio; this in itself necessitated the teaching of thousands of teachers throughout the country who had never spoken it. Dialects are not interfered with—many children in China today grow up learning both their local dialect and the "common speech." However, it is believed that in the course of time the "common speech" will be the spoken language all over China.

The Chinese Language Today: Romanization
by Molly Joel Coye and Jon Livingston

For one hundred years, since the time of the Western missionaries' first intrusion into China, Europeans and Americans have used a variety of conflicting and confusing methods to represent Chinese sounds. By now one set, the Wade-Giles system, has come to be used fairly regularly by American and British scholars, but it gives misleading and undependable indications of the true Chinese sounds. Twenty-four years ago the Chinese developed—and in 1979 put into formal use—a perfectly adequate system called *pinyin*.

The system is very simple. All vowel sounds are pronounced "pure," as they are in Latin. For instance, *ao* is pronounced to rhyme with "cow," *ai* to rhyme with "high," *ou* to rhyme with "throw."

On the following page is the official phonetic alphabet table published in Peking.*

A bit of further explanation is helpful toward understanding several sets of consonants for which we have only a single spelling and sound in English. For these the Chinese have two pronunciations and have thus chosen to use some English letters in unusual ways, as outlined below. We include these here in addition to the official chart because they are the most troublesome for English speakers. The letters, *c*, *z*, *x*, and *q*, when used for Chinese, do not correspond to common English sounds, whereas the others in the table generally do.

Pinyin	English	Similar English Sound
x	sh	*sh*eet (tongue lies flat)
sh	sh	*sh*ock (tongue touches roof of mouth)
j	j	*jee*p (*y* sound after *j*; tongue lies flat)
zh	j	*j*aunt (no *y* sound; tongue points up)
ch	ch	*ch*unk (no *y* sound; tongue points up)
q	ch	*ch*ew (*y* sound after *ch*)

Pinyin	Wade-Giles	As in ...
a	a	far
b	p	be
c	ts'	its
ch	ch'	church[a]
d	t	do
e	e	e in her
ei	ei	way
f	f	foot
g	k	go
h	h	her[a]
i	i	eat; sir[b]
ie	ieh	yes
j	ch	jeep
k	k'	kind[a]
l	l	land
m	m	me
n	n	no
o	o	law
p	p'	par[a]
q	ch'	cheek
r	j	z in azure[c]
s	s, ss, sz	sister
sh	sh	shore
t	t'	top[a]
u	u	too[d]
v	v	[e]
w	w	want
x	hs	she
y	y	yet
z	ts, tz	zero
zh	ch	j in jump

---

*Beijing Review, no. 1, 1979.

---

[a] Strongly aspirated.
[b] In syllables beginning with c, ch, r, s, sh, z, zh.
[c] Or pronounced like English r but not rolled.
[d] Or as in French tu or German München.
[e] Used only in foreign and national minority words, and local dialects.

Three other letters vary from English: *z* is harder than English *z* and is closer to *ds* in "ads." *c* is equivalent to *ts* in "hats." The Chinese *r* is not quite comparable to the French *z*, as claimed; rather it is closer to the combination *r* + *zh* sound in Czech represented by ř, as in the name Dvořák, without rolling the *r* too much.

The Chinese make only a few exceptions in their new romanization of Chinese words: Sun Yat-sen, China, and Confucius remain the same. But most familiar people and places now look quite different, even Peking and Mao Tse-tung. Here is a list of common new spellings with the old ones to the right.

Deng Xiaoping	Teng Hsiao-ping
Hua Guofeng	Hua Kuo-feng
Jiang Qing	Chiang Ching
Lin Biao	Lin Piao
Liu Shaoqi	Liu Shao-ch'i
Mao Zedong	Mao Tse-tung
Zhou Enlai	Chou En-lai
Beijing	Peking
Chongqing	Chungking
Guangzhou	Canton
Sichuan	Szechuan
Tianjin	Tientsin
Yan'an	Yenan

For other place names, see the map in the front of this book.

The *New York Times* (Feb. 4, 1979) made the following comments while announcing its switch to *pinyin*:

> Although it is difficult for any system to render the sounds of Chinese in the Roman alphabet, Pinyin in most cases comes closer than other forms. Deng, for instance is a better approximation of the family name of the Deputy Prime Minister than Teng. . . .
> The rendering of Chinese names in other languages has long posed a problem because the Chinese language is not written with an alphabetic script. . . . As many as 20 systems have been devised to convert the characters phonetically into the sounds of English, French, German and other languages.

A common system in English has been the Wade-Giles system. It was designed around 1860 by Sir Thomas Wade, a British diplomat and professor of Chinese at Cambridge University, and was applied by Herbert A. Giles, another Cambridge scholar, in a basic Chinese-English dictionary. The system found its way into English-language reference books, maps and atlases. . . .

As for the place names of China, the spellings most familiar to Western readers evolved in the 19th century for international postal use and are known as "conventional forms." The city of Nanking, a former capital of China, owes its spelling to the post office style; the Wade-Giles form is Nan-ching, and the Pinyin form is Nanjing . . .

Two Chinese introduced the Pinyin system in 1958 for two purposes. It was to serve as a teaching aid in studying the characters, which continue to be the basic form of writing, and in fostering the standard spoken language, known historically as Mandarin. Pinyin was also intended to provide a unified system of rendering Chinese names in Western languages, eliminating the various existing styles. Since it is written in the Roman alphabet, it is not suitable for languages using other scripts such as Russian, Greek, Hebrew or Arabic.

After having applied Pinyin for teaching over the last 20 years, the Chinese Government decreed last September that the system be extended to communication with foreigners. As of Jan. 1, both the Foreign Ministry and the official press agency were instructed to adopt the system in contacts with other countries.

What is good health? Certainly most of China was far from healthy in 1949. Yet today travelers in the People's Republic are amazed to find that although China is still a poor and developing country, her people are healthy and robust. China's first steps toward good health did not require advanced medical work, but rather spirit and organization, to produce enough food, clothes, and housing for all. At the same time, new basic programs attacked other problems, such as drugs, venereal disease, and child labor. These were the most serious obstacles to good health in China, and almost all of them were "social diseases"—that is, diseases or health problems which could not be cured with medicine alone. Instead they required action by the whole society to change the conditions which allowed these diseases and problems to exist. Joshua Horne is a British doctor who lived and worked in China from 1954 to 1969. In these selections from his book *Away With All Pests* (referring to the famous campaign to wipe out the "four pests": flies, rats, bedbugs and mosquitoes), Dr. Horne describes how China's new health workers organized mass campaigns to combat venereal disease. Campaigns of this type were used for health education and to control diseases such as schistosomiasis, a snail-borne parasite which is very difficult to eradicate completely. This is followed by a selection in which Dr. Victor and Ruth Sidel explain the early policies in public health which enabled China to make her unparalleled advances in preventive health and the delivery of health services.

Health Work in China
by Joshua S. Horne

The history of venereal disease in China. Until 1504, venereal disease was unknown in China, and this was not because it had not yet been correctly diagnosed, for at that time Chinese Traditional Medicine was already well advanced and hundreds of diseases had been accurately described in manuscripts which are still extant.

In that year, the old colonialists introduced syphilis into Canton and it soon spread widely thoroughout the whole land. . . . What were the political and social factors responsible for the hold gained in China?

Firstly, imperialism and colonialism, the forcible occupation of her territory by invading countries, the subjugation of her people and the wrecking of her economy. In 1877, more than three hundred years after the introduction of syphilis into Canton, the British Admiral in Shanghai, concerned about the mounting incidence of venereal disease among the sailors under his command, summoned his Surgeon-Commander and between them they devised a scheme to protect them. They instituted a totally illegal system of compulsory medical examination of prostitutes with a fee for examination and a money fine for noncompliance. In the first year the revenue from fines and fees totaled 2,590 taels of silver. But the syphilis rate was unchanged.

Secondly, war, inseparable from imperialism and from

the fragmentation of Chinese society consequent upon it.

Invading armies, and indigenous armies in the service of exploiters and oppressors, habitually loot, ravage and rape. They become infected with syphilis and they spread syphilis. The Kuomintang armies had a syphilis rate of about twenty percent. The incidence of syphilis in Chinese villages was directly proportional to the size and the duration of stay of invading U.S., Japanese and Kuomintang armies.

Thirdly, poverty, a result of feudal and capitalist exploitation and of the economic backwardness and insecurity they caused. . . .

Fourthly, drug addiction. Until the British East India Company sent the first big shipment of Indian-grown opium into China in 1781, the drug was almost unknown in China. . . .

Drugs and prostitution are co-partners in depravity. Most brothels were also opium dens and the girls, who had been sold into prostitution at an early age and who were not free to leave, also became addicts and lost their will to resist.

Fifthly, an attitude to women characteristic of class society which sees women as inferior to men, as their chattels and playthings. In feudal society with its polygamy, concubinage, child-marriage and a complete absence of legal and property rights for women, there was no attempt to disguise the inequality between the sexes. . . .

The present venereal disease situation in China. The present position can be stated in one short sentence.

ACTIVE VENEREAL DISEASE HAS BEEN COMPLETELY ERADI-CATED FROM MOST AREAS AND COMPLETELY CONTROLLED THROUGHOUT CHINA.

This is a sweeping statement but I am convinced that it is true. . . .

An investigation of infectious syphilis in seven major cities between 1960 and 1964 showed that by the end of this period, the early syphilis rate was less than twenty cases per hundred million of population per year; that is, it had very nearly reached the point of extinction.

How the victory was won. Since, as has been shown, the spread and persistence of syphilis in any country is due to social and political factors, it can only be eliminated by tackling these factors. That is to say, only an all-round political, as opposed to a purely technical, medical or legislative approach, can ever solve the problem.

The conquest of syphilis in China within a few years of the conquest by the Chinese working class is an outstanding example of the decisive role of politics in tackling major health problems.

There were two essential preconditions for the elimination of syphilis from China. The first was the establishment of the socialist system which ended exploitation and made the oppressed masses the masters of their fate. The second was the equipping of all those involved in the campaign, whether lay or medical, with a determination to serve the people and help socialist construction, with the method of thinking of Mao Tse-tung, so that they would be able to surmount all difficulties confronting them.

The following measures were carried out on the basis of these two prerequisites:

The elimination of prostitution. Within a few weeks of Liberation, most of the brothels were closed down by the direct action of the masses. The vast majority of the people recognized that prostitution was harmful and that it constituted crude exploitation of the prostitutes who, for the most part, had been driven into prostitution by poverty or by brute force. Brothel keepers who were scoundrels, drug-peddlers or gangsters were dealt with directly by the angry masses or handed over to the Public Security forces. The few remaining brothels were closed down by Government order in 1951 when prostitution was made illegal.

The prostitutes were treated as victims of an evil social system. First it was necessary to cure the venereal diseases which affected more than ninety percent of them and then to embark on their social rehabilitation. Those who had been prostitutes for only a short time were encouraged to go home and were found jobs. It was patiently explained to their families that no shame was attached to having been a victim of the old society and that now everyone who did an honest job was worthy of respect. Those who were deep rooted in prostitution were asked to enter Rehabilitation Centres where they studied the policy of the Government toward them, the nature of the new order, the reasons why they had become prostitutes and the new prospects which were opening up for them providing they themselves were willing to make a contribution. The floodgates of the past were opened at "Speak Bitterness" meetings which revealed the reasons for their former oppression and degradation. At the same time they were taught a trade and spent part of the day in productive work for which they were paid at the same rate as other workers. . . .

The transformation of the position of women. The closure of brothels and legislation outlawing prostitution cannot, of course, be equated with the elimination of prostitution or with the complete emancipation of women. The only fundamental way to do this is first to change the structure of society and then change the thinking of those who comprise it. This first found expression in the Common Programme of the Chinese People's Political Consultative Conference of 1949 and the Marriage Law of 1950 which freed women from feudal bondage and gave them equal rights with men.

Changing the moral values and deep-rooted customs of millions of people takes a very long time and necessitates unremitting effort. Great progress has been made since Liberation and Chinese women are now approaching genuine equality with men. They occupy important posts in every sphere of governmental, political, productive, and cultural work, and sex relations based on inequality are disappearing. Although it would be an exaggeration to say that they have already achieved 100 percent emancipation, it can be confidently stated that history has never before witnessed such a transformation in the status of women as has happened in China since 1949. . . .

Mass campaigns against syphilis. . . . To find and treat millions of cases of syphilis and change the attitude of tens of millions of ordinary folk towards venereal disease, the existing corps of medical personnel was totally inadequate. A new approach was needed involving the mobilizing and training of thousands of paramedical workers and immediately a number of highly controversial questions arose. What sort of people should be trained? What minimal educational standards should they possess? How, where and in what should they be trained? Were qualified doctors from the old society able to train others or did they themselves need to learn more before they could teach? . . .

To find the millions of cases of latent syphilis scattered

throughout the country was an immense undertaking which could not be tackled along orthodox lines.

Opinions were divided as to how it could be done. Those with conservative, stereotyped thinking urged greater working efficiency, more personnel, better and speedier methods of blood testing and more expenditure. Theirs was a purely technical approach. Those who could think in a bold, revolutionary way urged a political approach, with reliance on the initiative of the masses as the key to success. The political approach won out, although not without a struggle. . . .

In a county in Hopei province, after prolonged discussions between political and medical workers, a form was drawn up asking ten questions, an affirmative answer to any one of which would suggest the possibility of syphilis. These ten questions contained "clues" such as a history of a skin rash, falling hair, genital sore or exposure to the risk of infection. To draw up the questionnaire was one thing; to persuade tens of thousands of people to fill it in, honestly and conscientiously, was quite another thing. To do this intensive propaganda and education was carried out by anti-syphilis fighters who were able to make close contact with the people, give them the concept that they should liberate themselves, and enlist them as allies in the struggle. Propaganda posters were put up in the village streets, one-act plays performed in the market place, talks given over the village radio system and meetings, big and small, held night after night at which the purpose of the questionnaire was explained and the cooperation of the peasants gradually won. The opening talk would be brief and to-the-point and would go something like this: "Comrades, syphilis is a disease that was bequeathed to us by the rotten society we have thrown out. It's no fault of yours if you have syphilis and no shame should be attached to it. It's only shameful if you cling to your syphilis when you can easily get rid of it. We've got rid of the landlords and the blood-sucking government that looked after *their* interests and now we have a government that looks after *ours*. We have a Party that speaks for us and shows us how to go forward. Now it calls on us to get rid of syphilis and we should seize the opportunity. This form asks ten questions and you should answer them honestly. We will be glad to help any of you who can't read or write. If you don't remember the answers to some of the questions, ask your friends and relatives. In fact, there's nothing wrong with friends and relatives jogging your memories even when they're not asked. This is *our* country now and we should all be concerned about the well-being of everyone else.

"Comrades, we're going forward to Communism and we can't take this rotten disease with us."

At first in some places the response was slow; few villagers filled in the questionnaire and some of those who did so, concealed one or other of the "clues". More propaganda was done and more meetings were called at which the main speakers were those who had already been diagnosed as having syphilis and had been cured by a few injections. They told of the mental struggles they had gone through before admitting to the clues, and of their feelings after they had been cured. They recalled the brutality and indifference of the old days and contrasted it with the present.

The trickle of diagnosed cases increased until it became a torrent. News of the questionnaire, spread by political workers, attracted peasants from far and wide who came to the treatment centres eager to be diagnosed and treated.

Health Care from Liberation to the Cultural Revolution
*by Ruth and Victor W. Sidel**

Experiments in meeting the overwhelming health needs were started during the 1930s and 1940s by Mao Zedong and the People's Liberation Army, first in the Jiangxi Soviet and then, after the Long March, in the areas around Yan'an (Yenan) in Shaanxi Province. Mao and his colleagues gave health care relatively high priority, both as a method of organizing the peasants and winning them to the Communist side and as a method of maintaining the strength of their forces. Their efforts included mobilizing the people to educate themselves and encouraging them individually and collectively to provide their own health care and medical care services. It was during this period

* Sidel, *The Health of China*

that a few physicians from abroad, such as Norman Bethune from Canada and George Hatem (Ma Haide) from the United States, joined Mao's forces and provided direct services, training, and valuable advice.

When the Communist government assumed power over the entire country (with the exception of Taiwan) in 1949, high priority was given to the establishment of an efficient health care system organized so as to cover the entire population. Four basic guidelines for the organization of medical care were enunciated at the People's Republic of China's first National Health Congress in August 1950:

1. Medicine should serve the workers, peasants and soldiers
2. Preventive medicine should take precedence over therapeutic medicine.
3. Chinese traditional medicine should be integrated with Western scientific medicine
4. Health work should be combined with mass movements

Some of the efforts of the 1950s and early 1960s were in large measure based on models from other countries, particularly the Soviet Union, which provided a large amount of technical assistance to China during this period. A number of new medical schools were established, some of the older ones were moved from the cities of the east coast to areas of even greater need further west, and class size was vastly expanded. "Higher" medical education usually consisted of six years, following the completion of some twelve years of previous education, although some schools accepted students with less previous schooling and were said to graduate them after only four or five years of medical education. One school, the China Medical College, located in buildings of and employing much of the faculty of the former Peking Union Medical College, had an eight-year curriculum and was devoted to the training of teachers and researchers.

These efforts produced a remarkably large number of "higher" medical graduates, including stomatologists, pharmacologists, and public-health specialists as well as physicians. It has been estimated that more than 100,000 doctors were trained over fifteen years, an increase of over

250 percent. But by 1965 China's population had increased to about 700 million, and the doctor/population ratio was still less than one per 5,000 people compared to more than one per 1,000 in the industrialized countries at that time.

At the same time large numbers of "middle" medical schools were established to train assistant doctors (modeled largely on the Soviet *feldshers*—medical workers similar in many ways to military corpsmen[12]), nurses, midwives, pharmacists, technicians, and sanitarians. These schools accepted students after nine or ten years of schooling and had a curriculum of two to three years. It has been estimated that some 170,000 assistant doctors, 185,000 nurses, 40,000 midwives, and 100,000 pharmacists were trained.

During the period from 1949 to 1965 the number of hospital beds increased from approximately 84,000 (one for every 6,500 people) to approximately 650,000 (one for every 1,200 people) (see Table 3). This was still far less than the ratio of approximately one hospital bed for every 100 people in technologically developed countries, but considerably higher than in other countries at China's level of technological development. In 1965, India, for example, had one bed for every 1,600 people.

In addition to these efforts to rapidly produce many more professional health workers and health facilities, people in the community were mobilized to perform health-related tasks themselves. A large-scale attack was made on illiteracy and superstition. By means of mass campaigns, people were organized so as to accomplish together what they could not do individually. One of the best-known of these campaigns (which were often called the Great Patriotic Health Campaigns) was the one aimed at eliminating the "four pests," originally identified in some areas—but not all—as flies, mosquitos, rats, and grain-eating sparrows. When the elimination of sparrows appeared likely to produce serious ecological problems, bedbugs (and in some areas lice or cockroaches) were substituted as targets. People were also encouraged to build sanitation facilities to keep their neighborhoods clean.

Campaigns against specific diseases were also mounted. Thousands of people were trained in short courses to recognize the symptoms and signs of venereal disease, encourage treatment, and administer antibiotics when necessary. At the same time the brothels were closed or turned into small factories, and the prostitutes were treated and then retrained or sent back to their homes in the countryside. There were also mass campaigns against opium use. Epidemic-prevention centers were established to conduct massive immunization campaigns and to educate people in sanitation and other disease-prevention techniques.

Another example of the use of mass organization in health was the campaign against schistosomiasis, a parasitic illness acquired from working barefoot in contaminated water. Part of the development of the parasite takes place in snails, hence the term "snail fever." This campaign was based, according to Joshua Horne, a British surgeon who worked in China for fifteen years, on the concept of the "massline"—"the conviction that the ordinary people possess great strength and wisdom and that when their initiative is given full play they can accomplish miracles."

The idea behind the antischistosomiasis program was not only to recruit the people to do the work but also to mobilize their enthusiasm and initiative so that they would fight the disease. The antischistosomiasis effort is particularly illustrative of mass participation, since it mobilized the population in several directions: to move against the snails, cooperate in case finding and treatment, and improve environmental sanitation.

In all these health campaigns it was repeatedly stressed that health is important not only for the individual's well-being but also for that of the family, the community, and the country as a whole. The basic concept of the mass health campaign is said to be the recognition of a problem important to large numbers of people, the analysis of the problem and recommendation of solutions by technical and political leaders, and then—most important—the thorough discussion of the analysis and recommended solutions with the people so that they can fully accept them as their own.

In therapeutic medicine, modern technology was being introduced, but change was relatively slow and was concentrated in the urban areas. A campaign to integrate Chinese medicine with Western medicine was initiated and designed to: (1) make full use of those elements of Chinese medicine that were found effective; (2) provide greater acceptance of Western techniques among those, particularly in the rural areas, who mistrusted them; and (3) efficiently employ the large numbers of practitioners of Chinese medicine. The campaign met with some success, but there was said still to be considerable resistance on both sides and integration was slow and incomplete.

In sum, since 1949 health policy in China has reflected the dominant political ideology of the period. This has always been true, in China as in other countries, but is seen with extraordinary clarity in China. During the last five years after Liberation, in part because the Communist Party lacked trained people, physicians and professionals in the Ministry of Public Health largely shaped health policy. From 1955 through 1957 the Chinese leadership attempted to deal with the problem of "how to produce fundamental social change and simultaneously obtain the cooperation of the professionals necessary to make any such effort successful." The Ministry of Public Health was thought to be "divorced from Party leadership" and was attacked with increasing intensity, particularly for opposing traditional medicine. Consequently, party leaders were gradually placed in the Ministry and certain policy-making decisions were removed from the Ministry's authority.

The late 1950s was a period of further division between the Party and the Ministry of Public Health. While the Ministry was frequently criticized for deemphasizing rural health care, Mao's concern about the discrepancy between life in the cities and living conditions in the countryside and his concern about the consequent alienation of the peasants led to an attempt at rapid transformation of the rural areas. During the period of the Great Leap Forward (1957–1958), the responsibility for health care was further fragmented by the development of people's communes. Commune clinics that were almost completely independent of the Ministry (unlike those of the post-Cultural Revolution period) were organized and mass mobilization efforts were often under Party control. Mao's analysis of health policy focused on the undersupply and underutilization of health resources: the analysis of the Ministry of Public Health was that the problem was excess demand and constricting resources under its control. Because decision-making had been fragmented during the Great Leap Forward in health and in other areas, program coordination had become all but impossible.

The economic difficulties of the late 1950s resulted in diminished decision-making power over health policy by the political sector and by commune leadership. During the early sixties, therefore, the Ministry of Public Health once again became the primary decision-making body vis-á-vis health issues and during this period the emphasis once again was on "quality" care and on urban services.

These policy shifts seemed major to many within China, and to many outside, but in retrospect they were relatively modest adjustments in a fundamental policy that emphasized preventive medicine and integrated development of health care with economic and social development. The results of these fifteen years of effort were extraordinary. Diseases such as smallpox, cholera, typhus, and plague were completely eliminated. Diseases such as malaria, filariasis, tuberculosis, trachoma, schistosomiasis, and ancylostomiasis were still not under full control, although their prevalence was markedly reduced. In short, the successes in the prevention of infectious disease over a span of only one generation were truly monumental, but there was still much preventable infectious disease, particularly in the rural areas.

The Great Leap Forward and the Early 1960s

In its broadest sense, the Great Leap Forward was intended to achieve greater productivity in agriculture and independence in industrial development. By the mid-1950s the farming cooperatives had proved their worth, but even larger organizatons were needed to construct dams and irrigation networks, to clear new land, and to provide self-sufficient health and education programs. If every cooperative waited for the government to solve these problems for them—in a country still very poor—development would have been delayed for many years. The only alternative was for the cooperatives themselves to devise means to attack the difficulties. But even a cooperative was not big enough for the large-scale efforts required, and so the first communes were created, each combining several cooperatives. When the first experiments with the communes appeared to be successful, they were publicized, and the idea soon spread through China.

In the initial excitement, many of the new communes went to extremes. Some villages decided to eat in communal dining halls and to pay everyone equally no matter how much work they did. When it became clear that in agriculture the Great Leap had gone too far too fast, the Party reassessed its experiment and partially retrenched. The communes, it was decided, should continue, but the most "advanced" communes should return to paying everyone on the basis of work done. Later some communes decided they were too large and should be reduced to a manageable number of villages. At the same time, the communal dining halls died out except at harvest time, for most families decided they would rather eat in their own homes.

In the West, the communes were widely reported to have failed. In fact, the communes survived and remained the largest unit of organization in the countryside until the early 1980s. But the economic crisis during the years 1959–1961 was real. The Chinese later called the period the "Three Hard Years." The cause was a series of natural disasters combined with the Soviet pull-out, compounded by poor planning in the initial years of founding the communes.

Another aspect of the Great Leap Forward emphasized decentralization in industrial development. Soviet advice had been invaluable in establishing major industrial installations, but China often needed somewhat simpler industries with less complicated technology spread more thinly over the countryside. This campaign was symbolized by the "backyard furnaces" that the Chinese built everywhere to make low-grade steel for local industries. Although many of these industrial experiments are now recognized as failures, many rural factories that began this way during the Great Leap Forward now manufacture agricultural implements and small machines.

In the following selections, we trace the formation of the communes and the economic policies pursued during the Great Leap. There is also an outline of the Sino-Soviet split and an assessment of the Great Leap by C. P. Fitzgerald.

The People's Communes
by Christopher Howe

Mao's impact on agricultural collectivization was dramatic. By March 1956 over 90 percent of the Chinese peasants were in Cooperatives, and by 1957 virtually all were in the 680,000 Higher Stage Cooperatives. Thus a revolution planned to take fifteen years was completed in little more than one. The results, however, were unsatisfactory. Mao's expectation that changes in ownership and organization would produce immediate economic effects was belied by events. In autumn 1957 it was apparent that the growth of agriculture was still too slow, that urban unemployment was serious, and that relations with the Soviet Union (on which industrial assistance depended) were worsening. This crisis led Mao to launch the most extraordinary economic adventure that the world has ever seen—the Great Leap Forward of 1958. Abandoning all caution (and all Soviet advice) Mao took his argument one step further. He now urged that spectacular development could only be achieved if changes in ownership and organization *were combined with* a radical psychological transformation of the population—a transformation that would stimulate people to work more intensively, more creatively, more selflessly. If this could be achieved, Mao anticipated a wave of investment and development—a Great Leap Forward.

Apart from this central theme, the Great Leap embodied many other ideas and policies. For example, the Leap encouraged local initiatives, especially in developing small-scale industry and local economic self-sufficiency. This policy followed from Mao's conviction that Central Government bureaucrats were ill-informed of local conditions, and that neither they, nor the Party, nor he himself, had an infallible grasp of the laws governing the success or failure of human enterprises. The way the Leap was organized also reflected Mao's belief that chaos and imbalance were progressive, i.e. that a surge of activity in one area or sector created tensions that stimulated progress elsewhere.

In narrower economic terms, the Leap can be seen as a movement to improve employment and to make use of underutilized local resources such as coal and iron ore. It was also an attempt to narrow the gap between industry and the large-scale urban economy on the one hand, and rural life and the primitive handicrafts of the countryside on the other....

In agriculture, the framework for the Leap was a new form of agricultural organization—the People's Commune. The typical commune was a grouping of twenty to thirty Higher Stage Cooperatives; thus whereas in the Cooperatives the framework of peasant life had usually remained the relatively familiar village, it could now in some cases become an organization of up to 50,000 people incorporating villages and regions with which many peasants were unfamiliar. In many instances the Commune also revolutionized family life by introducing public mess halls, and there was a widespread campaign to limit incentives by paying incomes in relation to need as well as to effort.

The atmosphere during the summer of 1958 was extraordinary. Officials who for years had made cautious, pragmatic speeches about China's economy suddenly announced that grain, steel, and other commodities could be produced in almost unlimited quantities. Mao himself, visiting a Commune in August, advised the peasants that the time had come when the surplus of food grains might prove impossible to dispose of. By December there was some awareness that the Leap was running into problems. Nonetheless, a Party meeting held in that month published the most amazing claims for 1958. These included grain production of 375 million tons—more than double the output achieved in 1957. And at the same meeting the targets set for 1959 indicated that the Leap was to continue. Steel output was to rise from 11 to 18 million tons; coal from 270 million to 380 million; and grain from 375 million to 525 million. As the Leap went on into 1959, administrative confusion deepened and the consequences of strain, of the misuse of resources, and of sheer human exhaustion, became increasingly serious. When the end came it coincided with the withdrawal of Soviet assistance and a succession of natural disasters. The results were appalling; the Period of Fastest Growth [1952–1959] concluded with disaster....

By 1960 Mao and the Party leadership began to make fundamental changes. The most important was the priority given to the development of agriculture. Resources were ruthlessly allocated to the chemical fertilizer industry, and machinery plants all over China were converted to the production of agricultural equipment. Incentives to the peasants were increased and this required radical changes in the Communes. At first the smaller Brigade (previously subordinate to the Commune, and frequently equivalent in size to the old Higher Stage Cooperative) was made the main unit of planning and accounting. Later, in autumn 1962, the Team (which had been the smallest component of the Commune and which was usually equivalent to a village) was given this central role. Moreover, in many parts of China collective organization was completely dismantled and the land was handed over to family management on condition that certain basic tax and state purchase targets were met. . . .

In spite of his own flexibility, Mao found that political retreat from the Great Leap Forward was difficult. Not only was he criticized by his senior colleagues; but local leaders responsible for handling the day to day situation were scathing about him and his Great Leap Forward. 'A blind man riding a blind horse' was one description, and accusations thrown up in the Cultural Revolution claimed that Provincial leaders after the Leap were openly saying that they were 'too busy to read Mao's thought', and that the best political action was 'growing potatoes' and 'applying fertilizer'. . . .

The Sino-Soviet Split
by the Committee of Concerned Asian Scholars

It is easy in retrospect to discover the seeds of the present conflict between China and the Soviet Union. The myth of monolithic communism has been dead for well over a decade, and the Sino-Soviet split is a familiar part of our political vocabulary. More surprising, perhaps, is the fact that so few observers—in America—saw it coming.

Territorial Integrity. Just as Japan had demanded China's Shandong Province as spoils for helping defeat Germany in

World War I, so Russia demanded and received Dairen and Port Arthur from Japan after World War II. Their value as, respectively, warm-water port and naval base, were evidently well worth angering the Communist Chinese, then fighting a civil war against the Kuomintang. When the Chinese won Liberation, they found these territories still occupied by the Soviet Union and that—having driven out the Westerners—they still shared control of the Far Eastern Railroad in Manchuria with Russia through joint-stock companies. In December 1949, Mao went to Moscow to spend almost three months negotiating. At the end of that period, the Sino-Soviet Treaty of Friendship, Alliance, and Mutual Assistance was signed (aimed primarily at mutual defense against Japan); in 1950 Dairen was returned to China, in 1952 the joint-stock companies were liquidated and ownership reverted to China, and in 1955 the Russians withdrew from the Port Arthur base. Khrushchev came to visit in Peking, and good relations appeared to have been restored.

But the Chinese resented what they consider the refusal of the Soviet Union to offer adequate support in two major crisis involving their territorial integrity. The first, in 1958, was the Quemoy-Matsu crisis, in which the Russians pointedly did not support Chinese efforts to blockade the islands. The second was the equally serious clash between the Indians and Chinese in 1962. In both of these cases China was quite genuinely threatened, and Soviet unwillingness to aid China left a bitter suspicion in Peking.

To this day China resents the Soviet position on their mutual border. The border, fixed in 18th century treaties between the Manchu (Ch'ing dynasty) and czarist courts, transferred a large portion of what had formerly been considered Chinese territory to Russia. Despite Lenin's early promises to renounce all czarist treaties, the Soviets have continued to assert those borders. Compounding the border problems, there are large populations of "national minorities" (Uighurs, Kazakhs, Kirghiz, and other groupings of Mongol and Turkic stock) on both sides of the Sino-Soviet border. Both Russia and China fear attempts by the other to "stir up" these minority groups, some of which number in the millions....

Economic Aid. Economic relations between the two nations have at times been even rougher than those of a military nature. The brief period of Soviet support—barely a decade in all—ended in bitter recriminations and increasing mutual criticism of domestic policies in both countries.

Soviet assistance took two forms. All materials and financial aid were loans—and not particularly long-term loans. It has been a great point of pride for the Chinese that they were able to repay all of these loans fully, exporting cloth, raw materials, and foodstuffs in order to do so. Today they have no foreign debt. But this type of aid, although it undoubtedly contributed to China's impressive growth, was far less crucial than assistance in the guise of technical expertise. In the fifties, hundreds of Russian engineers, designers, production advisers, and other technically trained persons came to China. With their help the first huge hydroelectric stations and modern heavy industries were constructed and placed in operation.

By the late fifties, however, the Chinese were beginning to feel they had made a mistake. The economic model of development which the Soviets exported, and the Chinese had imported, was dysfunctional. Because the Soviet model was very capital-intensive, where China's greatest resource was its large labor pool, and also because the Soviet Union heavily emphasized development of urban areas and urban-related facilities, where China was still overwhelmingly agricultural, the Russian model simply did not fit. Recognition of this failure led to the Great Leap Forward, in an attempt to reverse the pattern adopted from Russia and to develop a unique Chinese model.

The Great Leap Forward was taken as a serious affront by the Russians. Not only were the Soviet economic models rejected, but the Chinese seemed to be claiming that they had pulled ahead of the Russians on the road to communism. In creating rural communes, the Chinese experimented with the "free-support system," in accord with the Communist idea of "from each according to his abilities, to each according to his needs" (as opposed to the less-advanced socialist stage in which each worker is rewarded according to his productivity). In asserting the unique value of its experience for other underdeveloped nations, China again directly confronted the Soviet model.

The Soviet response in July 1960 was to withdraw all technicians and personnel from China. Only about 150 of the approximately 300 industrial plants and other major projects the Soviets had taken responsibility for were finished—and many of the Russian technicians took the blueprints with them when they went. Coupled with three years of natural disasters (the "three hard years") and bureaucratic mismanagement, the Soviet pullout helped to offset the economic progress of the early years of the Great Leap Forward.

Ideological Disputes. The fierce ideological battles of the early sixties between Peking and Moscow revolved around three questions. First, what attitude should Communist nations take toward non-Communist, but neutralist, governments in the third world? The Russians supported these governments; the Chinese supported more radical liberation movements. Secondly, was there a possibility of coexistence with the United States? The Russians said yes; the Chinese, no. And thirdly, were Russia's changing domestic policies "revisionist," departing from progress toward communism and returning to capitalist forms? In 1964 a major article, "On Khrushchev's Phony Communism" (probably edited personally by Mao), provided a summary of the revisionist tendencies that China perceived in the Soviet Union. From this perspective, the Cultural Revolution can be seen as an attempt to eliminate similar tendencies in China: the adoption of material incentives, increasing bureaucratism, lack of control of bourgeois intellectuals, and increasing inequalities in wages and income. Significantly, Liu Shao-ch'i was commonly called "China's Khrushchev" during the Cultural Revolution.

China's relations with Russia—as with other countries—deteriorated markedly during the Cultural Revolution. But by the late sixties only the last of the three questions outlined above was still a bone of contention. Both China and Russia have a united front with regard to "national democratic" forces and governments, and China has dramatically demonstrated its willingness to coexist with the United States by inviting Nixon to Peking. But the Chinese still reject Russian domestic policies as a deviation from the path to communism.

Accomplishments of the Great Leap Forward

by C. P. Fitzgerald*

Thus both programmes [the communes and industrial development] ran into serious difficulties. Mao, it is now known, was blamed for these mishaps, and probably did not at that time get the credit for what was in fact achieved. This can be summed up briefly; the Communes had hardly been set up for one year before north and central China were stricken by the worst drought for more than 100 years. The Yellow river was almost dry in 1960: a vast region remained virtually without rain for over two years. Under previous systems of government and land tenure this would have meant a very major famine, the migration of millions of starving people, and the death by starvation of millions more. Great disorder, possibly a major rebellion, would have been the political consequence. There are many historical examples, some not so very long ago. In 1960–62, not even the most virulent critics of Mao Tse-tung's China claimed mass deaths by starvation, or mass migrations. There was certainly no political disorder. There were severe food shortages, rationing, especially of vegetable oils, malnutrition, though not among the children, and great hardships in many rural areas. But the Commune system, clumsy though it was, and resting on the more effective cooperatives, saved the lives of millions simply because resources were centrally controlled, and rationing made possible; and also because of the water conservancy works which had been carried out after the communization of all land in previous years.

One result was a modification of the system, reduction in size of the Commune unit, and a new plan by which labour was employed in its own local setting and advantage taken of local knowledge. The Commune system, fifteen years later, remains the Chinese land tenure system; it has outgrown its teething troubles and is now accepted as the normal way of organizing agricultural life. The Great Leap,

* *Mao Tse-tung and China*

which was certainly also a stumble, did not come up to expectations; but it was not a wholly disastrous misadventure as some critics have claimed. It had side consequences which were more beneficial than the projected targets. In 1960 as a phase in the developing Sino-Soviet quarrel, Russia suddenly without notice withdrew her scientific and technical experts, and with them their plans and blueprints. A heavy blow at Chinese industrial development, it resulted in the closure of plants and the abandonment of projects under construction. What the drought had done to the Communes, the Russian withdrawal of all aid did to the Great Leap Forward.

In many ways the results, over the years, proved comparable. The reshaped Communes have become a lasting and viable method of organizing rural society and economy; the stimulus given to Chinese technology and invention by the Russian act—intended to cripple such activity—has had the result of promoting a much more rapid industrial advance based on a wider technical foundation of skill among the Chinese people rather than reliance on foreign aid. 'Standing on two legs', as Mao puts it. In 1964, only four years after the Russian experts had departed, and the Great Leap had been disrupted, China exploded her first nuclear device—without Russian or any other assistance from abroad. . . .

It is perhaps necessary to put the Commune system into intimate focus because it was to become a subject of violent polemic, extreme criticism, and false deductions. There is no doubt, since the Cultural Revolution disclosed so many secrets, that the Commune plan was opposed by an important section of the leadership, and that it was supported by extremists who were largely responsible for projecting their own theoretical plans as established facts of Commune life. As has been shown, the men on the Communes were, it would seem, often as unaware of the theories as they were ignorant of the existence of an overall plan. They just did the necessary work, and organized the labour force. But it was this work and the organization of labour which was in fact the major weakness of the system as it was at first applied. The Communes were too large; men had to be moved about by bus and lorry to distant lands with which they were not familiar; the advice of elderly farmers was not regarded, because it was necessarily local. Local knowledge and skills were not acknowledged. Too many young cadres sent down from the ministries in Peking meddled with matters of which they knew too little. They advocated deep ploughing, often when the soil was not suitable for this treatment; they also advocated close sowing, when local knowledge did not agree; the workers, engaged on land with which they were not familiar, did not object, or know enough to point out the dangers. Thus crops were often below average instead of above it, and the cadres from the ministries were not very accurate in their assessments of what yield was being obtained. In fact they grossly exaggerated successes and covered up failures.

The economic setbacks that followed the Great Leap Forward temporarily reduced Mao's influence over the direction of politics in China. Yet Mao had begun laying the groundwork during this period for the Cultural Revolution—China's greatest mass political movement—in his work on the Socialist Education campaign. In the first selection Fitzgerald describes the campaign and its political implications, as well as the move toward democratization of the People's Liberation Army begun by Lin Biao. The reform of the army was marked by Lin's use of the *Little Red Book* of Mao's sayings, a book he had compiled. In the second selection the political career of Liu Shaoqi is contrasted with the political values of Mao Zedong. The "Two Lines", the opposing political forces that clashed later in the Cultural Revolution, had their roots in the opposing political views of Mao and Liu on many topics as Fitzgerald notes.

The Socialist Education Campaign
by C. P. Fitzgerald*

In 1962, through to 1964, a new movement was launched by Mao, called 'Socialist Education'; its purpose was to implant more radical ideas in the minds of the younger generation, the youths who had never really known or could hardly remember the old régime before the Communists came to power, and also those children who had

---

* *Mao Tse-tung and China*

actually been born since the revolution. Mao did not confront the hierarchy at that time; he was planning to undermine it by building a base of support for his own policy in the younger generation. This was a strategy which could not easily be thwarted by the men in power: no Communist could object to 'Socialist Education' by which the young were to be taught to understand the objectives of the Party, and the policies of the régime. It might well be that the government was not actually going to pursue some of these policies very vigorously, nor expecting to attain those objectives very quickly, but it was impossible to deny that such were the objectives, and such the policies. So Socialist Education thrived, more particularly in the rural areas, where the central hierarchy was less immediately powerful and young cadres of the Party were in local positions of control and influence. The movement also developed a strong bias against some of the intellectuals, who were accused of having bourgeois ideas and ways of life. This was a theme which was to gain strength and importance, foreshadowing the Cultural Revolution itself.

It now seems strange that the hierarchy did not perceive their danger, or if they did, that they could devise no plan to avert it. But one real difficulty stood in their way: the army. Lin Piao was a key figure in Mao's plan; he was the War Minister, and, whatever may now be said of him, he was at that time a radical, and the trusted instrument of Mao Tse-tung. He was making the army into a revolutionary force with egalitarian ideas. In 1965, ranks were abolished. Henceforward, there were no officers as such, and no differences in uniforms. Commanders of units of any size, and even the commander-in-chief himself, dressed in the same way as privates, and were simply known as 'Comrade So-and-so commanding such-and-such force.' It seems cumbersome, and must in practice have often been shortened to a simpler phrase. Lin Piao also issued the army with the famous *Little Red Book*—complete with a Preface by him—which is a selection from Mao's major writings, emphasizing discipline, service to the people, and maxims drawn from the experience of the guerrilla wars. It became a compulsory training manual for the troops. Thus the army was being brought to believe in the supreme wisdom of Mao, and the essential value of his leadership. The *Little Red Book*, not being a defence of the Communist

Party as such, but a collection of quotations from Mao's writings, makes little or no mention of the other leaders of the Party.

Mao's Attack on Revisionism
by C. P. Fitzgerald*

Personalities were in conflict; the record and personal history of Mao and Liu [Shao-ch'i] differed in important aspects. Mao had always fought and worked openly with the armed guerrilla branch of the Communist movement; Liu had been the underground leader and organizer in Kuomintang territory, the secret conspirator, an elusive figure whose activities were little known to the world at large, whose very name was almost wholly unknown to the Western press. Liu had had much closer contacts with Russia; it was certainly he who, in 1948, came back from Moscow to attend the conference held in that summer at Shihchiachuang (Hopei province). The advice he brought from Moscow, to continue guerrilla war and to abstain from taking the large cities, was rejected in favour of the opposite strategy, which within a year gave total victory to the Communist cause. This event cannot have bred confidence between the two men.

A deeper cause for conflict seems, from the accusations later made against Liu, to have been their differing conceptions of how the future policy of the government and movement should proceed. Liu was the 'apparatchik' type; a firm believer in hierarchy, discipline and strict obedience to the line laid down by the central organs of the Party. Such had been his methods in the long years of secret revolutionary work, and he could well believe that success and survival had been due to them. Mao has always been unorthodox in these matters; he believes in the creative force of mass opinion, he distrusts hierarchy and has actually encouraged rejection of the official line and open criticism of the higher Party organs and their leaders. Liu believed that the economy and its development was the first priority, and ideological and social transformations a

---

* *Mao Tse-tung and China*

second objective, only to be achieved at a time and pace which did not disrupt the economic programmes.

Mao clearly holds the opposite view; that too much attention to the development of the economy at the expense of social change ends in the 'revisionism' of which he accuses the Soviet Union, the gradual abandonment of truly socialist aims and the adoption of 'bourgeois' ways of thinking and living. The career open to the talented was the ideal of the followers of Liu, and there can be no doubt that among the many thousands who had found such careers opened to them by the Communist revolution, he had wide support. But Mao considers that such an ideal is esentially 'bourgeois', favouring the growth of new élites, and having an inherent link with the old Chinese society, in which, at least in theory, this was the ideal and as far as possible the practice aimed at by the old imperial Civil Service examination system. Differences founded on such antithetical ideas could only, sooner or later, result in an open conflict. The pretexts for the breach are far less significant than the fundamental causes.

The Great Proletarian Cultural Revolution

The Cultural Revolution was the second great mass campaign and was directed against problems even more basic than those addressed by the Great Leap Forward. The essential goal of the Cultural Revolution, as expressed by Mao, was to prevent the Chinese leadership from becoming a Soviet-style bureaucratic ruling class. This was the main thrust of the tumultuous political movement that peaked during the years 1966–1969 and lasted a full decade—until 1976. The Cultural Revolution was loosely orchestrated, though often not controlled, by Mao, and it was opposed by a large part of the Communist party leadership. In the end, Mao was only partly successful in his attempt to shake up an ossifying structure of government. Moreover, the costs are now known to have been enormous: in the uncontrolled violence and turmoil, China's economic development was severely stunted, and many thousands of lives were lost. Current Chinese views of the Cultural Revolution are overwhelmingly negative—as are those in the selections here by Christopher Howe and Fox Butterfield. The early course of the movement is drawn by David and Nancy Milton, a couple who were teaching English at the Peking First Foreign Languages Institute in Peking, and the aims and achievements are addressed by C. P. Fitzgerald. John K. Fairbank puts the effects of the Cultural Revolution on intellectuals and education in a historical perspective. It is important to point out that the Chinese have already gone through several phases in their evaluation of the Cultural Revolution, which has been a source of major dispute between different groups in China. Writings by Americans and other foreigners or by the Chinese about the Cultural Revolution should be seen as products of their own time periods.

Aims of the Cultural Revolution
by C. P. Fitzgerald*

The Cultural Revolution, when it began in 1966, was subject to many interpretations, most of which were to be disproved by events. It was seen as a power struggle between Mao and Liu Shao-ch'i; as a revolt of the young against the privileges and pretensions of the 'Old Comrades from Yenan', as the senior members of the Party had come to be called. It was also suggested that it was an upsurge of the regionalism which had characterized China in the years following the fall of the Manchu dynasty, and it was believed that the interval of unity which the Communist victory had imposed in 1949 was breaking down; a new warlord era was predicted.

The explanation which received the least credit was that which was given by Mao himself and those who were closely associated with him. The revolution must have various stages: first the political, by which the 'bourgeois' state is overthrown and the Communist Party, champions of the masses, comes to power. Next comes the economic revolution by which the capitalist economy and the 'feudal' land system are first modified, and finally replaced by new socialist forms of economy and land tenure. This was accomplished in the years following the military victory, and culminated in the Commune system and the virtually

---

* *Mao Tse-tung and China*

complete nationalization of industry and commerce. There remained a further stage; the government had been changed and the economy transformed, but the Chinese themselves, their thoughts, their tastes, their outlook on life and their personal hopes and ambitions, remained largely unaltered. The last step was to be a cultural revolution, whereby these characteristics were to be remodelled, culminating in genuine socialists to whom the way of life and thought of their ancestors would be as alien as those, for example, of the pagan world to the Christian era which followed it.

That this intention was the core of Mao Tse-tung's outlook and the inspiration of his policies is the clue to the Cultural Revolution. Indeed, it also involved a power struggle: Liu Shao-ch'i and those who, like him, believed in a firm hierarchical system (which, in Mao's opinion, must inevitably harden into a new class system) had to be driven from power. Their ideals were ultimately incompatible with Mao's aims. It also involved calling upon the younger generation—which had its own frustrations—to rally in an assault on the senior men of the hierarchy, and serve as Mao's shock troops in what he intended to be a wholly political and social movement, without violence....

It is also clear that the course of events was not exactly what Mao intended or expected. Using the revolt of the young, which he actively encouraged, he was able, very early on, to eliminate his opponents from power. But he did not foresee that the forces which he had unleashed could not be led or controlled by words alone. He had to call in the aid of the army, which, under Lin Piao, had been one of the main instruments for promoting the Cultural Revolution, and the principal political base of Mao and his supporters. The army had to restore order between contending factions, and by doing so came to occupy positions of power in all fields of activity which had hitherto been dominated by the Party organization. The army, or rather Lin Piao, made the error of thinking that this situation was permanent and could be consolidated by the elimination of Mao. This Mao probably did not foresee at the beginning, but there is evidence that he came to suspect Lin well before the final conspiracy, and therefore took his own precautions.

Revolution from Below
by David Milton and Nancy Dall Milton

Origins

As we were to learn, a bitter conflict between Chinese leaders over which road to follow had existed within the Communist Party from the beginning of the revolution. Even seventeen years after the victory of the Chinese Revolution, the dispute remained unresolved. We had come to China at the decisive stage of that massive effort to appropriate, translate, and then break loose from the Russian revolutionary experience. Like many non-Chinese observers in the fall of 1964, we believed that the Chinese Communist leadership constituted a monolithic, veteran group, united in policy and direction. Despite periodic arguments at the top and the occasional replacement of individual national leaders, the Chinese Communist Party was noted for possessing the most stable group of leaders of any political organization in the world. Within two years, not only would that "stable" leadership divide into hostile camps, but the nation would move to the brink of civil war. Believing that the debate with the Russians was just about over, we found that among the Chinese themselves it had just begun. Along with millions of ordinary Chinese, we were drawn into a political struggle over the meaning of a half century of Chinese history. The Chinese political war of the mid-Sixties was, in fact, a conflict over the two models of revolutionary development produced by the fundamentally different experiences of the Russian and Chinese revolutions. Which model should China choose? Which would be more relevant to its future development? It was a political struggle rooted not only in theory, but in the historical experiences of the two great revolutions of the twentieth century. Labeled by the Chinese as "the struggle between the two lines," it was a contest among leaders influenced by the model of revolution developed by Mao Tse-tung in his guerilla capital of Yenan and those determined to follow the classic Moscow formula for modernization.

Throughout the whole protracted course of the Chinese Revolution, the effort to synthesize the experience of the Russian Revolution produced strains and tensions within the ranks of the Chinese Communist Party. Mao's writings clearly reflect the search of generations of Chinese thinkers for a formula to revive a collapsing civilization. Mao once described how he had himself engaged in that search:

> From the time of China's defeat in the Opium War of 1840, Chinese progressives went through untold hardships in their quest for truth from Western countries [...] every effort was made to learn from the West. In my youth, I, too, engaged in such studies. They represented the culture of Western bourgeois democracy, including social theories and natural sciences of that period, and they were called the "new learning" in contrast to Chinese feudal culture, which was called the "old learning."
>
> Imperialist aggression shattered the fond dreams of the Chinese about learning from the West. It was very odd—why were the teachers always committing aggression against their pupil? The Chinese learned a good deal from the West, but they could not make it work and were never able to realize their ideals.

According to Mao, the Chinese finally discovered a universally applicable truth from the Russian October Revolution of 1917—"The salvoes of the October Revolution brought us Marxism-Leninism."

If the salvoes of the October Revolution brought the Chinese Marxism-Leninism, then the history and traditions of peasant revolt that had existed for centuries provided the social forces and indigenous form for China's revolutionary transformation. Hunan had been the center of Chinese revolutionary thought for over half a century prior to the 1911 Revolution. Moreover, Hunan, unlike Peking, was influenced directly by the concepts of peasant revolt, specifically the Taiping rebellion of the 1860's. It was in Hunan that Mao developed intellectually and where he spent more than eight years of his youth as a student and teacher at the Hunan Normal School in Changsha. It required a peasant intellectual to lead China's peasant revolution.

The scholars of Hunan, isolated from the main currents of Chinese history and thought during the eighteenth and early nineteenth centuries, developed their own pragmatic and interpretative approach to the Confucian classics. These writings, stressing economic and political aspects of Confucianism, challenged the scholasticism predominant in the rest of the country. It was Wang Fu-chih (1619–92), the anti-Manchu philosopher of Hengyang, who first developed an evolutionary approach to Chinese political institutions asserting that each historical period produced its own unique form of political organization. He therefore argued that it was futile to attempt to revive ancient institutions. This notion was, of course, an attack on a fundamental tenet of Confucian philosophy. For Wang, political and social systems, as well as human nature, and social customs were all subject to change.

> What is not yet complete can be completed; what is already completed can be reformed. There is not a single part of human nature already shaped that can not be modified.

The ideas of Wang Fu-chih were not well known outside his own province during his lifetime, but by the second half of the nineteenth century they influenced a whole generation of scholars and officials in Hunan, and during Mao's youth these ideas were widespread in the progressive school system with which Mao became associated.

Wang Fu-chih had stated, "Action can reap the result of knowledge, whereas knowledge might not lead to action." His theory of knowledge, while embracing a theory of observation and deduction, placed the weight on action. In 1937, Mao Tse-tung wrote in his famous essay "On Practice":

> If you want knowledge, you must take part in the practice of changing reality. If you want to know the taste of a pear, you must change the pear by eating it yourself [...] If you want to know the theory and methods of revolution, you must take part in revolution.

Did this come from Wang Fu-chih or Marx and Engels, from the Chinese dialectical system or the dialectics of

Hegel? Undoubtedly Mao was influenced by both Western and Chinese schools of thought and found them compatible. What he could not digest from the West he discarded, and as he and other Chinese Communists gained experience, they discarded more and more of the theory which did not fit their own environment. . . .

The first great revolutionary manifesto of the Chinese Revolution, written by the young Mao in 1927, contained the seeds of the unique Chinese view of modern revolution:

> The present upsurge of the peasant movement is a colossal event. In a very short time, in China's central, southern, and northern provinces, several hundred million peasants will rise like a mighty storm, like a hurricane, a force so swift and violent that no power however great, will be able to hold it back. They will smash all the trammels that bind them and rush forward along the road to liberation. They will sweep all the imperialists, warlords and corrupt officials, local tyrants and evil gentry, into their graves. Every revolutionary comrade will be put to the test, to be accepted or rejected as they decide [. . .] Every Chinese is free to choose, but events will force you to choose quickly.*

Mao put the revolution before the Party; the Party was to be tested by the revolution. Thirty years later, Mao would use the same concept to test the Party once more in the fires of revolution from below, and we as foreign teachers would find ourselves with the rest of the Chinese urban population submerged in a mass politics involving millions of activists. This was hardly the concept of the role of the vanguard party developed by the Russians.

Concepts of revolution from below were further elaborated and developed by the Chinese communists when they sank roots once again in the peasantry after their epic Long March to secure Northwest China base areas. For more than a decade, Mao and other Chinese leaders learned the rudiments of popular rule in the vast Liberated Areas the Chinese Communist armies carved out for themselves. The new political system worked out by Mao and his followers from the caves of their capital town in the

---

* "Report on an Investigation of the Peasant Movement in Hunan."

dry plateau region of Shensi Province included: an anti-bureaucratic style of simplified administration, reliance on local-level organization, the dispatch of intellectuals to the countryside, cooperative forms of production, mandatory cadre labor at the point of production, and the systematic spread of popular education. All these were to become the hallmarks of the new Maoist revolutionary theory and practice, very different indeed from the Russian bureaucratic system of top-down rule. The new popular forms of Chinese communist government grew naturally in the decentralized environment of protracted revolutionary guerrilla war.

The Early Stages

Although Chairman Mao sparked much that was new in China, he also stirred up much that was deep in the Chinese tradition of rebellion. Taking their cue from one of Mao's poems, these youths of Peking chose the classical symbol of Chinese rebellion, the Monkey King, to express their new spirit of defiance:

> Revolutionaries are Monkey Kings, their golden rods are powerful, their supernatural powers far-reaching, and their magic omnipotent, for they possess Mao Tsetung's invincible thought. We wield our golden rods, display our supernatural powers, and use our magic to turn the old world upside down, smash it to pieces, pulverize it, create chaos, and make a tremendous mess, the bigger the better! We must do this to the present revisionist middle school attached to the Tsinghua University, make rebellion in a big way, rebel to the end! We are bent on creating a tremendous proletarian uproar and hewing out a proletarian new world.

We heard reports of Chairman Mao's gigantic meeting [August 1966] with more than 1 million Red Guards in T'ien An Men Square, where he had put on a student's red arm band to legitimize their movement and told them, "Pay attention to state affairs and carry the Cultural Revolution through to the end." For more than two years, the youth of China would do little else.

When we returned to Peking at the end of August, we entered a dramatic and colorful world that had become a political festival of the masses. At the Institute, we found ourselves strangely unemployed. The gates to the school were now open, but the campus was almost deserted after ten o'clock in the morning as students and teachers disappeared into their intense study sessions, organizational meetings, and perusal of Cultural Revolution editorials and documents. Everywhere, on the walls of buildings, thousands of big-character posters stared out at us. We were now to live amid a sea of language, a lively world of large blue, red, and yellow ideographs. Freaks, monsters, demons, sinister soldiers, and gusts of evil wind were some of the charged phrases that energized a formerly tranquil atmosphere with the tension of conflict. No one could tell what the next morning might bring as new waves of words washed over the city. It was obvious to us that the revolution in our school had begun, but how far it had gone beyond the overthrow of the open vestiges of inequality was difficult to determine. In particular, it was not clear whether the walls of power had yet been breached.

Whatever the stage of the movement, the basic routine of political activity for the student population was now established for the duration of that movement. Students, teachers, and a few cadres would work late into the night, either individually or in groups, writing the posters which would then be pasted up the next morning. After breakfast, a great quiet reigned over this city of universities as the student population, numbering in the hundreds of thousands, silently read the posters of the previous night. And it was not only the students who participated in this orgy of writing and reading. Shop clerks, workers, office employees, and bus drivers somehow carried on their work while following the same basic routine as the students. It was a most impressive sight—the population of a country which only twenty years before had been 80 percent illiterate conducting a national debate through the written word. Late in the morning and in the afternoon, the students and teachers would break up into study or strategy sessions, participate in demonstrations, or visit other organizations throughout the city to learn the latest news and read their posters. The formidable organization of the Chinese Communist Party, built up methodically over the decades, had been suddenly overturned and replaced by a communications and organizational network which embraced millions of ordinary citizens in a decision-making apparatus of their own. In the evenings, thousands of mass meetings occurred simultaneously throughout the capital. There, the latest political developments were discussed, analyzed, and acted upon.

Within six months, every wall in Peking was plastered with an outpouring of big-character posters. Hastily constructed fences lined with reed matting flanked the paths and walkways of every organization to provide additional space for the torrent of words and argument. When this space ran out, wires were strung across large dining halls and meeting rooms. As this deluge continued, it grew more sophisticated, and one quickly learned which posters were important and which could be passed by. All were signed by their author or authors, and unwritten rules stipulated how long they must remain before they could be taken down—usually two weeks. Undoubtedly, the traditional veneration of the Chinese for the written word and the fact that in the past it had been a crime to destroy written material—in each community, a man was specifically delegated to dispose ceremonially of all such paper—contributed to the respect shown the big-character posters during the Cultural Revolution. The posters varied in content, length, and style. Some consisted of one sheet of denunciation, affirmation, or analysis; others, twenty-five or thirty consecutive sheets, often containing a detailed history and evaluation of an institution and its leading groups. One or two each week became famous. Everyone talked about them, and many replies were made to the specific arguments of these key documents, which sometimes turned the movement from its present course....

By late September, massive numbers of "traveling" Red Guards from all over the country were arriving in the city daily, complicating what was already an extraordinary outburst of mass activity. The *"Ch'uan-lien"* (literally, to exchange experience) was one of the great social inventions of the Cultural Revolution. Young rebels on "Long Marches" and extensive travels throughout the vast country spread the revolutionary fever to all sections of the population. Free transportation for any who wished to travel in the name of the revolution soon preempted the country's railway network. The economic cost may have been heavy, but the youth in their millions came into contact with the larger society. Within a few months, these travelers, carrying their little red books, bedrolls strapped to their backs, penetrated every nook and cranny of China. Many learned more than they taught, and, despite some irritation at youthful intrusion into the ordinary workaday life of the adult population, the young Red Guards, at least in the early stages of the Cultural Revolution, were received with warmth and encouragement by the Chinese citizenry.

The population of Peking, spurred by Premier Chou's personal concern for the welfare of the crowds of visitors, saw to it that food, clothing, shelter, and medical care were provided for the youngsters who poured into the revolutionary Mecca to catch a glimpse of "the reddest sun" himself. It seemed as if every resident of the city was engaged in preparing the traditional northern steamed buns to feed the young pilgrims of the Cultural Revolution. Everywhere on the gray walls of the city was to be seen the famous quote from Chairman Mao: "The world is yours, as well as ours, but in the last analysis, it is yours. You young people, full of vigor and vitality, are in the prime of life, like the sun at eight or nine in the morning. All hopes are placed on you." Mao Tse-tung had succeeded in tapping the roots of rebellion among the nation's youth. That elixir of revolution, that feeling of ordinary people that they are making history, had taken hold.

The famous mass meetings where the Chairman met with a million or so Red Guards in T'ien An Men originally had the purpose of mobilizing the youth. Soon such meetings became a necessity. Despite repeated instructions from the central leadership that the young people from afar could not remain in Peking and must return to their home provinces, the visitors refused to leave until they had seen Chairman Mao. No sooner had a million boarded the outgoing trains after their meeting with the Chairman than another million would arrive. When the giant square of the revolution could no longer contain the flood, Mao rode throughout the city in a jeep and so accommodated the hopes of 2 or more million youngsters at one stroke.

Observers in the West, who shuddered at the thought of turning the youth loose on any country, failed to realize that, in the long run, the march of the Chinese youth during the 1960's contributed to the unity of a nation which had long been geographically fragmented. The experience of the wandering Red Guards helped to undermine the parochial notions characteristic of a people just emerging from a past shaped by the peasant village. How many times had we urged our own students to seek out the museums and parks of Peking on a Sunday and how many times had they decided against venturing out of the school gates? Many of them had turned the walls of their universities into new villages. It seemed that only their Chairman was able to convince them to go out into the larger world in order to learn that all of China was their home. . . .

The months of December 1966 and January 1967 were a period of great chaos in China. Red Guards crisscrossed the country in the millions and continued to pour into Peking. Inspired by the editorials of the day, they rushed on in their search for class enemies. From the time it became clear that the Cultural Revolution was, in the Chairman's words, a "class struggle," the masses turned to past struggles for a form which fit the realities of this one. The primary class struggle of the people's experience or knowledge was the land reform movement, and it was from this struggle against China's landlords that so many of the forms of the Cultural Revolution were derived. So, when students began to attack either "bourgeois reactionary authorities" or Party officials, they fell back on the archaic forms of earlier struggles or simply on China's long historical tradition. Enemies were paraded through the streets wearing dunce hats and signs around their necks, a strange contemporary manifestation of the traditional Confucian "rectification of names." Criminals in early imperial China had been branded with a mark which indicated not only the nature of their crime, but their class status. The Communists themselves, before being executed by the Kuomintang, had been forced to wear signs defining them as "bandits."

The tendency to replicate the past was intensified by such mass study campaigns of the early Cultural Revolution as the one to reread Mao's 1927 classic analysis of China's class structure, "Report on the Investigation of the Hunan Peasant Movement." In it, Mao, describing the mass rising of the peasants, said, "At the slightest provocation they make arrests, crown the arrested with tall paper hats, and parade them through the villages saying, 'You dirty landlord, now you know who we are!'" In 1927, Mao, more than other revolutionaries, understood the historical necessity and indeed inevitability of the Hunan peasants' violent wrench with a past of subservience and class fear; but in 1966, he had no wish to preserve such methods. Stressing the difference between the recommended "struggle by reason" (*wen-tou*) as opposed to the emerging "struggle by force" (*wu-tou*), Mao wrote to Chou En-lai a little later that winter:

> Recently, many revolutionary teachers and students and revolutionary masses have written to me asking whether it is considered struggle by force [*wu-tou*] to make those in authority taking the capitalist road and freaks and monsters wear dunce caps, to paint their faces, and to parade them in the street. I think it is a form of struggle by force [*wu-tou*]. These goals cannot achieve our goal of educating the people. I want to stress here that, when engaging in struggle, we definitely must hold to struggle by reason [*wen-tou*], bring out the facts, emphasize rationality, and use persuasion before we can reach our standard of struggle and before we can achieve our goal of educating people.

However, new forms do not easily evolve. Although the use of hats and signs gradually began to diminish, what they symbolized was never entirely absent from the Cultural Revolution. . . .

"Empires wax and wane; states cleave asunder and coalesce"—so begins the Chinese classic *The Romance of the Three Kingdoms*. It would be difficult to find a Chinese who has not in some way internalized the political and historical concepts expressed in this most popular of all Chinese novels. The notion of politics as a process, an ebb and flow of power constellations, an unending struggle leading to splits, consensus, and coalition remains firmly rooted in the Chinese consciousness. By the spring of 1967, after one year of uninterrupted revolution, millions of ordinary citizens had entered a realm of power which for thousands of years had been restricted to the elites. After nearly a half century of experience in political struggles, Mao had come to the conclusion that "apart from uninhabited deserts, wherever there are groups of people, they are invariably composed of the left, the middle, and the right. This will be the case for ten thousand years." Yet, he added, while a clear left, right, and center rapidly emerge at the beginning of a social movement, in the course of time the early left may well degenerate and transform itself into the right. Thus, in Maoist theory, the three political categories are not fixed but changing, and the true left is formed and consolidated only through a process of protracted political struggle. After observing the complex politics and patterns of the Cultural Revolution for more than a year, Mao reached a deceptively simple formulation of one of the main laws of the movement: "There is one main tendency in a given period, and it may cover up the other tendency. While opposing the right erroneous tendency, the left erroneous tendency appears; while opposing the left erroneous tendency, the right erroneous tendency may appear."

Our lives, like those of all the citizens of the capital city, were now governed by the ebbs and tides of a social movement which had in time assumed an elemental ambience. It was as if the posters, the marching columns, and the blare of the loudspeakers had always existed. Riding our bicycles down the back road leading to the Institute, we were no longer startled by the sight of the once flat, now upturned, white granite slab marking the grave of the renowned painter Ch'i Pai-shih. The grave-stone had been set askew by the youthful rebels long ago and would no doubt in calmer times be restored to its original place so that the children could once again play ping-pong on its smooth broad surface.

The division of the half-million student population of Peking into the Heaven and the Earth factions was both a demographic fact and a way of life. Even the foreign community, following the social law of the movement, divided like an amoeba under the microscope. Our students who belonged to other factions no longer spoke to us nor invited us to their meetings, and we learned of their activities only through the filter of our own faction, which kept a close watch on the activities of its opponents. Despite the new political concepts and ideas which flooded the society, it was clear that the ancient Chinese adage "He who wins power becomes a king; he who loses power becomes a bandit" had not lost its grip on the popular consciousness. . . .

During the hot summer of 1967, a state of semi-anarchy prevailed in the most populous country in the world. Work went on, the buses ran, there was no interruption of water and electricity, but administration had virtually ceased. The whole middle organizational level had been wiped out. There was only the very top and the bottom. No ordinary official dared to give orders. Even orders issued by the highest officials in the land, including Premier Chou, Vice Chairman Lin, the Military Affairs Commission, the State Council, and the Cultural Group, were often ignored. The command to desist from marching cadres around in the streets in paper hats was ignored, as was the order prohibiting storming into public buildings and rifling state documents. Although the Red Guards were told not to go to Sinkiang and Tibet, they went anyway.

On June 16, *People's Daily* published an article entitled: "Masses Demand Stop to the Use of Broadcasting Vans and Deafening Loudspeakers." Reporting that the loud-speakers were making "such a big noise" that people were unable to sleep, the article condemned the use of high-pitched amplifiers as weapons in a civil war between mass organizations. The peasants of the Evergreen Commune next to our school sent a delegation to register a complaint with our rebel organizations stating that the commune members were unable to sleep because of the night-long cacophony from the school loudspeakers. By the time the Red Guards were ready to turn them off in the early hours of the morning and go to bed, the peasants were just about ready to get up and begin their day's work. But the direct protests of the masses, the *raison d'être* of the Cultural Revolution, had no more effect than any others. . . .

An atmosphere of extraordinary freedom and purpose existed in those days, an intensity of life which has been noted in all the great revolutions. People talked about everything, speculated endlessly, and read everything they could get their hands on; ordinary folk had become political philosophers contemplating the years to come. It was a time when everything came to the surface—the past, the present, and the future all jumbled together. When one of our students came to our apartment one day to borrow *Moby Dick*, we had a long discussion about China and the world. He asked us whether we thought the Americans would land on the moon and when we replied we did, he said that that was all right, since the Americans were part of the human race and could represent it there. Our young friend, possessed by the speculative mood of the time, told us that he thought there would always be factions in China now that they had emerged during the Cultural Revolution. We asked whether this meant a two-line struggle or a two-party system. He simply replied that he did not know how the system would operate, but that factions would continue to exist. It was evident that at least one Chinese rebel in the summer of 1967 was toying with the idea of institutionalizing the struggle between the left, right, and middle that the Chairman said would exist for 10,000 years.

The PLA Steps In

Perhaps it is only in retrospect that the role of the Army in the Great Proletarian Cultural Revolution can be properly assessed. At the beginning of the movement, the PLA [People's Liberation Army] established itself as the fountainhead of the Maoist orientation and line in opposition to the policy and work style of the old Party machine. The Army newspapers played the leading role in disseminating Maoist ideology. With the suspension of the Party organization in the fall of 1966, the PLA emerged as the only viable organizational structure possessing a monopoly of coercive power. Assigned the contradictory tasks of maintaining law and order, promoting productions, and supporting the revolutionary left organizations in their seizure of power, the Army soon found itself in the position of supervising factory and administrative management at every level of authority. Since the task of supporting the left proved to be the most elusive of goals, the others were given priority, and an organization committed to radical ideology soon found itself in a functionally conservative stance, often wedded to the preservation of the status quo.

Historically, the PLA, the instrument of peasant revolutionary war, had served as the organizational vanguard of a vast movement of social transformation. Political power in the Chinese Revolution had indeed "grown out of the barrel of a gun." In those long years of revolutionary war, it was hard to determine whether the Party organized the Army or vice versa. From the very beginning, Mao recognized the distinction between the two organizations when he stated that the Party commands the gun, while the gun should never command the Party. Nevertheless, despite the fact that, during the Cultural Revolution, it was the Army which played the historic political role and not the Party organization, it was a long time before the Chinese would admit that the People's Liberation Army had developed its own unique power interests.

The official position on the legitimacy of the Army's political stance during the Cultural Revolution was stated by Premier Chou En-lai in response to a 1970 suggestion by Edgar Snow that perhaps there was a tendency toward military dictatorship in China:

"Absurd," says Premier Chou. "How could that be?" The PLA is an instrument of the Party and the servant of the proletariat. "The Army is loyal to the Party; the Party within the Army has always held leadership through its own organizations right down to the company level." Chou added: "We are all connected with the Army." Chairman Mao had himself organized the Army, and Chou had also been a general, therefore it was wrong to make distinctions between military and nonmilitary individuals in positions of leadership.

Consolidation

The students had been the full-time professional rebels of a vast social movement, and though many were the victims of "petit bourgeois factionalism," egoism, and "small-group mentality," they had served loyally the causes of political leaders suffering from the same diseases. They had enjoyed the heady excitement of "participating in state affairs," had taken advantage of their own power, and had been used by others, both kings and pawns in a great game. But their role was over, the people were sick of the din and enraged at the destruction of state property and equipment in privileged institutions, paid for by the sweat of the workers and peasants. It was under these circumstances that Chairman Mao sent the workers, those "masters of our time," by the thousands into the schools to restore calm and thus end the great "*luan*" (chaos). In the last week of July [1968], when Mao sent the massive "Workers' Mao Tse-tung Thought Propaganda Teams" into the universities, a sudden blissful silence settled over the city. For the first time in more than two years the incessant din of loadspeakers ceased. Peking, a city of some four million souls, breathed a collective sigh of relief. The workers saw to it that the students went to bed at ten o'clock, an accomplishment that drew applause from a grateful populace....

Mao Calls in the Student Leaders

The decision to end his own student revolution by sending in the workers must have been a bitter one for Mao. It had been delayed long past the time when the Peking man and woman on the street thought it should have been taken. In front of the young leaders, Mao began to muse aloud about the possibilities which he had felt were open to him. Perhaps he was explaining his decision to them; perhaps also, he was reviewing it for himself. "How do you deal with fighting in the universities?" he asked rhetorically. "One way is complete withdrawal. Leave the students alone. Let everybody fight if he wants to. In the past, the Revolutionary Committee and the Garrison Command weren't afraid of the disorder created by fighting in the universities. They didn't interfere, didn't get upset, and didn't put it down. I still think this was right."

Another way to solve the problem, the Chairman said, was to give the students a little help. The dispatch of workers and soldiers to the universities was meant to accomplish this and "...has won the support of the workers, the peasants, and the majority of the students." Mao pointed out that, although there were more than fifty institutions of higher learning in Peking, fighting was severe in only five or six. If they couldn't handle the problem, he told the four student leaders, then the military under Lin Piao or Chief of Staff Huang Yung-sheng would have to handle it. Although he spoke in the language of possibilities, it must have been quite clear to all present that Mao had already decided that the young leaders couldn't "handle the problem." . . .

Hours went by as the elders discussed the problem of fighting in the schools, and the younger members of the family sat silently and kept their thoughts to themselves. On more than one occasion, Chiang Ch'ing, placing the problem within the ancient and familiar structure of patriarchal authority which these young rebels had been called upon to overthrow, interjected: "Disgrace to the family!" But when her criticism of Han Ai-ching grew intense, Mao stepped in and stated, "Don't criticize him. You always blame others; you never blame yourself." And to Chiang Chi'ing's reply that Han Ai-ching lacked "a spirit of self-criticism," the Chairman commented thoughtfully:

> Young people cannot stand criticism. His character [Han Ai-ching] is something like mine when I was young. Kids are very subjective, incredibly subjective. They only criticize others.

Perhaps speculating on what the young leaders must also have been thinking—that they had begun their rebel careers with encouragement from above and that their factionalism reflected the struggles of those with far greater political experience than themselves, Mao said:

> Who could have foreseen this kind of fighting? Suspension of classes for half a year was originally planned. It was so announced in the newspaper. Later the suspension was extended to one year. As one year was not enough, it was extended to two years, and then to three years. I say, if three years are still not enough, give them as many years as necessary. After all, people are growing older every year. Suppose you were a freshman three years ago, you are now a junior. The schools may be suspended for another two, four, or eight years, you get promoted all the same, so what?

The old revolutionary had moved into one of his favorite areas, the subject of education, and the fact that Engels, Stalin, and Maxim Gorki had had little education, which was also the case of most of the Chinese leaders, including himself. A great deal of what he said was reminiscent of, sometimes identical to, his remarks so widely circulated among the students in the early days of the Cultural Revolution: "Knowledge is not gained in schools. When I was in school, I did not obey the rules. My principle was just to avoid getting myself dismissed. As to examinations, my marks hovered between fifty or sixty percent and eighty percent, seventy percent being my average." He spoke as he had done many times before of his lack of specialized training: "I have never attended any military school. Nor have I read a book on military strategy." And he reiterated once again his ideas on educational methods:

> ... Teaching is harmful. Organize a small group for self-study, a self-study university. The students may stay half a year, one year, two years, or three years. No examination is required. Examination is not a good method. Who examined Marx? Who examined Engels? Who examined Lenin? Who examined Comrade Lin Piao? [...] The needs of the masses and Chiang Kai-shek are our teachers. This was the case for all of us. Teachers are needed in middle schools, but everything should be made simple. [...] To study in a library is a good method. I studied at a library in Hunan for half a year and in the library of Peking University for half a year ...

"Red" or "Expert"?
by John K. Fairbank*

Mao's last decade was as full of confusion and surprises as the 1790s in France. In size and complexity the Cultural Revolution was of course a much bigger event than the French Revolution. . . . Probably its most arresting feature, in retrospect, was its disastrous attack on learning and intellectuals in the very land that had exalted scholarship and invented civil service examinations thirteen hundred years before. In fact, the two were not unconnected—

---

* The New York Review, Dec. 2, 1982.

learning was attacked in China because it seemed to be so entrenched in the establishment. . . .

To understand the origins of the Cultural Revolution we have to get some picture of the establishment it was attacking—not merely the Party apparatus under Liu Shaoqi and Deng Xiaoping but the Chinese bureaucratic habits Mao saw reappearing in the Party. This leads naturally back to the Chinese invention of bureaucratic government two thousand years ago in the Han period, and their subsequent inventions of paper, printed books, and civil service examinations. By one thousand years ago, under the Sung dynasty, the examination system was a major arm of the state. Down to its abolition in 1905 it recruited the indoctrinated elite needed to govern the masses—how to govern peasants having become the great Chinese speciality in the world's most stable empire. . . .

This is what made education so important. Once in power in 1949 Mao needed to establish institutions for his regime through an indoctrinated elite such as the examination system had formerly provided down to 1905 (when he was twelve years old). He needed persons trained in his state orthodoxy who could propagate his new social order. Since Party dictatorship had supplanted dynastic despotism as China's system of government in the 1920s, Mao's new elite had to be the Chinese Communist Party (CCP) and its cadres, "reds" committed to his revolution. How to train such activists through China's educational system was a top priority.

It was not as easy as one might think. Until 1905 those who wanted to rise in the world had prepared for the old government examinations through private instruction in family and village; and the elite had also used some 300 semi-official academies, which were the only residential schools or colleges in the country. The examination system's many-tiered, multi-channeled structure had fostered an "examination psychology" among men of worldly ambition, but it was not a public-school system and did not aim at mass education. It rewarded literary skill, orthodox thinking, and conservative morality if not bigotry, while offering little chance for technical specialization. But during the 1911–1949 interregnum of central power between the end of the Ch'ing dynasty and the takeover by the CCP,

Chinese education had been rebuilt in modern style, first by organizing a school system on Japanese lines and then by setting up universities on largely liberal American models.

The products of this modern education, China's twentieth-century intellectuals trained in science, technology, and the humanities, have been generally regarded as the nominal and sometimes spiritual successors of the traditional literati who won degrees in the old examination system. But this appearance is deceptive. China's literati after 1905 had in fact proliferated and branched out to form a new intelligentsia that included journalists, writers, teachers, doctors, engineers, and all the other professionals. They were no longer mainly a talent pool of local gentry when out of office or civil servants when selected for state employment. They did not think with one mind; nor were they primarily devoted to propagating the state ideology and its doctrines of virtuous conduct. They were specialists, modern people whom leaders like Liu Shaoqi and Deng Xiaoping after 1949 wanted to recruit as experts to help modernize China.

In short, it can be argued that the old examination degree-holders' functional successors were not such modern experts but were really the new red Party cadres, a selected elite morally committed to the leader of the state and his vision of egalitarian revolution. For many centuries government in China had relied upon indoctrinated cadres. They were not a Soviet invention even though many of them thought they were. The fact that their ideas were now anti-Confucian could not change their function in the system. In some ways China's modern diversified intelligentsia were more novel than the CCP cadres. Thus the stage was set for the "class struggle" of red versus expert.

Viewed in this historical perspective, the Cultural Revolution was a product of more than an old man's frustration. It represented an inevitable conflict between the new ruler's customary need for ideological loyalty and the modernizer's need for special skills. Mao was highly traditional in conceiving of education as indoctrination. He deplored even the modern specialization that the CCP modeled on the USSR system in the 1950s, because it gave the specialist a basis for being independent-minded and potentially unorthodox, at least in his own specialty. . . .

Economic Effects of the Cultural Revolution
by Christopher Howe

From 1962 to 1964 the Chinese economy improved slowly but surely. Central control was reasserted in many spheres; planning was cautious; output rose; trade was restored; and the standard of living began to regain the level reached at the end of the First Five Year Plan. In everything moderation and proportion were the key words. In December 1964 Chou En-lai addressed the Third National People's Congress. He reported the recovery of the economy and urged that China pursue the 'Four Modernizations' (of industry, agriculture, defence, science and technology). Chou also urged that trade be expanded and that foreign technology be studied. In 1965 China's economic position improved further. Self-sufficiency in oil was achieved, and debts to the Soviet Union were finally cleared off. Visitors to China in the autumn of that year have described a calm, confident, and prosperous atmosphere.

Politically, however, the situation remained difficult. Mao believed that the retreat from the Leap had led to corruption, to selfish anti-socialist economic behavior, and to the entrenchment of his enemies (notably Liu Shao-ch'i and Teng Hsiao-p'ing) in the bureaucracy. As early as 1962 he had launched a Socialist Education Movement to correct these tendencies in the countryside, and in 1964 Mao supported moves to enhance the role of the People's Liberation Army in trade and industry. By mid-1966 the revival of the economy finally made it possible for Mao to launch a campaign against his enemies in the Party and State administrative apparatus without risking disastrous economic consequences. Thus, unlike his Leap, Mao's Cultural Revolution was *not* launched to remedy economic problems. It was mainly a political struggle, although economic issues were argued about and the economic crimes of Mao's enemies were condemned.

The Cultural Revolution had two economic consequences. One was that general dislocation led to a decline in industrial output in 1967—the first for many years; the other was that it halted the tentative revival of foreign trade. Between 1963 and 1965 China renewed imports of large industrial plants, but between 1966 and 1970 trade was frozen at existing levels. Outbreaks of anti-foreign hysteria (such as the burning of the British Embassy and the maltreatment of foreigners) created a climate within which new trade possibilities could not be explored. From mid-1968 the economy began to make progress again, although by the end of the 1960s it was encountering problems for which there were no purely domestic solutions.

Liang Heng was born in 1954 in Changsha, the capital of Hunan province in central China, where Mao Zedong was born. His father was a reporter for the major provincial newspaper. Liang Heng grew up during the Cultural Revolution. He was married in 1980 to Judith Shapiro, an American whom he met when she taught in China, and now lives with his wife in New York City. He is working toward a doctoral degree at Columbia University. The book they have written about Liang Heng's life is one of the first personal accounts published in the West about life in China during the Cultural Revolution.

Liang Wei–ping and Liang Fang are Liang Heng's sisters.

A Personal Experience of the Cultural Revolution
by Liang Heng and Judith Shapiro

By the time I graduated from primary school—in May of 1966 when I was just twelve—the Cultural Revolution was already approaching. The newspapers were full of criticism of the "Three-family Village," a group of writers whose works they called "poisonous weeds." After I had been at home only two weeks, I was summoned back to school for a meeting, just like a real grownup. This was the first time my classmates and I participated in what came to be known as "political study," an activity now as integral to urban Chinese life as lining up at the dining hall for a breakfast of rice gruel and *mantou*.

Our teacher read to us from the newspapers about how

our class enemies were working from within to deliberately attack and smash the Party and Socialism. These "enemies" had derided the Great Leap Forward of the late fifties as "just a lot of boasting." They had slandered the dictatorship of the proletariat, and even told our great Party to "take a rest." Our teacher explained that workers, peasants, and soldiers must join together to fight against these insidious "black" intellectuals, and not be taken in by their devious and subtle methods. Even though we were still small, he said, we too had a part to play. We should begin by writing compositions denouncing our enemies. We should take out our notebooks and "open fire." . . .

Then one morning when I was sitting at home with nothing special to do, Little Li walked in. He was the smartest of my playmates and my good friend, and I was pleased to see him. He sat down with his customary seriousness on the edge of the bed and said, "You know, everyone has been quoting Chairman Mao, saying, 'There is no wrong in Revolution; it is right to rebel.' We should do something too. There are a lot of Capitalist tendencies in our old primary school. Remember how Teacher Luo was always quoting the Russians? We should organize the other students and launch a Cultural Revolution there, too."

I thought this was a great idea. We would be following Chairman Mao just like the grownups, and Father would be proud of me. I suppose too I resented the teachers who had controlled and criticized me for so long, and I looked forward to a little revenge.

As it turned out, so did many of the other students, and they were delighted to be able to use Chairman Mao's stamp of approval to do what before they could only do under the cover of darkness with a slingshot and a window. Our unity was instantaneous, and we met at Little Li's apartment that evening. We had the place to ourselves because his mother lived at her own unit and his father was a proofreader who worked the night shift.

Little Li went to the newspaper to get some paper and ink and returned with his arms full.

"They support us!" he told us excitedly. "They say we can have all the supplies we need, and maybe later even an office!"

This was more than we had dared to dream of. We

divided up the paper happily, one sheet for each person and a pile for me since I was to draw satirical cartoons. But then, faced with the vast open spaces before us, we suddenly discovered we didn't know what Capitalism and Revisionism really were. Little Li was the only one able to come up with anything, and he painted with a flourish ANGRILY OPEN FIRE ON THE *HUNAN DAILY'S* ATTACHED PRIMARY SCHOOL'S CAPITALIST REVISIONIST LINE!!! We all thought this was just fine, but it was obviously not enough, and we sat in worried silence until my friend Gang Di's older brother, Gang Xian, made a good suggestion. "Why don't we go out to the street and see what other people have written?"

That was the first time in my life I didn't go home to bed. We spent half the night wandering around writing down the words on the big character posters. The low gray buildings along Changsha's main streets were literally white with paper, shining in the dull yellow lamp-light. The glass shop windows were unrecognizable, and posters even hung from between parasol trees, rustling like ghosts in the night. Even at that hour people were rushing about shouting and putting up new posters, as if all the grievances that had been suppressed for so many years were coming out at once, shaking the city.

I suppose the workers felt somewhat the way we did, and were using the Cultural Revolution to get back at their superiors for everything from tiny insults to major abuses of policy. The posters on the Sun Yat-sen Road Department Store attacked the leaders for allowing the workers no freedom of discussion and willfully speaking for all. They accused the leaders of taking home government property and using influence to get scarce goods and special privileges. They denounced one leader for insulting women by touching their shoulders when he spoke to them, and another for wearing slippers to work and taking off his shirt in the office. . . .

The list of crimes went on and on, and it was clear to us that everything was fair game. . . .

In early September, all college students and the more Revolutionary teachers and middle school students received permission to travel free throughout the country for what was called "exchange of experiences." Within a short time, trains and buses were hopelessly crowded. At this point a new phase began—long-distance walking. It was started by some students from the Dalian Shipping Institute in Manchuria who hiked all the way to Peking to visit Revolutionary sites. Their journey was heralded as a way for young people to "temper" themselves (and save the country money on transportation fees). Suddenly it was as if China had been turned into a nation of soldier-actors, at least so far as young people were concerned. We were to re-create for ourselves the hardships suffered by the Red Army more than thirty years before, either by marching as they had through the Jinggang Mountain and Ruijing District (where they fought their first successful guerrilla wars against the KMT in 1934), or by following the 25,000-*li* route of the Long March (during which 300,000 men were reduced to 30,000), or by walking all the way from Yanan to Peking, the road taken by our victorious troops in 1949. During all of this we were to wear facsimiles of their coarse gray uniforms and straw sandals, carry heavy burdens as they had done, and travel at the forced march pace of an army at war.

Since I was only twelve, I would normally have had no chance to become involved in such things, but one day the oldest son of the neighbors who shared our kitchen with us came home from Peking, where he was a composition student at the Central Institute of Music. . . . Peng Ming was about eight years older than I, and had always been the person my sisters and I looked up to; he was confident, determined, brilliant, and a little hyperactive; his sentences poured out end to end, as if his mind worked much faster than his mouth could produce the sounds. When I heard he was home again, I felt the thrill of excitement a young boy can feel only when his hero is at hand.

Peng Ming looked taller and bonier than ever, and he now wore thick glasses, perhaps a result of the nighttime hours he had spent filling empty staves with Revolutionary music. He was, of course, a Red Guard, and he soon proved that he knew more about everything than we did, including how to organize a New Long March team. As he talked, he moved his long thin arms as if he were working magic, describing how we would walk from our doorway all the way to the very top of the Jinggang Mountain 800 *li* away (about 240 miles). We would follow exactly in the Red Army's footsteps, suffering every hardship they had suffered, learning from them, turning ourselves into worthy inheritors of the torch of Revolution by journeying to the very spot where it was first lit. Liang Fang decided to go and at last agreed to take me. When Father approved, glad to get me safely out of the house again, I was in raptures. From then on I would have died for the right to follow Peng Ming.

There were eight people on our team, including Peng Ming's younger brothers and sisters and several other neighbor children, all of them much older than I. We prepared for three days, learning how to fold our things inside our blankets in a neat little square of army green, how to tie our Red Army-style straw sandals and wrap our leggings around our calves. We prepared a red flag with yellow characters in imitation-Chairman Mao calligraphy reading "Long March," fitted placards on our bundles with Quotations so the people walking behind us could see them and take inspiration, collected a first-aid kit, a map, and canteens. My proudest moment was when Peng Ming pinned on my red armband, not a makeshift paper one, but one of finest red silk, with the shining snow-white words "Red Guard" painted onto it. Then he attached a beautiful Chairman Mao button to my jacket, a noble yellow profile with metallic red rays emanating from it and Tian An Men Square in red relief below. I think I grew ten inches.

It was a beautiful crisp winter morning when we set out through the gates of the *Hunan Daily*, the eight of us in formation, Peng Ming's younger brother in the lead carrying our red flag. Father and the other parents saw us off, anxious but not regretful, proud but afraid to show their feelings before the small gathering of onlookers. Tears were controlled on my part as well, for I was determined not to show my age. I marched proudly and quickly, without looking back even once.

The people in the Changsha streets stared at us with respect and envy, and this made us walk even taller and faster. We had soon passed through the suburbs and entered the countryside itself. Within half a day we began to encounter other New Long March teams, some from as far away as Guangxi and Guangdong provinces, and I felt prouder than ever to be from Hunan, Chairman Mao's home province and the fountainhead of the whole Communist

movement. Some of these other groups had better costumes than we, with real gray uniforms and caps with red
stars, and most of the teams were larger than ours, but our
excitement and purpose were the same. We struck up an
instant camaraderie, singing songs together, encouraging
each other, exchanging information about what lay ahead.
The walls of the peasants' houses had been painted with
slogans like ONLY 750 LI TO THE JINGGANG MOUNTAIN and
REVOLUTION TO THE END, so we felt more than ever that
we were all engaged in a common pilgrimage, that we
were all part of an exalted tide being pulled inexorably
toward some sacred moonlight.

The peasants in the communes we passed through
were warm providers. There were roadside stands where
we could replenish our canteens with boiled water, and
each commune had a major hospitality station where there
was hot rice in huge wooden barrels, of which we could
eat as much as we wanted free. There was never much in
the way of meat or vegetables, but none of us complained,
since it was our purpose to suffer the hardships of the Red
Army. We were probably better off than they anyway, since
at most stations there was a shelter in which rice straw
beds had been spread for tired wayfarers, and the peasant
women prepared hot water for washing and drinking. We
must have depleted their stores and taken up an enormous
amount of their time, but the peasants seemed glad to
make sacrifices for Chairman Mao, and always urged us to
eat more as if we were their own invited guests. Many of
them already had small collections of buttons and printed
slogans, souvenirs of the many groups who had passed
before us.

We covered most of Changsha County by the first night
and stopped at a district hospitality station. It was an old
Qing dynasty meeting hall, with a curved roof and eaves
like the flip of the hair of a girl in a foreign movie. We
soaked our blistered feet and crawled into bed two by two,
one person's blanket below and the other's above, our
body heat raising the temperature in our cocoons enough
above freezing to let us pass a comfortable night. We had
walked close to eighty *li* (twenty-four miles).

The days passed and we soon got into a rhythm, sometimes climbing high mountains where we could see the
original slogans of Revolution carved into the rock faces.

WE WANT LAND, they read. DOWN WITH THE LANDLORDS.
There were pretty little pavilions where we could rest, and
the forests rang with the cries of teams calling to each
other. Liang Fang and one of our other girls dropped back
to walk with a team from Hubei Province, but I kept up
with the boys, although I often wept with the pain of
blisters and exhaustion. Later we began to follow the Red
Army's custom of traveling at night, burning torches to
light the way and walking until we were asleep on our
feet. The more we suffered, the prouder we were, and
some groups even bypassed the hospitality stations to
sleep in the open and dig sweet potatoes from the peasants'
fields with their bare hands. We saw the ditches where
Chairman Mao had lain to fight the KMT, and the towns
and villages were like museums, with the Red Army's
meeting rooms, guns, sandals, and documents all preserved with faithful reverence. We could get precious
Chairman Mao buttons at these sites, those invaluable
souvenirs that had become national symbols of fervor and
sincerity. Sometimes we were lucky and came upon some
town square where an old graybeard, a member of the
original Red Army, was speaking to the gathered Red
Guards about his experiences in the Liberation. The excitement of such times was tremendous; I had never felt
closer to the glorious Revolution, which had saved China
from a thousand evils. When Peng Ming stopped our team
once so we could carve our names into a thick bamboo, I
took the knife and cut as deeply and as beautifully as I
could.

I did find one thing strange, though. To judge by the old
slogans and by what the Revolutionaries had to say, the
peasants seemed to have been more interested in getting
land for themselves than in Communism or Socialism. I
realized, too, that if they had understood so little about
the goals of Liberation, they understood even less about
the Cultural Revolution. They were treating us so warmly
because they adored Chairman Mao for driving out the
landlords and he had told them to welcome us; but they
really didn't seem to know why we were there or what was
happening in the cities, nor did they really seem to care.
This was a little disturbing to me. We were struggling to
develop Communist thought and ideals, while it seemed
as though they had been selfish and materialistic. And for

so many years we had been taught about our great Socialist peasant Liberation!...

[Later Liang Heng returned to his home in Changsha.]

One of our ex-comrades walked by and sneered at us and then spat on the cement at our feet. "You sons of Reactionary Capitalist stinking intellectuals. Run and look at your fathers' big character posters. Then hurry home and criticize *them*, why don't you."

I was simply unable to comprehend his words. My father wasn't a powerful official, had never accepted bribes or used public furniture, had never used power to criticize a worker unfairly. He was just a low-ranking cadre working for a Party newspaper, and no one in the whole world loved Chairman Mao better than he. How could there be posters about him? How could anyone say he had Capitalist thought?

As in a dream, we hurried to the office building. There had been a lot of new activity. Now the posters stretched all the way up to the fourth floor, and ropes hung with still more had been strung from one wing of the L to the other. To get through, you had to push posters aside like hanging curtains. We began the painful search for our fathers' names. What would have been a game the day before was now a nightmare....

Then Gang Di pulled me by the sleeve. He had found my father's posters. I followed him numbly through the gaily painted paper, still believing there had been a mistake. But then I saw the terrible words, burning characters on brilliant yellow paper. EXPOSE THE PLOT OF THE REACTIONARY SCHOLAR LIANG SHAN TO THE LIGHT OF DAY!!!!!

There were too many sheets, maybe ten or more, each as tall as a man. And every word engraved itself on my heart with a blazing knife, every phrase struck me with a blow that was even greater than terror. I would never believe the ground was steady again.

Liang Shan is a thoroughly Capitalist newsman, our newspaper's Three-family Village. He has used the knowledge given to him by the Party to attack the Party, writing many Reactionary articles. In one of them, an essay about the growth of a sunflower, he dared to fart that the flower relies on its own lust for life. How evil, how poisonous! The Three-family Village said the sun had dark shadows, meaning the Party has made errors. But Liang Shan says the sunflower doesn't need the sun at all! His insidious idea is that China can be strong without the Communist Party. Isn't this singing the same tune as Capitalist KMT Reactionary Revisionism? Liang Shan is worse than Capitalism, fiercer than the KMT, more dangerous than Revisionism. Down with Liang Shan!!!!!

There was more, but the words wouldn't stay still. I was trembling all over. The bright paper posters floating about me had become walls of iron, the unknown sandaled feet glimpsed beyond them those of enemies. Everything was backwards, distorted, corrupted, insane. I didn't know if I was dreaming or if my life at home was a dream. I hugged myself, pinching my arms, but I didn't wake up. I closed my eyes and opened them but the words were still there. My Revolutionary father was an enemy. My father whose dream it was to join the Party was a Capitalist. How had things been ruined? Why had he ruined things? I didn't know where to put my misery and my hatred. I would never trust my perception of reality again. . . .

When the signal for dinner sounded, there was nothing to do but walk slowly home. . . .

Someone had taken the lock off our door, but it was shut tight. Our home presented a peculiar, sad, unfriendly appearance, which only deeped my misery. I pushed my way in and discovered Father sitting in a dense cloud of cigarette smoke, which he was concentrating on making thicker, the butts lying on the wooden floor like wreckage after some disaster. He barely moved when I came in. It hurt me to look at him, so I headed toward the drawer where the meal tickets were kept. My hand shook on the handle.

Then it was as if something swept over me, and I found myself swinging around, screaming out the question in my heart. "Father, is it true that you're a bloodsucker?" Suspicion, love, anger, sympathy, and hatred struggled against one another. I felt as if I would explode.

Father was silent, signaling that he had heard me only

by crushing out his cigarette and lighting a new one. I stared at the stub on the floor, long, white, and barely smoked.

"Tell me," I demanded. "Tell me, you should tell me. I have to know."

He remained silent, not meeting my eyes.

I wanted to shake him. "Why won't you say anything?"

He finally spoke, in what was close to a whisper. "You should always believe the Party and Chairman Mao."

He hadn't answered my question, and I stood staring and waiting.

He made another effort. "The Cultural Revolution is a mass movement. The people who criticized me have deep proletarian feelings and a great love for Chairman Mao." I could hardly believe my ears. It was all true, then. Father continued, "I've made a lot of mistakes. I should examine myself thoroughly. But as long as I'm faithful to the Party and Chairman Mao, it won't be long before I mend by errors." . . .

My father's hand trembled as he struck another match. Then in the silence we heard a great clattering on the stairs, and Liang Fang and Liang Wei-ping burst into the room. They were both crying, and they ran directly to their bed and threw themselves onto it, hugging the pillows. Their sobs were terrible in the silence.

Soon Liang Fang started accusing Father. "I'm so miserable being born into a family like this. First I had a mother who prevented me from joining the League. Now that I'm finally accepted as a Revolutionary, you have to ruin everything. Look," she cried, taking out a piece of paper. "Tonight I was supposed to be a marshal at the parades. This was the plan for the march. Do you think I can possibly face anyone now?" With a wail, she ripped her map into little pieces.

Father sat by the table with his head in his hands, passively accepting Liang Fang's fury as if he deserved it. He reached automatically for his pack of cigarettes, but it was empty. Liang Wei-ping, always the gentlest of us, nudged Liang Fang as if asking her to control herself and went into the other room and got another pack. As she handed it to Father I asked him, "Do you know what they called us today? 'Sons of Capitalist Reactionary stinking intellectuals.' They've cut us out of all their activities, kicked us out of the office. They won't let us do anything anymore."

Father raised his head and repeated, "You should believe the Party. Believe Chairman Mao." His words sounded like a prayer, a principle kept in his heart to invoke in times of trouble. They had been the key to his spirit for the past twenty years.

But Liang Fang raged. "Others don't believe *you*! They say you're a Capitalist, a bloodsucker, a foreigner's dog!"

Then my father stood up, his face white, his words tumbling out in one breath. "It's because I'm none of those things that I believe the Party and Chairman Mao. I've done nothing to wrong you. You can continue to participate in the Revolution. If you want to, you can break off with me. Go live at school if you like. But I'll tell you one thing. No matter how you hate me, I've always been loyal to Chairman Mao. And I've always supported the Party and Socialism."

"If I have to go, I'll go!" she shouted, grabbing at her bedding and clothing. "I don't want this counterrevolutionary family. I don't need this counterrevolutionary father and mother!"

Liang Wei-ping followed her older sister's lead. "I'm going too," she said with resignation. "Maybe it's better that way." She stood up and started gathering her things.

Father's eyes were red. "Go, go, all of you go. I won't blame you. I don't want to hold you back."

I don't know how the evening would have ended if the loudspeaker hadn't sounded outside our window. "The Red radio waves have happy news. Everyone please tune in and listen carefully. Everyone please tune in."

From force of habit cultivated only over the last few months, we rushed to the tiny transistor on the table. We arranged ourselves around it and laid our heads down so we could concentrate. Crackling from the radio came, "The August 8th Decision of the Central Committee of the Chinese Communist Party Concerning the Great Proletarian Cultural Revolution."

It seemed that one of the purposes of the statement was to clarify the targets of the Cultural Revolution. And as we listened the heavy stone that we bore on our backs became lighter and lighter, especially when we heard the Fifth Article.

> Who are our enemies and who are our friends?... The main target of the present movement is those within the Party who are in authority and are taking the Capitalist road. The strictest care should be taken to distinguish between the anti-Party, anti-Socialist Rightists and those who support the Party and Socialism but have said or done something wrong or have written bad articles or other works....

When all "Sixteen Articles" were finished, there were tears of joy in Father's eyes and he said triumphantly, "See, your father is no counterrevolutionary. I'm the third type of cadre, someone who has made serious mistakes but is not an anti-Party anti-Socialist Rightist."

My sisters smiled and looked embarrassed at having been so upset; I felt ashamed that I had thought so harshly of Father. We began to discuss the posters calmly and decided that since he had already talked with the Party about his membership in the KMT Youth League and about our mother, those problems wouldn't be regarded as serious crimes. His failure to quote Chairman Mao frequently in his writings would be considered a matter for education. The foul language and abuse in the posters merely showed the passion of the people and were not to be taken seriously.

Just as we were enjoying our renewed intimacy, we heard a blast of firecrackers and drums like an earthquake under our feet. Liang Fang jumped up as if she had forgotten something. "The parade!" she cried. "Oh Father, I *do* want to go live at school, but that's just for convenience in the Revolution, not because I want to move away from home."

So Father helped her to pack her bag, and tucked some cakes and sugar in the side to show he had forgiven her. She left in a great hurry because she was late, and we stood on the balcony and watched her go. From then on, she was always off making Revolution somewhere, and never really lived at home again....

Father spent every evening at his writing [self criticism], and Liang Wei-ping and I never felt much like talking. We were sitting silently like this, reading and writing, on the hot night that Liang Fang came home. I hadn't seen her in more than three weeks. She was a changed person. . . .

Father emerged when he heard voices and looked glad to see Liang Fang. "How have things been going?" he asked. "We haven't seen you in a long time."

"The situation is excellent," she answered in the language of Revolution. "We're washing away all the dirty water. But I never sleep. Every night we're out making search raids."

"What's a search raid?" I asked.

"You know, before you've been on a search raid you have no idea what's really going on in this society. People have been hiding all sorts of things. Counterrevolutionary materials, pre-Liberation Reactionary artworks, gold, jade, silver, jewelry—the trappings of Feudalism-Capitalism-Revisionism are everywhere."

My father looked surprised. "What do you care about those kinds of things?"

But Liang Fang was too involved in her story to answer. "We have a schedule to follow. Every night we go to a series of homes and go through every book, every page to see if there's any anti-Party material. It's an incredible amount of work. We have to check all the boxes and suitcases for false bottoms and sometimes pull up the floors to see if anything's been hidden underneath."

Liang Wei-ping brought her a basin of hot water and a towel to clean her face, and when she stood up to wash, her eye fell on a traditional painting of a horse by Xu Bei-hong. "What are you doing with *that*? Xu Bei-hong was denounced ages ago. You people are too careless." She went over to take it down, but Father's voice stopped her.

"What's wrong with it? That has nothing to do with any Capitalist-Revisionist line. Leave it be."

She said, "But you don't know what's been happening. It's not just a question of paintings, but of all the old things. Where do you think I've been all day? I was up on Yuelu Mountain with the Hunan University students trying to get rid of those old monuments and pavilions. And it wasn't an easy job, either. Half the stuff's made of stone.

We had to use knives and axes to dig out the inscriptions. Stinking poetry of the Feudal Society! But it's all gone now, or boarded shut." . . .

Father found his voice. "How could you destroy the old poetry carved in the temples and pavilions? What kind of behavior is that?"

"What kind of behavior? Revolutionary action, that's what. The Hengyang District Red Guards have already destroyed all the temples on the Southern Peak of Heng Mountain. So much for the 'sacred mountain'!" . . .

"Who asked you to do those things?" Father demanded.

"Father," she answered with exaggerated patience. "You really don't understand the Cultural Revolution at all, do you? We have to get rid of the Four Olds. That includes *everything* old. Don't you even read your own newspaper? You'd better keep up with things or you'll be in trouble."

Father protested, "It's one thing to get rid of customs and ideas, and another to go around smashing ancient temples."

"What good are they? They just trick people, make them superstitious. They're a bad influence on the young people."

"Who ever influenced you?" Father demanded. "No one in your whole life ever asked you to believe in any Buddhas."

Liang Fang didn't have an answer, which irritated her. "Well, anyway, they're all old things. Why aren't there Revolutionary poems, Chairman Mao's poems, statues of people's heroes, workers, peasants, and soldiers?" . . .

The search raids spread to the newspaper. It was a terrifying time, because every night we heard the sounds of loud knocks, things breaking, and children crying. Like every family with a member attacked in the posters, we knew the Red Guards would eventually come to our house, and we were constantly on edge. During the day we went to see the exhibits of confiscated goods; at night we lay dressed, sleeplessly waiting for our turn.

At eleven one night the knocks finally came, loud, sharp, and impatient. We sat up in bed automatically. Father emerged from the inside room and turned on the light. He motioned with his head for Liang Wei-ping to get the door.

There were seven or eight of them, all men or boys, and

the small room seemed very crowded. Despite the heat they were all wearing white cloths over their mouths and noses, and dark clothes. The one who seemed to be the leader carried a long metal spring with a rubber tip. He struck it against the table top with a loud crack.

"Liang Shan!" he said. "Is there anything Feudalist-Capitalist-Revisionist in your house?"

Father stammered, "No, no. I had pictures of Liu Shao-qi but I turned them in to the Work Team. Nothing else."

"Farter!" The man sliced at the table again.

Liang Wei-ping started to cry.

"What are you blubbering about? Cut it out. You and the boy, get over there in the corner."

We cowered there, trying to keep our sobs silent.

"What you must understand is that this is a Revolutionary action," the man announced. "Right?"

"Yes, yes, a Revolutionary action." I had never seen my father plead with anyone before. I had never seen him without his dignity.

"You welcome it, don't you! Say it!"

Something stuck in my father's throat.

"Shit. You've always been a liar!" Two Red guards took him by each arm and grabbed his head, pushing it down so he was forced to kneel on the floor. They shook him by the hair so his glasses fell off, and when he groped for them they kicked his hands away. "Liar!"

The others were already starting to go through our things, some going into the other rooms for the books, others to the boxes. For several minutes there was silence except for the rustling of paper and the opening of boxes and drawers. Then one of them cried out.

"Quite a fox, isn't he? We said he was a liar!" The Red Guard had two Western ties and a Western-style jacket. "What's the meaning of this?"

"Ties," my father mumbled.

They kicked him. "Ties! Do you think we're children? Everyone knows these are ties. Capitalist ties. Or hadn't you heard?"

Father was pointing excitedly. "They were ordered through the newspaper. For some jobs. It wasn't my idea. For receptions and—" The spring slammed down on his hand and he cringed in pain.

"Who told you to point your finger? Think you can order people around still, don't you? Stinking intellectual!"

Liang Wei-ping cried, "How can you go hitting people that way? He can't even see properly."

"Shut up, little crossbreed, or we'll be hitting you next," snapped the Red Guard standing by the bureau. "Look at this! Fancy pants and sleeves with three buttons!"

From the other room came two Red Guards with armfuls of books. They dumped them unceremoniously on the floor near where Father was kneeling and went back for more. Tang poetry fell on top of histories, foreign novels on the Chinese Classics. Our house had always looked very neat and spare; I had never realized we had so many books.

After an hour they had finished going through everything. My comic books of the Classics had been added to the pile; the Xu Bei-hong horse had been crumpled and tossed on top. Everything we owned was in disorder on the floor, and even our pillows had been slit open with a knife. Father had been on his knees for a long time, and was trembling all over. The Red Guards were stuffing things into a large cloth bag when one of them got an idea for another game.

He put our large metal washbasin on the floor and built a little mound in it out of some of the finest books. He lit a match underneath and fanned it until the whole thing was aflame. Then he fed the fire, ripping the books in two one at a time and tossing them on. Father turned his head away. He didn't need his glasses to know what was on the pyre.

"What's the matter, Liang Shan? Light hurt your eyes?" The leading Red Guard held the metal spring out in front of him like a snake. "'A Revolutionary action.' Say it. 'It's a good fire.'"

Father was silent. I prayed he would speak.

"You shitting liar. Say it!" The man grabbed Father by the hair and twisted his head to make him look at the flames. "'It's a good fire!'"

My father's face looked very naked without his glasses, and the light from the fire shone on it and glistened in the tear lines on his cheeks. I could hardly hear him.

"A Revolutionary action," he whispered. "It's a good fire!"

They let him go; it was over. They shouldered the bag and filed out, the last putting our transistor radio into his pocket as he passed the table. We three couldn't find a word of comfort for each other; we just put things back in order in silence. The next day we discovered they had also helped themselves to Father's salary for that month. . . .

It was hard to keep track of who was right and who wrong. "One day you're black and then you're red and then you're black again," he [Father] said. "Children, whatever you do please remember to be careful what you say. Never give your opinion on anything, even if you're asked directly. Just believe Chairman Mao's words, they're the only thing that seems to be reliable anymore."

I remembered his words for many years. They were another lesson in self-protection in modern society. And events showed that a lot of other people had learned the same lessons as I. . . .

That summer, things got even worse in Changsha: The Rebels began fighting among themselves. Those who had once been comrades became mortal enemies, and the streets of Changsha ran with blood in the hundred-degree heat of August. The Cultural Revolution lost all connection with its original crackdown on anti-Socialist elements, now long forgotten. A civil war was going on, with each side claiming to love Chairman Mao better than the other, to be protecting his Revolutionary line against the policies that threatened it. Both sides were willing to die for the right to wield power under Chairman Mao's name.

The Rebels had guns now, and more. They had grenades and bayonets and machine guns and cannon and tanks and anti-aircraft missiles, all the weapons that China's military arsenals had to offer. Jiang Qing and the Cultural Revolution Directorate's slogan "Attack with Words, Defend with Guns" had been interpreted throughout the country to mean that all questions should be settled through armed struggle, and since Chairman Mao himself had said that the Rebels should have arms, they felt they were entitled to all the weapons they could get. The guns distributed to the Rebels' small official militia by the 47th Army scarcely satisfied them. They added what they had seized from the Conservatives, stole from the local militias, stopped trains for weapons shipments, broke into arsenals, and attacked military bases. Then they started shooting at each other in order to decide arguments about who was going to be in charge. . . .

The real issue was the apportionment of power, the power to run the Great Proletarian Cultural Revolution in all of Hunan Province. Hundreds of thousands of Hunanese workers and students found themselves caught up in a battle for very confused goals, with our wise and beloved Chairman Mao at the center of the conflict. It was during this gory climax that people began to realize that the Cultural Revolution would never make sense.

It was absolutely terrifying. Bullets whistled in the streets, and the roar of a motorcycle or the wail of a siren meant violence and tragedy. The gateways of many units had broad white lines drawn across them, and armed guards waited on the other side to shoot anyone who stepped across without permission. There was a 9 P.M. curfew, and no one wanted to go out during the day unless he had to; there were many reports of the deaths of innocent vegetable-buyers by stray bullets. People crisscrossed their windows with tape to prevent their shattering as the city shook with explosions and gunfire, and at night the sky flashed light and then dark with the passing of rockets.

Every evening Father pushed a heavy bureau up against the door and sat down in his old bamboo chair with a volume of *Chairman Mao's Selected Works* open on his lap, his broad brow knitted in concentration. But he never read anything, for the sounds of war in the city beyond disturbed him. Then some alarm would sound, warning us to turn off all the lights, and we would wait in darkness wondering if this time the newspaper would succumb to attack, and what our fates would be. . . .

Beneath his immediate terror, Father was profoundly troubled. It seemed impossible to him that Chairman Mao could approve such violence, and he couldn't understand why it was that everyone seemed to have guns, or why they were fighting at all. There was no social order, he complained again and again. Those who were supposed to be protecting the peace were contributing to the chaos; even the police and procuratorial organs had gone to war. . . .

At last Father was "liberated" to become a peasant. The cadres had made errors, Chairman Mao said, because they had been away from the grass roots too long. Now they were to settle in the countryside for prolonged re-education; at the same time they would help to "cut off the tail of Capitalism" by bringing Revolutionary knowledge and construction to the most isolated regions of China. I would naturally go too.

Father believed he would now be a peasant to the end of his days, yet he was remarkably cheerful about it. He seemed to have lost all desire to resume his career. "It's too dangerous to live by the pen," he joked. "I'd rather have peasant bones. And you'll be a peasant's son, so no one will accuse you of having a bad background anymore."...

It must have been close to midnight when we arrived. Little Boy Guo took us immediately to the Team leader's home. A crowd of shaved heads was already waiting for us around the fire.

Team leader Guo came to the point. "Old Liang, Chairman Mao has sent you to us, so we should welcome you. But this Team has many members and very little land. If we have a good harvest, each person has only three hundred to four hundred *jin* per year, and that's including sweet potatoes."

Father knew his figures, having been an agriculture reporter so many years. He was astonished. "Then how do you live during planting time?" he asked.

"Sometimes the government helps, but it's never easy. Old Liang"—the Team leader drew a breath—"Maybe you should speak with the commune leaders and ask to go somewhere else. We simply can't support you."

The others chimed in. "There are so many of you."

"You have no experience."

And an angry voice: "Damned brigade leaders don't assign anyone to their own Production Teams!"

Father spoke gently. "Countrymen. You must understand that we have come not because we wanted to but because others wanted us to. We cannot ask them to send us anywhere else. Please forgive us. We'll help with the work as best we can."

"Help with the work? We've got to give you food, find you a place to live. What kind of help is that?" came the chorus.

Father was silent a moment, and then said, "We can't go

back. We don't have city residence cards anymore. But tomorrow, if you like, I'll go to the leaders and explain your difficulties."

The peasants seemed much mollified, as if they saw that Father was a good man and would do his best. "No need to discuss any further tonight," announced the leader. "Let our guests eat!"

They ushered us into another room where they had prepared big bowls of food in the traditionally hospitable manner of the countryside. My eyes bulged when I saw the thick chunks of pork. No sooner was I seated than I helped myself to two fragant mouthfuls.

For some reason, the peasants weren't happy about this. One of the women standing by the side watching the men and boys eat reached over and covered the pork with cabbage while another tried to distract me by urging me to drink some soup.

As we were led off to sleep, Father whispered to me, "That meat was Spring Festival meat for their gods. It was only on the table to show their hospitality. If we are to live here in peace, we must be careful to respect their customs." Then he and Zhu Zhi-dao were taken to one house and I was led to another, where I shared a bed with a peasant boy.

Father didn't have to go look for the leaders the next day. They came to the Production Team, the Party Secretary of the commune, foul-mouthed Brigade Leader Li, and our Company leader. Old Dai was the only one who didn't seem drunk, and he looked very professional with his red star on his military cap.

To our surprise, the peasants had lost all trace of their unfriendliness of the night before and now seemed strangely stolid. Team Leader Guo brought out rice wine and poured it into big teacups, urging the leaders to drink, and other people filtered into the meeting room, hanging back toward the walls. Father began to speak his piece on behalf of the peasants, but he had hardly finished his opening sentences when the commune Party Secretary exploded.

"What kind of attitude is this?" he demanded, slamming his thick hand against the table and addressing the crowd. "Is this the way to respond to Chairman Mao's call? Is this the way to understand his edicts? He teaches us, 'Do not fear hardship, do not fear death'—so what does it matter if you add a few mouths to your dinner tables? Chairman Mao sent them here. If you don't welcome them, you're opposing our great leader." . . .

Our discomfort at being thus forced on the peasants was acute. There wasn't a word of protest from them in the face of these imprecations; in fact, they didn't seem to be affected much one way or the other, mules under the whip who know they must eventually obey. No wonder I had heard so much about the autocratic "work style" of the leaders in the countryside! They were despots in their little kingdoms, armed with the sayings of Chairman Mao.

When they had gone on to another Production Team, Team Leader Guo took us to a room in his younger brother's house. "Guo Lucky Wealth and his wife have no children," he explained to Father, "so this room will be yours. You can set up a small bed in the kitchen for the boy." I wasn't too pleased with the thought of sleeping in the smokiest room in the house, but I was in no position to choose. At least the peasant couple, on first impression, seemed kind.

"Now I'll show you your vegetable plot," said Team Leader Guo, pleased by the satisfaction Father had expressed with our sleeping quarters. He led us out into the fields and I discovered the area looked familiar and lovely, a real, typical Hunan countryside, with iron-rich red earth and mud houses to match, yellow rice fields, and blue-silhouetted mountains not too tall in the distance. It was bitterly cold, of course, as Hunan is in February (there is no central heating south of the Yangtze, even in cities), but I was used to feeling always slightly chilled during the winter. When we came to our plot, I reached down and broke a piece of the cold, dry earth in my fingers. It was hard to believe this was to give us our cabbage and our sweet potatoes, our beans and our turnips. Then Father's freshly polished leather shoes caught my attention and I looked up past the tidy city clothes on his elegant frame to his bewildered intellectual's face behind its thick glasses. He looked bizarre in this place where everything was tinged with the color of the land. I suddenly wondered how we were ever going to make it.

In fact, although Father was a peasant in name, his situation was quite different from that of a peasant. It was more like that of the local leaders we had met, for he earned a government salary (issued by the study class and distributed by the commune) and he was given rice coupons, a meager but sufficient twenty-six *jin* a month. These entitled him to buy rice at the town food exchange, to which the peasants turned in their government quotas for shipment to the cities. Father's labor in the fields was expected as part of his re-education, of course, but it was not to be rewarded in any way. Thus, aside from this small vegetable plot that had been carved away from some other family, Father was not really a financial burden.

The problem was us, the family members. The coupons we received for twenty-one *jin* of rice were not enough and, like the peasants, we received no salaries. According to policy, we were to be allowed to earn work points with them when we labored in the fields. The system worked like this: A day's work brought a certain number of points, ten for a man, seven for a woman, three or four for a child or an old person. At the end of the year, the accumulated value of all a person's points was calculated; in our Production team ten points were worth only fourteen *fen*, an indication of the extreme poverty of our region. From this hypothetical sum of money was subtracted the value of the rice and sweet potatoes that had been issued to the person, leaving him or her either with a small amount of credit, which might be paid if the Production Team had funds, or in the Production Team's debt (an attempt could be made to work this off during subsequent years). Our participation in this system was unwelcome because the Team was already at peak production level, and more hands would not grow more rice or sweet potatoes. Even if it could, our inexperience made us all but useless. The collective wealth of the Team was thus fixed, both in terms of food and of cash. By stepping in we would be impoverishing everyone just a little bit. It was no wonder they hoped we would be transferred.

Ultimately, we bought our acceptance. The peasants' dissatisfaction was so widespread that a new edict came down ordering all cadres to "invest" part of their savings in their Production Teams, according to their own financial situations. In our case, the price was fixed at 200 *yuan*. It was steep, but it proved worth it. The Team members were delighted, since they needed to buy fertilizer and had found their own resources inadequate; Father's contribution bought a year's worth of chemicals. At the same time, the peasants were beginning to realize that we had really come to stay. It was Father's mission, as an educated man, to help "blow the spring wind of Chairman Mao Thought all over the land," and he devoted all his feeling and energy to it. Through this work, we became a real part of the community.

Political Leadership: 1969–1976

This period was punctuated by the death of many of the Yan'an-generation leaders. Lin Biao, appointed by Mao as his successor, died in an apparent plot on Mao's life in 1971. This event, as well as the mass campaign to "Criticize Confucius and Criticize Lin Biao" that followed, is described by Fitzgerald. The deaths in 1976 of Mao Zedong and Zhou Enlai are noted briefly by Jean Chesneaux and Ross Terrill. Alden Whitman, in an obituary written for *The New York Times*, gives details of the extraordinary life and times of Zhou Enlai.

Lin Piao

*by C. P. Fitzgerald**

Lin Piao, before becoming Defence Minister in 1959, had not been prominent in political life. He was well known as a leading general with a brilliant record dating far back to the first days of the Communist movement. . . . Even after he became Minister of Defence, it was thought by many that his weak health [tuberculosis] would terminate his career long before Mao Tse-tung was likely to die. He was known as a devoted supporter of Mao: he had made the Cultural Revolution possible by bringing to it the support and logistic resources of the army, and his reward, to be nominated, [in 1969] as Mao's 'closest comrade in arms' and designated his successor, was thought by some

---

*Fitzgerald, *Mao Tse-tung and China*.

to be a kindly gesture made to a close friend who would not in fact ever live to enjoy such an honour. . . .

One of Mao Tse-tung's best known and misunderstood remarks is, 'Power grows from the barrel of a gun . . . but the Party must always control the gun.' Power, indeed, in every country of the world, is either maintained by the gun, or originated by gaining control of it. The American Revolution was won by the gun, the English Revolution of 1688 was determined by the control of the gun. There is nothing sinister in this historical reflection of Mao Tse-tung; his contribution was to make the point, already illustrated in the history of other countries, that civil power established by the gun must thenceforward control its use, if a régime is to achieve stability and durability. In 1969, as the Cultural Revolution officially came to a triumphant conclusion, Mao must have realized that the control of the gun was hardly in the hands of the disorganized rump Communist party any longer, and was in danger of slipping from his own.

It was known at the time, April 1969, that the Ninth Congress of the Chinese Communist Party had sat for the unusually long period of three weeks. It was conjectured that this unusual duration meant that there had been real debates on issues upon which all were not in full agreement, and that the report which was produced by the Congress concealed some compromises. It was not thought, then, that Lin Piao was one of the obstacles to full and swift agreement. . . .

Lin wanted men in places of power who would support him; and Mao distrusted such men. There were divergences wider than places and power: Lin held a theory which has been later denounced in most vigorous language (proving that Mao Tse-tung did not accept it), although it was put forward in Mao's praise. This was the theory that once in many centuries there appears upon the scene a man of outstanding genius who can and will transform society and bring into being a new historical era. This, argued Lin Piao, was the case with Mao Tse-tung. Without such a man, it is suggested, any political and social movement, however well intentioned, will falter for lack of that inspiration of genius. . . .

It gradually became clear that Mao Tse-tung listed not to the voice of the charmer. He did not accept the theory of the rare genius; on the contrary he had always stressed the role of mass movement and support. He has often made plain his belief that the changes and transformations of society throughout history have not been the work of kings and rulers but of a congruence of the views and feelings of thousands, or millions, of ordinary men and women—the masses. . . .

It has not yet been disclosed when Lin Piao first began to hatch a conspiracy aimed at destroying Mao and usurping his position. Indeed, the Chinese régime has felt some difficulty in convincing the world that this is what he did intend to do. Yet it is now clear that there was such a plot, and the curious facts about it are related to the apparent inefficiency of the measures planned to achieve their end, the surprise and confusion when the plan failed and the hasty improvised flight—the suggestion that the fatal crash was due to inadequate fuel for the long flight is altogether of a piece with the rest of what has been made known. . . .

It has obviously been difficult to explain why a man with the record of Lin Piao, a famous tactician and victorious general, should in the supreme endeavour of his life have employed such amateurish methods and so little regard for possible mischance. He has, since the story was made public, been treated sometimes as a fool, almost an imbecile—wholly inconsistent with his record—or as a deeply deceptive traitor who had nourished his ambition and his plans for many years, waiting for the right moment. This, too, is not a satisfying conclusion. If it were true, then Mao himself is shown to be a political innocent who failed to detect the real character of the man he trusted and relied upon, to the point of virtually naming him as a chosen successor.

It would seem to be more consistent with what is known to suppose that Lin, indeed ambitious, believed that he could climb to the highest positon on Mao's back; he therefore professed loyalty to his leader, supported him in the great gamble of the Cultural Revolution, which removed other possible rivals from power, and at the same time brought the army into the forefront of political life. Only when it became clear to him at the Ninth Congress in April 1969 that Mao was not going to let the gun slip from his hands, and that the time was approaching when the predominance of the army would be curtailed, did Lin see that his position was in danger and that his hopes might prove vain.

The Campaign to Criticize Lin Piao and Confucius

by C. P. Fitzgerald*

[Following Lin's disappearance], the ideological purging took more time and needed still more care. Lin Piao was the first begetter of the famous *Little Red Book* of Mao Tse-tung's Thoughts. He had written the preface, and he had made it the training manual of the People's Liberation Army. Thousands of copies of that edition had to be recalled, and destroyed. But Mao's Thought could not be attacked, nor repudiated. The book must remain extant, purged of any trace of Lin Piao's hand. These were only material cleansing operations; what was also needed was a reasoned critique of the thinking of the traitor, as well as a condemnation of his actions.

It must have been a considerable task to work out what this new line should be: the difficulty of representing Lin Piao as an ambitious fool was self-evident—why then had Mao trusted him? . . . Lin Piao is not to be shown as a modern would-be military dictator, in the mould of so many contemporary leaders of the non-Communist world. This would suggest that such men could rise high and be trusted in a Communist society and still hold 'bourgeois' ambitions. Lin Piao must be revealed as an ideological heretic, a man who had perverted rather than failed to understand the truth. The theory of the rare genius provided the necessary base for this charge. It could not be denied that Lin had held that view; he had indeed pretended to place Mao in that sublime category, the better to obtain power for himself. But the ambition was only the consequence of the wrong ideology, not the prime motive. Lin was not a military *putsch* maker, but a man of ability who had been seduced by a false conception of the laws of history and society.

There was another man whom Mao saw as having held

---

* Fitzgerald, *Mao Tse-tung and China*.

the same mistaken view, and who imposed it upon the Chinese people for more than 2,000 years: Confucius. Confucius was a man of great talent; he was not influential in his own lifetime, but his views became the orthodox ethic of the Chinese civilization within a few centuries of his death. Mao could see that had he accepted the theory of rare genius, he, Mao, would also soon qualify for the title of sage! His writings would become classics, his words treasured in a new Analects. Lin Piao would most certainly have used Mao, once dead, in this way had he succeeded. A rigid orthodoxy would once more have been imposed upon China, enshrined in a hierarchical Party. The error of Liu Shao-ch'i would have been revived with even greater strength than it promised to have when Liu was in power.

Mao never believed in rigid orthodoxies nor trusted hierarchies; his revolutionary instinct was too strong, his disbelief in élite rule too deep-rooted. For him the masses were the real leaders, from them came the true decisions, the lasting developments of society. Again and again he emphasized his faith in man rather than in material, and in men rather than in organizations and institutions. Confucius and his followers built up a complex structure of institutional and ideological traditions which ruled China, no matter who sat on the throne, for two thousand years. It may once have had its value, but in Mao's opinion that time passed centuries ago. His revolution was directed more against the old ideology than against the ephemeral figures, emperors or presidents, who embodied it in his own lifetime.

So Confucius, the supreme exponent of the old reaction, can be matched with Lin Piao, the latest exponent of the selfsame error. The theory of genius in history was essentially Confucian; the sage had always held up as examples the partly or wholly mythical rulers of remote antiquity, and in particular the real, if rather shadowy, men who founded the Chou dynasty, the feudal régime, far gone in decay, under which Confucius lived. Lin and his long-dead predecessor have, in this explanation, the same basic erroneous ideas. They both believed that man could be taught by the example of a small élite of supreme power holders: that, as the Chinese proverb put it, 'As the wind blows, so the grass bends.' . . .

Thus if Lin and Confucius shared the same basic errors

their association as twin examples of reactionaries ancient and modern makes sense. It shows that, as Mao continually pointed out, revolutions are not won in a day; the need for vigilance is constant, the final victory of the new society is still not wholly certain. It might seem to observers who are not Chinese that the very fact that it has been found useful and effective to associate such disparate men as Lin Piao and Confucius in a shared condemnation is a striking proof of the continuity in ways of thought, if not in conduct, between the old China and the new. To turn to historical examples drawn from a volume of record longer, more detailed and more accurately recorded than any other in the world, is characteristic of the literature of old China; and to outside observers of China and the Chinese people it seems to be a cultural trait which is so much a part of the national heritage that no revolution can uproot it, and revolutionaries, even Mao Tse-tung himself, are unaware of its essentially Chinese nature.

From Lin Biao to Deng Xiaoping
by Jean Chesneaux*

On the surface there was no major political crisis in China between the fall of Lin Biao (1972) and the [temporary] fall of Deng Xiao-ping (1976). But latent tensions remained very strong and appeared suddenly after Mao's death. Basic conficts between the conservative management line and the radical line often entailed personality conflicts. The "Shanghai Four" [better known as the Gang of Four: see next section] (Zhang Qun-qiao, head of the political department of the army, Wang Hong-wen, number three man in the party hierarchy, Yao Wen-yuan, in charge of ideological affairs and information, and Jiang Qing, who had inspired the campaigns for proletarian culture), who were the very active promoters of the campaigns against Confucius and the bourgeois right, were also on very bad terms with Zhou En-lai and attacked him in private. Their propaganda was more defensive than offensive, which was probably an expression of their growing isolation. Little by

---

* Chesneaux, *China: The People's Republic*.

little it seemed that they were reduced to factional intrigues, which was a prelude to their brutal fall in October 1976. Did this isolation reflect a certain organic weakness in the leftist line, a certain weariness after so many shake-ups and ideological campaigns? Or did it mean that the "Four" themselves had been gradually cut off from the mass line that they had been defending with such vehemence since the glory days of the Shanghai Commune? And at what point did Mao, weakened by illness, finally stop supporting them, and even approving of them?

Between 1972 and 1976 these conflicts remained hidden and openly affected only isolated cities or provinces.... The potential seriousness of these conflicts can be measured by the fact that in order to delay them as long as possible many top-ranking leaders did not retire from their jobs in spite of their advanced age. But in the space of less than a year many of them died: Deng Bi-wu (born in 1886), Zhou En-lai (born in 1898), Kang Sheng (born 1896), Zhu De (born in 1886), and finally Mao Tse-tung, who died in September 1976 at the age of 83.

Chou En-lai Leaves a Gap
by Ross Terrill

The death of Chou En-lai—the first of the trio of deaths that was to shake China in 1976—came as a shock all over the nation and beyond. Chou's ability and length of service had made him the anchor of Chinese politics.

The announcement came in the freezing cold of January 8, 1976, as a grim prelude to the Year of the Dragon. Dead of cancer at seventy-eight. From the hospital where he had died, Chou's body was taken to the gilded splendor of the former Imperial Palace. A weeping crowd in overcoats watched the cortège with its hearse draped in rosettes of black and yellow.

The next forty-eight hours brought out, as if the gods were in charge of symbols, the three big reasons why Chou En-lai was a great politician. (Even in China new events cannot be hidden to the point of obliterating the outward shape of inner workings.)

In the first place, the very size of the crowd bore witness to the Chinese people's affection for their premier. The rows of common folk numbered close to one million. No death in China for decades, whether Communist or pre-Communist, nor the deaths of the other two red titans, evoked visible mass feeling on such a scale.

At one point during the procession, according to an eyewitness, a large group of Chinese moved onto the road to try to prevent the vehicle bearing the coffin from going forward. They suspected that the plan to cremate the body was a wish, not of Chou himself, but of Chiang Ch'ing and her friends. Only when the widow, Teng Ying-ch'ao, stepped forward to explain to the group that cremation was Chou's own wish did the concerned citizens let the vehicle pass.

The Chinese masses believed in Chou. He never had a credibility problem and even Mao, in the last years, was a less vivid figure to people in the street than this man of steely will who also had a personal touch. Ms. Teng's direct and effective communication with the funeral crowd seemed a symbol of Chou's credibility. The outlook was a shade bleaker for almost everyone in China—there were some striking exceptions—without Chou En-lai.

Then too, unexpectedly, the somber funeral room beneath the orange tiles of the Imperial Palace was thrown open to foreigners. Not many non-Chinese reside in Peking, but almost all of them—ambassadors, newsmen, students, brothers in the faith who work for the Chinese government—came to view the jar of Chou's ashes and the boyish portrait behind it. This was an unusual intrusion of foreigners into the sealed courtyard of Chinese grief, but fitting too, for Chou was the international face of the Chinese Revolution.

And thirdly, it was announced at the ceremony in the Great Hall of the People a few days later that Chou had asked for his ashes to be "scattered upon the rivers and soil of our motherland." No gaudy mausoleum to freeze history into granite for this forthright man without airs. It was a typical gesture. The *way* Chou did things was always as important as what he did.

So Chou towered over most other figures of the Chinese Revolution in that he evoked affection from ordinary people; he was China's bridge to the international community; and he was a selfless man whose quality of character made him able to get fractious people to compromise with each other.

Chou En-lai: China's Man for All Weather

by Alden Whitman*

Chou's life bridged traditional and revolutionary China. He was born in the waning years of the Manchu Dynasty, in 1898—the exact date is unclear—in the eastern city of Hwaian, in Kiangsu Province. His family was of the gentry and well-to-do; its seat was Shaohing, about 100 miles southwest of Shanghai. Both his parents were versed in the Chinese literary classics. His mother died in his boyhood and his father, a minor bureaucrat fond of rice wine, was thought ineffectual by members of the Chou family. It was agreed that the youth would be reared by an uncle, Tiao-chih, in Shanghai.

Chou's attachment to his extended family was in the traditional manner. In 1939, for example, he made a special trip to Shaohing to pay his respects—by bowing three times—to the then head of the clan. And when his father died in 1942, the son saw to it that the obituary notice in the Communist Party paper conformed to ancient custom, quite contrary to general party practice.

When Chou was ten, still another uncle undertook his upbringing, and took him to live in Mukden, where he passed his elementary school years. At home and in class he became acquainted with the writings of Chinese reformers and Western political thinkers. He also learned some English.

From 1913 to 1917 Chou was at the Nankai Middle School in Tientsin, where his nationalist feelings were further fortified. With the crumbling of the Manchu Dynasty and the concomitant rise of foreign influence in Chinese internal affairs, the spirit of reform and nationalism grew in the 19th century, especially among the country's educated élite. One expression of the nationalist movement's

New York Times, Jan. 9, 1976.

force was the Boxer Rebellion which was crushed by foreign (mostly European and American) troops in 1900 and which cost the Chinese people additional losses in pride and sovereignty.

Ultimately, in 1911, the crumbling Manchu rule was overthrown, and the long and often chaotic and halting process of establishing a new China began. Lacking strong, coherent leadership, the country was initially divided by the contentious aspirations of various provincial generals and warlords; and it took more than 10 years for a significant national authority to emerge under Dr. Sun Yat-sen.

Meantime, Chou was making his mark at the Nankai school as a writer and editor of the student journal. His articles stressed China's need for unification and industrialization, as well as the importance of enrolling youth in the political and social process. Completing four years at Nankai and in search of new knowledge, Chou went to Tokyo, then a center for many Chinese students with nationalist leanings. In two years in Japan, the young man was introduced to socialism through the writings of Kawakami Hajime and audited courses in social science. And in constant discussions with his fellow students his nationalist fervor mounted. In one such conversation, Chou reportedly said:

"You cannot salvage the situation with strong leadership alone. You have to have strong followers to support the leadership. You have to start with a thorough re-education of the younger generation—of the students, the workers and even the peasants. You have to have them all with you before you can push a revolution to a successful conclusion."

The transition from talk to action came in the May Fourth Movement, which grew out of a violent student demonstration in Peking on May 4, 1919. The protest was against a decision at the Paris Peace Conference (ending World War I) that awarded Germany's economic concession in the Shantung Peninsula to Japan.

The movement took Chou back to Tientsin, where he was named editor of *Chueh-wu* (The Awakening), an organ of the strongly nationalist Awakening Society. This society and others like it in other parts of China were the taproots of the Chinese Communist Party, organized in mid-1921.

Some nationalists, Mao and Chou among them, were deeply influenced by the Bolshevik Revolution of 1917 in

Russia, articles about which appeared from time to time in the student press. Chou's link with the Communists was not immediate, however, although the drift of his thinking shifted leftward.

After spending a few months in jail for his agitational activities, Chou left China in mid-1920 for France. The object was further study, but he spent much of his four years in Europe in organizing other Chinese students and in absorbing Marxist thought. Some time in this period he joined the Chinese Communist Youth Corps, a training ground for potential party members, and then the party itself, of which he became a leading member....

The Communists cooperated in the Expedition that captured Shanghai in early 1927. Almost immediately, however, Chiang turned on the Communists, and in a coup staged on April 12, 1927, arrested and shot hundreds of Communists and their associates. Chou barely escaped with his life, as did Mao. Chou's role in the capture of Shanghai and his flight were immortalized in André Malraux's *Man's Fate*, in which Chou, thinly disguised, is the novel's principal character.

In the Communist Party congress that met in Wuhan shortly after the Shanghai disaster, Chou was elected to the Central Committee and then to its Politburo, a group that did not then include Mao. In the brief but celebrated Nanchang Uprising of August, 1927, he was a member of the city's Revolutionary Committee. But this revolt also fizzled, and Chou went underground.

He emerged in Moscow in the summer of 1928 for a congress of his shattered party, becoming then second in rank to Li Li-san, de facto chief of the party. And at the Comintern meeting that September he was elected a candidate member of its executive committee. Returning to Shanghai, he lived a shadowy existence, trying to reconstitute the party on "the proletarian base" proposed by the Comintern and by Stalin.

Meanwhile, Mao and some party associates were becoming convinced of the crucial importance of the peasantry to the revolution, a point of view he developed from 1927 onward. It differed fundamentally with the Comintern position, which argued for a revolution based on the working class. This difference was the nub of the often-fierce doctrinal dispute between Mao and Soviet Communists, a quarrel that was exacerbated as Mao's theory and tactics proved correct for China. Organizing the countryside and surrounding and capturing the cities, the essence of Maoist tactics, proceeded from the assumption that the exploited peasantry, the bulk of the country's millions, were the ones who had nothing to lose but their chains.

Mao created a peasant and guerrilla base at the remote town of Chingkangshan, shifting later to Kiangsi Province, where a soviet republic was set up in 1931. Chou, who had been adhering to the Moscow policy with rising doubts, finally joined Mao in the Kiangsi fastness in 1931 and was elected a member of the soviet's Central Executive Committee. The election attested his consummate ability to adapt to political reality at the right time.

During the growth of the Kiangsi soviet in the face of at least four Chiang "bandit suppression" campaigns against it, Mao's stature in the party shrank temporarily in a complex argument over the nature of guerrillaism. He was, in fact, replaced as political officer for the military by Chou, who also became a vice chairman of the Central Revolutionary Military Council, whose chief was Chu Teh....

Along the way to Yenan, at Tsunyi, in Kweichow Province, the Red Army paused for a political reassessment, in the course of which Mao asserted his supremacy as party leader. Although Chou slipped from chairman (the post was given to Mao) to vice chairman of the party's Military Affairs Committee, the two men worked in harmony. The conference—its details are still murky—not only put Mao's imprint on the Chinese Revolution, but also consolidated behind Mao the important intellectual-nationalist forces represented by Chou.

In the last stages of the Long March Chou was seriously ill and had to be carried in a litter, but he retained his authority as a senior commander. He was still commander in 1936 when Edgar Snow interviewed him in Yenan. "Like many Red leaders [Chou] was as much a legend as a man," Snow wrote later, continuing:

"Slender and of medium height, with a slight wiry frame, he was boyish in appearance despite his long black beard, and had large, warm, deep-set eyes. A certain magnetism about him seemed to derive from a combination of personal charm and assurance of command. . . . Chou left me with an impression of a cool, logical, empirical mind."

After 1936, when the Red Army position in Shensi was secure, Chou relinquished his military role for that of a diplomat, a step facilitated by restiveness in northern China over Japanese aggression and a renewed general sentiment for a domestic peace that would permit a united front against the invader. . . .

[After 1949] Chou applied himself to the two tremendous tasks that were to occupy the remainder of his life: that of chief diplomat in China's foreign relations and that of administering the vast state bureaucracy. . . .

On the world stage, Chou—the name is pronounced jo—became visible to millions of Americans in February 1972, when they watched him on television acting as host to President Nixon during the historic journey to China. Erect in his military posture, trim in a well-tailored gray tunic and trousers, Chou, whose dark face was dominated by brown eyes and black eyebrows, was witnessed as a relaxed and evidently tireless banqueter.

Off camera, he was reported to have been a supple negotiator of an easing of Chinese-American tensions. These talks paved the way for a substantial increase in commercial and cultural relations between the two nations as well as for limited diplomatic ties. Chou, however, did not succeed in persuading the United States to terminate relations with the Chinese Nationalist regime on Taiwan.

Chou's skill in negotiation was well regarded even by those who differed with him or sat on the other side of the table. General of the Army George C. Marshall, who dealt with him on a post-World War II mission to China, expressed esteem. And Dag Hammarskjold, the late Secretary General of the United Nations, once said that Chou had "the most superior brain I have so far met in the field of foreign politics."

As China's principal face to the world, Chou attended the Geneva conference on Vietnam in 1954 and the Bandung, Indonesia, meeting of the so-called third-world countries the following year. Later he traveled widely in Asia, Africa and East Europe in search of goodwill and wider influence for Peking, although not always successfully. He negotiated diplomatic recognition with Japan. He played an important role, moreover, in the delicate dealings with the Soviet Union, whose relationship with China was exceedingly tense from 1960 onward. With patience and adroitness he brought China out of her virtual diplomatic isolation in 1949 into ranks of the great powers, a process culminating in China's admission to the United Nations in 1971.

Foreigners who met him were struck, above all, by his combination—rare among Chinese leaders—of toughness and sophistication. He was always immaculate, his tunic creaseless and shoes gleaming. His right arm was permanently crooked as a result of a riding accident in the 1930s, but his handshake was vigorous.

He remembered enough English and French from his student days, which he spent in England, France as well as Germany, to correct his interpreters.

As Foreign Minister, Chou enunciated to the world that henceforth China was the sovereign in her own house and expected nothing less than absolute equality among other nations—a position he persistently adhered to until other nations, at first hostile, accepted those principles.

At the outset China was virtually a pariah except among other Communist states, obliging her to make relations with the Soviet Union a cornerstone of policy. With Mao, Chou negotiated the key 1950 treaty of friendship with the Soviet Union and an ancillary accord that provided for the return of Port Arthur and Dairen to China and $300 million in credits.

One of the tension points of Chinese-Soviet relations even in 1950 was that it was China that went cap in hand to Moscow. Indeed, no significant Soviet leader visited Peking until after the death of Stalin in 1953; nor was Mao recognized by Moscow as the great revolutionary leader he believed himself to be.

Chou's efforts to gain non-Communist friends for China suffered a serious setback with the Korean conflict in 1950. The Chinese backed the North with matériel and men, a step that led to serious American battlefield reverses and a truce in July 1953, the intricate details of which Chou helped to work out.

While one war raged in Korea, another was being fought in Vietnam. The French were decisively beaten by Communist-led forces at the historic battle of Dien Bien

Phu, leading to the Geneva conference of 1954. Chou headed the Chinese delegation to that meeting, blossoming for the first time as a world statesman.

Sitting as an equal for the first time with diplomats of the great powers—the United States, the Soviet Union, Britain and France—Chou chose the conference as the occasion for an approach to John Foster Dulles, the Secretary of State. Dulles's refusal to shake Chou's extended hand in a room outside the conference chamber was taken as an unforgiveable affront by Chou, who mentioned it frequently in later years.

At the conference, he demanded an end to colonial rule in Asia, saying: "We hold that interference in the internal affairs of the Asian nations should be stopped, all foreign military bases in Asia be removed, foreign armed forces in Asia be withdrawn, the remilitarization of Japan prevented and all economic blockades be abolished."

He also accused the United States of "creating an aggressive block" in Asia, using the island of Taiwan as one base.

The Geneva accord, which the United States did not sign and subsequently did not observe, called for a temporary division of Vietnam and elections in 1956 to determine a unified national government. In later years Chou expressed deep regret that he had signed the agreement, for he had come to feel that the Ho Chi Minh nationalists had been obliged by the Chinese to make too many concessions and had been swindled.

Chou was also disturbed because, in 1954, the United States sponsored the Southeast Asia Treaty Organization and signed a mutual security pact with the Chiang regime on Taiwan. Both actions seemed to Chou directed against China.

Partly in reaction to these developments, Chou led a delegation to the 29-nation African-Asian (Bandung) Conference in early 1955. At this meeting in Indonesia, Chou's performance was again impressive.

Chou exploited the Bandung meeting in several ways: by saying that China would "strive for the liberation of Taiwan by peaceful means so far as it is possible"; by inviting Asian heads of state to Peking; and by embarking on a spectacular tour of Asia.

Meanwhile, Chinese-Soviet relations were outwardly correct. Chou did make some references to "great-power

chauvinism," and Soviet leaders did criticize the Great
Leap Forward, China's 1958 attempt to spur the pace of
industrialization. Despite these differences, Chou went to
Moscow in 1959 and negotiated expanded economic and
technical aid that was supposed to carry through to 1967.
A year and a half after the accord was signed, Soviet aid
and technicians were abruptly withdrawn, leading to open
bitterness between the two countries.

The strife had many manifestations on both a state and a
party level, not the least dramatic of which was Chou's
walkout at the 22d Congress of the Soviet Communist
Party in 1961. The incident arose over Soviet remarks
critical of Maoism, part of the war of epithets that has
symbolized the doctrinal division of world Communism.

Also in the foreign field, China's relations with India
suffered a fracture, ostensibly over the Chinese-Indian
border. There were armed clashes in 1962, which left a
residue of ill will for many years. This coldness was further
intensified in March 1972, when China sided with Pakistan
in the fighting over Bangladesh, in which India sided with
the Bengalis.

After the Ninth Congress of the party in 1969, which
signaled the winding up of the Cultural Revolution, Chou's
activities intensified as he began to remend China's fences
abroad and to get the economy rolling again.

Chou's long and delicate foreign initiatives bore fruit in
China's admission to the United Nations in 1971 and in
Mr. Nixon's dramatic visit to Peking and other cities in
1972.

Although Mao had often hurled invectives against United
States "imperialism" and was a vigorous opponent of
American involvement in Southeast Asia, it was agreed in
August and September 1970 to feel out the United States,
with which there had been some liaison over the years
through ambassadorial meetings in Warsaw. Thus it was
that in December 1970 Mao indicated in an interview with
Edgar Snow, the American journalist, that President Nixon
would be welcomed in Peking.

The United States, it was contended, would respond not
only in the interest of a more stable Asia but also because
a Nixon visit could strengthen its hand with the Soviet
Union. The Peking sessions of early 1972, conducted
largely by Chou, lightened the atmosphere between the

two nations, but fell far short of establishing diplomatic relations. Even so, Chou was credited with helping to relax tensions and with opening the door to significant commerical and cultural interchanges. . . .

Although Chou succeeded in creating conditions for a détente with the United States, he did not solve the thorny problems of Taiwan. He wanted explicit United States recognition of Peking's sovereignty over that island. Nor was he able to resolve the border issue with the Soviet Union, although talks were kept alive, if only barely.

China's door is now partly open and if China is indeed on the road to acquiring the industrial and technological substance of a great world power, much of the credit must go to the foresighted and adaptable Chou, his country's man for all weather.

Mao Zedong's life spanned the death of Imperial China, the warlord years and the consolidation of the KMT, the war against the Japanese and civil war, Liberation and almost thirty years of struggle to build China into a modern, independent, and socialist nation. Through all of this, he was philosopher, guerrilla fighter, party theoretician, charismatic center of the new political leadership, and above all—as he wanted to be remembered—a teacher. For years before his death in 1976, both Chinese and foreigners speculated about it and about China's subsequent course. John K. Fairbank discusses Mao's death, writing only months afterward, in terms of Mao's own hopes for China.

The Death of Mao
by John K. Fairbank*

The word came ominously: "Power fight is on in China. 900 million mourning Mao" (*Daily News*, New York, September 10).

The reporting of the death of Mao told us as much about ourselves as about China: 1) Good news is not news; only when Mao dies can we devote much space to him. 2) We

---

New York Review of Books, Oct. 14, 1976.

focus on Mao personally, not upon the vast revolution that gave his genius its opportunity. 3) Vaguely aware that, unlike us, China has no crisis of inflation, unemployment, crime, or corruption, we find what bad news we can in the Peking "power struggle." All bits of news can fit this interpretation. Does the Central Committee make a statement? "As if anticipating a power struggle for Mao's mantle, the Central Committee of the Communist Party issued an appeal for unity" (CP-UPI Peking, September 9).

Are "capitalist-roaders" attacked as usual? "The simmering power struggle among his political heirs broke into the open with demands for further purges of Mao's enemies... even as the official mourning began" (UPI Hong Kong, September 10). Evidence? The Shanghai party committee vowed to "deepen the criticism of Teng Hsiao-p'ing," which has been going on for six months. What is this power struggle? On examination it turns out to be a *policy* struggle. (Mao taught struggle, of course.) It is between factions, to be sure, but over real issues that confront the revolution, in brief, whether to persist in the effort to change the character of people or settle down to material development. Ford vs. Carter is a more naked power struggle than anything going on in Peking. The policy differences are greater between the Peking factions than they are between Democrats and Republicans. "Power struggle" fits our 1976 election process. We understand it as a legitimate contest for power, with platforms and promises tailored to get votes and win power. But the Central Committee in Peking is not holding an election. It has power already. It confronts policy problems on which honest revolutionaries disagree.

By calling the conflict between the Peking policy factions a "power struggle," we do several things at once: we cut down dedicated revolutionaries, whose thinking condemns selfishness and personal aggrandizement, to the size of ambitious individualists of a type we know well— Chang Chun-chiao,* for instance, is implied to be no more than John Connally with chopsticks. We impose our self-image on the distant Chinese scene.

"Power struggle" as an explanation of what is happening also eliminates the whole field of policy options and ideology,

---

*One of the Gang of Four later deposed.

which we therefore need not try to understand. The "who succeeds Mao?" approach sidesteps the great issues of the revolution. It reduces Peking's problems to the level of a contest among individual competitors. . . .

Peking's policy issues have inhered in the distinction between the industrial revolution and the social revolution. The industrial revolution of modern times applied to China has increased production in both industry and agriculture through new technology, literacy, public health, capital investment, and new forms of organization. This is the province of those we label "pragmatists" or "moderates," whom we like to think we understand and can even identify with. . . .

The social revolution in China has been *sui generis*, quite beyond our experience, a struggle against China's most persistent heritage, the ruling-class tradition. This included the Confucian teachings of social order based on the natural inequality of status between elders and youth, men and women, rulers and ruled. The tradition was highly elitist, expressed in ancient China's inventions in bureaucratic government, perfected by the T'ang build-up of the examination system, which for twelve centuries down to 1905 funneled Chinese talent into official life. The small ruling class produced China's great literature and philosophy, patronized her arts and commerce, and ran her affairs both local and imperial while living off the peasantry.

The attack on China's outworn social structure has been Mao's province from the beginning, ever since his heterodox report of 1927 on the peasantry as the real vanguard of revolution. "Liberation" during the Yenan decade from 1936 to 1946 brought the peasant a sense of freedom, literacy, and some technology. But primarily Yenan trained new party cadres to mobilize the peasantry for production, war, and politics. After 1949 the great mass organizations and national campaigns retrained the bureaucrats and scholars, and gradually eliminated both landlords and capitalists.

But Mao found to his dismay that it was not enough to eliminate the old ruling-class leftovers. The elitist virus was encysted with the body politic. The revolution's newly liberated peasants were not only incipient capitalists, European fashion, they also had it in their bones to rise in the social scale and make a new ruling class. Special privilege reappeared in the Communist Party apparatus, sprouting from the deep soil of China's tradition. . . .

"Class struggle" thus has a special meaning in Chinese social history. "Serve the people" means no more upper-class privilege.

Yet this supremely Maoist slogan makes plain the problem it seeks to overcome. Chinese officialdom, now so extraordinarily swollen in size (the party alone is some 28 million), is heir to its own tradition of avowedly benevolent manipulation of the masses. In updating this upper-class responsibility to "bring order to the empire," Mao as sage and teacher has led in a process of tutelage, bringing the masses into political life, setting them upon the road of self-reliant development. The need for tutelage, to nurture self-government among a politically inert though often rebellious peasantry, was obvious to reformers like Liang Ch'i-ch'ao at the start of the century. Sun Yat-sen made tutelage central to his program. Mao has put it in other terms, but his would-be egalitarian order is still managed by an elite party. Travelers in the People's Republic are struck by the strong sense of hierarchy still remaining as a necessary component of social order and by the party cadres' sense of duty to "serve the people" as a special calling. . . .

Our handicap is our public ignorance of the secretive China we are dealing with. (Find a China specialist who does not feel ignorant and you have a fool.) To rely on "power struggle" as the key to understanding Peking is simplistic, a cheap way out. Underlying the competition for leadership, which may indeed produce disruptions at any moment, are policy problems so stark as to make Washington's seem like peanuts. And if, as seems not unlikely, our problems prove largely insoluble with or without peanuts, we can only begin to imagine those that burden the Central Committee in Peking. Mao and Chou with all their faults may look better and better as times goes on.

How to judge Mao Tse-tung will inspire a large literature among us. He was not a small man. Look at his treatment of the United States. Nineteenth- and early twentieth-century Americans in China did much to stir up the great revolution, but when it came to power in 1949 we opposed it. We fought the Chinese quite unnecessarily in Korea: after MacArthur landed at Inchon, and before he went for the Yalu to conquer North Korea, Chou En-lai explained to us that China could not let a friendly buffer state be supplanted by an avowed enemy on the border of her Manchurian industrial base. In Korea we shot a million Chinese casualties. We later compounded this by bombing North Vietnam with many invasions of Chinese air space, a humiliation to all patriots. But Mao stayed out, and in the end—because we had become less of a problem than the Russians—he invited the leader of our defeat [Richard Nixon] to visit Peking. . . .

With help from Chou En-lai and some millions of others, Mao has led the People's Republic through a phase of history that has now come to an end. Will we be able to achieve any greater understanding of China's problems now that he and his generation are gone? The new generation will be equally absorbed in domestic issues, as usual in China, and we shall have to understand them largely by our own efforts through barriers of language and ideology.

Daily Life in the 1980s

The Chinese government maintains strict control over each of its more than a billion citizens. This is accomplished by a rigid system of formally identifying everyone with his workplace, school, or commune. Fox Butterfield relates his experience with the system when he arrived in China in 1979 to set up *The New York Times* bureau. He goes on to describe how street committee representatives oversee the people's home lives.

Identity

by Fox Butterfield

The Workplace

A balding, slightly stooped clerk in a loose-fitting brownish-gray tunic stood behind the reservation desk, which was identified by a sign in English that said, "Accommodation Center."

"Do you have a room?" I asked in my best Chinese.

After examining me for what seemed several minutes, he replied, "Where are you?" or *"Ni nar"* in Chinese.

Thinking I had heard wrong, I repeated my question. But he answered again, "Where are you?"

Finally, sensing my confusion, he amplified. "We only give rooms to units, not to individuals," he said, using the Chinese word *danwei*. *Danwei*, I knew, meant a person's workplace, their office, factory, school, or commune. "Where are you?" therefore meant "What is your unit?" But I had just arrived in China as a U.S. journalist; I didn't have a *danwei*.

"Everyone in China has a *danwei*," the clerk said definitively. "You must find your *danwei*, or we can't give you a room."

Thus began my first task in China, to find my *danwei*. The Information Department, which had granted me my visa, disclaimed responsibility. The China Travel Service said they couldn't help because I was a resident in China and not a tourist. The Diplomatic Services Bureau, which arranges housing for foreigners in Peking, turned down my request because they said they gave out only apartments, which they didn't have, and not hotel rooms. The American Embassy was reluctant to become involved because the press and the government in the United States are supposed to keep their distance from each other. Eventually, I did appeal to the American ambassador, Leonard Woodcock, who wrote to the Foreign Ministry suggesting they should take the awful responsibility and adopt me as part of their *danwei*.

This adventure was a useful lesson. *Danwei*, I quickly discovered, are the basic building blocks of Chinese society, almost a second citizenship for most Chinese. A Chinese is more likely to be asked his *danwei* than his name when he goes someplace new. Chinese telephone conversations usually begin "Where are you?" not "Who is this?" When I stopped for a night in the remote industrial city of Qiqihar in the far northeastern corner of China, the first question on the registration form of the local hotel asked for the guest's unit. Only the second line inquired about his name. . . .

The reason for this stress on *danwei* is that a *danwei* to a Chinese is far more than just his workplace. A tall thirty-five-year-old woman who worked in the semisecret Fourth Ministry of Machine Building, which produces electronics for China's defense industry, explained how the system works. She lived in an apartment in a vast compound of five-story gray-brick buildings managed by her ministry. All her neighbors were also employed by the ministry. To go in or out of the one entrance, she had to walk past an army guard in uniform, and if she brought any visitors into the compound, they had to register in the sentry box. The woman's nine-year-old son went to school in another building inside the compound; she shopped for groceries in the compound store; when the family was sick there was a clinic in the compound. The ministry also issued her her ration cards for rice, cooking oil, cloth, and what the Chinese call "industrial goods," including radios, watches, sewing machines, or bicycles.

But the *danwei's* authority over her went even deeper, as she related one summer afternoon when we drove by her compound. It would have been impossible for me to go in past the sentry, she apologized. When she wanted to get married a decade ago, she recalled, she had been required to apply to the Party secretary of her *danwei* for permission, a standard procedure. Her *danwei* then ran a security check with her boy friend's unit, and only after both *danwei* approved, could they wed. If she wanted to try to transfer to another job, her unit had to agree. When an elderly neighbor died recently, she added, the *danwei* had arranged for his funeral and cremation. To talk to me, a foreigner, she was supposed to receive permission from her *danwei* beforehand, and she was to report back on whatever we discussed.

Not every *danwei* in China is so well equipped that it can provide this full range of cradle-to-grave services. Some units don't have their own housing; only the largest have both their own school and hospitals. But for the government the *danwei* structure means that society is organized as much as a security system as it is a social or economic system. If the hallmark of the feudal system in medieval Europe and Japan was the peasant's inescapable bondage to the land, the essence of the Chinese system, I sometimes thought, was the individual's ties to his *danwei*, a kind of industrial feudalism.

There was no exact counterpart for the *danwei* in traditional China. Earlier dynasties did practice a mutual guarantee organization called the *bao-jia* system: families were organized in groups of tens and hundreds with each unit responsible for the acts of all the others. But the real antecedent probably lies simply in the Chinese penchant for bonding the individual to his group. . . .

The Street Committees

If the *danwei* exercises control over Chinese in their workplaces, the street committee provides the government with a mechanism to watch them at home. In the five-story concrete building where my friends Hong and Weidong lived, the representative to the local street committee was a rotund, graying, illiterate woman in her fifties named Ma whose husband had been a poor waiter in a restaurant before 1949. Mrs. Ma was not a Party member, but she was energetic, shrewd, and had carefully cultivated good relations with the police by offering them a cup of tea or a cigarette whenever they happened to stop by the building. In time, at the annual meeting of all the adults in the building, Mrs. Ma was put forward by the neighborhood office, the lowest level of government, as the official candidate for street committee member. The ballot was not secret, and everyone knew whom they were supposed to vote for, Weidong related. Mrs. Ma won all the votes.

In action, Mrs. Ma was a cross between a building superintendent, police informant, social worker, and union-hall hiring boss. The powers of the street committee are not codified in law, for they are considered representatives of the "masses" rather than the police, but that only gives them more authority Weidong said.

"Their most terrifying power is that they can search your house whenever they want," Weidong related. "The police are supposed to have a warrant, but the street committee cadres can come in when they please." Usually three or four members of the street committee, middle-aged women like Mrs. Ma, would just barge in without knocking after midnight when Hong and Weidong were asleep. "Their excuse is that they are here to inspect our *bu-kou*," the household registration certificate. The street committee was checking for any people living in Peking illegally from the countryside, relatives of the family, perhaps, or rusticated youth who had snuck back into the capital. "I give them our certificates, but then they always look around the apartment and examine anything they are interested in."

"If we have friends over, even for dinner, Mrs. Ma may walk in and ask who they are," Hong interjected. "It is very humiliating. If you don't cooperate, she can call the police and they will come over and ask the same questions." Once when Hong and Weidong quarreled late at night, Mrs. Ma stopped by the next day to chastise them for not resolving their domestic problems. "There is no way to be alone, she even watches what time we go to bed," Hong complained. "We are like caged animals."

Mrs. Ma also keeps a strict eye on the residents' neatness and sometimes reprimanded Hong for not washing the dishes or sweeping the floors. Often during the winter, when dusk falls early, Mrs. Ma and the other street committee cadres would hide in the unlighted entryways to the buildings to watch for strangers, Weidong cautioned me. He had seen her carrying a club. For me, it gave each of my nocturnal visits to their house an added and unwelcome sense of adventure. One evening, when walking through a dark field toward their apartment, I was accosted by two young men in ordinary blue workers' clothes. They demanded to know what my *danwei* was and what I was doing in the area. I offered the fiction that I was a foreign teacher on my way to visit the home of one of my students. Weidong explained that they were members of the local urban militia, another link in the security network.

The street committee cadres are not paid a regular salary, but they can count on small gifts of meat, vegetables, and rice from residents who want to keep on their good side. More important, their posts put them in position to help their families and friends, for it is the street committee that passes on recommendations about job assignments to the city labor department for unemployed young people in the neighborhood. It is also the street committee that advises the municipal housing office about which families need new quarters.

"Just look around and see whose children come back first from the countryside and get good jobs, and you'll know who the street committee people are," Weidong said.

In recent years the street committee has gained a further and extraordinary power—the right to decide which couples in the neighborhood may have chlidren. This prerogative is part of the government's tough new birth-control campaign that aims to reduce China's rate of population increase to zero by the year 2000 by encouraging families to limit themselves to one child. Under the drive, each privnce and city has been awarded quotas for the number of babies they are allowed to sire per year, and the street committee then determines which families may use the quotas.

"We give first preference to couples without children," said Mrs. Tian, another energetic middle-aged woman street committee member I got to know. She took pride in her job and pointed out that she had helped establish a small cooperative for unemployed youngsters in her building making soles for shoes. She also made sure that elderly people in the building without children to support them got their small monthly welfare subsidies. But she took a firm attitude toward birth control.

"If a family already has one child, we ask them to wait at least four years before having another, or better, not to have a second baby. If a couple already has two children or more, we tell them not to have any more."

For those who agree to have only one baby there is a package of rewards: a monthly bonus of five yuan ($3.30) for each parent until the child reaches fourteen (or about 8 percent extra pay for an average urban worker), preference for their child in school enrollment, and, theoretically, the right to housing space normally allotted to a family of four.

Mrs. Tian was frank about how her street committee administered the program. "We assign a person to keep track of each woman's menstrual cycle. If someone misses her period and isn't scheduled to have a baby, we tell her to have an abortion. There isn't room for liberalism on such an issue."

In October 1982, the Chinese announced the results of the largest census ever conducted anywhere. The People's Republic of China totals 1,008,175,288 people, or nearly one-fourth of the world's population. This selection describes what the Chinese are trying to do to solve their vast population problem.

Family Planning
by Ruth and Victor W. Sidel

China's population policy has undergone numerous swings since the Communists took power in 1949. Due to increased and more equitable distribution of food, intensive sanitation, and other efforts to bring infectious disease under control, the combination of malnutrition and infection that kills so many people—particularly children—in poor countries was rapidly diminished. Mortality levels therefore fell sharply during the 1950s. At the same time an increase in marriages that had been postponed during the turmoil of the 1940s was followed by a sharp upsurge in births. There was consequently a significant rise in the rate of natural increase in the population of China by the mid-1950s. Although Mao and others within the government had dismissed birth control programs based on Malthusian fears as a program to "kill off the Chinese people without shedding blood," by 1956 birth control efforts were being promoted, though primarily in the urban areas. This effort was short-lived, since it was essentially terminated during the Great Leap Forward in 1958.

A second birth control campaign was begun in 1962 but had almost no impact on the rural areas and, apart from major cities such as Shanghai, only slight impact on the urban birth rate. This campaign was disrupted in 1966 by the Cultural Revolution. In fact, it has been reported that during the late 1960s young people in some areas took advantage of the relaxation of administrative controls over marriage to marry and a significant increase in the number of births followed.

The third nationwide birth control campaign got underway in the early 1970s, just after medical and other institutions were reorganized following the upheaval of the Cultural Revolution. Late marriage was promoted (ages 24 to 26 for women, 26 to 29 for men); two or three children were considered the maximum, popularized through the slogan "two children per couple are enough, three are the limit and four is too many"; and lengthy spacing between children was encouraged. Workers at all levels of the political system and at all levels of the health care system were mobilized to educate the population about Chinese citizens' obligation to China to limit their number of children and the consequent need for family planning.

Contraceptives of various types were made available free of charge, were distributed by the barefoot doctors and midwives in the rural areas and by the Red Medical Workers in the cities, and were freely available in pharmacies. The most frequently used methods, based on limited data, were condoms, intrauterine devices, and oral contraceptives. Diaphragms were used relatively rarely. Carl Djerassi estimated in 1973 that 15 million women in China used the pill, more women than in any other country in the world. Furthermore, the Chinese had introduced a low-dose combination pill at least five years earlier than its introduction in the United States. Inexpensive methods were used, such as dipping a square of rice paper into the contraceptive steroid and ruling off 25 small squares, one to be torn off and taken on each of the first 25 days of the month. Sterilization was also made easily accessible for both sexes but, as in all countries, the number of tubal ligations far exceeded the number of vasectomies. Abortion during the first trimester was free and easily available, but women were urged not to use abortion as a primary contraceptive method and to attempt to limit its use to contraception failures.

These efforts led to a significant further fall in birth rate, from about 27 births per 1,000 population in 1973 (already, of course, markedly down from a reported high of 44 per 1,000 in 1963) to 18 per 1,000 in 1979. The overall death rate remained fairly constant during the decade, despite a relative aging of the population, at about 6 deaths annually per 1,000 population (compared to 14 per 1,000 in 1953). The natural population growth rate (the difference between birth rate and death rate) therefore fell from 21 per 1,000 in 1973 to 12 per 1,000 in 1979.

Despite this remarkable achievement, when the Second Session of the Fifth National People's Congress met in June 1979 it was clear that China's population growth would still be enormous. New population projections calculated within China—a resumption of work that was said to have been interrupted during the Cultural Revolution—had become available. Data published in the *People's Daily* in March 1980 indicated, for example, that if an average of three children per couple were maintained, China's population (not including that of Taiwan), which was estimated at 970 million at the start of 1980, would reach 1.4 billion by the year 2000 and 4.3 billion (the total *world* population in 1980) by 2080. Projections, shown in the figure, were also made for a variety of other fertility rates. They showed, to take an example from the other extreme, that if the number of children born were reduced dramatically to one child per couple by 1985 and maintained at that level thereafter, China's population would continue to grow for another 25 years and peak at just over 1 billion in 2004; it would then begin to fall, down to 370 million, approximately one third of China's current population, by 2080. . . .

Faced with these projections, the National People's Congress in June 1979 decided to launch a massive campaign to promote the one-child family. On June 18, 1979, Premier Hua Guofeng stated, "The State demands that each couple should ideally have only one child and not more than two. To produce a third child is to violate the State regulations." Elaborate and varied incentives and disincentives have subsequently been developed to encourage couples of childbearing age to limit the number of their children to one. Couples who have had one child and then pledge that they will have no more are issued a "Planned Parenthood Glory Certificate" that entitles them to benefits in health care, housing, food allowances, and work assignments. Those who have two children will essentially break even; they will neither be rewarded nor lose benefits. Those who have three or more children after 1979, however, will lose benefits in a variety of ways. By late December 1979 the Chinese reported that over 4 million married couples of childbearing age with one child had pledged to have no more children and in January 1981 the number was said to be over 10 million. China's natural growth rate

Population Projections for China*

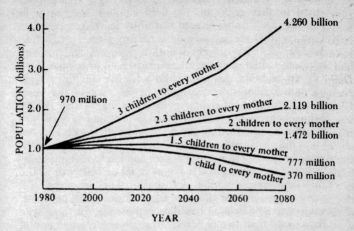

POPULATION (billions)

4.0

3.0

2.0 — 970 million

1.0

3 children to every mother — 4.260 billion

2.3 children to every mother — 2.119 billion

2 children to every mother — 1.472 billion

1.5 children to every mother

1 child to every mother — 777 million
370 million

1980 2000 2020 2040 2060 2080

YEAR

* Source: Gerard Chen: *Population Forecasts for China's Coming Century,*
Eastern Horizon 19 (4): 29–31, April 1980.

was reported as "less than 11 per 1,000" in 1980 and
eighteen provinces and municipalities had reduced their
growth rates to "less than 10 per 1,000."

The rewards for agreeing to have only one child vary
somewhat from city to city and from province to province.
While material rewards have received the greatest amount
of attention both in the Chinese and the Western press, in
part because the use of material incentives for this purpose
was such a departure from long-standing principles in
China, the importance of nonmaterial incentives should
not be minimized. In a society in which consensus, mass
support of public campaigns, particularly health campaigns,
neighborhood and workplace pressure to conform, and the
esteem of one's neighbors are of great importance, active
participation in an effort such as the one-child family
campaign brings the couple praise and recognition both
within their neighborhood and within their place of work.

According to the Committee for the Defense of Children,
a Chinese governmental group concerned with issues involving children and families, the material incentives offered
in Peking for those who have signed the "one-child pledge"

include a monthly stipend of five yuan from the birth of the first child until that child turns fourteen, living space equal to that given to two-child families or priority in housing, six months of paid maternity leave (compared to the usual fifty-six days of paid maternity leave), totally free medical care for the child until age seven, and priority when the child seeks admission to school or applies for a job. In addition, an only child who lives in the city is exempted from future assignment to work in the rural areas. In Shunyi County, a rural county in the Peking Municipality, the economic rewards include five yuan per month from the birth of the first child until the child is ten years old, six months paid maternity leave for the pregnant woman, priority in nursery school and kindergarten admission and in housing and a bonus of 60 or 100 yuan at the time the couple applies for the single-child certificate. Some areas—but not all—have adopted provisional penalties, subject to modification based on experience, for those who have more than two children. In some areas, for example, workers who have more than two children may not receive promotions or increases in pay. It has also been reported from some areas that for those couples for whom the cost of delivering children is paid by the state or by the parent's workplace the cost of having any child beyond two children must be borne by the parents. In addition, a third child may not receive subsidized medical care and there is a limit on the number of children from a single family who can attend a university simultaneously. Some of the penalties used in parts of China have recently been criticized; health workers have been urged not to resort to "coercion and commandism" but rather to focus on guidance and education. . . .

There is one major exception to the intensive campaign for population limitation in China, which is largely directed at its ethnic Chinese population, also known as the Han people, who comprise 94 percent of China's billion people. The remaining 60 million are divided among 55 groups referred to in China as "national minorities." For them the population policy is quite different, as stated by the Xinhau News Agency in 1977: "In areas inhabited by the minority nationalists, many of whom were once dying out, the policy is to encourage population increase . . . However, guidance is available for those who wish to limit the number of their children. . . .

In the next two selections, three Americans who have spent time in China discuss improvements in the lives of women since 1949, current marriage laws and customs, and the role of women in the changing economy of the 1980s.

Women and the Family in China Today
by Saundra Sturdevant

Whether as a daughter, daughter-in-law, wife, mother, or widow, the Chinese female lived in a state of dependence and subservience. As a child her feet were bound; as a teenager her marriage was arranged and she entered her husband's household (Chinese women married out of their village) as a vulnerable stranger; as a daughter-in-law she was expected to submit to the authority of all in the household, especially that of her mother-in-law, who supervised her work. Status in the family was gained through the production of sons. If a woman survived her husband, she fell under the authority of her in-laws or her sons. Her position is summarized by Fu Hsüan's poem:

> How sad it is to be a woman!
> Nothing on earth is held so cheap.
> No one is glad when a girl is born,
> By her the family sets no store.

Through the process of change and revolution, beginning before Liberation and continuing since the establishment of the People's Republic, the position of women in China has greatly improved. To assess these changes we must look at woman's relationship to the family, especially in the question of marriage, and at woman's relation to work.

The Family: Marriage was one of the main pillars of China's feudal system. Through its provisions, half of the population was in bondage, often literally. The Marriage Law of May 1, 1950, prohibited forced marriage, concubinage, bigamy, child betrothal, dowries, and interference with the remarriage of widows. It provided for marriage based on the free choice of both partners, equal rights for both sexes, and protection of women and children. Either party could initiate a divorce, but both parties had to agree to it. Both parents have the duty to support and educate the children, and each person is responsible for debts incurred during the marriage.

The social change promised by this broad new law was dramatic—one of the greatest changes ever made in the world in the legal status of women—but it was also threatening to many forces in China's traditional peasant society. Enforcement of the new marriage law was often difficult. Tremendous educational campaigns—including touring drama groups, newspaper articles, posters, leaflets, party pronouncements, and educational classes for cadres— were launched to publicize and enforce it in the early 1950s, but implementation was slow and resistance often great. For many years after Liberation arranged marriages remained the norm and divorce met so much opposition that deaths of women, either by suicide or homicide, after family disputes concerning marriage or divorce were a major problem. Yet in the process, hundreds of thousands of women won divorces, and the nature of the Chinese family began to change substantially.

Nevertheless, old feudal marriage customs die slowly. Reports of campaigns against arranged or forced marriage, dowries, and expensive weddings have continued through the 1960s and 1970s. Divorces remain difficult to obtain, and arranged marriages are still apparently the norm in the countryside, with the progressive feature that now the parties meet each other before the wedding. As in many societies, the urban areas offer women relatively greater freedom and independence, and arranged marriages are less common than in the countryside.

Work: In an agricultural society, land is the primary source of income. Traditionally, women were prohibited from inheriting or owning land. Responsible for all the work associated with the household, limited physically by bound feet, and continuously pregnant or caring for young children, women participated in agricultural labor only marginally. Women's field work accounted for approximately 13 percent of farm labor, depending upon the crop under cultivation (greater in the labor-intensive double-cropping rice areas), and the type of work which women did was secondary, mostly weeding. The Hakka women of southern China were the exception that proved this rule. Hakka women never had their feet bound, they participated significantly in field work, and they are known throughout China for their physical strength and for their participation in village affairs.

The Land Reform Law of the People's Republic provided that women and men should receive equal shares of land. But there were many obstacles to the development of an independent role for women in agriculture: women's lack of agricultural skills; differences of strength in a labor-intensive economy; women's lack of self-confidence; and direct male opposition. These problems were deep-rooted and their solution was piecemeal. Educational campaigns, training courses in basic agricultural skills, nurseries, and child-care facilities were developed, made possible by changes in the organization of agricultural production.

The progression of agricultural organization and development—from mutual aid teams to cooperatives to the communes of the late 1950s—also led to increased participation by women in labor. Simply put, the labor and skills of both men and women were needed to feed China's population and to provide the economic surplus for heavy industry. At the same time the women's associations began to point out that until women were full participants in the labor force they would not be able to win full participation in the social and political life of the country.

But contradictions remained: women were given fewer work points than men, at least partly because of their lesser physical strength; their work points were totaled with the family's, and men represented this joint family labor unit in work-team decisions; and women were increasingly caught in the classic double burden of housework and field work. Mothers-in-law often eased this burden by assuming household tasks, which freed the younger women to engage in agricultural labor but created even greater conflicts with the mothers-in-law.

Gradually these contradictions were lessened, if not completely resolved. In the mid-1960s the development of commune industry, designed to support agricultural development, provided increased opportunities for women to participate in labor. Light industry does not require as much physical strength, it is located in villages or towns (where child care can be shared and the home is more accessible), and it was new, without traditional roles. The Cultural Revolution also brought greater attention to women's health problems, including birth control, enabling women to devote more time to work and commune activities.

Urban Areas: Women's life in the urban areas has been markedly different from that in the countryside. At the time of Liberation the most important tasks in the cities were restoration of production and creation of political and social stability. Women's role in the creation of political and social stability was central. It was the working-class women who formed the core of resident or street associations in each urban area. These associations made house-to-house checks for rats, bugs, lice, and dirt, led vaccination and sanitation campaigns, administered relief, found employment, organized literacy and math classes, aided discharged soldiers and their families, counseled on marriage and divorce, ran kindergartens, and played an important role in security work by aiding new arrivals.

As part of the Great Leap Forward in the late 1950s, the associations formed neighborhood-based small-scale light industries, often in conjunction with previously existing heavy industrial plants in the area. The establishment of the neighborhood industries attempted to solve some of the contradictions endemic to women's labor: lack of technological skills, competition for employment with men, and prejudice against women working. Most of these light industrial plants have continued to be productive; many new plants have been established and some have developed into relatively large concerns.

Since 1949 the condition of women has greatly improved— no longer is it true of Chinese women that "nothing on earth is held so cheap." Women's role in the family and in the work place has changed substantially. There is widespread agreement in China that this is good, and that the worst inequalities of traditional society have been struggled against and overcome.

There is also considerable agreement that much remains to be done. Women hold *more* than half the sky: their burden is double, their pay is not equal for the work done, and the positions of responsibility they hold are not proportionate to their numbers. Critiques of the Gang of Four acknowledge many of these shortcomings. In other rapidly developing Third World societies, women—who have less education and fewer technological skills in the earliest stages of development—are often by-passed in training and promotion for technical/engineering and leadership roles. China has done a great deal to combat this pattern in the first three decades since Liberation, and the question now is what the next stage—the Four Modernizations— will mean for women's work and the position of women in future Chinese society.

Marriage
by Ruth and Victor W. Sidel

Women now receive equal pay for equal work (although hard manual labor still merits more work points than lighter manual labor) and are, therefore, not as dependent upon their families or their husbands as they once were. But the role of women is closely linked to the economy; when employment drops, women workers are the first to be laid off. The liberation of women, therefore, has been inextricably tied to the fluctuation of employment in China since 1949. While women work in a wide variety of jobs and seem to have gained a significant amount of power at the local administrative level, the number of women drops sharply at higher levels of government and Party structure.

The Chinese family today is most often three-generational; the most common pattern is still for the young couple to move into the husband's parents' home. Since virtually all women under retirement age work outside the home, grandparents play an important role in child-rearing and homemaking. In fact, the Chinese family can best be viewed as a minimutual aid group in which, as the Chi-

nese say, the old take care of the young and the middle-
aged take care of the old. But while the elderly have
retained much of the respect that was traditionally accorded
to them, they do not have the unquestioned power they
once had.

The vast majority of Chinese people marry, usually in
their early to midtwenties, and the divorce rate seems to
be exceedingly low. A new Marriage Law which went into
effect on January 1, 1981, stipulates that although later
marriage should be encouraged the minimum age for marriage is currently 22 for men and 20 for women, that
marriage must be completely voluntary, and that husband
and wife should enjoy equal status in the home. It also
maintains the mutual responsibility of family members by
stating that parents are responsible for rearing and educating their children and that children are responsible for
supporting and assisting their parents.

In addition, the new law stipulates that divorce should
be granted if one party insists, in cases of "complete
alienation" or when mediation has failed; this is a change
from the 1950 law which did not require the automatic
granting of divorce in those cases. Divorce is now becoming somewhat more widespread because of these new
regulations, especially in Chinese cities. The new law,
following the pattern of the old law, states that the husband may not apply for a divorce while his wife is pregnant
or within one year after the birth of a child.

Although both the 1950 and the 1981 Marriage Laws
state, "Marriage must be based upon the complete willingness of the two parties. Neither party shall use compulsion
and no third party is allowed to interfere," and "The
exaction of money or gifts in connection with marriage is
prohibited," there is evidence that arranged marriages and
the exchange of money or gifts remain widespread, particularly in the rural areas. In urban areas marriage is commonly
based on love and mutual attraction but in the countryside
it is more difficult for young people to meet and get to
know one another.

In some rural areas a go-between introduces the two
sets of parents; the parents then "consider how many
members in each family share the family income and
property, how many people in each family can work, and

its annual income before they ask their children's opinion."
If after the couple meet the man is satisfied with the
match, he will leave a gift, usually money; if the woman
accepts the gift, they are engaged. A survey of two rural
counties in Anhui Province in 1979 indicated that of the
14,586 marriages studied, 15 percent were by free choice,
75 percent were arranged but agreed to by the couple,
and 10 percent were arranged only by the parents.

Marriage arrangements appear to be less dependent on
the parents in the cities. In urban areas young people may
meet with the aid of a Marriage Introduction Service such
as the one affiliated with the Shanghai Shipping Bureau.
Interested individuals fill out a questionnaire, attaching a
photograph, and the Service attempts to introduce single
people to one another.

Getting married in revolutionary China is not inexpensive.
A recent survey of a typical village in the North China
province of Hebei indicates that it costs an average young
peasant male 3,000 yuan to marry, most of that money
earmarked for building a three-room home and buying
furniture. Betrothal gifts and the wedding banquet will
cost the groom's family at least another 1,000 yuan. After
the engagement, the young man is expected to give his
fiancée money for new clothes and sometimes a wristwatch,
a bicycle, and a washing machine. In Peking a television
set, it is said, has become de rigueur. Considering the fact
that the average peasant in China only earns from 100 to
400 yuan per year and the average beginning worker earns
approximately 50 yuan per month these gifts clearly represent a hardship for young men and their families.

While there have been efforts to democratize relationships within the family and to move away from rigid role
differentiation—men are being encouraged to participate
in housework and child-rearing as women have been encouraged to work outside the home—there is also substantial evidence that the revolution has actually strengthened
a "reformed version of the traditional peasant family."
According to a recent analysis of the modern Chinese
family, "Patrilocality, a semi-arranged marriage system,
and even a form of bride-price appear to be durable
survivals in postrevolutionary rural China. There are a
variety of indications that . . . this modified traditional fami-

ly system and the muted version of patriarchy that it supports, are strong, stable and remarkably unquestioned in the People's Republic of China."

Furthermore, the potential consequences of the new responsibility system in the rural areas on the role of women are as yet unclear. The establishment of an individual work point system at the time the communes were organized in the late 1950s provided women with independently determined income. Each worker, rather than each household, earned work points based on the kind and amount of work he or she performed. Women were therefore not necessarily economically tied to their husbands. Under the new responsibility system, the household as a unit contracts with the production team to farm a specific amount of land and to meet specific production quotas. It is ironic that while the Chinese are moving from collective responsibility for farming the land to individual household responsibility, they are at the same time moving from individual income calculation within the collective commune structure to income calculation for the household as a unit.

The production team negotiates with the head of the household (who is very likely to be the male adult) and, from published reports of areas in which the responsibility system has been tried, income and produce are earned by the household as a single unit rather than by individuals within the household. Will this system, if widely adopted, tie women even more closely to their husbands? Will they, once again, be working under their husband's authority? What will be the economic options for women who may wish to divorce their husbands?

The new responsibility system may, in addition, be in direct conflict with China's intensive drive to lower the birth rate. A household with several children would appear to have an even clearer economic advantage over one with the strongly recommended single child.

This selection discusses the changes in the educational system since the end of the Cultural Revolution and the death of Mao and the difficulties the Chinese face in obtaining higher education.

Education

by Fox Butterfield

Reverence for education, which dated to Confucius, made Mao's reforms of the school system one of the most contentious issues in China. Like some progressive American educators in the 1960s, Mao felt the schools had become too elitist, that they discriminated against children from less-advantaged families like those of peasants and workers. That was why he had abolished the college entrance exams and simplified the curriculum in the schools. To lessen the traditional authority of the teachers, which Mao also believed was elitist, he had encouraged student attacks on teachers. And to make education more practical, he called for combining study with work in the fields and factories.

But since his death, most Chinese agree Mao's experiments only ended up lowering standards. The New China News Agency stated in one sensational report that China now has 140 million illiterates, 120 million of them under forty-five. In another article, the *People's Daily* revealed that while 95 percent of Chinese children do start out attending primary school, as the government has long claimed, "in reality only 60 percent finish their five years of primary school and only 30 percent can be said to have reached the five-year primary school standard." The problem lies with the poor quality of rural schools, the severe shortage of government funds for them, and the continued belief among many peasants that it is more useful for their children to work in the fields than go to school. As a result, the Chinese school system, like many American schools, is turning out functional illiterates.

Education is also an emotional subject in China because along with membership in the Communist Party and promotion to the officer corps in the armed forces, it is one of the three main avenues for moving up in society. Competition for survival starts early. The Communists have rapidly expanded the number of schools—there are 210 million Chinese in school today. But 12 percent of those who finish primary school are unable to go on to junior high, and there is no room in high school for 50 percent of the students who complete junior high. At the top of this pyramid, only 3 percent of the college-age population in China, about a million students, can get into university. In the United States, by comparison, 35 percent of the population between eighteen and twenty-one are in college; 23 percent of young people in the Soviet Union go to college, and even in the Philippines, which has a total of 40 million people, there are 1.27 million college students, more than in all of China. The *Guangming Daily* groused that China ranked 113 out of a list of 141 countries in the world in percentage of its young people who get a post-secondary education.

This figure startled me, given the value Chinese place on schooling. The major reason is money. Peking has not released exact data for its expenditure on education, but some rough calculations can be made. The 1980 national budget for education, plus health, culture, and science, of which over half went to scientific research, was 14.8 billion yuan ($9.87 billion), or about $10 per person. The real total would be somewhat higher, since Peking requires the villages to finance their own schools out of local revenue. But another article in the *Guangming Daily* disclosed that in the late 1970s, after the downfall of the Gang of Four, the government invested only 1.12 percent of China's gross national product in education. That would put China about 110th on the United Nations list of spending for education, after such countries as Somalia, 2.7 percent, Guatemala, 1.7 percent, and Bangladesh, 1.2 percent. The United States invests 6.4 percent of its GNP in education, the Soviet Union, 7.6 percent. Chinese friends traced Peking's miserly appropriations to Mao's contempt for expertise and the Communists' failure to understand the role of technology in the modern world. Mao had derided intellectuals as "the stinking ninth category," after landlords, capitalists, and assorted other bad elements. The Chairman's view became national policy. "For quite some time," the *People's Daily* said in a revealing 1980 article, "some people considered education as an item of consumption that had no connection with production. When they thought of expanding production, they considered building factories, buying machines, constructing irrigation works. They seldom considered, or simply did not consider, the question of training people."

For the lucky few who do get into college, the rewards are immense. Unlike those young people who finish only junior or senior high school and may have to wait a year or two before being assigned to work in a neighborhood cooperative or at best a factory, they are assured some of the most prestigious jobs in China: as scientists, engineers, interpreters for the China Travel Service. "It is a lifetime meal ticket," said an affable professor at Fudan University in Shanghai who had been trained in the United States. "You have to realize that under our system, almost no one flunks out once they get into college. Professors just don't fail students. It would go against the idea of a guaranteed lifetime position once they make it into college."

The key to success, since Mao's death, is passing the national university entrance exams, twelve and a half hours of tests in six subjects spread over three days. In 1980, of the 3.3 million students who qualified through a preliminary screening process to sit for the tests, only 285,000 were admitted to college. Most were high school seniors, seventeen, eighteen, or nineteen years old, though there were a few people in their mid- or late twenties whose schooling had been disrupted by the Cultural Revolution or who had flunked earlier exams. Americans are familiar with the ordeal of taking the college boards—the competition, the preparation, the anxiety; but the Chinese exams involve even more tension. The very word for test in Chinese, *kao-shi*, resonates with a hallowed significance, evoking memories of the old imperial exam system where thousands of scholar-candidates steeped in years of study of the Confucian classics were locked in cubicals for several days at a time. Those who succeeded became the Emperor's mandarins. Exams to Chinese are almost a religious ritual, admitting priests to a cult, a kind of theocracy. . . .

One of the consequences of the return to a conventional exam system has been the open creation of the kind of elite that Mao abhorred. Just as in America, children from families with a higher standard of living and better educational backgrounds now have an advantage in getting into college. The New China News Agency conceded that of the entering class of 2,000 students at Peking University in 1979, 39 percent came from families of cadres and soldiers, though these two groups make up only 2.2 percent of the overall population. Another 11 percent of the freshmen were offspring of intellectuals, who constitute perhaps 2.5 percent of the population. Friends who taught at Peking University, however, cautioned that the situation was not really that different while Mao's reforms were in effect— the only change was that his successors were more candid about the figures.

The government also returned to the pre-1966 system of "key schools" in which it could concentrate its scarce resources on the individuals with the greatest intellectual potential to provide the economy with talent in the speediest, most efficient fashion. . . .

Ever since 1949, graphic arts in China have been affected by government policies.

Art

by John Gittings

The images of art in the Chinese Cultural Revolution were bold, affirmative political statements about Mao Zedong's "New Socialist Man". In propaganda posters issued in print runs of up to a million, workers and peasants always smiled as they effortlessly built bridges or levelled the land—unless they were "smashing the class enemy", when their faces became stern and pitiless. Youth was a cheerful girl bus driver cleaning her windscreen, a barefoot doctor picking herbs in the countryside, students with backpacks making their own Long March to see Chairman Mao.

Traditional artists had been condemned by Jiang Qing (Mao's wife) for their "gloomy pictures" and forced to clean out lavatories with other Chinese intellectuals. But in villages and factories groups of amateur artists began to produce their own posters, woodcuts, and papercuts collectively, illustrating with rough enthusiasm the contrast between China's Bitter Past and her Present Happiness.

Today, with the Cultural Revolution officially regarded as nothing but ten years of disaster (1966–1976), arts belong to a different world—where economic modernization is the goal, and traditional pine and bamboo art is back in favor. Satellites and space-ships fill the air in the new propaganda posters. And the atomic symbol is held aloft, replacing the Red Lantern (a popular motif from one of Jiang Qing's revolutionary operas) and the Little Red Book. The faces are mostly serious too. Students are no longer depicted marching into the countryside. Wearing spectacles again (symbols of the bourgeois bookworm during the Cultural Revolution) they comtemplate a sky filled with logarithmic signs beneath the Leninist slogan: "Study, Study and Study Again!"

Mao first formulated the rules for socialist literature and art in his famous *Talks to the Yan'an Forum* in May 1942. Young intellectuals fleeing from Chiang Kaishek's censorship trekked into the barren highlands of Mao's northwestern stronghold to join the revolution. Mao welcomed them but soon made it clear that revolutionary society makes its own demands upon the artist.

Literature and art, said Mao, must be "subordinate to politics" and must "serve the people," providing the cultural cogs and wheels for the machine of revolution. What ordinary people needed, Mao said, was not "more flowers on the brocade" of China's elegant high culture, but "more fuel in snowy weather" to provide cultural warmth in a language they could understand.

This imposed on the Chinese artist a set of rules which, when rigidly interpreted by Communist Party bureaucrats (as in the four decades since then) have restricted and confined. Yet Mao also encouraged Chinese artists to discover what until then had been ignored—the rich traditions of folk art and oral story-telling, which had always been regarded as "common stuff" by the pre-revolutionary elites.

This inspired Chinese woodcut artists to relearn their art in the villages from peasants' woodblock prints that used to be pasted up at the Chinese New Year. Musicians and writers similarly turned to the dance rhythms and ballad metres of the rural areas. A new directness of style began to bridge the gap between intellectual and peasant....

What went wrong during the Cultural Revolution, in art as in all other fields, was the "one hundred and ten percent" insisted upon by the cultural bosses. In Beijing (Peking), Jiang Qing personally inspected every line of the handful of "model" revolutionary operas and plays allowed on stage.

The result was the strange blend of innovation and conformity that I saw in 1976 at the Nanjing Fine Arts College. Young graphic artists there, like Chinese students everywhere, "went down" to the countryside or factory floor for their inspiration. . . .

But the peasant paintings of Huxian country in Shaanxi province offer an example of the sort of propaganda overkill which undermined the Cultural Revolution. In Huxian, and many other places, local art had been encouraged during the Great Leap Forward of the late 50s. New People's Communes had extended the collective concept to culture and education as well as agriculture: art classes were organized at night schools and the meaning of socialist cooperation was depicted in everyday terms—digging a new well or shifting loads of pig manure to make the fields fertile.

Huxian became the national model for peasant art and an exhibition of the best (and politically most correct) works went on international tour. A two story gallery was built in the small county town with a hotel and restaurant behind it for foreigners and high-level Chinese officials.

In Huxian . . . I discovered that the little gallery is now regarded as an extravagance. Huxian's unique collection of peasant paintings is being casually sold off to stray tourists at prices between 50 and 300 *yuan* ($30–$180), calculated quite arbitrarily as the visitor goes around. Wall murals in the villages are fading too—vanishing because they cannot be sold.

Peasants still paint at evening classes, and their style is still arresting. But now they paint contemporary themes of modernization and the good life—hairdressers, furniture shops, new houses. "What will happen to these new pictures?" I asked. The best will be chosen for exhibition in the Huxian art gallery—where they may catch the wealthy tourist's eye.

The values of the market place are now regarded, not as

an invitation to "restore capitalist practices," but as a healthy component of the socialist economic system. Intellectuals are no longer obliged to go to the countryside, and the difference between mental and manual work is now officially justified as reflecting a "natural" division of labor. And so the gap between elite and popular art reappears and widens.

Once again the scholar artist paints his traditional mountain landscapes, no longer obliged to place a hydroelectric dam in the foreground. Meanwhile the peasant artist can rediscover the traditional woodblocks of centuries old pre-revolutionary Door Gods and Hearth Gods, or cut new blocks from faded original prints. No one is any longer obliged to show proletarian modesty by not signing a work of art and presenting it as the product of a collective group.

There is a positive side too. Chinese art magazines—closed during the Cultural Revolution—now offer examples of foreign art and a forum for Chinese artists to discuss previously unmentionable topics such as abstract art.

In Beijing, the city's art gallery has allowed the "Single Spark" group of young experimental artists to stage two shows. In a culture where Abstract Expressionism is hardly known, and even Impressionism remains controversial, much of their work is inevitably derivative—here a sort of Picasso, there something like Munch—and to the Western critic simply second-rate. But it is a phase through which the Single Spark artists have to work if Chinese art is ever to break free from the stultifying traditions of "national painting". "Today the only new continent lies within ourselves", says their manifesto. "To discover a new angle, to make a new choice, that is an act of exploration."

Yet these are but a small urban elite—or counter-elite. Art reflects life, and the great majority of Chinese people now look towards the billboards and the press, where political slogans and propaganda posters have been replaced by advertisements of another kind.

Young ladies of vaguely Eurasian appearance fondle pots of face cream or flourish badminton racquets. Medical panaceas are recommended by the kindly faces of traditional Chinese doctors with wispy beards. These more commercial images, along with rockets, spaceships, and megalopolitan visions of the future, now appear widely in popular magazines and in the work of school children and other amateurs.

A poem by a "spare-time artist" in Shanghai, displayed outside a workers' club next to his sketch of the busy Nanjin Road, sums up the new mood:

Oh, multicolored spread of advertisements.
Smilingly stretched along the ten league road.
Citizen quartz watches; Phoenix face cream,
Victory Song TV sets; Turtle shirts...
You are a set of bright medals on the chest of Shanghai!
You are a branch of flowers hanging over our new road,
In the colors of China's new spring of the 1980's!

Art, said Mao, must serve revolution. Now in China it serves the policies of modernization and the growing consumerism of a society which feels it has been poor long enough. These are familiar—perhaps inevitable—cultural phenomena in the Third World. We wait to see whether a "socialist" developing country can offer more.

Feeding her vast population has historically been one of China's most difficult problems. Today's government utilizes a complicated coupon rationing system for all food, household necessities, and consumer goods.

Rationing

by Fox Butterfield

Before 1949 the Chinese had long practiced a form of petty corruption that foreigners call "squeeze," demanding a little extra money or a cut of any deal before it is consummated. The Communists claimed with pride they had eradicated such malfeasance. But the very nature of the Chinese Communist economy and its inefficiencies—the shortages, the endless waits in line, the shoddy quality of goods—reproduced "squeeze" in a new guise, the back door. In 1957, when the population of China stood at 600 million, the *People's Daily* reported, there were about one million stores in China, grocery shops, bicycle repair shops, laundries, barbers, cobblers. But by 1981 the population had swollen to one billion, an increase of 400 million, almost equal to the total of the United States and Western Europe combined, yet the number of stores had shrunk to only 190,000. The rest had fallen victim to the Communists' distaste for private enterprise and zeal for unified central control. In Peking alone the number of restaurants plummeted from 10,200 in 1949 to 679 in 1981. Mao had proclaimed, "Serve the People," a slogan emblazoned on the walls of thousands of offices and stores. But less than 10 percent of the Chinese work force are employed in the service industry compared to 48 percent in the United States and 42 percent in France and Japan. For Peking had decided to copy the Soviet model of industrialization and put emphasis on the expansion of heavy industry, like steel, rather than on agriculture, consumer goods, and housing. This produced glamorous annual statistics of growth in the gross national product and added to the leaders' sense that China was becoming a modern industrial power. But it did not keep up with the needs of a swiftly growing population. It was a costly mistake in priorities avoided by other nations in the region, including Japan, South Korea, and Taiwan.

To cope with the resulting shortages, the Communists have devised a rationing system so Byzantine in its complexity that many Chinese themselves are at a loss to understand it. In Peking people have to carry as many as seven or eight different types of coupons and ration booklets, explained Fuli, a soft-spoken woman factory worker with a weathered face and prominent teeth. First, she said, is your grain ration book, in a red plastic cover; new pages for it are issued each month by your local government grain store, if you are a legal resident of the neighborhood and have a valid household registration. The Communists have added to the intricacy of the rationing system by an egalitarian attempt to tie a person's food allotment to the energy they expend in their work. Fuli herself, as a worker in a musical instrument factory, got thirty-five catties a month (a catty is 1.1 pounds, or half a kilogram). Her father, a cadre, got thirty-one catties, since his work is less physically taxing; her younger brother, a construction worker, got forty catties. Infants get six catties a month, she said, with the maximum of sixty catties for men tending blast furnaces in steel plants. In Peking, she added, people get 50 percent of their grain ration in wheat flour (northern Chinese prefer noodles and steamed bread to rice), 20 percent in rice, and 30 percent in coupons good for buying bowls of rice or noodles in restaurants. The first time I went out to eat with Chinese I was surprised when the waiter asked them for their grain coupons before accepting their orders. As a foreigner, I was exempt. If a Chinese cadre is sent on a business trip, there are special national grain tickets which he has to use on trains or in restaurants outside his hometown.

In effect, the system means that any time you go out and get hungry, you have to have your grain coupons with you as well as cash. . . .

Next come a series of separate coupons: for cooking oil (a catty a month in Peking, but as little as two ounces a month in Yunnan), for cotton cloth (sixteen feet seven inches a year, in Peking), for coal, and for cooking gas. Since 1979 meat has not been rationed in Peking, but in some other provinces the allowance is as little as a pound or two a month.

In addition, each neighborhood state grocery shop issues another type of ration booklet. It includes monthly allotments of soap, sugar, bean curd, corn starch, some types of fish, and several Chinese delicacies like sesame paste and vermicelli noodles made from green beans.

Finally, Fuli explained, her factory gave each worker four industrial coupons each January good for purchasing manufactured products. Two or three of these coupons could buy enough wool to knit a sweater; half a coupon was necessary for some brands of tea. Ten industrial coupons, two and a half years' worth, were required to make the most important purchase of all, a bicycle, as indispensable to a Chinese as a car to twentieth-century Americans. But that was not all. To buy a bike you also had to have a special bike purchase coupon. In her factory, Fuli said, out of every one hundred workers, only two were given these treasured certificates each year.

"The chance to buy a bike is so important to us," she said, "that when a new worker is assigned to the factory, the first thing they do is go to the quartermaster to put their name on the bike list. Some of my friends who already have bikes of their own register their names on the list again when they have a baby. That way, by the time their kids are in their teens and old enough to need a bike, they will be able to get one.

"If you lose your coupons, it is a real disaster," Fuli continued, contorting her face into a grimace. Once a friend of hers had all the family's coupons in an envelope and his wife threw them out by accident. The government wouldn't replace some of them till the next year; but in Chinese fashion, their friends and colleagues chipped in and shared some of their own coupons. It was the kind of generosity I was to witness several times.

An astonishing example of the rationing system is that to buy a light bulb a Chinese has to turn in his old one. Each bulb bears a serial number—those used in factories are different from those intended for home use, and those sold in Peking are marked with a different sequence from those in other places. That way, you can't cheat and bring in a light bulb from any place but your home. If your bulb is stolen, you have to get a letter from the police before you can replace it.

In a developing country like China with a population of one billion, some rationing may be essential to prevent inequalities, Chinese I knew conceded. But Fuli saw another purpose to the government's program. "It's really a way to control you," Fuli remarked. "If you don't have the proper residence certificate, you can't get your ration cards, and, without them, you can't live."

After Mao's death and the arrest of the Gang of Four in 1976, Deng Xiaoping began to consolidate his power and implement his Four Modernizations policy. The shift in political direction encouraged urban workers and intellectuals to hang wall posters (on "Democracy Wall" in Beijing) that publicly attacked the excesses of the Cultural Revolution and Mao Zedong himself. Some even went so far as to criticize the Chinese communist system as a whole. In the spring of 1979, the Deng government cracked down on this movement, arresting many of the dissidents. In the following selection, historian John Israel discusses the dissident movement and China's attitude toward the concept of human rights.

Human Rights

by John Israel

The smashing of the Gang of Four and resurrection of Deng Xiaoping produced a sense of euphoria and gave rise to unrealistic expectations in many areas of Chinese life. In the economic realm, visionary planners drew up blueprints based upon resources that simply were not there. In the political realm, young men and women dared to act upon the conviction that the Gang's downfall would open the way to an overall democratization of Chinese politics.

The planners went back to the drawing board. The human rights advocates went off to jail. . . . Focal point for political protest was Beijing's Democracy Wall at the Changan Jie-Xidan intersection but the movement was by no means confined to Beijing; it encompassed at least thirty organizations and publications in some half dozen cities. In addition, issues raised by the young dissidents were discussed in the official press and among government and Party cadres— albeit in more subdued tones. . . .

Just as the struggle for human rights was not limited to freedom of speech, press, assembly, and due process of law, neither were tactics confined to the written and spoken word. During the cold Beijing winter of 1978–79, the Democracy Wall publicists were but the tip of an iceberg, the bulk of which consisted of thousands of ordinary men and women who flocked to the capital to beseech China's highest leaders to rectify wrongs perpetrated by their underlings.

Significantly Ms. Fu Yuehua, who supported and marched with the petitioners, was the first activist to be arrested. The event shocked her comrades and demarcated the early euphoric phase of protest from the later angry phase. An extreme example of the latter is Wei Jingshen's essay, "What is Wanted: Democracy or New Despotism?" which raises the ultimate question of the regime's legitimacy and suggests that only freely elected representatives of the people have valid claim to political power. . . . Wei Jingshen emerged as the most radical and articulate of the young rebels—if not necessarily representative of the mainstream of their opinons. Now serving a fifteen-year prison sentence, he is also the movement's most famous martyr. . . .

If human rights are conceived as absolutes, based on natural law, there is little support in China's heritage for the values incorporated in the first amendment to the U.S. Constitution. Chinese tradition offers a few examples of rulers who permitted intellectual controversy and many of brave subjects who risked life and limb to struggle for the right to speak out—but Chinese tradition denies human rights advocates the kind of sustenance that Western thinkers draw from the Judeo-Christian tradition, the Greco-Roman heritage, the Enlightenment, or the liberal-humanitarian thought of the 19th and 20th centuries. "Liberalism" can be identified in the Chinese political tradition only if we give the word an unacceptably broad definition of "principled resistance to unrestrained authority." Members of the Enlightenment Society were close to the truth when they lamented that "the words 'human rights' cannot be found in China's history—not in two thousand years, not six thousand years, nor eight thousand years." . . .

In the eyes of many Chinese, a liberalism that takes as its point of departure the moral autonomy of the individual is still regarded with suspicion, as a foreign import. Natural rights doctrine denies a fundamental precept of Chinese political thought: that individual rights (or, more accurately, individual interests) must be subordinated to the needs of the group. Chinese liberals, therefore, are hard put to reconcile their cry for individual freedom with the priorities of the body politic.

How do Chinese human rights advocates attempt to justify themselves to their fellow citizens and (more important in the short run) to their rulers? . . .

Since modernization has become a virtually sacrosanct precept in China, anything that can be sold as "modern" stands a better chance of moving public opinion and winning official approval. If democracy somehow can be seen—like science and technology, industry, agriculture, and defense—as an irreducible feature of the modern world—a "fifth modernization"—then a China intent upon becoming a modern state should adopt democracy. The problem is that the regime's ultimate reason for pursuing the Four Modernizations is not simply that they are modern but that they are essential to the building of a strong state.

It is hard to demonstrate that human rights are essential to the building of state power or to material and military modernization. In fact, from the point of view of China's rulers, a contrary series of propositions seems more logical: (1) modernization requires unity; (2) human rights activists threaten to undermine unity with dissent and agitation; (3) therefore, human rights run contrary to modernization. This syllogistic reasoning has been devastatingly effective, first, because it appeals to Chinese principles of unity, order and harmony (especially in vogue since the Cultural Revolution); second, because it invokes sentiments of national loyalty and patriotism, irrefutable arguments for modern Chinese; and because it is backed up by a state monopoly of police and judicial power....

By the fall of 1981, the wave of suppression that began with the destruction of the underground press, the outlawing of the Democracy Wall, and the arrest, imprisonment, or disappearance of human rights activists was moving toward a new crest with the campaign to tighten the permissible limits of literary expression and to reassert the ideological authority of the Party. The campaign to vilify liberal ideas has sometimes attained a stridency equal to that of the Cultural Revolution. For example, in the September 21, 1981 issue of *Beijing Review*, Vice-Minister of Culture Chen Huangmei blasted writers who "resort to bourgeois human feelings, humanism and human rights; eulogize the abstract dignity of humanity, the value of man, human freedom, and the position of mankind."...

The Government and Economy Under Deng Xiaoping

The direction of China's development since the death of Mao has been marked by abrupt shifts and major changes in economic policies. At the end of 1976 not only was Mao gone, so also were Zhou Enlai and many others of the Yan'an-period old guard. The new leadership that took control of the party and government was, if not young in age, of a different outlook. Since consolidating their position, the group headed by Deng Xiaoping has proved determined to shift China's economic policies away from accepted "Maoist" doctrines and toward decentralization and incentives designed to improve productivity. China clearly remains communist, yet the Deng reforms conceivably could, if pursued successfully, produce a Yugoslav- or Hungarian-style economy. What cannot be predicted is whether the Deng policies will prevail.

Deng Xiaoping
*by John Gittings**

Politically Deng is a very tough character who is unique among the Chinese leadership in having risen twice from political death in the space of the last five years.

During the Cultural Revolution Deng was denounced by the Red Guards as the "Number Two Party Person in Power Taking the Capitalist Road," second only to Liu Shaoqi (Liu Shao-chi). Then after a return to authority in 1973-76 he clashed with Mao's wife, Jiang Qing (Chiang Ching) and the rest of the populist leadership now known as the Gang of Four. This time he was labelled as an "Unrepentant Capitalist Roader" who was responsible for the "Right Deviationist Wind" which sought to undo the achievements of the Cultural Revolution. He returned to power a second time in the spring of 1977 only months after Mao Tse-tung's death and the overthrow of the Gang. . . .

Deng's commitment to the modernisation of China is shared by most of his generation of revolutionary leaders, men and women who spent 20 years and more living and fighting in hardship before the Liberation, and who feel strongly that socialism should be an age of plenty, not poverty.

Because of his later experience as Party Secretary-General, Deng has been too easily type-cast in the West as the arch-bureaucrat of China. In fact he has a long and distinguished record in the revolution.

After the 1927 split between Chinese Communists and

Manchester Guardian Weekly, Jan. 21, 1979.

Nationalists, Deng worked for two years underground in Shanghai, then helped form one of the original Red Armies in Southern China. He took part in the Long March (1934–35) as head of the Political Department in the First Army Corps—then led by Lin Piao. Throughout the anti-Japanese War (1937–45) he served as the Political Commissar of the 129th division of the main Communist Eighth Route Army, fighting a guerrilla war in and around the Taihang mountains—a key area of north China.

In 1938 Deng met an American military observer, Evans Carlson, who described him as "short, chunky and physically tough," with a mind "as keen as mustard." Carlson was also impressed at the extent of Deng's information "over the entire field of international politics."

For Deng, like Chou En-lai but unlike Mao Tse-tung and many other home-bred revolutionaries, had also had experience abroad. Born in 1904 Deng spent five years (1920–25) in France on a work-and-study scheme for Chinese students, and was active first in the Chinese Socialist Youth League and then in the Communist Party which he joined in 1924. On his way home to China he studied for several months in Moscow, though he never became one of the "Returned Bolsheviks" who were groomed in the Soviet Union to run the Chinese Party and clashed with Mao in the 1930s.

By the end of the Chinese Civil War (1946–49) Deng was Party Secretary of the Second Field Army, one of the five Communist armies which liberated China. His talents as an administrator and fixer were quickly recognised and he became Secretary-General of the Party as early as 1954.

Men with this sort of experience do not take kindly to criticism from young "revolutionaries" who were still wearing slit pants at the time of the Liberation. They are also more likely to treat others of their generation, even including Mao, as their equals. Deng's relationship with Mao was stormy but almost until the end the Chairman seems to have accepted, reluctantly, Deng's talents. "See that little man there," Mao told Khrushchev in 1964 according to the Russian leader's memoirs, "he is highly intelligent."

Later Mao complained that Deng had for years failed to keep him properly informed as Chairman of the Party. "He treated me like his dead ancestor," said Mao. In October 1966, Deng made an abject self-criticism where one cannot help detecting a note of expediency. (Liu Shaoqi was firmer—his critics called him more stubborn—and maintained that everyone in the leadership, including Mao, was open to criticism.)

"I have become accustomed to lording it over others and acting like something special, rarely going down among the people or even to make the effort to contact cadres (officials) and other leaders to understand their working situation and problems," said Deng in his self-criticism.

He described himself as an "unreformed petit-bourgeois intellectual who has failed to pass the tests imposed by socialism," and confessed that he had not been "a good student of Chairman Mao." Deng then disappeared from public view for the next six years, until 1973, when he was reelected to the Party's Central Committee. But it must have been Mao who personally approved the choice of Deng, on his return to the leadership, to be his spokesman on foreign affairs. It was Deng who at the United Nations General Assembly in April 1974 unveiled Mao's "Theory of the Three Worlds."

Deng's second self-criticism, made in April 1977, after Mao's death, was a good deal more perfunctory. He declared that he had "done some good work" in 1975— before his dismissal after the Tienanmen Incident*—though he had some "short-comings and had made mistakes."

Deng clearly feels that he has little to apologise for this time. Indeed his current popularity stems not from the past, but from his emergence in the last years of the Cultural Revolution as the only man prepared to take on the Gang of Four. In the summer of 1975 Deng quite deliberately declared war upon this ultra-left group in the Party who persisted in putting the class struggle and the political goals of the Cultural Revolution ahead of China's economic requirements. He called them "sham Marxist political swindlers" and announced his intention of purging them from the Party.

"These anti-Marxist class enemies," it was stated in the first important document (the General Programme of Work) which Deng inspired, "have stepped into the shoes of Lin

---

*Mass demonstration in the main square of Beijing in memory of Zhou Enlai and in support of Deng's policies. Force was needed to put down the crowd in April, 1976.

Piao" (Mao's former "chosen successor" who had died fleeing China in September 1971).

"They take over our revolutionary slogans all the time, distort them, twist them and appropriate them for their own use, mix up black and white, confound right with wrong. Thus they have confused the thinking of some of our comrades and some of the masses, and confused the organisation of the Party in some places and units, splitting the Party, splitting the working class and splitting the ranks of the masses."

The events of 1976 including the Tienanmen Demonstration of April, Mao Tse-tung's death in September, and the ousting of the Gang of Four by Hua Guofeng (Hua Kuofeng) in October, can only be understood if we realise that the political battle was a two-sided affair in which Deng Xiaoping had declared war first.

And Deng engaged the enemy with the sort of sarcastic and sometimes scatological wit which only the most confident can afford, riling the Gang where he knew it would hurt most, just as Monkey in the legend hunted the demons and ghosts before striking them down.

The Gang and their followers, as Deng described them more than once, were the sort of people who would "sit on the lavatory and not do a shit." The young ex-Red Guards who had been recruited into the Party under their radical banner were "political helicopters," spiraling up the ladder of promotion into jobs for which they were incompetent.

"There is a group of people who want to make their name by criticising others," said Deng contemptuously. "They climb up on other people's shoulders to get themselves on stage."

And he mocked the campaigns led by the Leftists to focus upon the political or "superstructural" aspects of building a Socialist society, to "restrict the bourgeois rights" which still exist in such a society where differentials have not yet been eliminated. "There are some people," he commented in September 1975, "who say it is raining when they hear the wind, just as if it was something big." Who cares, argued Deng, whether some people are not "red" or politically pure, so long as they do a decent job of work to help modernise China. . . .

The Chinese are quick to tell you that "Stability and Unity" is a slogan which was raised by Chairman Mao

Tse-tung himself in 1974. But it was Deng who took it over and elevated it to take precedence over the "class struggle" which Mao always put first (and it was Mao who criticised him for doing so).

At the moment a large number of Chinese, jaded by the factional politicking into which the Cultural Revolution degenerated, will agree with Deng's interpretation. But they will also want to see results from the policy of the Four Modernisations for which, they are told, stability and unity are essential.

The more that the Chinese people are reminded that their country has stagnated economically in the past ten years, the more they will expect changes for the better soon. This is the new standard which Deng has raised and which, if he remains politically active into the 1980s, he will have to match with goods in the shops and cash in the workers' and peasants' pockets.

The following selection by Deng Xiaoping outlines the Chinese modernization plan of the late 1970s known as the Four Modernizations of agriculture, industry, national defense, and science and technology. The economic reforms have been sweeping and potentially revolutionary. Deng's program was calculated to modernize China on almost a crash basis. Trade with the West was to be increased dramatically, and the basis for major industrial complexes was to be imported whole. However, China's planners realized that China had neither the infrastructure for assimilating and using these plants nor money to pay for them, and these plans were largely scrapped. Only in the area of petroleum is development proceeding rapidly.

The Four Modernizations
by Deng Xiaoping*

In order to make China a modern, powerful socialist country by the end of the century, we must work and fight hard in the political, economic, cultural, military and

---

Documents of the First Session of the Fifth National People's Congress of the People's Republic of China (Peking: Foreign Languages Press, 1978).

diplomatic spheres, but in the final analysis what is of decisive importance is the rapid development of our socialist economy.

At the Third National People's Congress and again at the Fourth, Premier Chou, acting on Chairman Mao's instructions, put forward a grand concept for the development of our national economy which calls for the all-round modernizations of agriculture, industry, national defense and science and technology by the end of the century so that our economy can take its place in the front ranks of the world. By the end of this century, the output per unit of major agricultural products is expected to reach or surpass advanced world levels and the output of major industrial products to approach, equal or outstrip that of the most developed capitalist countries. In agricultural production, the highest possible degree of mechanization, electrification and irrigation will be achieved. There will be automation in the main industrial processes, a major increase in rapid transport and communications services and a considerable rise in labour productivity. We must apply the results of modern science and technology on a broad scale, make extensive use of new materials and sources of energy, and modernize our major products and the processes of production. Our economic and technical norms must approach, equal or surpass advanced world levels. As our social productive forces become highly developed, our socialist relations of production will be further improved and perfected, the dictatorship of the proletariat in our country consolidated, our national defence strengthened, and our people's material well-being and cultural life substantially enriched. By then, China will have a new look and stand unshakably in the East as a modern, powerful socialist country.

The ten years from 1976 to 1985 are crucial for accomplishing these gigantic tasks. In the summer of 1975, the State Council held a meeting to exchange views on a prospective long-term plan. On the basis of a mass of material furnished by investigation and study, it worked out a draft outline of a ten-year plan for the development of our economy. . . .

According to the plan, in the space of ten years we are to lay a solid foundation for agriculture, achieve at least 85 percent mechanization in all major processes of farmwork, see to it that for each member of the rural population there is one mu of farmland with guaranteed stable high yields irrespective of drought or water-logging, and attain a relatively high level in agriculture, forestry, animal husbandry, side-line production and fisheries. The plan calls for the growth of light industry, which should turn out an abundance of first-rate, attractive and reasonably priced goods with a considerable increase in per capita consumption. Construction of an advanced heavy industry is envisaged, with the metallurgical, fuel, power and machine-building industries to be further developed through the adoption of new techniques, with iron and steel, coal, crude oil and electricity in the world's front ranks in terms of output, and with much more developed petrochemical, electronics and other new industries. We will build transport and communications and postal and telecommunications networks big enough to meet growing industrial and agricultural needs, with most of our locomotives electrified or dieselized and with road, inland water and air transport and ocean shipping very much expanded. With the completion of an independent and fairly comprehensive industrial complex and economic system for the whole country, we shall in the main have built up a regional economic system in each of the six major regions, that is, the Southwest, the Northwest, the Central-South, the East, the North and the Northeast, and turned our interior into a powerful, strategic rear base.

China's Political Pendulum
by Ruth and Victor W. Sidel*

Since the autumn of 1976 Chinese politics has been characterized, according to one observer, by "a consensus within the leadership to depart from Mao's revolutionary radicalism and to promote the program of 'four modernizations,' i.e., the modernization of industry, agriculture, science and technology, and the military." As part of Deng's consolidation of power and his emphasis on pragmatic modernization programs, he and his supporters have

*The Health of China

attempted to destroy what they call the "cult" of Mao and to dilute Mao's ideological authority. Recent statements [1981] in *Renmin Ribao (People's Daily)* have described Mao as a "great Marxist" but as only one of dozens of outstanding Chinese leaders, "including Sun Yat-sen, Confucius and Genghis Khan." In a recent article in the *Liberation Army Daily* a senior Communist Party official evaluated Mao's role over the years. While the late Chairman was charged with having pushed "socialist revolution and socialist construction" too far and too fast, with having followed policies that led to "great disorder" during the Cultural Revolution and with having lost "contact with the day-to-day life of the masses," the article urged that he be judged with "compassion, love and respect." "Defaming Chairman Mao can only demean the party and our socialist motherland," the article continued. In May 1981 Huang Hua, China's Foreign Minister and Deputy Prime Minister, stated that the current consensus of party leaders is that while Mao made mistakes, such as his initiation of the Great Leap Forward of 1957–1958, he was a "great Marxist and a great revolutionary who was the first to combine the universal principles of Marxism with the concrete conditions of the Chinese revolution." The "consensus," according to Mr. Huang, is that Mao's contributions were primary and his mistakes secondary.

Since the spring of 1978, Deng has been promoting a new ideological tenet which is essentially one of pragmatism: "practice is the sole criterion of truth." In essence this means that a policy is correct if it produces positive results. Perhaps the clearest expression of Deng's pragmatic ideology is his now famous remark made in 1962 that he did not care whether a cat was black or white so long as it could catch mice. According to a recent analysis, "Deng's clarion call is to 'seek truth from facts.' In a system in which party and state constitutions have sanctified Marxism–Leninism–Mao Zedong Thought as the guiding ideology, the idea that Deng has been trying to foster is truly iconoclastic and revolutionary." In conjunction with efforts to promote a new ideological framework Deng has attempted to gain control of the main decision-making bodies by purging Maoists and others opposed to his policies. Despite opposition from Hua and others, Deng has been able to purge many of those who had collaborated with the

Gang of Four and to consolidate a network of support both at the national and provincial levels. After the Third Central Committee Plenum in December 1978 it was clear that Deng was the most powerful leader in China and the primary architect of China's modernization policies and programs. In June 1981 Deng's consolidation of power was further realized as Hua was replaced as Chairman of the Chinese Communist Party by Hu Yaobang, a protégé of Deng's, and Deng himself was named Chairman of the Party's Military Commission, which controls the army.

The current phase of China's development strategy stems from the December 1978 meeting of the Communist Party, during which principles of "readjustment" were adopted. This process has been described as "a major readjustment of the economic relations between the state, the collective and the individual." Official statements in 1981 gave the governmental view that China's plan for economic growth developed soon after the fall of the Gang of Four was overly ambitious and that future plans must be more realistic. China is now openly examining its "previous mistakes, backward methods and outmoded beliefs and practices left over from 'feudal' thinking."

The current official goal is to establish priorities among the economic sectors—agriculture to be given first priority, light industry second, and heavy industry third. Economic management is being transferred from administrative units to economic organizations and the role of market forces is being widely debated. Some Chinese economists are suggesting a greater interplay between central planning and market forces in the hope that local initiative will be more greatly stimulated. At the same time there has been a shift toward smaller economic units, such as breaking down what were viewed as relatively large units at the commune and production brigade level, and a more flexible policy that would take into account local strengths and regional differences of climate and natural resources. One consequence of the smaller units and decentralized planning is that some localities will develop faster than others, exacerbating the already existing differences between relatively affluent and poor areas. Some 3,000 enterprises have been given a larger measure of self-management, and it has been reported that the Chinese have examined the Yugoslav system of worker-management.

During the 1976–1977 period there was a startling policy shift toward importing foreign technology, utilizing foreign loans, and developing heavy industry. Since 1978 emphasis has shifted somewhat from the "microchips with everything" plans for modernization toward what appears to be a more realistic and self-reliant approach of modernizing existing enterprises. For instance, one of the most important symbols of the Four Modernizations policy, development of the huge Baoshan Steelworks near Shanghai, was postponed in 1980, after construction had already begun, because of a shortage of foreign currency, inadequate planning, and a lack of raw materials.

With the current stress on material rewards and the raising of incomes of both peasants and workers, increased production of consumer goods and improved housing and other elements of daily living are being emphasized. The proportion of heavy industry to light industry will be altered in favor of light industry. In Shanghai, for example, the emphasis will be on "sectors requiring technical expertise, precision and skills, areas of high technology involving relatively lower consumption of energy, imposing less of a burden on transportation and not requiring massive inputs of raw materials with which the municipality is not well endowed." In contrast, the province of Anhui, which has little industry and is rich in natural resources, will significantly increase its development of heavy industry.

In agriculture, which has been given highest priority in China's most recent modernization plans, the focus is now on mechanizing those areas in which farm machinery can be used to greatest advantage and encouraging further modernization through a combination of state financial assistance and local efforts. To maximize local input into rural development, communes and brigades are being encouraged to raise their own development funds, in part through increasing the output of their local factories. Peasants are being given greater freedom to choose the crops they will grow, and a new agricultural "responsibility system," adopted since Deng Xiaoping's victory at the Party's Third Plenary Session in December 1978, sets responsibility for crop goals and production at far lower levels of social organization—including the household and individual level—than ever before. Intended to raise the peasants' agricultural production by providing individual

and family incentives, the new agricultural policy also
supports the extension of peasants' private plots and the
reopening of free markets in the city and countryside.

Current Chinese development policy has led to an
increased emphasis on technical expertise over political
consciousness—an emphasis on being "expert" over being
"Red." It has led to a new frankness about the extent of
the damage due to natural disasters—such as 1980 droughts
in Hebei Province and floods in Hubei Province—and
requests for foreign aid from the International Red Cross,
the United Nations, and Western countries. It has also led
to increased foreign trade with the United States, Japan,
and other countries and to a markedly increased exchange
among scholars between China and the United States and
with other countries.

The changes instituted by Deng Xiaoping extend beyond the
economy and into many areas of public and private life,
including the legal system. China has no independent judiciary,
and there are very limited human rights compared to the
West. In China, for example, one is not presumed innocent
until proven guilty. The current trend toward a fairer legal
order is examined here by Fox Butterfield. Jiang Qing and
the "Gang of Four," mentioned below, were a political group
that lost out in the power struggle following Mao's death.
Jiang is Mao's widow.

The Legal System
by Fox Butterfield

When they emerged from years of exile or prison after
Mao's death and returned to power, Peking's current leaders like Deng Xiaoping clearly had a personal stake in
preventing a recurrence of the trauma of the Cultural
Revolution. They also knew that the persecutions of the
past decade had shattered popular confidence in the
Communist Party. So one of their first priorities was to
create a more equitable system of justice, or restore
"socialist legality," in their own term. Hence in 1979 the
Communists promulgated China's first criminal code since
1949. It promised that trials would be public; it prohibited

the courts from using forced confessions as evidence; it gave defendants the right to a lawyer—the legal profession had been abolished in 1958—and it fixed strict limits on the time the police could detain suspects before bringing them to trial. Ominously, however, the new criminal code and a revised constitution passed in 1978 made no provision for judicial independence. Instead, the constitution reaffirmed that "the Communist Party of China is the core of leadership of the whole Chinese people" and that "citizens must support the leadership of the Communist Party." In other words, the Party is the law. And while China's tiny group of 2,000 lawyers was allowed to come out of the closet, the National People's Congress in 1980 passed regulations declaring them to be "state legal workers" who must "protect the interests of the state" as much as their clients. They should not act like their counterparts in the West and get bogged down in arguing against the prosecution. China's chief prosecutor gave an indication of how Peking regarded the new legal system when he disclosed in 1980 that 95 percent of all those arrested in the past year had been convicted. In essence, for those people who have been arrested and undergone police examination, by the time they get to trial innocence is no longer an issue. The question is, were the proper procedures followed to prevent arbitrary arrests, frameups, and torture. That was what the Chinese people hoped.

The trial of Jiang Qing, her cohorts in the Gang of Four, and five senior generals who had been associated with Lin Biao was to be the showpiece of the new legal system. The trial carried high risks—it couldn't help but look like personal vengeance and it would give Miss Jiang a political platform she had not had since her arrest in October 1976. But, friends said, Deng believed the trial would demonstrate to Chinese that he would not stoop to the low road the radicals had taken in dealing with their adversaries and he wanted to win back popular support from many disillusioned Chinese. . . .

When the verdict finally came—after a month's delay to allow the Politburo time to debate the sentence—it was almost an anticlimax. Jiang Qing and Zhang Chunqiao, the two who refused to confess, were sentenced to death, but with a two-year reprieve to see if they reformed. The two-year stay of execution is a Chinese Communist legal innovation. The other eight defendants were given prison terms ranging from sixteen years to life. Some Chinese considered the verdicts fair, since Mao was really to blame and it was time to exorcise the ghost of the Cultural Revolution. But other Chinese I knew grumbled; to them it was another example of the Communists' double standard—one set of rules for the masses, another for Party members. . . .

New Attitudes Toward the Chinese Communist Party
by Fox Butterfield

Peking's leaders are acutely aware of this growing disenchantment with their rule. Few Communist regimes have been as blunt about recognizing their own faults. The *People's Daily* in 1980 called it "a crisis of faith" in Marxism. The paper, which is distributed nationally with a circulation of 5.3 million, blamed it on distortions of Marxism by the Gang of Four and the appearance of "some new situations and new questions" for which Marxism does not yet have an answer. Among these, the paper said, is the problem of why capitalism has not yet collapsed, as Marx had predicted, and why most socialist countries are poorer than capitalist ones. These were questions most Chinese I knew were already asking among themselves.

The Party's theoretical journal, *Red Flag*, confessed in another 1980 article, "The Party's prestige is not high—this is a fact." Echoing Lord Acton's dictum that power tends to corrupt, *Red Flag* suggested there may be a "basic difference between a ruling party and an underground or nonruling party. What is the danger to a party after it has assumed power? The danger is that it will degenerate if it works carelessly. After it has assumed power, the party cannot order the masses and must not become the rulers and the ruling class of the old society." It is theoretically possible for a Communist party to degenerate into a fascist party, the journal added. "This is a very serious problem."

The Party seemed to hope that such candor would help recoup its declining prestige. In 1980 and 1981 the

Communists also took several steps to try to return to their earlier, more democratic and popular ways. Peking called for an end to the system of lifetime tenure which allowed senile patriarchs to keep their posts in the Party, the government, or the army no matter how infirm or incompetent they became. It instituted limited local elections for people's congresses, the first since 1949. It promulgated China's first criminal code since Liberation to create a more equitable system of justice. And it installed a new team of leaders, including Hu as Party Chairman and Zhao Ziyang as Prime Minister. They succeeded the hapless Hua Guofeng, whose major claim to legitimacy was that a dying Mao had told him "With you in charge, I'm at ease."

Even among the country's leaders there is a ferment, an uncertainty, about what Marxism means for China. "We are having trouble defining what our system is," an official in Yunnan province, in the southwest, told an American diplomat visiting there. "We are trying a number of experiments. Those that work, we will call socialism. Those that don't, we will call capitalism."

Deng Xiaoping himself has defined Marxism simply as the principle of "seeking truth from facts." As a corollary to that, he has added, "Practice is the sole criterion of truth." Some older cadres I met abhorred this as reducing socialism to mere pragmatism.

Perhaps to help compensate for the reduced appeal of Marxism, Deng has dusted off the old nationalistic slogan of the reform-minded mandarins of the late nineteenth century who wanted to modernize China to catch up with the West. Their goal was to make China *fu-qiang*, or "rich and strong." In a 1980 meeting with a Rumanian delegation, Deng said concisely, "The purpose of socialism is to make the country rich and strong." At bottom, that is what most Chinese I knew really wanted out of communism.

During 1981 and 1982, Deng Xiaoping strengthened his control of the Communist Party and state machinery. The long-awaited Party statement on Mao Zedong symbolized Deng's victory, as the replacement of Mao's chosen successor, Hua Guofeng, with Deng's protégé, Hu Yaobang, cemented that achievement.

Deng's Consolidation of Power
by David Bonavia

The sixth plenum of the 11th Central Committee, which met [in Beijing] from June 27–29, 1981, was one of the really crucial meetings in 60 years of the party's history and 32 years of Communist rule. The very ease with which it was carried out, once it was assembled, indicated how meticulous the preparations for it were, and how long it took to put together. . . .

To the surprise of no one, Hua Guofeng, Mao Zedong's nominated successor for the leadership of the Chinese Communist Party, was toppled from his position with barely a nudge. But though accused of such serious errors as trying to foster a personality cult around himself, Hua was allowed a face-saving place in the leadership with the rank of vice-chairman, albeit the lowliest of the six holding this title.

Hua was also accused of trying to oppose Vice-Chairman Deng Xiaoping's pet slogan "practice is the sole criterion of truth." But he was given credit for his role in helping to overthrow the Gang of Four in 1976 when he was premier and acting chairman. The plenum—delayed fully six months since the original date for its convocation—replaced Hua with Hu Yaobang, a strong supporter of Deng and hitherto secretary-general of the party. . . .

Hu Yaobang, the new chairman of the Chinese Communist Party, sees eye-to-eye with his ally and sponsor, Vice-Chairman Deng Xiaoping, in more ways than one. They are both the same height, around 5 ft.

But there the resemblance ends. Deng is rugged-featured and often looks grim. Hu is lively, almost birdlike, and smiles easily. Hu, aged 68 or 69, is Deng's junior by seven or eight years. . . .

Hu's experience has been mostly in work with the Communist Party's Youth League until it was virtually disbanded and he was purged (not on grounds of age, but of politics) in the Cultural Revolution. Since then he has made a measured comeback, obviously under Deng's patronage, to his exalted role as party chairman.

Born in Mao's native province of Hunan, he is believed to have taken part in the 1935 Long March as a youth leader.

After 1949, Hu made a successful career as a party administrator in Deng's native province of Sichuan. In the 1950s he was a member of delegations which visited East European countries, and has been active in united front work with other national communist parties, with further short spells of provincial administration. . . .

Just as the accession to the Party chairmanship of Hu Yaobang represented the shift of power to Deng concretely, the issuance of a lengthy Party statement on Mao was a potent symbol of change. The document effectively rewrites the history of the entire Communist period. In particular, by criticizing Mao's Great Leap Forward and Cultural Revolution policies, the statement gives ideological support for Deng's political and economic programs. In addition, it coincides with the apparent widespread revulsion among ordinary Chinese toward Mao's mass campaigns. A new constitution adopted in December 1982 further reinforced Deng's new direction.

Reassessing Mao

by David Bonavia

A nearly 20,000-word document issued after the sixth Central Committee plenum [June, 1981] contains some of the most stinging and uncompromising denunciations of the late chairman Mao Zedong's leadership yet printed in Peking. But it also gives him full credit for his early revolutionary role and his practical and theoretical contributions. The document—the most important historical text to be published for many years—says Mao succeeded in rescuing the Chinese Communist Party and the Red Army at two critical points—in the 1927 encirclement campaign by the Kuomintang, and during the 1935 Long March when the Zunyi conference firmly established his leadership.

But on Mao's role in the Cultural Revolution, in the last decade of his life, the report is uncompromisingly hostile, calling the entire movement a "long-drawn-out and grave blunder." It dates Mao's serious errors from 1957 and the anti-rightist movement he launched then after the Hundred Flowers campaign. Mao and other leaders had become "smug about their successes, were impatient for quick results and over-estimated the role of man's subjective will and efforts." It goes on: "The Great Leap Forward and the movement for rural people's communes were initiated without careful investigation and study and without prior experimentation."

Deng Xiaoping has seen his life's work come to fruition with the Chinese Communist Party endorsing at its 12th congress the aims and work-style which he has long stood for. A mere six years after the death of Mao Zedong, the party has repudiated some of the old chairman's best-known ideas as well as the methods of government he evolved in the last tumultuous decade of his life. The congress, which started on September 1, 1982, passed new statutes for the party constitution, aimed at making it more democratic and less self-serving.

The congress rubber-stamped the work report of Hu Yaobang who, as secretary-general, leads the 39-million-member party. Hu's report—delivered on September 1 and filtered out on successive days until the release of the full text on September 7—dwelt heavily on the need for practical solutions to China's problems and on the party's guiding—not dictatorial—role. How far the party will follow these unimpeachable intentions is another matter, which only time will make clear. . . .

Hu announced that from the second half of 1983, party members would have to be re-registered—a polite way of describing a nationwide purge of dishonest, over-age or inept cadres, and especially those who rose to power on the leftist surge of the Cultural Revolution.

The secretary-general, who will have the power to convene and preside over sessions of the politburo, gave a realistic appraisal of the state of the Chinese economy, not pulling any punches when he spoke of waste and inefficiency. Words like "appalling," "rather low," "shortage and strain," "lagging behind," and "backward" fell often from his lips. . . .

[Hu] announced no drastic changes of course for the sixth five-year plan (1981–85), but confirmed that present policies would continue, especially the liberal responsibility systems in agriculture. But he gave a warning that productivity must rise faster than incomes if China were to develop and grow.

The 1982 Constitution
by David Bonavia

For nearly three decades, China's constitutions have been a barometer of its political and social climate. The forecast after the most recent one—adopted on December 4, 1982—is for mild, sunny weather, with overcast patches. The more than 3,000 delegates to the fifth session of the fifth National People's Congress (NPC) predictably approved the draft of socialist China's fourth constitution, as presented by Peng Zhen, the top authority on legal and constitutional affairs.

Among its most notable innovations is the creation of the post of president of the republic, which vanished with the last incumbent, the late Liu Shaoqi, in 1967. It is evidently quite a strong post, though not as strong as an American president. The new constitution has also created a Central Military Commission which becomes a state organ. The new basic law states that China is "a socialist state under the people's democratic dictatorship led by the working class and based on the alliance of workers and peasants." Members of the NPC, provincial and local congresses are elected in pyramid style.

The constitution addresses itself early on to the question of ethnic minorities. Any discrimination against minorities is forbidden, as well as "acts that instigate their secession"—a surprising possibility for the drafters to have considered. Everyone, including every member of the Communist Party, is enjoined to obey the laws as defined by the NPC, and no organisation or individual may be above the law.

The removal of political power from the People's Communes is laid down in Article Eight, which also guarantees the peasants' right to farm land over and above the fulfilment of procurement contracts. Urban land belongs to the state, while rural and suburban land belongs to collectives, principally village-level production teams, unless the state decides otherwise. The right to lawful inheritance and to ownership of earned income, savings and houses is underlined. Article 18 supports the right of the state to let foreign enterprises and individuals invest in China. . . .

The constitution is clearly intended to win public support in China through its relatively liberal provisions for the defence of civic and ethnic rights, on paper at least. It is closer in spirit to the first constitution, promulgated in 1954, though mellow even by comparison with that. The second constitution, passed in 1975, was leftist, and vague about political institutions. It was scrapped in 1978 in favour of a draft which pointed China along its present road, but was perfunctory and paid more lip service to the "thought of Mao Zedong," now omitted except for a single reference in the preamble.

As with the constitution of all totalitarian states, the latest one must be treated with caution. Its fundamental weakness is that it does not spell out the electoral processes at the bottom of the pyramid. The entire edifice from there upwards is plainly open to mutual back-scratching on a massive scale.

The People's Liberation Army takes a big step down in prestige and political power. Article 29 says the tasks of the armed forces "are to strengthen national defence, resist aggression, defend the motherland, safeguard the people's peaceful participation in national reconstruction, and work hard to serve the people. The state strengthens the revolutionisation, modernisation and regularisation of the armed forces in order to increase the national defence capability." . . .

Alluding to the problems of Taiwan, Macau and Hong Kong, the new constitution says the state "may establish special administrative regions when necessary." This is in line with the softer tone being taken recently by the Chinese leaders over Hong Kong.

On religion, the document states: "No organ, public organisation or individual may compel citizens to believe in, or not to believe in, any religion, nor may they discriminate against citizens who believe in, or do not believe in, any religion." In an obvious reference to the Vatican's attempts to assert its authority over the Catholic church in China, it adds: "Religious bodies and religious affairs are not subject to any foreign domination."

According to the constitution, only public security organs may arrest Chinese citizens and then only with the approval of a procurator or court. Unlawful house search is banned. The privacy of correspondence is decreed, but "to meet the needs of state security or of investigation into criminal offences, public security or procuratorial organs are permitted to censor correspondence in accordance with procedures prescribed by law."

Citizens supposedly have the right to make complaints or criticisms of state functionaries or organs, without threat of unfair retaliation. Article 42 lays down the duty of Chinese citizens to work—which will raise a hollow laugh among the several million unemployed young Chinese. Family planning is laid down as a duty though it is detested by some three quarters of the population in rural areas.

Since 1949, China has gone through a series of dramatic changes in its relationships with the Soviet Union, the United States and the rest of the world. Harry Harding, associate professor of political science at Stanford University, reviews the history of the People's Republic's foreign relations.

China's Foreign Policy
by Harry Harding

Seen through Western eyes, Chinese foreign relations over the past 30 years have shown great change and volatility....

Radical Aligned State

In the 1950s, China could best be described as a country interested in defending its newly completed revolution against threats both at home and abroad. After it extended its power nationwide in 1949, the most pressing tasks facing the Chinese Communist Party (CCP) were the consolidation of political control over the world's most populous country and the initiation of a program of socialist transformation and sustained economic development. Both of these goals had significant international implications. The consolidation of political power required that the new regime ensure its security against the two external forces that seemed determined to eliminate it; the Nationalist government on Taiwan and the Nationalists' ally in Washington. Socialist transformation and economic development required that Beijing seek capital, technology, and advice from abroad, particularly from the more advanced Communist nations.

These imperatives led China into an alliance with the Soviet Union. Under this arrangement, Moscow developed a program of economic and technological aid to China that one American scholar has described as "the most comprehensive technology transfer in modern history." The USSR also provided extensive military assistance to Beijing, including the extension of its nuclear umbrella over China, the export of weapons and military doctrine to help modernize the Chinese armed forces, and the development of the PRC's capacity to produce its own conventional weapons. The degree of trust between the two countries at the height of their alliance was reflected in a 1957 agreement on nuclear cooperation, in which the Soviet Union may have agreed to provide the PRC with a sample atomic bomb and the technical data concerning its manufacture. In return, Beijing agreed to align China with the socialist camp, acknowledge (and, at crucial points, promote) the Kremlin's leadership of that camp, and coordinate China's foreign policy with that of the Soviet Union.

Yet, China never seemed completely comfortable with this alignment with the Soviet Union. For one thing, it was not the first choice of a number of leaders of the CCP, including both Zhou Enlai and, at least for a time, Mao Zedong. The relationship between Moscow and the Chinese Communists during the CCP's struggle against the warlords and against Nationalist government had been quite strained, with Stalin repeatedly giving his Chinese comrades unwise and self-serving advice. As a result, by the mid-1940s, some Chinese Communist leaders were hoping for some kind of accommodation with the United States that would allow a victorious Communist movement to take a more balanced position between Washington and Moscow, gain access to American capital and technology, and reduce the chances that the United States would take a hostile position toward a Communist government in China.

Furthermore, while the Soviet Union was generous to

China in many ways—particularly in its willingness to help the PRC develop nuclear weapons—Moscow also struck a hard bargain in its relations with Beijing. In exchange for the military alliance of 1950, Stalin demanded, and received, continued privileges in China, including the formation of four joint-stock companies and the retention of Soviet port facilities and naval bases in Dairen and Port Arthur. During the early 1950s, complained the Chinese, the Soviet Union gave China no economic grants, insisted that Beijing pay for all the economic and military assistance it received, interfered with China's economic plans, and sought to integrate the PRC into a "socialist international division of labor." And once Nikita Khrushchev began to speak of "peaceful coexistence" with the United States at the 20th Congress of the Communist Party of the Soviet Union in 1956, Beijing began to worry that Moscow might choose to sacrifice Chinese interests for the sake of improving its relations with the United States.

Thus, even during this period of alliance, China gradually began to stake out a somewhat more independent foreign policy, focused on attempts to weaken the American strategic position in Asia by undermining U.S. ties with the smaller developing states in the region. In the early 1950s, Beijing supported national liberation movements in Asian countries aligned with the West, providing large amounts of military and economic assistance to Viet Minh forces in French Indochina, and rhetorical support and small amounts of material aid to Communist movements in Burma, Malaya, and the Philippines. Later in the decade, China sought to improve its relations with virtually all independent Third World governments, in the Middle East as well as in Asia. Through China's "Bandung Line," named after the conference of Asian and African governments in Indonesia in April 1955 at which it was announced, Chinese leaders tried to persuade Third World governments to adopt a position of neutrality in cold war rivalries and to attenuate their political and military ties with the United States.

These actions, however, did not make China a truly revolutionary state. Essentially, Chinese foreign policy during this period was defensive: it aimed at discouraging the smaller countries of Asia from participating in the American strategy to isolate China diplomatically and economically and to encircle it militarily. China certainly did not accept the international status quo, but it had not yet launched a frontal challenge against it, as it would begin to do in the early 1960s.

Radical Nonaligned State

By the end of the 1950s, serious tensions had emerged in Sino-Soviet relations. The Chinese had become convinced that the model of development they were importing from the Soviet Union was inappropriate to Chinese conditions, but their attempt to break away from the Soviet model, through the Great Leap Forward, led the Kremlin to order the withdrawal of Soviet advisers from China. A Soviet proposal in 1958 for a joint naval fleet in the western Pacific confirmed Chinese suspicions that Khrushchev wished to establish control over the Chinese armed forces. And lukewarm Soviet support for China in the Quemoy crisis of 1958 and the Kremlin's indecisiveness in the Sino-Indian border conflict of 1959 also seemed to justify Beijing's concern that the Soviet Union would compromise its support of basic Chinese territorial interests for the sake of either avoiding conflict with the United States or improving its relations with nonaligned states such as India.

While the formal Sino-Soviet alliance would remain in effect until its expiration in 1980, the actual relationship between the two countries deteriorated rapidly. Trade between the two countries dropped markedly; the Chinese accepted no further credits from Moscow and spared no effort to pay off their outstanding debts ahead of schedule. While the Soviet Union continued for a time to sell some conventional military equipment to China, Khrushchev renounced his earlier agreement to assist China in developing its own nuclear weapons.

The main arena of the Sino-Soviet split, however, was in the realm of polemics between the two Communist parties. Even though China continued to claim membership in the socialist bloc, it began to express its opposition to a wide range of Soviet initiatives, especially Moscow's "revisionist" package of domestic policies and its policy of peaceful coexistence with the United States, which Beijing claimed was nothing less than a disguised attempt by the two superpowers to share global hegemony. At the same time, each side vied for the leadership of the international Communist movement: the Soviets attempting to drum China out of the Communist camp and to extend their influence in the Third World; the Chinese trying to mobilize Communist parties against the USSR and to exclude the Soviet Union from participation in conferences of Third World states.

Yet, the emergence of the Sino-Soviet dispute did not produce a rapprochement between China and the United States. Throughout the 1960s, and particularly as American involvement in the Vietnam conflict grew, Beijing still regarded Washington as the most dangerous imperialist power and the major threat to Chinese security. Thus, instead of shifting its alignment from the Soviet Union to the United States, China pursued an independent foreign policy. With relations with the United States frozen, and those with the USSR in decline, China sought to develop diplomatic ties with Western Europe, achieving success in 1964, when it established formal relations with Gaullist France—the first European nation to recognize the People's Republic since the early 1950s. In the security sphere, Beijing became convinced that it could take on both superpowers simultaneously by making preparations to fight a "people's war" against foreign invasion and by developing its own independent nuclear capability, which it achieved in minimal fashion with the explosion of its first atomic bomb in October 1964.

But the main theme of Chinese foreign policy in this second period was a radical attempt to mobilize the Third World to join an international united front against both superpowers, and against the international system they allegedly dominated. Accordingly, Beijing adopted a more strident and disruptive policy, encouraging Third World countries to support Indonesia's call for the creation of a new United Nations, organized around the "newly emerging forces" of the developing world; to refuse economic assistance from the Soviet Union and the United States; to support national liberation movements working against the remaining colonial and apartheid regimes in Africa; and to oppose the partial nuclear test ban treaty that had been negotiated by the Soviet Union, the United States, and Great Britain. China also began to provide greater support for revolutionary movements in countries whose governments refused to recognize the PRC, voted against Beijing's admission to the United Nations, or maintained close military and political ties with the United States.

Chinese efforts, however, did not yield many results. China simply did not have the military or economic capability to provide large amounts of assistance to most national liberation or revolutionary movements, except the one in Vietnam. And the issues around which Beijing chose to construct its united front—opposition to the United States, to the Soviet Union, and to all pro-Western developing countries—were not attractive to many Third World governments. . . .

Revolutionary Isolationist State

With the advent of the Cultural Revolution in late 1966 and early 1967, Chinese foreign relations underwent a further radicalization, reflecting the heightened radicalism of Chinese domestic politics. That radicalization, which was reinforced by the chaos in China's foreign affairs bureaucracy, produced a nearly complete break of China's international diplomatic and economic ties. In the early part of the decade, China, though independent from the two superpowers, had been actively involved in world affairs; at the height of the Cultural Revolution, the PRC turned almost completely inward, isolating itself from the rest of the world. . . .

Chinese policy toward the Third World was redefined in ways that made the qualifications for membership in the united front against the United States and the Soviet Union even more restrictive than in the early 1960s. Beijing thus stopped making appeals to established Third World governments, choosing to regard all of them as little more than political instruments of American imperialism and Soviet revisionism. Even relations with North Korea became strained, as Red Guards accused Kim Il-song of "revisionism"; and practically the only governments with which China remained friendly were those of Albania and North Vietnam. Beijing encouraged Maoist insurgents to carry out armed struggle against the governments of virtually every developing country, in order to create "storm centers of world revolution" throughout the Third World. In an analogue to China's own Communist revolution—

and in accordance with the Maoist doctrine reemphasized by Lin Biao in 1965 in his "Long Live the Victory of People's War"—armed insurgents were to seize control of the "countryside" of the world, surround the developed "cities," and thus cause the collapse of both the Soviet Union and the West.

Reformist Semi-Aligned State

By the end of the 1960s, however, Chinese leaders concluded that the international isolation produced by the Cultural Revolution was becoming increasingly dangerous. Throughout the latter part of the decade, both China and the Soviet Union had reinforced the military forces deployed along their common frontier, thus introducing a military element into what had originally been a political and polemical conflict. Ultimately, in 1969, the two sides engaged in serious armed clashes over several small islands in the Ussuri River, which separates Chinese Manchuria from Soviet Siberia, as well as at other points along the Sino-Soviet frontier. Those clashes, plus the precedent of the Soviet intervention in Czechoslovakia in August 1968, raised the possibility of a large-scale Soviet attack against China, in the name of preserving socialism in Beijing.

At the same time, the Chinese also concluded that the changing tide in the Vietnam War was producing a major shift in the international balance of power, away from the United States and toward the Soviet Union. It was clear to the Chinese leadership that the United States was losing its stuggle in Vietnam and had decided to disengage from the conflict. And a new American administration, under Richard Nixon, seemed willing to seek an accommodation with Beijing as a means to bolster what the Chinese considered a deteriorating U.S. strategic position.

In this context, China began to redefine its foreign policy in the early 1970s, taking three initiatives that departed sharply from the isolation and radicalism of the Cultural Revolution. First, over the opposition of some of China's military commanders as well as of the radicals who had come to prominence during the Cultural Revolution, Beijing began to explore the possibility of an accommodation with the United States. The rationale for this policy lay in the need to stabilize the situation along the Sino-

Soviet frontier and to create a new global alignment to contain the Soviet Union, which Chinese leaders viewed as rapidly becoming more ambitious and more powerful. Second, again over the opposition of leftist leaders at home, Beijing abandoned the radicalism that had served it so poorly throughout the 1960s, in favor of a kind of international reformism more in harmony with the thinking of most Third World governments. Instead of an international revolution, China began to propose sweeping, but more moderate, changes in the international political and economic order, becoming, in short, a vigorous proponent of a "new international economic order" (NIEO). Third, the PRC rejected the economic autarky characteristic of the Cultural Revolution period and began to resume active commercial transactions with the rest of the world, particularly with the West. But largely because of the concern of radical leaders with the danger of economic dependence on foreigners, the types of economic relationships in which China was willing to engage remained severely limited. The PRC would never accept, it was said, foreign loans, foreign investment, or imported consumer goods.

Chinese foreign policy in the early and mid-1970s was summarized in the "theory of the three worlds," formulated by Mao Zedong in February 1974 and presented publicly by Deng Xiaoping in a speech before the United Nations General Assembly two months later. According to that doctrine, the main characteristic of international affairs was the growing resistance of the developing countries (the Third World), supported by the more developed countries of Eastern and Western Europe and Japan (the Second World), against the economic and political "hegemonism" of the two superpowers (the First World). All Second and Third World countries, regardless of their social or political systems, were welcome to join Beijing in a united front against these two superpowers. Opposition to hegemonism—rather than "people's war" or "armed struggle"—was now viewed as the essence of a "progressive" foreign policy.

Theoretically, therefore, China still considered both the United States and the Soviet Union as adversaries. But Beijing subtly incorporated its partial alignment with the United States into its formal foreign policy doctrine, first by reversing the order in which the two superpowers were listed so that the Soviet Union always appeared before the United States, and then by explicitly declaring that the Soviet Union represented the more "ferocious" and "treacherous" of the two.

Conservative Aligned State

Developments both at home and abroad led to the further moderation of Chinese foreign policy in the late 1970s. The purge of the "Gang of Four" in October 1976, one month after the death of Chairman Mao Zedong, removed the leaders of the opposition to alignment with the United States and to expanded economic relations with the West. The establishment of formal diplomatic relations between Beijing and Washington in December 1978 seemed, at least temporarily, to eliminate the Taiwan issue as an obstacle to the further improvement of Sino-American relations. And the continuing expansionism by the Soviet Union and its allies—exemplified by the Vietnamese invasion of Cambodia in December 1978 and the Soviet invasion of Afghanistan one year later—raised the threat of a Soviet diplomatic and military encirclement of China. As a result, Chinese leaders introduced significant modifications into each of the three initiatives that had been adopted in the early and mid-1970s, in ways that produced a closer alignment between China and the United States, and that gave the impression that China had become, for all practical purposes, a status quo power. . . . Moreover, China seemed to drop the United States from its list of hegemonic powers, leaving in that category only the Soviet Union and such proxy states as Cuba and Vietnam. While Beijing never said so formally, some Chinese scholars implied that the United States had, in effect, been so weakened by its experience in Vietnam that it was no longer an active imperialist power, but had fallen, like Britain and France before it, into the ranks of the Second World.

Whatever Beijing's informal assessment of American intentions and capabilities, it was clear that China was now willing to move into closer alignment with the United States on a number of issues. The two countries began to consult on a wide range of regional and global questions of common concern and to devise parallel or coordinated policies on such issues as Indochina and Afghanistan. They also initiated a limited cooperation on security problems, with the United States agreeing to relax its restrictions on the export of military technology to China, and China agreeing to establish a joint surveillance facility to monitor Soviet missile tests. The United States noted its interest in a "secure and strong" China, and Deng Xiaoping spoke, just before his visit to the United States in early 1979, of the need for China, the United States, Japan, and Western Europe to build a strong anti-Soviet united front.

Neither side expressed any interest in creating a formal military alliance comparable to the Sino-Soviet alliance of 1950, seeming satisfied to remain, in the words of the Carter Administration, "friends, rather than allies." But the two countries began increasingly to speak of their parallel international objectives and common foreign policy interests and worked to narrow (or at least to tone down) their differences on remaining points of disagreement. All this amounted, if not to an alliance, at least to a reasonably close alignment between Beijing and Washington.

Finally, in the economic sphere, China significantly relaxed restrictions on commercial relations with the West, having concluded that its economic and scientific modernization could be promoted better by cooperation with the West than by self-reliance. The Chinese therefore began to explore a variety of economic relationships with the West that had previously been proscribed, including joint ventures with foreign investors; management consulting contracts and licensing agreements with foreign firms; technical assistance from intergovernmental organizations; and loans from commercial banks, foreign governments, and international financial institutions. . . .

Reformist Independent Leanings

By the beginning of 1983, however, the policy of close cooperation with the United States seemed to be undergoing significant modification. . . .

To begin with, serious strains developed in Sino-American relations. The immediate cause of the problems between Beijing and Washington, of course, was the reemergence of the Taiwan issue. The Chinese suspected the Reagan Administration of wishing to upgrade American relations with Taipei, which in effect was tantamount to following a "two China" policy. . . . In the fall of 1981, China began to demand that the United States agree to a timetable for halting the sale of all weapons to Taipei.

In early 1982, the Reagan Administration responded, announcing that it had decided not to sell an advanced fighter aircraft, the so-called F-X, to Taiwan. Then, in August 1982, China and the United States issued a joint communiqué in which the United States pledged that its future arms sales to Taiwan would not exceed, in quality or quantity, the level that had been maintained since normalization, and that it intended gradually to reduce those sales over an unspecified period of time. For their part, while still refusing to renounce the use of force against Taiwan, the Chinese described their proposals for a peaceful reunification of Taiwan and the Mainland as representing a "fundamental policy." . . .

Chinese foreign economic relations have undergone less change than has its geopolitical posture. To be sure, Chinese leaders have become increasingly concerned about the effects of contact with the West on Chinese society. They blame the rise in political dissent at home, defections of Chinese to foreign countries, growing corruption within the Chinese bureaucracy, and even an increase in the crime rate at least partially on China's wider relationship with the rest of the world. But they still seem eager to reap the benefits of China's new "open door." While placing increasing restrictions on unofficial and informal contacts between Chinese and foreigners, and reducing some opportunities for Chinese to study abroad, Beijing has not limited the wide range of economic and commercial transactions with the West that were inaugurated in the late 1970s.

The new directions in Chinese foreign relations, therefore, might tentatively be summarized as a kind of "independent reformism." In terms of its orientation toward the international system, China has decided to reassert its support for reform of the international economic and political order, although the practical steps it plans to take remain to be seen. In this regard, Beijing's foreign policy, rhetorically at least, will be similar to that of the mid-1970s.

China's relations with the two superpowers, however, may have little precedent. Unlike the late or even mid-1970s, indications are that China will seek to avoid the impression that it is closely "aligned" with, or a partner of, the United States, and will attempt to strike a more independent posture. But the independence of the early 1980s will probably be very different from that of the early 1960s, when it was China's position to oppose vigorously the initiatives of both superpowers. China may feel that it is now possible to engage in an active diplomatic dialogue with both the United States and the Soviet Union, and to pursue parallel policies with Moscow on some issues and still join with Washington on others. . . .

What is more, it remains to be seen whether China will seek a true equidistance between the United States and the Soviet Union, or whether, as is more likely, its national interests will lead it to find "points of meeting" with Washington more frequently than with Moscow. Much will depend on the policies that the United States and the Soviet Union adopt on issues of interest to the Chinese, as well as on the overall strategic balance between the two superpowers. . . .

Overview

From a position of weakness three decades ago, China has become a "candidate superpower," both politically and economically. In the early 1950s, for example, the PRC enjoyed formal diplomatic relations with only 12 countries outside the socialist camp and was denied representation in the United Nations. In the 1960s, however, many of the newly independent nations of the Third World chose to recognize Beijing rather than Taipei. As a result of this and of the signs of Sino-American rapprochement, by the fall of 1971, the People's Republic was able to gain a seat in the United Nations, thereby replacing Taiwan as China's representative to that body. By the end of 1982, Beijing had established diplomatic relations with 125 nations and claimed membership in most international economic organizations.

There has been a similar increase in China's economic activity. Since 1970, China's international trade has been rising rapidly, both in absolute terms and as a proportion of the PRC's gross national product. In the 1970s, China's two-way trade increased nearly tenfold, from around U.S.

$4 billion to about U.S. $38 billion in current prices. Over the same decade, trade grew also from an estimated 3.5 percent of China's GNP to approximately 9.4 percent. Moreover, as its trade has grown, the PRC has become a significant trading partner of an increasing number of states. In 1981, China became the third largest importer of American goods in Asia (Japan and South Korea are first and second). And, in the same year, it was Japan's fifth largest trading partner, after the United States, Saudi Arabia, Indonesia, and Australia.

How has China been able to transform itself from what Mao Zedong called a "semi-colony" to a "candidate superpower" in the space of 30 years? In part, it is the result of China's sheer size: the PRC has the world's largest population and, not coincidentally, the world's largest standing army, third largest navy, and third largest air force. The change is also due in part to the substantial economic development that has occurred since 1949, giving China, at about U.S. $400 billion, the world's sixth largest GNP, an industrial sector equal to that of Japan in the early 1960s, and the world's third largest strategic nuclear force. Moreover, these resources are at the command of a powerful central government, a situation in sharp contrast to the political fragmentation of the country before 1949.

Also, Chinese leaders have employed their available material resources with great skill. Despite the PRC's somewhat limited resources, China's leaders have throughout the years undertaken a surprisingly large foreign economic aid program. Through their ability to impress and persuade both official and unofficial visitors, they have made their country a major commentator on world developments. On numerous occasions—in Korea, in the Taiwan Straits, along the Sino-Soviet and Sino-Indian frontiers, and in Vietnam—they have shown a willingness and resolve to use their limited conventional military resources in active support of their foreign policy goals, even against more powerful adversaries. And, accurately or not, it is widely believed, both in Asia and in other parts of the world, that China is likely to become an increasingly significant force in world politics over the rest of the century.

These trends, to be sure, should not be overstated. On

many dimensions of national power, China remains a poor country, with a low GNP per capita, obsolescent industrial technology, and relatively primitive weaponry. There are, as well, real limits to the speed with which China can develop its economy and modernize its armed forces. For the foreseeable future, China will remain an Asian, rather than a global, power. Nonetheless, China has been able to attain—and is likely to maintain—a degree of influence in world affairs far beyond what one might expect, based on the PRC's actual material resources alone.

Following American diplomatic recognition of the People's Republic of China in 1979, the United States removed its military personnel from Taiwan, abrogated previous treaties with the Republic of China, and converted its embassy in Taipei into a nondiplomatic office for trade matters. Having accepted unofficial relations, the United States and Taiwan enjoy a high volume of trade and personal exchanges. Moreover, under the Reagan Administration, the United States continues to supply "defensive" weapons to the Republic of China. Thus, the Taiwan problem that bedeviled American domestic politics in the 1950s seems abated. Yet the basic PRC-Taiwan stalemate remains unresolved, as Ross Terrill discusses in this selection.

The Problem of Taiwan
by Ross Terrill

Taiwan is an island province of China which became separated from the motherland for half a century because of Japanese conquest. When the Chinese civil war was nearing its end, the Chiang Kai-shek forces went to that island, set up a mainland Chinese régime over the Taiwanese people, and thus introduced them into the fight between Mao Tse-tung and Chiang Kai-shek. That was the fate that overcame the Taiwanese.

Since 1949 they have been part of the Chinese civil war question. The U.S. commitment to them was not a commitment to the island as a polity, nor to the people of Taiwan, but to the régime of Chiang Kai-shek, with its claim to be the government of China. . . .

The problem of Taiwan has three parts. So long as there is a régime in Taipei that pants to recover the twenty-nine provinces it fumbled with and then lost, the Chinese civil war will smolder on. But this "two Chinas" pain has eased since 1972. The United States and Japan have acknowledged that there is only one China. Taipei's threats to invade the mainland lose credibility as new generations arise. Some fifty nations have stopped regarding the government in Taipei as the Republic of China and begun to treat it as an entity with which there can be plenty of private—but no official—dealings.

A second part of the problem is the existence in Taiwan of U.S. soldiers and bases that were originally a by-product of the outbreak of the Korean War in 1950. A solution to this problem was laid down at Shanghai when the United States stated that "it affirms the ultimate objective of the withdrawal of all forces and military installations from Taiwan." . . .

A third part of the problem is the view held both in Taipei and Peking that Taiwan is a province that should be reunited with the mainland. Merger seems about as possible as mixing one unit of water with 55 units of whiskey (that is the population ratio of Taiwan and the People's Republic of China) and achieving a drink that differs in any noticeable way from pure whiskey. Yet I have subdivided the Taiwan problem for a reason which is important and lends hope.

As a matter of historical fact, the third part of the Taiwan issue was not an urgent matter until the first and second parts intruded. (Mao Tse-tung told Edgar Snow in the 1930s that Taiwan might or might not come back to China.)

The Taiwan question was turned into the emotional core of Chinese foreign policy, and the chief bilateral quarrel between Peking and Washington over twenty-nine years, by Chiang Kai-shek's claim that his remnant in Taiwan was the government of China, by the American backing for this claim, and by the decision of President Truman in June 1950 (reversing previous policy) that led to making the island a U.S. military base. . . .

It was *our side* that helped destroy the hope of a peaceful resolution of the Taiwan issue. Forgetting this, some people as a consequence allow themselves to forget how horrendous in every way a *non*-peaceful solution would be from Peking's point of view.

Peking knows that it would be a big and risky task to integrate Taiwan with the southeastern provinces. The island has a higher standard of living than does the PRC. Its defense forces could cause a lot of damage if they chose to fight.

Far more important, there are few signs that public opinion in Taiwan is "turning red" in the way Peking has hoped for. This is the often-overlooked crux of the hope for peace in the Taiwan Strait. The Chinese are deeply attached to a concept of Liberation as a people's movement. A decade ago, Peking rather carelessly used the expression: "We shall surely liberate Taiwan," but friendly Taiwanese objected to it. The Taiwanese must basically liberate themselves, it was pointed out. Peking cannot be the prime mover.

Fortunately this is now the view in Peking. Today the PRC typically states: "The Chinese people [i.e., including those on Taiwan] shall surely liberate Taiwan," or "Taiwan shall certainly be liberated." This seems to rule out invasion and large-scale war.

All this suggests that once Taipei ceases to pose as the government of China, or is no longer acknowledged as such by Washington, and once Taiwan is no more the site of foreign planes and joint war games between U.S. and Taiwan forces, the question of Taiwan as a separated province may not be as urgent to Peking as many people now assume. . . .

China says that full normalization with the United States will be achieved when three steps are taken: an end to diplomatic ties between Taipei and Washington; U.S. military withdrawal from Taiwan and an abrogation of the 1954 Security Treaty between the United States and Chiang's Republic of China. In other words, Peking seeks the de-internationalization of the Taiwan issue and asks that the United States not perpetuate the Chinese civil war. That is all the Chinese ask.

Of these demands, it is the treaty which is the sticky one. Military withdrawal is a stated goal of the United States and in fact it inches ahead. Since it is clear that the United States could keep an "unofficial" office in Taipei even after breaking relations with the Republic of China, the diplomatic switch is unlikely to be more momentous for Taiwan than was the similar step taken by Japan in September 1972. By 1977, *no less than eight of Taiwan's top ten trading partners* were among the ranks of countries that had established diplomatic relations with Peking....

It is not a question of "abandoning Taiwan" or of "handing Taiwan over to Peking." Taiwan is not the fifty-first state of the United States; it has never been America's to "abandon," any more than China in the 1940's was America's to "lose." To suppose otherwise is to undermine the very Taiwanese people we mean to befriend. We should not "hand over" Taiwan, nor is Peking asking for that....

If normalization is reasonably handled, not only will relations between Washington and Peking enter a more serious era, but Taiwan will probably be better off. To live on a myth is to live on the edge of a cliff. It is very likely that, as the year 2000 arrives, Taiwan will be living essentially its own life, if with growing bonds to the PRC. Our grandchildren will puzzle that the "Taiwan issue" should have bedeviled American foreign and domestic politics alike for thirty years.

Agriculture: The 1980s

The agricultural experimentation now happening in China is audacious. If successful, it bids well to create a newly prosperous peasantry and a semicapitalist private plot economy at the village level. Capital generated by growth in agriculture would provide the base for needed expansion in industry and trade, for, with the exception of oil, China has limited means to finance her plans for modernization. Should Deng's program fail, the outcome is likely to be continued rural poverty and lowered expectations—with social consequences that are unpredictable but daunting. Deng's political survival may well depend on his success in China's villages.

While the experiments are now under way to restructure China's agricultural system, most Chinese peasants still live on agricultural communes. In the following 1981 essay, Victor Lippit describes how communes are organized, as well as their uniqueness in the context of the Third World.

The People's Communes and China's New Development Strategy
by Victor Lippit

In China, unlike most third world countries, rural development has been a central component of the overall development strategy. The key institution making this possible is the People's Commune, which combines agriculture, capital construction and local industry with health, welfare, education and cultural activities. The commune is a unique institution which, by combining farming and other productive activities with the activities of local government, integrates the social, political and economic life of the countryside within a single unit.

China's overall population is over 1.008 billion [as of the 1982 census]. Approximately 80 percent of the population live on communes, which now number 50,000. The communes average about 16,000 persons or 3,800 households each; individual commune sizes vary widely from the average, with communes in mountainous regions typically much smaller than the average while those in flat, densely-populated plains areas not uncommonly reaching 60-70,000 members. When the entire countryside was first organized into communes in 1958, 26,000 communes were established. These proved to be too large for efficient administration and the number was increased to a peak of 78,000 in the early 1960s before a new round of consolidation brought the total down to the present number around the end of the decade.

The communes are divided into four levels, each of which has its own sources of income and each of which has its own sphere of decision-making autonomy. The four levels are the commune, the brigade, the team and the household. The commune level is typically responsible for providing secondary school education, maintaining a hospital, organizing cultural activities and carrying out the functions of local government. At the same time, it carries out larger-scale industrial activities, capital construction and some farming activities. . . . In China as a whole, commune and brigade enterprises together employ 28 million rural workers out of a total commune labor force of 300 million.

An average commune has 15 brigades, which in turn average about 253 households or 1,067 people. The brigades operate enterprises that are smaller in scale than those of the commune and sometimes receive income as well from assessments levied on teams which are members. The brigades, which are typically organized around natural villages, carry out smaller-scale capital construction projects and provide smaller-scale educational and health facilities; elementary schools and clinics, for example, are normally operated at the brigade level. . . .

The teams are the basic units for agricultural production and, with the exception of a limited number of instances in which brigade-level accounting is practiced, of income-distribution as well. The average team in China has about 38 households or 160 people. . . .

In addition to their collective activity, commune members have a right to maintain private plots, which typically amount in the aggregate to some 5 percent of the collective lands. At the Sino-Japanese Friendship Commune, each family has about 66 square meters of land, yielding an estimated cash income of about 150 *yuan* per family. In China as a whole, the per capita income from collective labor in agriculture was 83.4 *yuan* in 1979, roughly half in kind and half in cash, and the Ministry of Agriculture estimates that family sideline activities and private plots added about 30 to 40 *yuan* more to this figure. Peasants can use the plots to grow food for their own consumption or for sale to the state or, except for grain and cooking oil, at local free markets, where somewhat higher prices prevail. Many urban consumers buy agricultural produce both at state stores, where prices are lower, and at free markets, where the food is fresher. . . .

It is common to find team and brigade leaders elected by their members, but commune-level cadres are typically appointed by the state; their charge is to see that the commune as a whole operates in accordance with public policy and party principles. Thus the commune blends in a unique way not only different aspects of social life but also grass-roots self-determination with state power. Other government agencies also play a role, but the point here is to emphasize the character of the vertical linkages. Thus the county, for example, stands in relation to the commune much as the commune does to the brigade; communes are not isolated, discrete units. Important targets like those for grain will be determined by the State Council in consultation with the State Planning Commission, Ministry of Agriculture and other competent bodies. . . .

The communes were first formed in 1958, and by September of that year, 98.2 percent of China's rural households were commune members. The main drive for the formation of communes came during the summer, by which time favorable weather conditions seemed to assure a bumper crop. This materialized as expected in 1958, but in the succeeding three years output fell sharply, creating near-crisis conditions in the agricultural sector and forcing a sharp shift in national policy toward agriculture. Whereas the development of heavy industry had been stressed in the 1950s, from 1960 agriculture was supposed to have been accorded priority. The terms of trade between industry and agriculture shifted gradually in favor of agriculture and the development of industries which provided inputs for agriculture (chemical fertilizer, farm machinery, etc.) was accorded priority. At the same time, reorganization of the communes emphasized making the production team, rather than the commune, the basic unit of accounting and distribution, thus linking income more closely to productive effort. . . .

Between 1960 and 1965, the changes in agricultural policy had primarily been pragmatic, but these were reinforced from 1966 by the broader vision of social change which the Cultural Revolution incorporated. Self-reliance, the development of local industry and elimination of the three great differences (between town and country, agriculture and industry, and mental and manual labor) gave a distinctive cast to rural development in China.

The common pattern in capitalist countries and in the Soviet Union has been to focus on urban-industrial development, usually at the expense of the countryside, which provides resources and cheap labor but begins to draw some benefits from the development process only when it is relatively far advanced. China, by contrast, has been trying to make the development of the countryside one of the central pillars of the overall development effort. Peasants are not free to migrate to the cities; improvement in their lives must come through the transformation of their own environments. The development of industry at the brigade and commune levels is a part of this process. These local industries provide cash income for the collectives (which can use this to purchase agricultural machinery), employment opportunities for the commune members, important agricultural inputs and everyday consumption necessities. The state will provide technical guidance in the establishment of these local industries and sometimes help with the financing, but they rely on a combination of state and local initiative to get under way.

A major element in China's new agricultural program is the repudiation of established models—most notably the Dazhai commune—which China's peasants had been encouraged to follow during the Mao years. Dazhai stood for farmers' self-reliance vis-à-vis the state and a high level of political awareness among the peasantry. Recently, many of Dazhai's accomplishments have been questioned as fraudulent, as Jack Gray points out. In many parts of China the government is experimenting with the abolition of the commune's economic functions and trying to encourage lower-level agricultural production. Personal incentives and the chance to grow prosperous by means of family farming, it is hoped, will produce higher crop yields. The selection by James Wallace examines this new direction. What success or failure might mean is discussed by John K. Fairbank.

Whatever Happened to Dazhai?
by Jack Gray*

For twelve years—from 1964 until the fall of the Gang of Four at the end of 1976—the Dazhai Production Brigade was the unassailable model for rural socialist development in China. This little community, buried among the harshly eroded slopes of the mountains of north west China, had created a new life for itself by heroic and heroically persistent effort. Its people toiled year after year to move masses of rock and earth by hand. They created and irrigated terraces of soil where, before, there had been

---

New Society, March 1981.

nothing but semi-desert. Three times flash floods destroyed all their work, and three times they began again.

No wonder the village was taken as living proof that even the poorest can transform their lives, if they have the will to win and the solidarity to make a common effort.

Mao took it up as the model of self-reliant socialism. His followers, less discriminating, turned it into a model of everything, China was urged and pressurised to emulate not only Dazhai's admirable fighting spirit, but Dazhai's wage policy, its fervent study of the Chairman's works, its schools, its policy towards women, and every other aspect of its life. Its achievements—inspiring enough in truth—were grossly exaggerated for political purposes. Its reputation for successful self-reliance was falsely bolstered by secret state subventions. Its party secretary, Chen Yongguei, was made a vice-premier. China's half a million villages were pressured to imitate it, even though their conditions were seldom poor enough to require such heroic and drastic solutions.

Soon the whole movement got badly out of hand, quite beyond the control even of the Cultural Revolution authorities in Peking. Private plots and rural fairs were abolished in many places, just because Dazhai had dispensed with them. The small teams on which collective agriculture was based were merged into the bigger brigade, because Dazhai had done so. This happened even if it meant (as it did not in Dazhai's case) putting richer and poorer villages into one unit of account, to the disgust and dismay of the richer.

Dazhai's wage policy was an equal share-out of the results of the common effort. This was natural enough in an all-out drive, from which every participant ultimately gained so much that immediate rewards for individual contributions were of little interest. The wage policy was applied to collectives which depended for success not on a million-men-with-teaspoons transformation, but simply on maintaining incentives for regular individual participation in routine farming.

Dazhai did not immediately cease to be a model when the Gang of Four were arrested. The new party chairman, Hua Guofeng, though he took the initiative in arresting the maoist radicals, is himself a maoist—though a sober one. He had already chosen Dazhai as the site for his national conference on agriculture. Even Deng Xiaoping (the prime minister) was compelled to pay lip service to the model. He had to visit the place, and take foreign ambassadors there to observe it. Gradually, however, as Deng Xiaoping's influence grew, and that of Hua Guofeng waned, Dazhai came under attack. This took place with the usual mixture of good sense and vicious nonsense which such campaigns produce in China. It included the arrest of the son of Dazhai's leader, Chen Yongguei, for alleged rape, robbery and several other crimes of that kind. Chen himself is no longer a vice-premier, and is said to be "undergoing re-education."

Deng and his supporters were determined on a new agricultural policy which was, at almost all points, the antithesis of what Dazhai represented. They saw its egalitarianism as the culmination of a long process, stretching back almost as far as the 1955 origins of collective agriculture itself. In support of this, Chinese peasants had been dragooned into a system of excessively collective organisation and remuneration, which few of them liked. It had damaged incentives, discredited socialist agriculture, and demoralised peasants and local communist leaders alike.

The picture of the collectives' failure, which China's new leaders paint, is a black one. It is black enough to dismay even those who, while hoping that Chinese socialist agriculture would succeed, still retained some commonsense reservations about its claims so far. In one in six of China's 2,000 counties, they say, production has increased little since the early 1950s and the days of individual farming. But population has meanwhile doubled.

In China as a whole, *per capita* grain supplies were less when the Gang of Four were arrested in 1976 than in 1957—the year before the communes were created. A quarter of the rural population still have incomes averaging less than £14 per head a year.

Only in Manchuria and the Yangtse estuary has collectivised agriculture really succeeded to the satisfaction of both the peasants and the party. And these are the rich areas, where individual agriculture might have succeeded just as well, or better. It is now admitted that, in many places, the masses have "lost confidence in the collective." These places are not specified, but it is hard to believe that any peasant, among the 50 percent whose incomes fall below the average of about £22 a year, is brimming over with enthusiasm.

We cannot know how far these strictures on past policy are entirely true, and how far they are exaggerated in order to justify the new policies. It has probably proved much more difficult than China's leaders expected to im-' prove the conditions of the poorest communities whose resources are so scant. And these might well represent as much as one in six of China's counties—though no doubt a much smaller proportion of her population, as the poorer counties are less densely settled.

What is more shocking is the comment in *People's Daily* on the future prospects for creating a truly socialist agriculture. That is that these prospects will no doubt take care of themselves "when the peasants have enough to eat and to wear." Were we wrong in assuming that China had guaranteed the fulfillment of basic needs for all? Not quite. What it does mean, however, is that too many of China's more backward rural areas are still dependent on state handouts.

The new government's answer is that collective management of agriculture should be largely given up. Farm work and local enterprise generally (excluding local industry) will now be carried on by small work-groups, under contract to the collective. In many places—those where collective farming has manifestly failed to raise incomes and where the peasants have "lost confidence"—the contracts will be given to individual families. In a few cases, the land, though remaining formally in collective ownership, will be divided for cultivation, along with tools and beasts, among individual families. These families will themselves meet the state's grain-purchase quotas and state taxes, pay a small rent to the collective in return for its maintenance of social overheads, and keep the rest of their product, to sell if they wish at freely negotiated prices.

Such policies are, from a socialist point of view, regressive. It is admitted now (after two years of mealy-mouthed evasion) that the new system is not just a matter of changes in administration of labour organisation, but "an adjustment of production relations." In other words, a substantial social change. Why is it necessary? Because, apparently, the problem of incentives is so great that it overwhelms every other consideration. . . . This new policy of contracting for farm labour was not first invented at the top, but imposed by peasants who refused to work on any other terms.

The authorities are keenly aware of the damage that may be done to the socialist organisation of agriculture by the new system. *People's Daily*, in an article which gave top-level approval to the new ideas, at the same time listed disadvantages. The list reads like a denial of everything for which socialism has so far stood in rural China. The new system, says *People's Daily*, will be bad for the prospects of agricultural mechanisation, the rational use of water resources, the care of draft animals, and the defence against crop pests and diseases. It will hamper scientific innovation in agriculture, increase the difficulty of coping with natural disasters, and be an obstacle to the mobilisation of labour for farmland construction. It will discourage the diversification of agriculture and the development of local small-scale enterprises. It will prejudice soil and water conservation. And it will make it difficult for the collective to care for those in need.

In spite of this devastating case against the system, it is being applied. Resistance is being worn down. Provincial authorities which, six months ago, were expressing dissent are now issuing orders to the counties and the communes to get on with it.

It is a long way from Dazhai. Yet perhaps it is not the end of socialism in the Chinese countryside. The problems which collective agriculture has faced in China—the destruction of personal incentives, the low level of collective management, the relatively poor productivity, the limited surplus produced for the national market—are common, in varying degrees, to collective agriculture everywhere.

Socialist agriculture has not, on the whole, been a rousing success. It has not created a more productive technology which compels acceptance of collectivisation. It is trapped in the contradiction that, at any likely price paid to the farmers for grain, growing almost anything else (on the private plot) is more profitable. So while the state looks to the collective to maximise the marketed grain surplus, the peasants look to it merely for subsistence.

In these circumstances, a system in which the collective becomes contractor rather than manager—while retaining the responsibility for capital accumulation, investment in infrastructure and economic diversification, general planning, and welfare services—may possibly work better than the old. If it increases productivity sufficiently, it may even provide more, rather than fewer, collective resources to be used for development and for redistributive action. The next few years will tell.

End of an Era for China's Communes
by James Wallace

A rural revolution in China is sweeping aside one of Mao Tse-tung's most cherished institutions—the farm communes that the late Communist leader intended to be homes, workplaces and political centers for 800 million peasants.

The idea that no member of a commune should work harder and earn more than the others—in reality, shared poverty—is giving way to the concept that individual enterprise, initiative and productivity should be rewarded.

Also on the way out is Mao's belief that slogans, not cash benefits, would turn every peasant into a model worker. The long-term implications of these revolutionary changes are uncertain. Some observers predict that they eventually could undermine the Communist system in China. . . .

Ever since Mao dramatically launched the communes in 1958, they have dominated life in China's rural areas. Commune leaders controlled political affairs, oversaw farm production, were responsible for education and health care. Among their tasks: Selecting a few bright young people who would be permitted to move to the industrialized cities to work and further their education.

Communal kitchens were to feed everyone from infants to the aged. Housewives were told to throw away their pots and to eat in the common dining halls. They did—but not for long. By the early 1960s, the communal facilities were beginning to disappear. Families preferred to cook at home where they could eat their breakfasts of rice gruel and pickles, a lunch of rice and vegetables with a tiny slice of meat or an egg and then have the leftovers for dinner.

Now, the communes themselves are beginning to fade out of sight rapidly, with nearly 3,000 already abolished.

More and more, a visitor to rural areas finds family units, even individuals, doing tasks that formerly were the responsibility of the entire commune. Land is available to workers willing to sign production contracts or to join other private enterprise-style systems. Cooperatives and corporations process and sell whatever contractors have agreed to produce. Above-quota output belongs to the tiller or the toiler.

This does not mean Peking equates private enterprise with democracy. No thought is given to surrendering the Chinese Communist Party's power in the countryside. Where communes have been broken up, elected governments take charge of management at county and township levels. The party, however, still sets and oversees basic policies.

Few analysts argue that China's 54,000 communes served no useful purpose. One of their major successes was elimination of the age-old threat of recurring rural famine.

Moreover, the system combined discipline, new technology and state investment funds to produce significant increases in grain production. Harvests that peaked at 332 million tons in 1979 had for years been crawling upward at a slightly faster rate than the increase in population.

If communes had value, why are they being eliminated?

The short answer: China's leaders—most of all Peking's foremost realist, Deng Xiaoping—are convinced that sharp increases in production of food and raw materials are vital if the nation's overall economy is to be modernized.

To accomplish that task, central agricultural planning in Peking is to be curtailed and inefficient communes closed. Instead of blind dependence on ideology, efficient Chinese peasants will be turned loose to plan their own production, to earn bonuses for higher output and to have access to expanding markets wherever profits can be made. . . .

For the vast majority of peasants in rice-bowl provinces such as Sichuan in western China, life still is mostly a day-to-day grind of transplanting rice seedlings in chilly, knee-deep water, tilling the fields with heavy hoes, shivering or sweltering in dimly lit houses, eating simple food.

One advantage of being on the farm is that families may have up to five times more living space than city dwellers.

But a peasant's home may be nothing more than a cave in a clay hillside, a mud-brick hut or a simple prefabricated building. Electric fans to ease the discomfort of blistering summers are rare. In winter's cold, heat other than from a primitive stove, used only to cook meals, is a luxury. Clothing more often than not is a collection of patches.

Nevertheless, a brighter future lies ahead for Sichuan's Qionglai county, a pioneer in contract farming and other reforms. There, individual enterprise by farmers is paying off in brick houses, some with two-burner stoves and lamps using energy from biogas generators.

Take Gu Yueming, 30, and his pretty 27-year-old wife Li Zhiying. They farm slightly less than an acre of fertile bottomland under a contract, renewed annually, that gives Gu exclusive use of the plot of state-owned land. His contract calls for him to turn over a fixed quota of grain to the Phoenix Integrated Company, which took over forty communes in 1979. Any surplus from Gu's labor is his.

Gu's total yearly earnings from his commune a decade ago amounted to just $40 in cash and "enough grain to get by on." In 1979, when rural reform began taking hold in Qionglai, his cash income rose to $250.

Through hard work and more extensive use of fertilizer and pesticides, Gu's output in 1982 rose to five tons of grain, of which two tons of rice and 1.2 tons of wheat were delivered to Phoenix to fulfill his contract. By selling the surplus of 1.8 tons or using it to fatten pigs for the market and by producing yeast for a local distillery, the family's one-year cash income tops $2,000—four to five times the pay of most urban factory workers.

When they were married in 1973, the young couple lived in a cramped mud-brick dwelling "and never even thought about building a house because our income was so low." Now the family, since grown to four with a school-age son and a daughter, has a 1,440-square-foot house made of kiln-dried clay bricks that cost $4,000 for materials and outside labor. They own two bicycles, two wristwatches, a radio-cassette player and some new furniture, and they have plans to buy a 14-inch TV set for which they will pay $635.

The Phoenix collective has a unit that does the plowing for everyone. But Gu and his wife do their own seeding, transplanting of rice shoots and harvesting. He and three neighbors jointly own an $80 foot-powered threshing machine that saves labor and reduces waste.

Although Gu's plot of land is neatly marked off from those of his neighbors, he does not feel he "owns" it. Others, especially older farmers with memories of pre-commune times, hope contract farming eventually will lead to return of land to private ownership. Officials insist there is no reason to believe that this dream ever will come true. . . .

Gu knows that officials probably will set higher quotas and lower purchase prices in 1985 when reform programs will be reviewed. But he believes they are working and will not be reversed. Confidently, he says: "Yes, I will be happy if my children become farmers. It is a good life now. . . ."

China's rural revolution raises many questions: Will economic freedoms revive class distinctions, erode party control and generate pressure for political and social liberties that no Communist regime can accept?

Some Chinese, especially once powerful commune leaders, see grave dangers ahead. They want to return to the philosophy of "let everyone eat from the same rice pot"— meaning no individual should earn more than his co-workers. . . .

Another headache for Peking: As remaining communes are phased out in the next three years, their economic tasks will be taken over by companies and cooperatives. At the same time, political administration will return to the counties, which, for centuries in pre-Communist times, had been China's basic political-economic units in rural areas.

County-level Communist Party committees will continue to implement decisions made by national and provincial leaders. But new local governments, elected by peasant associations, will set up independent agencies to handle irrigation projects, schools, hospitals and other functions that had been the responsibility of the communes.

These changes may not undermine the Communist Party's monopoly of power. Yet the authority of local party chiefs will be reduced, and opportunities to challenge the political system will grow. Tests of how well the new agencies perform will come when problems arise. What happens if public works are mismanaged or a rural enterprise misses its targets and loses money? . . .

Reforms are spreading with none of the signs of violence

that mark most revolutions. Still, resistance is being encountered, mostly among the million or so commune leaders who will lose their jobs.

Their most common complaint is that farmers who grow crops to be sold for cash sooner or later will turn into bosses who "behave like landlords" and hire others to do their dirty work. And it is a fact that some peasants, and some regions, rapidly are getting richer than others.

Stripped of official jargon, the new style of farming in China is not very different—although much more profitable—than sharecropping. And the techniques of the budding agribusinesses owe more to the experiences of free-enterprise corporations than to socialist collectives.

Some ideologists warn that reforms create "contradictions" that threaten the Communist system. An American analyst agrees. "It's like trying to be a little bit pregnant," he says. "No Communist country has ever managed a major relaxation of one set of controls without it threatening to spread through the entire system. That, in turn, usually ends up with the original relaxations being abolished."

But few people in areas where reforms are moving fastest seem worried. Watchwords are more of everything—incentives, output, profits and consumption. . . .

The New Two China Problem
by John K. Fairbank*

Chou En-lai and Teng Hsiao-p'ing's program for modernization of industry, agriculture, science-and-technology, and defense [the Four Modernizations] is the latest revolutionary solution to China's age-old problem, how to govern the villages from the cities. The villages today contain 800 million people, the cities 200 million. By the year 2000, whether or not the Four Modernizations are completed, China's villagers are likely to total one billion, her city dwellers perhaps 300 million. Food and government will still be major problems. Americans accustomed to farmsteads more than villages, whose countryside has generally disappeared into suburbs, can only try to imagine China's

*New York Review of Books, March 8, 1979.

situation. The press of numbers creates problems of economy, government, and values including human rights that are all very strange to us.

If we repeat our experience of the 1930s with National-ist China, trading, investing, educating, and touring main-ly in the cities, we can again be startled, embattled, and embittered by what comes out of the villages. China's farming people are not going to disappear like ours into urban centers. They were there in their villages before America began and will no doubt outlast us. The modern revolution is only beginning to reach them. Now that the Chou-Teng program seeks our investment of technology in training, equipment, and joint ventures, we must get our minds out of the familiar cities like Canton, Shanghai, and Peking and into the less known countryside. To help China blindly, knowing only what we are told in English, una-ware of what our Chinese friends are up against, is a prescription for another American disaster in China remi-niscent of the 1940s.

Having got beyond our thirty-year-old Two Chinas prob-lem by agreeing that Taiwan is a self-governing, armed province over which Peking has latent sovereignty, we now face another Two Chinas, urban and rural. The Chinese revolution, not yet finished, is really two revolutions, one social and one technological, that sometimes coincide and sometimes conflict. This is what produces the policy zig-zags that always amaze us. They are built into the revolu-tionary process like "walking on two legs," as the man said.

Mao Tse-tung's social revolution aimed to liberate the villagers from second-class citizenship, ignorance, and want. It tried to wipe out the old ruling-class elite of privileged literati, officials, merchants, landlords, and city-dwelling exploiters in general. But mobilizing peasants for this egalitarian purpose inevitably created a great cult of Mao something like a folk religion, and his latter-day followers led by the so-called Gang of Four wound up as anti-intellectual dogmatists. With "politics in command," they attacked "bourgeois tendencies" like Calvinists routing out original sin. They decried material incentives as unworthy of true socialism. The result was a failure to educate or to produce, which led to an economic stagnation and another shift of course once the Gang were thrown out of power.

Under Teng Hsiao-p'ing the other revolution, to apply modern technology to all aspects of Chinese life, now has its day and opportunity. We must help it to succeed, but how far it succeeds and how long it lasts as Peking's dominant policy will depend to some degree on how we do our part. Foreigners of all stripes have always found their counterparts in China. Our opium traders found Chinese opium distributors, our missionaries found Chinese devoted to good works. Even without the help of rip-off specialists in our General Services Administration, Chinese purchasers in capitalist America will truly be in enemy territory. To sup with us, they will need long chopsticks. Even the ten-dollar bills of eleemosynary tourists in China's new 1000-room hotels will be corrupting. With all due respect to one of America's inexpugnable claims to fame, we may also wonder whether Coca-Cola can really hit the spot in Honan province. In summer Shanghai, yes, but will it increase crop acreage in Lin Hsien, or irrigate more than the purchaser?

In the midst of plans for steel, coal, and oil production to build up industry, we have to wear bifocals that can keep in view the rural 800 million. They have doubled in numbers since 1949 but are still bone poor. If the new city elite that we help to train should lose touch with the villages, Mao's ghost may well appear and cry "Remember me!" in more than one rural hamlet. Literacy and transistors are spreading expectations among the most cohesive and the largest bloc of people ever to appear on earth. Teng Hsiao-p'ing's program for a controlled chain reaction in the Chinese countryside has its dangers. We can expect in ten or twenty years to be feeding China's cities in exchange for consumer goods we cannot produce competitively. But this symbiosis will be with the modern international fringe of China, a mere 200 or 300 million, while the billion farmers of the Chinese countryside, still poor, may be mobilizing anew. In short, we have reason to study more than China's technological needs, appreciate more than the tourist cuisine, and offer more than audience enthusiasm for the Chinese people's great achievements. They have troubles too, and in the global future we cannot escape a connection with them....

Overall, the People's Republic has done very well. Gross national product has grown about 5½ percent annually as a whole and 9 percent in industry—rates that we can envy. *If* politics can remain stable and *if* military costs can be restrained, the prospects are bright for a continued slow rise in living standards. But this will not happen of itself and several things may impede it—not only political turmoil or a military buildup but also bad weather or natural disaster like the great Tang-shan earthquake of 1976.

One critical problem is that China has run out of crop land. Leveling and combining fields, terracing mountains, reclaiming wasteland are all meeting diminishing returns. Some of the plans for creating new land will boggle the American mind—for example, farming a riverbed by dint of putting the river in a tunnel underneath it. The hand work involved in cutting and carrying the stone for such a river tunnel is the same cheap labor that built the Great Wall, labor that is still the major resource in the country and still low in productivity without more capital equipment. Teng's program for farm mechanization aims mainly to free labor for the rural small-scale industries that are beginning to provide cement, chemicals, iron, power, machinery, and consumer goods for local consumption in the countryside. By American or Soviet standards these small plants are of poor quality and uneconomic. But industry has to go to the villages and the economy of mass production in central cities must be forgone because no feasible transport system could possibly deliver the goods to 800 million consumers. The villages have to industrialize *in situ*.

The basic problem is that, while industry has built up rapidly, grain production has grown only about 3 or 3.5 percent a year. It has barely kept ahead of population growth at 1.8 to 2 percent. The agrarian product left over for commerical and industrial use and for export to earn foreign exchange has been very thin. Plans call for 4.5 percent annual growth in grain production even though from 1964 to 1974 it was under three percent and no other major grain producer has been able to maintain a rate of 4.5 percent growth. New fertilizer plants coming "on stream," as the economists so vividly put it, will help. Another tactic in the struggle for grain is to intensify land use by raising not merely two but three crops a year. One analyst, Thomas Wiens, sees this multiple cropping as a doctrine in need of cost analysis. It requires such early ripening seeds and so much labor, fertilizer, and irrigation that it may in fact be uneconomic.

Overall, however, the economists—piecing together data which Peking regards as nobody else's business—see great potentialities, probably beyond reach at the breakneck speed now planned for but vast and imposing nevertheless. The command economy of the People's Republic has done so much better than India that there is no longer any question of competition between the "communist" and "free" systems—or should one say, more realistically, between China and India?

Annotated Bibliography

Most books included here are simply written and accessible to the general reader. *Unless noted* (**), they are paperbacks.

Imperial China (1765 B.C.–A.D. 1800)

Dun Li, *The Ageless Chinese: A History* (3d ed. New York: Scribners, 1978). A straightforward, well-written history of China from the earliest era to the present day.

Dun Li, *The Essence of Chinese Civilization* (Princeton, N.J.: Van Nostrand, 1977). An excellent collection of readings, divided into sections on philosophy, religion, government, economics, and family and society.

Edward H. Schafer, *Ancient China*** (New York: Time-Life Books, 1967). Schafer deals with Chinese history up to A.D. 907—and simply describes China's cultural, scientific, and social accomplishments. The book is beautifully assembled and includes photographs, art reproductions, and drawings.

Wolfram Eberhard, *Folk Tales of China* (New York: Washington Square Press, 1973). Arranged by topic, with notes and historical commentary.

Michael Sullivan, *The Arts of China*, rev. ed. (Berkeley and Los Angeles: University of California Press, 1978). Profusely illustrated, much in color, perhaps the best short history of Chinese art available.

Joseph Needham, *The Shorter Science and Civilization in China* (Cambridge, England, and New York: Cambridge University Press, 1978 and 1981**), 2 vols. A partial abridgment of the monumental, multivolume study of China's scientific achievements. Rather dense, it is the only easy access to this area for English speakers.

Wu-chi Liu and Irvine Yucheng Lo, eds., *Sunflower Splendor: Three Thousand Years of Chinese Poetry* (New York: Doubleday Anchor, 1975). A large collection, with many new translations; reasonably priced.

Lo Kuan-chung, *Three Kingdoms: China's Epic Drama* (New

507

York: Pantheon Books, 1976), trans. and ed. Moss Roberts. A classic, newly translated and abridged.

Moss Roberts, trans. and ed., *Chinese Fairy Tales and Fantasies* (New York: Pantheon Books, 1979). A fresh selection of Chinese fables in engaging translations.

Jacques Gernet, *Daily Life in China on the Eve of the Mongol Invasion 1250–1276* (Stanford, Calif.: Stanford University Press, 1970). A colorful and authentic recreation of life in the capital of the Southern Sung dynasty, this book conveys not merely the facts but the texture of life in thirteenth-century China.

Jonathan D. Spence, *Emperor of China: Self-Portrait of K'ang-hsi* (New York: Knopf, 1974; Vintage paperback, 1975). A fascinating "recreation" of the life of a famous Manchu emperor of the Qing dynasty, in his own words, by creatively interspersing official documents. This almost seems like a contemporary biography.

China and the West (1800–1937)

C. P. Fitzgerald, *The Birth of Communist China* (Baltimore: Penguin Books, 1964). This is the most concise and readable short history of the final decades of the Manchu empire and the early years of the Republic from 1911. It also includes good descriptions of the rise of the Chinese Communist party.

Franz Schurmann and Orville Schell, *The China Reader* (New York: Vintage Books, 1967). This is a collection of readings with explanatory introductions. Volumes I and II cover the late Imperial and Republican periods.

Pat Barr, *Foreign Devils: Westerners in the Far East, The Sixteenth Century to the Present Day* (Baltimore: Penguin Books, 1970). *Foreign Devils* is a delightful assemblage of photographs, documents, and readings illustrating the ways Westerners and Asians have viewed each other—often in exactly opposite ways. It is colorful and tries to show the Chinese people's own perceptions.

Ida Pruitt, *A Daughter of Han: The Autobiography of a Chinese Working Woman* (Stanford Calif.: Stanford University Press, 1967; originally published in 1945). Ida Pruitt shows in graphic and direct language the life of Chinese women in the old society. Though written about women in the 1920s and 1930s, it is also applicable to the situation of women in the late Imperial period. It is the autobiography of one woman as told to the author.

Jean Chesneaux, Marianne Bastid, and Marie-Claire Bergère, *China from the Opium Wars to the 1911 Revolution* (New York: Pantheon Books, 1975).

Jean Chesneaux, Françoise LeBarbier, and Marie-Claire Bergère,

China from the 1911 Revolution to Liberation (New York: Pantheon Books, 1976). Two concise texts.

Barbara Tuchman, *Stilwell and the American Experience in China, 1911–45* (New York: Bantam Books, 1972). History written in broad sweeps and in the lively style for which Ms. Tuchman is renowned. Does for Republican China what *The Guns of August* did for World War I.

Theodore H. White and Annalee Jacoby, *Thunder Out of China* (New York: Da Capo Press paperback reprint; originally published in 1946). An exciting, on-the-spot account by two journalists of the 1930s and 1940s in Nationalist China. It includes descriptions of the Kuomintang-Communist civil war and the disastrous effects of the Sino-Japanese War on the Chinese people. Highly readable.

New China (1937–   )

Edgar Snow, *Red Star over China* (New York: Bantam Books, revised and enlarged edition, 1978; first published in 1938). Snow's account, written after his trip to the Communist capital at Yan'an in the late 1930s, contained the first solid information about the Long March of 1934–35, Mao Zedong's life, and the kind of society that the Communists were building. Set amid the confusion of the Nationalist-Communist civil war and the early years of the Sino-Japanese War, it is by far the most readable book on the 1930s.

Snow was a remarkable journalist, and he continued to chronicle China's course and to serve as personal friend and occasional spokesperson for Mao, Zhou Enlai, and many others among China's leaders. His early experiences in China are recorded in *Journey to the Beginning* (New York: Vintage, 1958). *Red China Today* (New York: Vintage, 1970) is a detailed and comprehensive report on China's society, economy, and political life two decades after Liberation. In *The Long Revolution*** (New York: Random House, 1972) Snow contemplates the changes of the late sixties and early seventies in a more philosophical and analytic vein.

Jack Belden, *China Shakes the World* (New York: Harper & Row, 1949; reprinted as a paperback by Monthly Review Press). Belden wrote this book after a long trip through the war-torn Chinese countryside in 1948–1949. It is a journalistic report, written like a fast-paced novel, of the peasant revolution going on in the Communist "liberated" areas of northern China. With Snow's *Red Star*, Belden's book is one of the classic books on pre-1949 China.

William Hinton, *Fanshen: A Documentary of Revolution in a Chinese Village* (New York: Vintage, 1966). *Fanshen* is a highly detailed description of reforms and revolution in a single village after Liberation. It is long, but benefits from numerous individual portraits of peasants and stories of personal lives as told to Hinton.

Jan Myrdal, *Report from a Chinese Village* (New York: Pantheon, 1981, paperback) and *China: The Revolution Continued* (New York: Pantheon, 1970). Myrdal's two books tell the story of life in a village, first visited in the early 1960s and revisited later in the same decade. Many personal stories and a good overview of agricultural life on a modern commune. It is helpful to read the two books in sequence.

Dr. Joshua S. Horne, *Away with All Pests—An English Surgeon in People's China: 1954–1969* (New York: Monthly Review Press, 1969). The unusual experiences of a British doctor working in China. Shows how strikingly different the notion of meaningful health care is from the American medical system.

John Gurley, *China's Economy and the Maoist Strategy* (New York: Monthly Review Press, 1976). The best general discussion of the Maoist perspective on economic development in China up to 1976.

E. J. Kahn, *The China Hands: America's Foreign Officers and What Befell Them* (New York: Penguin Books, 1976). An objective account of this episode during the McCarthy period.

C. P. Fitzgerald, *Mao Tse-tung and China* (New York: Penguin Books, 1977). A compact and readable summing-up.

David Milton and Nancy Dall Milton. *The Wind Will Not Subside: Years in Revolutionary China—1964–1969* (New York: Pantheon Books, 1976). The most insightful and engaging account of the Cultural Revolution. The authors were on the scene and became personally involved in many of the exciting events they describe.

Ruth Sidel, *Families of Fengsheng* (New York: Penguin Books; 1976) and *Women and Childcare in China* (New York: Penguin Books, 1973). These warm and careful looks at how China has attempted to solve the social and family problems created by modernization, urbanization, and new socialist structures of community organization are both somewhat dated but still valuable.

Frederic M. Kaplan and Julian M. Sobin, with an introduction by John S. Service, *Encyclopedia of China Today***, 3d ed. (New York: Eurasia Press, 1981; distributed by Harper & Row). An exciting, wide-ranging attempt to provide a large amount of current information on China; in a manageable, well-organized format.

John King Fairbank, *Chinabound: A Fifty-Year Memoir*** (New York: Harper & Row, 1982). America's most respected Sinologist retells his decades-long interaction with China. In both private and official roles, Fairbank has been the foremost interpreter of China to Americans.

Ruth Sidel and Victor W. Sidel, *The Health of China*** (Boston: Beacon Press, 1982). Together with Dr. Joshua Horne's *Away with All Pests*, this is the best overview of the evolution of China's health system, from early development modeled on the Soviet system up to the present.

Fox Butterfield, *China: Alive in a Bitter Sea* (New York: Times Books, 1982; Bantam Books, 1983). Often poignant and generally thought-provoking, this is an up-to-date view of China by a Chinese-speaking correspondent of *The New York Times*.

Nancy Milton, *The China Option*** (New York: Pantheon Books, 1982). A lively thriller, somewhat in LeCarré style, this novel conveys faithfully the Chinese world of power struggles and intrigue as possible only by someone who has lived and worked in China.

Frederic M. Kaplan and Arne J. De Keijzer, *The China Guidebook* (New York: Eurasia Press, 1982/83). An excellent concise guide, updated, with many maps and photos.

Ross Terrill, *Mao: A Biography*** (New York: Harper & Row, 1980). One of the better new biographies of Mao, related in an episodic structure rather than analytically.

National Geographic Society, *Journey into China*** (Washington: National Geographic Society, 1982). Superbly produced, this volume visits the major regions of China, with essays by scholars and journalists. Included is the best available map of China—both must be ordered by mail from the National Geographic Society, P.O. Box 2174, Washington, D.C. 20013.

Keith Buchanan, Charles P. Fitzgerald, and Colin A. Ronan, *China: The Land and the People*.** Foreword by Joseph Needham. (New York: Crown Publishers, 1981). This sumptuously executed book looks like a coffee table item. Inside it has concise overviews of China's scientific achievements, geography, history, and relations with the West by several experts. Includes rare early photographs from nineteenth century.

Betty Bao Lord, *Spring Moon*. (New York: Avon, 1982). A novel by a Chinese-American about the life of a woman in China during enormous changes from the late nineteenth century through the Cultural Revolution.

Edoarda Masi, *China Winter: Workers, Mandarins, and the Purge of the Gang of Four*** Translated from the Italian by Adrienne Foulke. (New York: E. P. Dutton, 1978). An Italian woman writes perceptively of her experience teaching in China in 1976–1977, when Mao died and the Gang of Four were arrested.

Lois Wheeler Snow, *Edgar Snow's China: A Personal Account of the Chinese Revolution Compiled from the Writings of Edgar Snow*.** (New York: Random House, 1981). Selections from the reknowned American journalist's writings about his experiences in China from 1928 to 1949. Includes 450 fascinating photographs of the period.

Jonathan D. Spence *The Gate of Heavenly Peace: The Chinese and their Revolution, 1895–1980* (New York: The Viking Press, 1981). Spence presents the major themes of modern Chinese history by telling the stories of activist and Utopian theorist Kang Youwei, great writer Lu Xun, and novelist/feminist Ding Ling, shapers and interpreters of the revolution who sought not to control the revolution but to make sense of their lives within it.

From China: For books and magazines published in the People's Republic, contact China Books and Periodicals (West Coast Center, 2929 24th St., San Francisco, CA 94110; Midwest Center, 174 W. Randolph St., Chicago, IL 60601; East Coast Center, 125 5th Ave., New York, NY 10003).

Works Used in This Book

Adams, Leonard P., II, in Alfred W. McCoy, *The Politics of Heroin in Southeast Asia* (New York: Harper & Row, 1972).

Balazs, Étienne, *Chinese Civilization and Bureaucracy: Variations on a Theme* (New Haven: Yale University Press, 1964).

Barr, Pat, *Foreign Devils: Westerners in the Far East, The Sixteenth Century to the Present Day* (Baltimore: Penguin Books, 1970).

Bastid-Brugière, Marianne; Marie-Claire Bergère; and Jean Chesneaux, *Histoire de la Chine de la Guerre Franco-Chinoise à la Fondation du Parti Communiste Chinois 1885–1921* (Paris: Hatier, 1972). Translated as *China from the Opium Wars to the 1911 Revolution* (New York: Pantheon Books, 1976).

Belden, Jack, *China Shakes the World* (New York: Harper and Bros., 1949; Monthly Review Press, 1970).

Birch, Cyril, ed. *Anthology of Chinese Literature from Early Times to the Fourteenth Century* (New York: Grove Press, 1965).

Bodde, Derk, *Peking Diary, 1948–1949, A Year of Revolution* (New York: Abelard, 1950; Fawcett, 1967).

———, *China's Cultural Tradition* (New York: Holt, Rinehart and Winston, 1957).

Bonavia, David, *Far Eastern Economic Review* July 3–9, July 10–16, September 10–16, and December 10–16, 1982.

Butterfield, Fox, *China: Alive in a Bitter Sea* (New York: Times Books, 1982; Bantam Books, 1983).

Chang, Hsin-pao, *Commissioner Lin and the Opium War* (Cambridge, Mass.: Harvard University Press, 1964).

Chesneaux, Jean, *China: The People's Republic, 1949–1976* (New York: Pantheon Books, 1977).

———, *Secret Societies in China in the Nineteenth and Twenti-*

eth Centuries (Ann Arbor: University of Michigan Press, 1971).

Chiang Kai-shek, *China's Destiny and Chinese Economic Theory* (New York: Roy Publishers, 1947).

Cohen, Paul A., *China and Christianity: The Missionary Movement and the Growth of Chinese Antiforeignism 1860–1870* (Cambridge, Mass.: Harvard University Press, 1963).

Collis, Maurice, *Foreign Mud* (London: Faber and Faber, 1964).

Committee of Concerned Asian Scholars, *China! Inside the People's Republic* (New York: Bantam, 1972).

Congressional Quarterly Service, *China and U.S. Far East Policy 1945–1967* (Washington, D.C.: 1735 K Street, N.W., Washington, D.C. 20006).

Deng Xiaoping, *Documents of the First Session of the Fifth National People's Congress of the People's Republic of China* (Beijing: Foreign Languages Press, 1978).

Dickinson, Goldsworty L., "Chinese Response to the Boxer Rebellion as Imagined by a Westerner," in *Letters from a Chinese Official* (New York: McClure, Phillips, 1907).

Eastman, Lloyd E., "Fascism in Kuomintang China: The Blue Shirts," *The China Quarterly*, number 49 (January/March 1972).

Eberhard, Wolfram, *Folktales of China* (New York: Washington Square, 1973).

———, *A History of China* (Berkeley: University of California Press, 1950, 4th ed., 1977).

Fairbank, John K., "On the Death of Mao," *New York Review of Books*, October 14, 1976.

———, "'Red' or 'Expert'?" *New York Review of Books*, December 2, 1982.

———, "The New Two China Problem," *New York Review of Books*, March 8, 1979.

———, *The United States and China* (Cambridge, Mass.: Harvard University Press, 1979).

Fairbank, John K., Edwin O. Reischauer and Albert M. Craig, *East Asia: Tradition and Transformation* (Boston: Houghton Mifflin, 1973). Currently titled *China: Tradition and Transformation*.

Fitzgerald, C. P., *The Birth of Communist China* (Baltimore: Penguin, 1964).

———, *The Chinese View of Their Place in the World* (London: Oxford University Press, 1964).

———, *Mao Tse-tung and China*, rev. ed. (New York: Penguin Books, 1977).

Fremantle, Anne, ed., *Mao Tse-tung: An Anthology of His Writings* (New York: Mentor, 1962).

Gernet, Jacques, *Daily Life in China on the Eve of the Mongol Invasion 1250–1276* (Stanford, Calif.: Stanford University Press, 1962).

Gittings, John, "Deng Xiaoping," *Manchester Guardian Weekly*, January 21, 1979.

———, "Not Just a Pretty Picture," *The New Internationalist*, April 28, 1981.

Gray, Jack, "Whatever Happened to Dazhai?" *New Society*, March 12, 1981.

Greene, Felix, *China: The Country Americans Are Not Allowed to Know* (New York: Ballantine, 1961).

Harding, Harry, "Change and Continuity in Chinese Foreign Policy," *Problems of Communism*, March–April, 1983.

Horne, Joshua S., *Away with All Pests—An English Surgeon in People's China: 1954–1969* (New York: Monthly Review Press, 1969).

Howe, Christopher, *China's Economy: A Basic Guide* (New York: Basic Books, 1978, paperback, 1982).

Isaacs, Harold R., *The Tragedy of the Chinese Revolution* (Stanford, Calif.: Stanford University Press, 1961; New York: Atheneum, 1966).

Israel, John, *Student Nationalism in China 1927–1937* (Stanford Calif.: Hoover Institution and Stanford University Press, 1966).

———, "Human Rights in China," *Bulletin of Concerned Asian Scholars*, July-September 1982.

Jacobs, Paul, and Saul Landau, eds., *To Serve the Devil*, Volume II: *Colonials and Sojourners* (New York: Vintage, 1971).

Lamb, Harold, *Genghis Khan: Emperor of All Men* (New York: Bantam, 1953).

Lattimore, Owen and Eleanor, *The Making of Modern China* (New York: W.W. Norton, 1944).

Li, Dun J., *The Ageless Chinese: A History* (New York: Scribner's, 1965; 3d edition, 1978).

———, *The Essence of Chinese Civilization* (Princeton, N.J.: Van Nostrand, 1967).

Liang, Chin-tung, *The Chinese Revolution of 1911* (Jamaica, N.Y.: St. John's University Press, 1962).

Liang, Heng, and Judith Shapiro, *Son of the Revolution* (New York: Alfred A. Knopf, 1983).

Lin Yutang, *Translations from the Chinese* (Cleveland and New York: World, 1963).

Lippit, Victor, "The People's Communes and China's New Development Strategy," *Bulletin of Concerned Asian Scholars*, July-September 1981.

Liu Ta-nien, "How to Appraise the History of Asia?" in Albert Feuerwerker, ed., *History in Communist China* (Cambridge, Mass.: MIT Press, 1968).

Loh, Pichon P. Y., ed., *The Kuomintang Debacle of 1949: Conquest or Collapse?* (Boston: D. C. Heath, 1965).

McAleavy, Henry, *The Modern History of China* (New York: Praeger, 1967).

McClellan, Robert, *The Heathen Chinee: A Study of American Attitudes Toward China, 1890–1905* (Columbus: Ohio State University Press, 1971).

Mao Dun, "Spring Silkworms," *Spring Silkworms and Other Stories* (Beijing: Foreign Languages Press, 1956).

Mao Tse-tung, *Poems of Mao Tse-tung*, trans. by Willis Barnstone (New York: Bantam Books, 1972).

———, *Selected Works* (Beijing: Foreign Languages Press, 1965).

Mende, Tibor, *The Chinese Revolution* (Worcester, England: Thames and Hudson, 1961).

Milton, David, and Nancy Dall Milton, *The Wind Will Not Subside: Years in Revolutionary China—1964–1969* (New York: Pantheon Books, 1976).

Mirsky, Jeannette, ed., *The Great Chinese Travelers* (New York: Pantheon, 1964; University of Chicago Press paperback).

Morse, Hosea Ballou, *The International Relations of the Chinese Empire*, Volume II: *The Period of Submission 1861–1893* (London: Longmans, Green & Co., 1910–1918); speech by J. Ross Brown.

Myrdal, Jan, *Report from a Chinese Village* (New York: Pantheon, 1963; paperback, 1981).

Payne, Robert, ed., *The White Pony: An Anthology of Chinese Poetry from the Earliest Times to the Present Day* (New York: Mentor, 1960).

Peck, Graham, *Two Kinds of Time* (Boston: Houghton Mifflin, 1950).

Pruitt, Ida, *A Daughter of Han: The Autobiography of a Chinese Working Woman* (New Haven: Yale University Press, 1945; Stanford, Calif.: Stanford University Press, 1967).

Russell, Maud, *Far East Reporter* (January, 1971).

Schafer, Edward H., *Ancient China* (New York: Time-Life Books, 1967).

Schurmann, Franz, and Orville Schell, eds., *The China Reader* Vol. 3 (New York: Vintage, 1966).

Service, John S., "Memorandum by Foreign Service Officer in China," *United States Relations with China, with Special Reference to the Period 1944–1949* (Washington, D.C.: U.S. Department of State, 1949).

Sidel, Ruth, *Families of Fengsheng* (New York: Penguin Books, 1974).

———, and Victor W. Sidel, *The Health of China* (Boston: Beacon Press, 1982)

Snow, Edgar, *The Other Side of the River: Red China Today* (New York: Random House, 1962).

———, *Red Star over China* (New York: Random House, 1938; Bantam Books, 1978).

Sociological Resources for the Social Sciences, *Social Change: The Case of Rural China* (Boston: Allyn and Bacon, 1971).

Strong, Anna Louise, *One-Fifth of Mankind* (New York: Modern Age Books, 1938).

Sturdevant, Saundra, "Women and the Family in China Today," original essay written for this reader.

Sullivan, Michael, *A Short History of Chinese Art* (Berkeley: University of California, 1967).

Teng, Ssu-yu, and John K. Fairbank, *China's Response to the West: A Documentary Survey 1839–1923* (New York: Atheneum, 1967).

Terrill, Ross, *The Future of China: After Mao* (New York: Delacorte Press, 1978).

Waley, Arthur, *The Analects of Confucius* (New York: Vintage, n.d.).

———, *Chinese Poems* (London: Allen and Unwin, 1948).

———, *A Hundred and Seventy Chinese Poems* (New York: Knopf, 1919; Vintage, 1973).

———, *The Poetry and Career of Li Po* (London: Allen and Unwin, 1950).

Wallace, James, "End of an Era for China's Communes," *U.S. News & World Report*, January 17, 1983.

Wheelwright, E. L., and Bruce McFarlane, *The Chinese Road to Socialism* (New York: Monthly Review Press, 1970).

White, Theodore, and Annalee Jacoby, *Thunder out of China* (New York: William Sloane Associates, 1946; Da Capo Press paperback reprint).

Whitman, Alden, "Obituary of Chou En-Lai," *The New York Times*, January 9, 1976.

INDEX

ABOUT THE EDITORS

MOLLY JOEL COYE, M.D., M.P.H., studied Chinese history in Hong Kong and Taiwan before receiving a master's degree in East Asian studies from Stanford University. She is coeditor of *China: Inside the People's Republic,* and author of articles on education and health in China; she has traveled in the People's Republic of China twice, in 1972 and again in 1978. In 1977 she completed the M.D. and M.P.H. degrees at Johns Hopkins University, and is now Medical Officer for the National Institute for Occupational Safety and Health, Region IX, in San Francisco, and Chief of the Occupational Health Clinic at San Francisco General Hospital.

JON LIVINGSTON received a master's degree in East Asian history from Harvard University. He is coeditor of the two-volume *Japan Reader* (Pantheon Books), has traveled in Asia and has lived in Japan. Presently, he is working in New York as a graphic designer.

JEAN HIGHLAND was a senior editor for twelve years at Bantam Books where she commissioned and edited the first two editions of this book. She now works as an independent editor. She traveled to China in 1978 in a group led by Molly Joel Coye. She was editorial director of the third editon of the *Encyclopedia of China Today* by Fredric M. Kaplan and Julian M. Sobin. In 1982 she traveled to India to prepare and edit two books by Sir Richard Attenborough, *The Words of Gandhi* and *Gandhi: A Pictorial Biography,* to tie in to his film "Gandhi."

We Deliver!
And So Do These Bestsellers.

SPECIAL MONEY SAVING OFFER

Now you can have an up-to-date listing of Bantam's hundreds of titles plus take advantage of our unique and exciting bonus book offer. A special offer which gives you the opportunity to purchase a Bantam book for only 50¢. Here's how!

By ordering any five books at the regular price per order, you can also choose any other single book listed (up to a $4.95 value) for just 50¢. Some restrictions do apply, but for further details why not send for Bantam's listing of titles today!

Just send us your name and address plus 50¢ to defray the postage and handling costs.